EARLY CHILDHOOD EDUCATION for EXCEPTIONAL CHILDREN

A Handbook of Ideas and Exemplary Practices

Edited by
June B. Jordan
Alice H. Hayden
Merle B. Karnes
Mary M. Wood

D1242227

Editorial Advisory Committee
Merle B. Karnes, Chairperson; Jane DeWeerd; Ernest A. Gotts; Alice H. Hayden; David E. Shearer; Mary M. Wood.

The Council for Exceptional Children, 1977

Library of Congress Catalog Card Number 76-52845

Published in 1977 by The Council for Exceptional Children
1920 Association Drive, Reston, Virginia 22091

Art and design by Angeline V. Culfogienis

Photographs by Nanda Ward Haynes

The work presented or reported
herein was performed pursuant to a
grant from the Bureau of Education
for the Handicapped, US Office of
Education, Department of Health,
Education, and Welfare. However,
the opinions expressed herein do not
necessarily reflect the position or
policy of the US Office of Education
and no official endorsement by the
US Office of Education should be
inferred.

CONTENTS

CONTRIBUTORS

Victor L. Baldwin earned his Ed.D. in special education at the University of Oregon. Since 1968 he has been the director of exceptional child research at Teaching Research, a division of the Oregon State System of Higher Education. In the past he has worked as a psychologist at Parsons State Hospital and Training Center in Parsons, Kansas. Before entering the doctoral program and subsequent to completing the degree he worked for two years in the Psychology Department at Fairview Hospital and Training Center, Salem, Oregon. He has been the author or coauthor of five books on special education. He is a past president of the State of Oregon Council for Exceptional Children and presently serves on the advisory board for several special education projects in universities throughout the country.

Jane DeWeerd, who received her M.A. in speech and hearing from the Central Institute for the Deaf at Washington University, St. Louis, is currently the coordinator of the Handicapped Children's Early Education Program administered by the Division of Innovation and Development, Bureau of Education for the Handicapped. Previously she worked briefly in the Title III and Deaf/Blind Centers program at BEH as an education program specialist. Her prior experience includes teaching nursery school, kindergarten, and primary classes for deaf children in public schools. She was a demonstration teacher at the Lexington School for the Deaf in New York City. She has designed and developed programed language development materials for use by young hearing impaired children.

Eugene B. Edgar received his Ph.D. from George Peabody College in the area of special education, and presently he is an associate professor of education at the University of Washington, Seattle. His professional activities include consultancies to several institutions, public school districts, and schools for handicapped children. Dr. Edgar's main areas of emphasis are special education/early childhood education and program design. Most recently, he has become executive editor of the *American Association for the Education of the Severely/Profoundly Handicapped Review*. His publications reflect his continuing concern over identification and remediation of handicapping conditions in the very young and the severely handicapped.

H. D. (Bud) Fredericks, who received his Ed.D. in special education with honors from the University of Oregon, is presently research professor at Teaching Research, a division of the Oregon State System of Higher Education. He is currently codirector of the Teaching Research Infant and Child Center which includes national model programs both in early childhood and severely handicapped. He has served as chairperson of an Oregon task force that revised the special education legislation in Oregon, and he is currently chairperson of the state's Developmental Disabilities Council. He also serves as consultant to various school districts, the Oregon Board of Education, and the Oregon Mental

Health Division. Dr. Fredericks has an extensive list of publications on educational methods and curriculum for the severely handicapped, parent training, and evaluation.

Ernest A. Gotts received his B.A. from California State University, studied at the University of Washington, and completed his M.A. and Ph.D. at The University of Texas at Austin. He is presently Associate Professor of Special Education in the School of Human Development at The University of Texas at Dallas. Dr. Gotts was formerly Director of the Special Preschool and Program Director for the Staff Training Program in Early Childhood Education at The University of Texas at Austin. He has served on the CEC Board of Governors representing the Division for Early Childhood as well as several national advisory groups. He has presented numerous papers and written a variety of reports, technical papers, articles, and chapters related to early education for exceptional children. Dr. Gotts has been active in Head Start as well as university level teacher training programs.

David N. Grove received his Ph.D. in developmental and child psychology from the University of Kansas in 1969, and he is presently a research professor at Teaching Research, a division of the Oregon State System of Higher Education. His current activities include being a codirector of the Teaching Research Parent Training Clinic and the coordinator of research activities within the Teaching Research Infant and Child Center. In addition his consulting activities include developing programs for emotionally disturbed children, assisting school districts in parent training and staff development activities, designing evaluation procedures for clinical programs, and developing viable models for training institutional staff. Upon graduation from the University of Kansas, he was selected to receive the Outstanding Young Psychologist Award from the American Psychological Association. Dr. Grove has an extensive list of publications ranging from basic research in motor development and in the development of program evaluation procedures to developing a curriculum for the severely handicapped and designing parent training programs based on the use of paraprofessionals.

Jasper Harvey received his Ph.D. in educational psychology in the area of exceptional children at The University of Texas at Austin. At the time he wrote his chapters for this publication, he was a professor in the Department of Special Education at The University of Texas. He is presently the director of the Division of Personnel Preparation, Bureau of Education for the Handicapped, US Office of Education, Washington, D. C. Dr. Harvey has held university faculty positions; has been the director of various national, state, and university projects; and has published widely on the topics of staff training and vocational rehabilitation of the retarded. For three years he served on the National Advisory Board to the National Center for Law and the Handicapped, Inc.; for two years he served as chairperson of the Governmental Relations Committee of The

Council for Exceptional Children; and he is a past president of CEC. He is listed in *Who's Who in the World* in addition to *Who's Who in the South and Southwest* and *Who's Who in America.*

Alice H. Hayden received her Ph.D. from Purdue University, where she was a Purdue Research Foundation Fellow, and she did postdoctoral work in education and psychology at Purdue and Boston Universities. Currently Dr. Hayden is professor of education and director of the Model Preschool Center for Handicapped Children at the Experimental Education Unit of the College of Education and the Child Development and Mental Retardation Center, University of Washington, Seattle. She is also project director for the Office of Child Development Region X Resource Access Project and director of the BEH funded research project on "Acceleration and Maintenance of Developmental Gains in Down's Syndrome School Aged Children." Her wide experience includes work in the areas of the gifted, early intervention, performance measurement, and special education/early childhood education. She is well known in the field of special education/early childhood education through her many publications and presentations.

Carl J Huberty, who received his Ph.D. in education from The University of Iowa, is presently an associate professor of educational psychology at The University of Georgia, Athens, where he teaches data analysis methods and educational measurement courses. Before receiving his doctorate, he served for several years as a high school mathematics teacher in the United States and in France. Dr. Huberty has had numerous papers dealing with statistical and evaluation methods presented at meetings and/or published in professional journals. He is an associate or consulting editor for three research journals, and a review editor for book publishers. Dr. Huberty has served as an evaluation consultant to Rutland Center, to Title III projects, and to Follow Through projects. He is a member of various professional associations and is listed in *American Men and Women of Science* and *Who's Who in the South and Southwest.*

Oliver L. Hurley, who received his Ph.D. in special education from the University of Illinois, is now an associate professor and head of programs in mental retardation in the Division for the Education of Exceptional Children, University of Georgia, Athens. Dr. Hurley has been a teacher of educable mentally retarded children and an educational diagnostician and consultant on an assessment team. He has been a consulting editor for four journals, a consultant for the Bureau of Education for the Handicapped, a major advisor for Technical Assistance Development System, and a professional advisory board member for the Association for Children with Learning Disabilities. He is a past president of the Division on Mental Retardation of The Council for Exceptional Children. In 1975 he was appointed special master for the *Mills v. Board of Education of the District of Columbia* decree in Washington, D.C.

Margaret H. Jones, M.D., Pediatrician, is a professor of pediatrics emeritus at the University of California at Los Angeles School of Medicine. Her special interest lies in chronic neurological conditions in young children. Prior to her retirement she served as medical director of the Cerebral Palsy Prenursery School—a research, demonstration, and training project at UCLA. Formerly she was director of Maternal and Child Health and Crippled Children's Services, State Department of Health in Wyoming, and subsequently in the private practice of pediatrics in the Los Angeles area.

Merle B. Karnes, with an Ed.D. from the University of Missouri and postdoctoral work in special education at the University of Illinois, is presently a professor of special education in the Institute for Child Behavior and Development, University of Illinois, Urbana-Champaign. Dr. Karnes has been a classroom teacher, a director of special services for Champaign Unit 4 Public Schools, and the director or codirector of several early childhood education projects. She has been president of the National Council of Administrators of Special Education, president of the Illinois Council for Exceptional Children, chairperson of the Publications Committee of The Council for Exceptional Children. Among other awards, she has received CEC's highest award, the J. E. Wallace Wallin Award, for her outstanding contribution to exceptional child education. Dr. Karnes's extensive publications focus on early childhood education, development of language skills, effects of various types of interventions, and the problems of disadvantaged children.

William G. Moore, who received his Ed.D. in special education from the University of Oregon, is currently codirector of the Teaching Research Infant and Child Center at the University of Oregon. Dr. Moore has been an elementary classroom teacher, a college assistant professor, and a consultant to state departments of education in early childhood education. He is currently involved in program development in the area of bilingual/bicultural education. This includes work in the area of curriculum development and implementation, staff development, and program evaluation. Dr. Moore has published and presented papers on a broad range of topics within the areas of early childhood education, bilingual/bicultural education, and reading instruction.

David E. Shearer, with a M.S. in special education from Indiana University, is currently the director of the Portage Project in Portage, Wisconsin. He is presently the president of the Wisconsin Division for Early Childhood CEC. His experience as a teacher has included a variety of settings—public schools, associations for retarded citizens, and institutions. Since 1965 he has directed several model development programs for parents and their children. He has served as consultant to early childhood programs such as public schools, day care centers, universities, medical centers, and Head Start programs across the country.

Marsha S. Shearer, who received her M.S. degree in behavioral disabilities from the University of Wisconsin-Madison, is currently the Bureau of Education for the Handicapped Outreach codirector for the Portage Project in Portage, Wisconsin. In this capacity, Ms. Shearer is responsible for planning training programs for replication sites and for providing technical assistance to state agencies. In the past, Ms. Shearer has served as a classroom teacher for trainable mentally retarded children, as a home teacher for preschool children with exceptional educational needs, and as the training coordinator for the Portage Project. She has also coauthored a developmental curriculum for preschool children and has published and presented papers on a broad range of topics including precision teaching, behavior modification, parent training, and home based teaching. She has also served as a consultant to a large number of First Chance projects primarily in the areas of parent involvement, curriculum development, and program evaluation.

William W. Swan, who received his Ed.D. in research design in education from the University of Georgia, is currently the Outreach project director for the Rutland Center at The University of Georgia, Athens. He has been the coordinator of program evaluation for Rutland Center and for the Technical Assistance Office to the Georgia Psychoeducational Center Network and was the program evaluation consultant for the Georgia Division of Mental Health's Study Commission on Mental Health Services for Children and Youth. He has also been a consultant for the US Office of Education's Bureau of Education for the Handicapped. In addition, he has assisted various special education programs in needs assessments, in designing and implementing program evaluation systems, and in developing and implementing Outreach technical assistance efforts. He has published and presented papers on observational instruments, developmental therapy, program evaluation, and Outreach technical assistance.

Mary M. Wood received her Ed.D. in special education from The University of Georgia and did postdoctoral training at Hillcrest Children's Center in Washington, D.C. Presently Dr. Wood serves as director of training for the Rutland Center and secretary to the CEC Division for Early Childhood (DEC). She has been on the faculty of The University of Georgia since 1963. There she established the first teacher training program in Georgia for the preparation of teachers of emotionally disturbed children and served as head of the emotionally disturbed child area for 4 years. For 6 years she directed the university's Special Education Clinic for Disturbed Children and served as director of the Rutland Center. She is the author of the Rutland Center model and *Developmental Therapy*. In 1972 Dr. Wood was appointed by the Secretary of Health, Education, and Welfare to the Child Development National Advisory Committee. She is a field editor for *TEACHING Exceptional Children* and a consultant to the Bureau of Education for the Handicapped and Technical Assistance Development System. She has served as consultant to numerous state and regional programs, and has presented professional papers on a range of subjects related to the emotional development and education of young handicapped children.

R. Reid Zehrbach, with a Ph.D. in school psychology from George Peabody College, is presently an associate professor in the Institute for Child Behavior and Development at the University of Illinois, Urbana-Champaign. Dr. Zehrbach has been a classroom teacher, a supervisor of school psychologists for the Champaign Unit #4 Public Schools, a professor in school psychology at Indiana University, and a professor and program evaluator associated with several early childhood education projects. He has coauthored extensive publications on early childhood education including intervention programs, dissemination, and most recently an early childhood screening process. Other publications have been in the areas of the gifted, the slow learner, and the culturally different.

1
INTRODUCTION

Jane DeWeerd

□The status of children in our society is viewed in different ways. Some believe ours is a child centered society, and the statement is often heard that children are our most precious resource. Marian Edelman of the Children's Defense Fund, on the other hand, says it is a myth that Americans are a child loving people: "As a nation we have failed to provide every child a chance to a decent life" (Children's Defense Fund, 1974).

No matter which view people hold, they are becoming more aware of the circumstances under which many of our children live—circumstances that are leading to unnecessarily high numbers of handicapped children.

One striking fact is that no one is sure of the exact number of handicapped children, particularly those under 6 years of age, in the United States today. The usual estimate is about one million, but regardless of the number, there is ample evidence that it could be lower. But first, what are some of the factors that contribute to the estimate?

EFFECTS OF POVERTY AND POOR HEALTH CARE

The United States ranks 14th in infant mortality, behind 13 other industrialized nations, and the mortality rate varies with poverty. Poverty is also a factor in malnutrition, low birth weight, mental retardation, and intellectual malfunction according to the Senate Select Committee on Nutrition and Human Needs.

In 1974, over 10 million children (15.5%) lived in families whose ability to rear children was severely handicapped by incomes below the poverty level (Solnit, 1976). Higher incidence figures are reported by some sources. A survey of Texas households in 1973 reported that 28% of all Texas families with children under 6 were in poverty and another 26% were in near poverty (Texas Department of Community Affairs, 1974).

Health care is a compounding factor, and one not confined to America's poor. According to Zigler (1976):

> It has been estimated that two-thirds of our nation's 66 million children receive inadequate medical attention, with 25 million of them receiving little more than marginal care. Many health experts are voicing concern about the possibility of future epidemics among America's children. Although vaccines have long been available, our nation has failed to develop a fail-safe system that guarantees inoculations for every child against an array of death-dealing and crippling diseases. The problem here as in other health areas is not lack of knowledge but rather a shortage of commitment and concern. (p. 40)

Add to this picture the increased prevalence of divorce and single parent homes and other social factors, and it puts the child, particularly the handicapped child, in a most vulnerable position. Recent investigations of the extent of child abuse, for example, indicate that one child in every hundred in America is physically abused, sexually molested, or severely neglected (Light, 1974). Although there are many factors that add to the number of children entering the ranks of the handicapped, there are some encouraging developments.

REACHING CHILDREN IN THEIR EARLY YEARS

There is evidence that programs providing early educational and therapeutic programing to meet the needs of young handicapped children and their families are reducing the number of children who will need intensive or long term help. The importance of reaching handicapped children early and working to help them reach their full potential cannot be overemphasized. With early help, the sooner the better, these children can often function at higher levels than had been dreamed possible in prior years.

One of the major ways that the Office of Education seeks to stimulate and improve specialized services for young children and their families is through the Handicapped Children's Early Education Program. Administered by the Bureau of Education for the Handicapped (BEH), the program has grown from 24 initial projects with a $1 million appropriation in 1969–70 to $22 million for 200 projects in 1976–77. To try to reflect the changes that have taken place, this introduction will discuss the nature of the program and how it sees children and will give some thoughts on the task still ahead. It is the hope of those who have compiled this handbook that what has been learned will be useful to others involved in the vitally important work of providing effective and timely assistance for young children. For it is through this specialized help that these youngsters can attain their full potential.

DEVELOPMENT OF THE FIRST CHANCE PROGRAM

In 1968 the Congress recognized that one reason for the paucity of services for handicapped children from birth through age 8 was the shortage of model programs. Ideally, such models would demonstrate effective ways to meet a variety of situations and would make their results generally available. To meet this need, Congress established the Handicapped Children's Early Education Program.

The purpose of this program, sometimes known as the First Chance program, is to develop experimental projects to serve as demonstration models for public schools and other agencies who need information on how to provide a variety of kinds of special help to handicapped children and their families. The legislation was brief, but it asked that each program to be funded present plans on the most effective ways to meet local needs. Not only was the project to develop a well rounded program for children, but also it was to include parents in its activities, run inservice training, evaluate the progress of both the children and the program, coordinate its activities with the public school and other agencies, and disseminate information on the project to professionals and the general public.

In preparing guidelines for the program, BEH gathered experts from many areas—special education, child development, early childhood education, pediatrics, psychiatry and child psychology, recreation, and rehabilitation. Also helping to guide the direction of the new program's emphasis were members of state departments of education, clinics, universities, private agencies, and public schools.

FUNDAMENTAL VIEWS OF THE HANDICAPPED

During the planning process, certain fundamental views of the handicapped child began to emerge. These views now permeate the program:

- The child is viewed as a person with the same basic needs, wants, and problems in growing up as other children, but with additional difficulties to overcome.
- The child is seen as an individual whose special needs can be met through diagnosis, assessment, and planned programing.
- The child is viewed in the context of his or her family or other living group, and not in isolation.
- The child is seen as a citizen with rights, which include the right to an education.
- The child has a related "civil right" to be included, to be visible.

In all of its efforts the First Chance program and the projects it supports follow these basic views.

The Child as a Person with the Same Basic Needs as Others

Each project has its own approach to meeting the needs of children. But all must provide for the social, emotional, language, and motor development of each child and not concentrate just on the cognitive area. Each project is encouraged to involve staff members and consultants with backgrounds in child development, as well as those with special education and other specialized expertise. Supplementary services to provide specialized therapy and meet nutritional needs are available. Transportation, often a major stumbling block to providing services for young children, can be arranged.

The Child Whose Individual Needs Can Be Met

Treating the child as an individual means he or she has the right to be viewed without stereotyping, without automatic ceilings on expectation. In diagnosing and assessing each child's needs, it is stressed that no one knows for sure what a child might become capable of until that child has had a chance. There are many children in First Chance projects who have disproved prognoses that they would never walk or talk. The striking developmental gains made by some Down's syndrome children, for example, attest to the value of approaching each child as an individual with unknown potential. Viewing the child as a unique person with strengths and weaknesses means that these abilities and needs must be taken into account in planning his programing.

Early intervention programing can meet the special needs of young handicapped children—which is shown by the finding that more children have "graduated" from First Chance projects to enter regular programs than to go into special education placement. Each year hundreds of "graduates" are successfully accepted by the same programs that could not take or keep them before they received special help in the First Chance projects. A third party evaluation of the gains made by a randomly selected sample of children (Battelle Center for Improved Education, 1976) showed that it was not uncommon for children to have gained 1½ to 2 times more than would have been expected in the absence of project experiences. Among graduates in the sample, 41.5% were rated by teachers in their past project placements as being more advanced socially than similarly handicapped peers who had not been in the program; 57.8% of the graduates were considered by teachers in their new placements to be more advanced in cognitive skills than similarly handicapped peers who had not been in the program. It does work, and this fact has positive implications for reducing human and financial costs for long term remedial care in the future.

The Child as Part of a Family Group

Parent and family participation is a vital component of all the projects. The program philosophy is in accord with Senator Mondale's (1974) statement:

My work on children's programs has convinced me that there is nothing more important for a child than a healthy family. Just as the ecology movement has sharpened our understanding that we cannot make policies and carry them out without considering the impact on the total environment, so we are beginning to recognize that we should not make decisions on taxes, transportation, housing and welfare without considering their impact on families and children. Policies in these fields directly impinge on the stability and strength of the family and so directly affect the development of the next generation. (p. 50)

Families of enrolled children have many opportunities to take an active part, from the moment a project is planned through the daily work with their own and other handicapped children. At this crucial stage in a child's life, parents work closely with staff members observing educational methods and using them, helping set objectives and plans, spreading information about the project and the children's needs, receiving counseling as needed, and helping evaluate the project. Often the project staff can assist family members with consumer, nutrition, health, job, or legal problems, thus strengthening the family resources to better meet the needs of the handicapped child. And parents have shown how much they have to contribute to the success of the program.

The Child as a Citizen

Right now, only about 50% of school aged handicapped children receive appropriate specialized educational services. The estimate for preschool children is much lower. But the picture is improving. One of the most useful changes has been a move from thinking that handicapped children received an education out of sufferance, as an expression of charity, to the view that every child has a right to an appropriate education (US Department of Health, Education, and Welfare, 1976).

Recent court rulings have furthered this change. In addition, new legislation goes one step further in the handicapped child's right to education. It requires that procedures be developed to locate all handicapped children and phase in services for them, moving toward the goal of full services. The Public Law 94-142 amendments to the Education of the Handicapped Act call upon the states to establish a policy of providing education to all handicapped children between 3 and 21 years of age by 1980 (with the reservation that states that do not offer programs for handicapped children between the ages of 3 to 5 and 18 to 21 are permitted but not required to provide services to handicapped children within those age levels).

As the states and local agencies with the major responsibility for providing educational services move to provide services for additional numbers of younger children with handicaps, a number of the First Chance projects have moved into cooperating and assisting roles to further this goal. Nearly all the projects' services to children, which were funded for a 3 year demonstration period, have been continued by state, local, or other monies. Many projects have received requests to provide training resource help, and consultations to other programs.

The Child's Right To Be Visible

In the past, there has been a tendency to isolate the handicapped from the general public. This made it difficult for many people to become familiar with handicapped persons as individuals. The legislation indicated that projects funded under this program are required not only to demonstrate their approach to professional people, but to "acquaint the community" with their work and the problems and potentials of children with handicaps as well.

Handicapped children have not often been pictured in books or seen on television. Recently, however, Sesame Street, Mister Roger's Neighborhood, and Captain Kangaroo have been including children with handicaps.

The emphasis on integrating children with handicaps into regular programs when feasible is giving the handicapped more visibility. In one large region, where handicapped children were included in Head Start projects and training was provided for teachers and administrators, a survey of a sizable sample group showed they felt considerably better about serving handicapped children after a period of exposure and training than they did before (Grossi, Pinkstaff, Henley, & Sanford, 1975). The consensus was that their experiences with handicapped children had a positive effect on their work with all children.

PROJECTS' ASSISTANCE TO OTHER PROGRAMS

The First Chance projects are all dedicated to helping others learn how to help the handicapped. The projects operate at many levels to do this: Some projects are making their areas aware of the needs, others are developing evidence of effective practices, and some have moved into the role of helping others adopt similar programing. In addition to providing information on what has worked for them and helping schools and other agencies set up similar programs this effort means in some cases helping coordinate efforts at the state and local level. The Technical Assistance Development System (TADS) of the University of North Carolina helps the projects provide visibility and improve their effectiveness through needs assessment and delivery of technical assistance, workshops, conferences, and publications. At the same time, BEH's program staff brings all the project directors together annually to share good practices.

THE TASKS STILL AHEAD

But through all of this activity it is possible to see how much remains to be done. More work on nutrition and preventive health care is needed. In 1961 a survey of cities with populations of 200,000 and over disclosed that the annual mean per capita expenditure for health services for mothers and children was 49 cents. There is a need for increased awareness of the circumstances under which some children live and for changes in the priorities for allocating national resources if there is to be an improvement in the conditions that are forcing some children into lives that are handicapped and delaying the amelioration of their handicaps.

There is a need to find and assess more of the nation's handicapped children. The new legislation will help, but it will take time to work out the procedures, especially for the child under age 5. Effective practices have been developed for improving the functioning level of youngsters with handicaps, but there is a need for more improved procedures for keeping up to date on new developments and disseminating the best of them in usable form. Improved techniques are also needed in the difficult task of evaluating the effectiveness of practices.

Finally, the emphasis should change from remediating handicaps to preventing them. The quality of life for the most vulnerable children, those in the early and formative years, could be vastly improved. A great deal of progress has been made, but there is much yet to be done.

REFERENCES

Battelle Center for Improved Education. *Final report on evaluation of Handicapped Children's Early Education Program (HCEEP)* (Report to Bureau of Education for the Handicapped, US Office of Education). Columbus OH: Author, 1976.

Children's Defense Fund. *Children out of school in America.* Cambridge MA: Author, 1974.

Grossi, J. A., Pinkstaff, D., Henley, C., & Sanford, A. *Impact of mainstreaming the handicapped child in Region IV Head Start.* Chapel Hill NC: Lincoln Center, 1975.

Light, R. J. Abused and neglected children. *The Rights of Children.* Cambridge MA: Harvard Educational Review, Reprint Services No. 9, 1974.

Mondale, W. F. A statement. *The Rights of Children.* Cambridge MA: Harvard Educational Review, Reprint Services No. 9, 1974.

Solnit, A. J. Changing psychological perspectives about children and their families. *Children Today,* 1976, *5*(3), 5–9;43.

Texas Department of Community Affairs. *46 things you need to know about Texas children, the darker side of childhood.* Austin TX: Author, 1974.

US Department of Health, Education, and Welfare/Office of Education. Education of the handicapped today. *American Education,* June 1976, p. 6.

Zigler, E. F. The unmet needs of America's children. *Children Today,* May-June 1976, pp. 39–43.

This chapter was written by Jane DeWeerd in her private capacity. No official support or endorsement by the Bureau of Education for the Handicapped is intended or should be inferred.

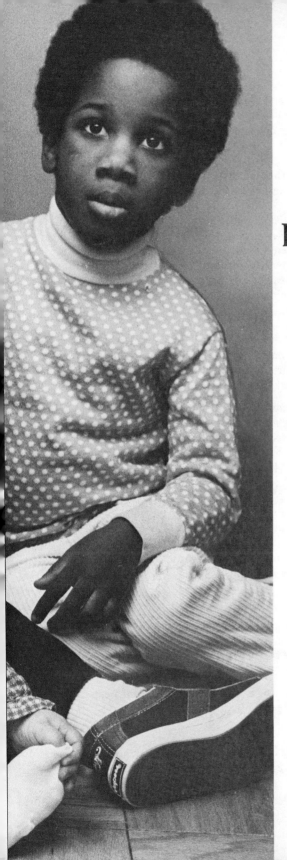

2
THE ENABLING LEGISLATION: How Did It All Begin?

Jasper Harvey

□ The Handicapped Children's Early Education Assistance Act (HCEEAA) was a landmark in that it was the first legislation in history approved by Congress exclusively for the education of all handicapped children without being attached to any other legislation (LaVor & Krivit, 1969). The intent of this act, Public Law 90–538, was to experiment with the process of educating young handicapped children and to develop models that could be replicated in other settings. Further, HCEEAA was directed toward planning, experimentation, and innovation.

LaVor and Krivit (1969) treated the legislative history of HCEEAA in detail in the first appearance of the Law Review department in the January 1969 issue of *Exceptional Children.* It was of interest to peruse various collections in the Lyndon Baines Johnson Library in order to compare views held by members of the executive branch, including the President, with those of members of the Congress. To present these various positions, a chronological presentation of events in both legislative and executive branches is made.

INTRODUCTION OF H.R. 17090

On May 7, 1968, H.R. 17090 was introduced in the House by Representatives Hugh Carey (New York) and Albert Quie (Minnesota). Regarding the significance of the HCEEAA, Quie remarked that:

although the need for early educational development is recognized, educators do not have a fixed, positive approach as to how they can solve these problems . . . . We must seek to set up model, pilot programs on an experimental basis and to attempt thereby to determine the best means for helping our handicapped children. (p. H3439)

S. 3446: INTRODUCTION AND PASSAGE

On May 7, 1968, S. 3446, a companion bill to H.R. 17090, was introduced in the Senate by Senators Winston Prouty (Vermont), Jacob Javits (New York), Wayne Morse (Oregon), and Ralph Yarborough (Texas).

Senator Prouty read the following statement into the *U.S. Congressional Record—Senate* as he introduced S. 3446:

I am convinced that of the several tools we have provided for the children in the past 2 years, none will have more promise for affecting their lives than this new program. For a parent who discovers in the first day or weeks of the new baby's life that his child is handicapped, it is too much to ask that he wait until that child is 6 before he begins to get special education and training. (p. S5045)

On July 11, 1968, S. 3446 was included as part of the 1968 Amendments to the Vocational Education Act and was passed by the Senate

HOUSE HEARINGS ON H.R. 18763

July 16–17, 1968, hearings were held on H.R. 18763 by the Select Subcommittee on Education. H.R. 18763, which replaced the original H.R. 17090, was sponsored by Representatives Daniels (New Jersey), Carey (New York), Quie (Minnesota), Perkins (Kentucky), and 21 other members. LaVor and Krivit (1969) pointed out that although House rules permit only 25 members to cosponsor any single piece of legislation, many additional members did indicate their desire to cosponsor.

The Council for Exceptional Children (CEC) was represented at these hearings by John Kidd, then President of CEC; William C. Geer, Executive Director of CEC; and Freeman McConnell, Chairperson of CEC's Early Childhood Education Committee. CEC's *Official Policy Statement on Federal Legislation* (1966) was included in the statement for the record by Kidd, along with a series of three sections from a November 1965 statement by Evelyn Deno and William C. Geer. After surveying authorities in special education to assess what the future would hold for the exceptional child, the Deno and Geer statements as presented by Kidd (1968) were as follows:

> In the years just ahead, adequate procedures for a continuing census of all children, including exceptional children, will be developed. Doctors, psychologists, and others will refer children to educational agencies as early in life as exceptionalities are discovered. Medical, psychological, and other diagnoses and treatment will be accomplished as early as possible. (p. 3)

> Each state will carefully manage its preschool census of handicapped children with a view toward early corrective measures and preparation for education. (p. 3)

> An emphasis on total social skills will prevail increasingly in education. The blind child or the deaf child at age six months will be provided with experiences designed to alleviate or ameliorate his handicap. Programs for other exceptional children will begin as early as practicable. (p. 3)

Kidd closed by stating:

> We have paid lip service to education . . . it is truly man's hope for coping . . . but as we are now operating education, it is much too little and far too late for many. (p. 5)

THE PERKINS REPORT TO THE HOUSE

On July 19, 1968, H.R. 18763, a clean bill, was reported by the subcommittee with amendments. Then on July 25, 1968, Congressman Carl Perkins (Kentucky), Chairman of the House Education and Labor Committee, submitted Report No. 1793 to accompany H.R. 18763. Congressman Perkins' report (1968) stated,

> As a result of the favorable findings by the Select Subcommittee the full Committee on Education and Labor reported this legislation unanimously and with bipartisan approval (p. 3).

That report also included a statement regarding testimony given the committee during its hearings:

The committee was extremely impressed by testimony of Dr. Samuel A. Kirk who reported his successful preschool intervention program which brought beneficial results to preschool mentally retarded children, confirming earlier research which also suggested the benefits of early intervention. The best time to attack a child's mental and emotional handicaps appears to be the period from birth through the early childhood years. (p. 2)

A summary of major provisions of the bill was included in the Perkins report:

This program should be viewed as a model demonstration program and not as a service program; however, programs that show promise of providing meaningful answers for education of handicapped should at the appropriate time be evaluated for permanent legislative approval. (p. 4)

It is intended that there be as great a diversity among projects as possible, so that models will be developed which are applicable to as many different handicapping areas and particular environmental areas as possible. Where professionals disagree upon the most advantageous methods to be used, for example, in the education of the deaf, the committee expects that all methods or systems which show promise of providing educational gain for preschool handicapped children will be consolidated. (p. 4)

Three specific stated aims were delineated by Perkins. The first of these was "to encourage the development in all its aspects of the handicapped child" (p. 4). This reflected the committee's conviction that the model preschool programs should provide programs that would stimulate all areas of development. These areas were to include "emotional, physical, intellectual, and social needs" (p. 4). The report urged that "programs encompass not only all disabilities, but all age groups from birth to 6 years of age" (p. 4).

The second stated aim was participation of parents, which had two major purposes: "first, to provide the parents with counseling and guidance on how they can effectively respond to the special needs of their handicapped children" (p. 4); and, second, to "enlist the help of the parents as allies and associates of educators to provide a total program" (p. 4).

The third aim was to

acquaint the community with the problems and potentials of handicapped children. This is included in the belief that society, including educators, too often underestimates the capacities of these children and, as a result, often limits their opportunities to develop and function as constructive members of our society.

. . . Where possible, new demonstration programs should be established in settings so that they may be used for the training of teachers, speech pathologists and audiologists, clinicians, psychologists, physicians, paraprofessionals, professional aides, and others whose contributions are required in effecting good early childhood education of the handicapped. (p. 5)

LaVor and Krivit (1969) summarized the essential elements in a total program as envisioned in the act:

Research—to provide a sound base of knowledge of the preschool handicapped child upon which to base programs.

Development—to develop curriculum and techniques designed to meet the particular needs of the preschool handicapped.

Demonstration—to create programs of excellence from which other communities and schools are able to pattern their activities, using the best of current wisdom and skills.

Training—to develop a cadre of well trained professional and supportive personnel to man new programs.

Implementation—to develop quality programs dispersed throughout all areas of the country (p. 381)

HOUSE DEBATE AND PASSAGE OF H.R. 18763

On September 16, 1968, H.R. 18763 was passed by the House. The *Congressional Record—House,* September 16, 1968, indicates that Congressman Perkins (Kentucky) moved to suspend the rules and pass the bill to authorize preschool and early education programs for handicapped children (p. H8734). Congressman Reid (New York) demanded a second. Without objection, Speaker Albert (Oklahoma) considered a second as ordered. Perkins, in discussing the bill, gave its three purposes (presented earlier in this chapter).

Then Congressman Daniels (New Jersey), Chairperson of the Select Subcommittee on Education, urged support of the bill:

Because of the absence of viable models for preschool and school-age handicapped children, States and local educational agencies overlook the fact that it may be less expensive to channel resources toward infancy and early childhood development, thus reducing the need for more expensive services later on in the handicapped child's life. (p. H8735)

Next Congressman Quie (Minnesota) spoke for passage of the bill:

It is my contention that a model preschool program should provide stimulation in all areas in order to meet his [the child's] emotional, physical, intellectual, and social needs . . . . it is essential that the focus . . . be directed toward the full range of the handicapped population under 6 years of age. (p. H8736)

Congressman Ayres (Ohio) also responded in support of the bill:

There is a body of sound research which indicates that the right intervention in the life of the young handicapped child, while it may not prevent the handicap, can prevent many of the disabling and dependency-producing consequences of the handicapped in later life. (p. H8736)

Congressman Carey (New York), who had earlier introduced H.R. 17090 on which H.R. 18763 was based, stressed the planning aspect:

Before the States begin to launch a comprehensive program of preschool services for handicapped children, they want to be able to answer certain questions, "what kinds of children might be grouped together for preschool program?"; "what kind of training and qualifications will be necessary for teachers and teacher-aides?"; "what will be the special problems connected with developing programs in rural areas or in inner city locations?"; "how effective are such programs?" (p. H8737)

In addition to these Congressmen, 11 others rose to speak in support of H.R. 18763.

Speaker Albert (Oklahoma) stated that the question was on the motion to suspend the rules and pass H.R. 18763. The question was taken, the rules suspended, and the bill passed (p. H8742).

REMOVAL OF S. 3446 AND SENATE PASSAGE OF H.R. 18763

On September 17, 1968, the Senate removed S. 3446 from the Vocational Education Amendments of 1968. The House version of the bill, H.R. 18763, was then passed by the Senate.

The *Congressional Record—Senate* of September 17, 1968, indicates that Senator Long (Louisiana) asked that the Chair lay before the Senate a message from the House of Representatives on H.R. 18763. The Presiding Officer, receiving no objection to Senator Long's request, laid before the Senate H.R. 18763, which was read twice by its title. Senator Long then asked unanimous consent for its immediate consideration. Senator Prouty (Vermont) rose in support of the bill:

H.R. 18763 is almost identical to S. 3446 which I authorized and introduced in the Senate on May 7 of this year. The measure received enthusiastic and bipartisan support from every member of your Education Subcommittee. This is attested to by the fact that the subcommittee recommended and the Senate approved incorporating S. 3446 as an amendment to H.R. 18366, a bill to amend the Vocational Education Act of 1963, which is now awaiting conference. (p. S10907)

The bill, H.R. 18763, then was ordered to a third reading and passed by the Senate.

STATEMENTS BY HOUSE AND SENATE SPONSORS

At the time of the bill's passage by both the House and Senate, Congressmen Hugh L. Carey (New York) and Albert H. Quie (Minnesota), the original co-sponsors of H.R. 17090, made statements that emphasized the importance of the legislation. These and other statements were cited by LaVor and Krivit (1969). Congressman Carey discussed the aim of the bill:

The Handicapped Children's Early Education Assistance Act is a significant step. It focuses attention on the most critical years for development of the intellectual and emotional facets of a child. If we are to prevent the situation of a child entering first grade, already sadly lacking in language development, in interpersonal skills, in familiarity with basic information, then we must vigorously pursue effective preschool education for handicapped children. (p. 381)

Congressman Quie said,

Legislation of this type is vital because the problems of handicapped children will not disappear with wishful thinking. The deaf will always have problems in understanding other people. The blind will not develop new eyes. The crippled may learn to walk, but not without many lost years. The mentally retarded will always be slow in learning to read.

These problems will not disappear but they can be softened. The deaf can be helped to communicate better, the blind can learn to work and play without eyes, the crippled may learn to walk, to play, to read and write without the lost years between hospital, school and home; the mentally retarded can learn new approaches to learning to read which will minimize the difference between him and his more fortunate peers. (p. 381)

Congressman Dominick V. Daniels (New Jersey), who sponsored H.R. 18763 and who was Chairperson of the Select Committee on Education, discussed the importance of the bill to parents:

Few parents are prepared to take care of a child who looks different, behaves in grossly unacceptable ways or fails to respond even to the sound of a mother's voice. Parents of handicapped children may have fears and are often frustrated and bewildered. They need help in understanding their child's disability. They need help in working with their handicapped child.

This bill will bring us into a new era of educating handicapped children. In addition, it is anticipated that this legislation will enlist the help of the parents as allies and associates of educators to provide a total program. (p. 381)

Congressman Carl D. Perkins (Kentucky), Chairman of the House Education and Labor Committee, discussed the principles of the bill:

Opportunities for handicapped Americans are often limited; and limited opportunities mean limited fulfillment. If the Nation is to offer its handicapped citizens the opportunity to develop their potentials to the fullest, it must first understand that these citizens, despite physical or mental disadvantages, contain potential as great as any American. The bill before us recognizes this principle; not only does it seek to help handicapped children realize their potential, but it also promotes a wider community understanding of what these children can do. (p. 381)

Senator Winston Prouty (Vermont), an original cosponsor of S. 3446, observed,

Mr. President, the program we are offering is designed to bring together all the accumulated knowledge and wisdom in the field of special education in a controlled, model environment so that we can begin to apply comprehensive considerations to the learning problems of the disabled child.

Mr. President, there is no child who deserves a First Chance, a helping hand, more than the child who enters this world with dim vision, with faint hearing, with difficulty in comprehending the nature of our world, or with any of the myriad disabilities which afflict our handicapped children. (p. 381)

To summarize the legislation and its rationale, LaVor and Krivit (1969) used Congressman William A. Steiger's (Wisconsin) statement:

It has been said that a handicapped child produces a handicapped family and even a handicapped community. Indeed, the magnitude of the effect on the family is difficult to understand. Not so many years ago parents, out of ignorance and futility, often locked their handicapped children in the closets of their homes. While in most cases the physical closets are gone, the closets of the mind still handicap children in regard to their families and communities. H.R. 18763 not only seeks solutions to the educational problems of the handicapped child, but also focuses on the problems of his family and community by encouraging parental participation in the development and operation of preschool experimental centers and efforts to acquaint the community with the problems and potentialities of such children. For it is only through such a coordinated attack that we can begin to open the closets of the mind in which we have all locked the handicapped.

Mr. Speaker, in addition to the five million school-age handicapped children in this country, it has been estimated that there are an additional one and one half million such children in the preschool years, ages 3 to 6. For years we have bowed to the magic age of six as the time for all children to begin their education. This belief has been based on the premise that children before reaching this age will learn naturally from their environment the skills they will need to succeed in formal education. Educators all over the world have proved conclusively that this contention is invalid and this bill also recognizes it by encouraging the establishment of experimental programs for handicapped children from birth to six. (pp. 382–383)

THE ROMMEL MEMORANDUM

On September 23, 1968, Wilfred H. Rommel, Assistant Director for Legislative Reference, sent a memorandum to the President on H.R. 18763. Included in this memorandum were agency recommendations from the Bureau of the Budget, the US Department of Health, Education, and Welfare (HEW), and the Office of Economic Opportunity. Rommel's memorandum stated,

The failure to develop preschool programs is due, in part, to the lack of widely distributed information about successful approaches which have been developed. The absence of model or prototype programs which could provide the basis for local planning has also inhibited larger investments in preschool programs. (p. 2)

The Rommel memorandum also included a letter from HEW Secretary Wilbur J. Cohen to Charles J. Zwick, Director of the Bureau of the Budget. In that letter Secretary Cohen (1968) indicated,

This legislation would provide a sensible and prudent approach to the problems of preschool education for the handicapped. It does not launch a massive program, but instead suggests a carefully evaluated program of approximately 100 model programs. The model programs would explore approaches to preschool and early education for the various discrete types of handicapping conditions, and also take into account geographic and cultural factors related to urban and rural environments.

Although this proposal was not part of the Administration's program, it would advance the cause of preschool education for handicapped children. It had strong bipartisan support both in the Congress and among those concerned with education of handicapped children. Consequently, we recommend that this enrolled bill be approved.

The Rommel memorandum included a similar letter to Mr. Zwick from Robert Perrin (1968) for Bertrand M. Harding, Acting Director of the Office of Economic Opportunity. Perrin's letter indicated,

The Office of Economic Opportunity favors the President's approval of this measure. The Head Start program, administered by this agency, has encouraged communities to develop the potential resources of economically disadvantaged children. This Act can provide similar encouragement to local organizations to increase the quality of education for physically, mentally, and emotionally handicapped children.

He continued,

We particularly approve of one feature of this Act . . . its recognition of the need to encourage parents to participate fully in the development and operation of a program for preschool children. This, as you know, is an integral part of the Head Start program.

Regarding some administrative aspects of the legislation, Perrin stated,

This legislation can, and we believe should, be administered in such a way as to provide needed assistance to community action agencies and other organizations which operate Head Start, Parent and Child Centers, and Neighborhood Health Center programs and which already serve, or would like to serve, handicapped children. These agencies can, we believe, provide important models and vehicles for programs funded under this act.

The bill was signed by John W. McCormack, Speaker of the House of Representatives, and Carl Hayden, President of the Senate Pro Tempore (1968), authorizing $1,000,000 for the fiscal year ending June 30, 1969, and $10,000,000 for the fiscal year ending June 30, 1970. The bill then was submitted to President Johnson for his approval.

SIGNING OF THE BILL INTO LAW

On September 30, 1968, President Lyndon B. Johnson signed H.R. 18763, which became Public Law 90–538. At the signing of the Handicapped Children's Early

Education Assistance Act President Johnson ("Remarks," 1968) made the following remarks:

> Secretary Cohen, Senator Morse, Senator Prouty, Congressman Carey, Congressman Daniels, Members of Congress, My Friends:
>
> One way we can measure our country's total concern for the individual is to measure our efforts to help the least fortunate—the least able.
>
> The bill we sign today is a testament to our concern for five and a half million of those least fortunate—five and a half million handicapped children: the blind, the mentally retarded, the crippled, the palsied.
>
> Those children and their plight touch us all. And I believe they have a special claim on us as public servants.
>
> We have learned that more than 50% of handicapped youngsters can have their conditions substantially improved—even cured—*if* they get help early enough. Yet only two million of the Nation's five and a half million handicapped children are reached now by special education programs. This bill will help us change all that.
>
> It will provide from 70 to 100 model educational centers for the handicapped. The centers will give an important boost to preschool education for the handicapped. And they will be a spur to local and state agencies to improve their programs for the handicapped. Most important, these new centers will bring hope to families and children who very much need—and deserve—our help.
>
> No one could doubt the determination of these youngsters—not if you have seen a crippled child struggle to walk across a room, or a little retarded girl trace a picture again and again, determined to get it just right.
>
> No one can doubt the value and wisdom of this law.
>
> It gives me pleasure to think about the good it will do: the lives it will touch. I'm glad to sign this bill.
>
> Thank you.

CEC'S ROLE IN PASSAGE OF HCEEAA

The foregoing legislative history is recorded in various bibliographical references. However, there is one basic and critical aspect of the legislative process that is not treated in published form—the function fulfilled by a professional organization such as The Council for Exceptional Children. Article III, Section 7, of the *CEC Articles of Incorporation and Bylaws,* states:

> Take positions on matters of current import coming before legislative bodies and make its views and positions known through direct communication, appearances, newsletters, and other appropriate means, to the legisla-

tive body concerned, to the members of the corporation, and to the general public. (*CEC Handbook,* 1974, p. 23)

A function of the executive director, as set forth in the bylaws, is "to administer the Council's program and direct the operation of its central office" (p. 33). For many years the Council's program has included governmental relations in its broadest meaning. A responsibility of the central office staff has been working with Senators and Representatives and their staffs in drafting legislation, working to provide information and testimony where needed, and in every sense furthering the cause of exceptional children. Such a continuing relationship is necessary to assure the Council's efficacy in legislation and governmental relations. Nowhere has there been quite the total involvement that existed to assure the passage of the Handicapped Children's Early Education Assistance Act.

REFERENCES

Statement of Congressman Hugh Carey, *Congressional Record—House,* May 7, 1968.

CEC Handbook. Reston, VA: The Council for Exceptional Children, September 1974.

Cohen, W. J. Letter to Charles J. Zwick, September 23, 1968, with Wilfred H. Rommel to the President, September 23, 1968, Reports on Legislation, Box 52, 9/20/68—10/4/68, Lyndon Baines Johnson Library.

Geer, W. C., & Deno, E. D. CEC and legislation—Now and in the future. *Exceptional Children,* 1965, *32,* 187–194.

Kidd, J. W. (President, The Council for Exceptional Children). Statement to Select Subcommittee on Education and Labor, US House of Representatives, July 16, 1968.

LaVor, M., & Krivit, D. The handicapped children's early education assistance act, Public Law 90–538. *Exceptional Children,* 1969, *35,* 379–383.

John W. McCormack and Carl Hayden, to the President, with Wilfred H. Rommel to the President, September 23, 1968, Reports on Legislation, Box 52, 9/20/68—10/4/68, Lyndon Baines Johnson Library.

Carl Perkins, Committee on Education and Labor, Report No. 1793, 90th Congress, 2nd Session, to accompany H.R. 18763, with Wilfred H. Rommel to the President, September 23, 1968, Reports on Legislation, Box 52, 9/20/68—10/4/68, Lyndon Baines Johnson Library.

Remarks, Signing of the Handicapped Children's Early Education Act, Lyndon B. Johnson, The White House, September 30, 1968, Box 62, Statements, 8/21/68—12/4/68, Lyndon Baines Johnson Library.

Robert Perrin, for Bertrand M. Harding to Charles J. Zwick, September 23, 1968, with Wilfred H. Rommel to the President, September 23, 1968, Reports on Legislation, Box 52, 9/20/68—10/4/68, Lyndon Baines Johnson Library.

Wilfred H. Rommel, to the President, September 23, 1968, Reports on Legislation, Box 52, 9/20/68—10/4/68, Lyndon Baines Johnson Library.

NOTE: References are cited in a form required for citing historical materials from the Lyndon Baines Johnson Library.

This chapter was written by Jasper Harvey prior to his joining the Bureau of Education for the Handicapped. No official support or endorsement by the Bureau of Education for the Handicapped is intended or should be inferred.

3 ALTERNATIVE MODELS FOR DELIVERING SERVICES TO YOUNG HANDICAPPED CHILDREN

Merle B. Karnes
R. Reid
Zehrbach

☐ Programs for young handicapped children have developed in highly individualized ways; and, as a result, attempts to summarize data often serve merely to obscure the uniqueness of a given approach. Instead, this chapter will begin by defining briefly four dimensions that appear to be critical in the development of programs for young handicapped children—the population served, the geographical area, the theoretical basis, and the delivery system. In the second and major section, selected programs for young handicapped children will be described under the following delivery system headings:

1. Home.
2. Home followed by center.
3. Home and center.
4. Center.
5. Technical assistance and consultative services.
6. Prenatal.
7. Intervention into higher level systems.

Data for this chapter were obtained from information provided by some 120 BEH First Chance model programs. As a rule, an initial 3 year period is funded in part by BEH; during the fourth year, some projects are funded for dissemination activities and are called Outreach projects. Some Outreach projects have been funded for as many as 3 years. In the discussion of funding in this chapter, it is assumed that BEH played a major role during the developmental stages of each project. The funding sources cited, therefore, are those responsible for the continued funding of the service component of the program.

CRITICAL DIMENSIONS IN PROGRAM DEVELOPMENT

The first dimension to be considered in program development is the *nature of the population* to be served, most particularly the range of handicapped children within that population. In brief, is the program to serve a broad range of handicapped children cross categorically and from all socioeconomic levels, or is it to serve only handicapped children from low income and/or bilingual families? Is it to serve only low incidence handicapped children, such as the blind, the deaf, or the trainable mentally retarded?

The second dimension is the *geographical area* to be included and the density of the population. If the area is large and sparsely populated, the tendency may be to attempt to serve all handicapped children within a given program. If, on the other hand, the population is dense and large numbers of low incidence handicapped children who are easily categorized can be identified, programs tend to provide for a more restricted group such as the blind or the deaf.

A third dimension in program development is the *theoretical basis* upon which it will operate, including the philosophy of its administrations and the viewpoint of its constituency, especially the parents of handicapped children. Six theoretical approaches are readily identified, although they do not usually exist in a pure or simple form: open education; precision teaching with a heavy emphasis on language development; precision teaching based on developmental guidelines in the areas of gross and fine motor development, self help and social skills, and cognitive language development; behavior modification; cognitive developmental instruction based especially on the work of Piaget; and the creation of a learning environment, with particular emphasis on the physical aspects of that environment.

The fourth dimension in program development to be reviewed here is *delivery of services.* A variety of delivery systems can be used in programs for young handicapped children with some overlapping and much variation, but four seem to be major: the home based system, the home followed by center, the home and center based system, and the center based system. Although many of these systems involve the use of a categorical or homogeneous grouping approach, there is an increased emphasis on mainstreaming—the inclusion of handicapped children in programs with nonhandicapped children. Three less commonly used delivery systems are the technical assistance and consultative services model, the prenatal model, and the intervention into higher level systems model. These seven systems and the concept of mainstreaming are discussed in depth in the next section.

PROGRAM SUMMARIES BY DELIVERY SYSTEM

It is impossible within the confines of a single chapter to discuss programs in great detail. Therefore, some are presented in greater detail while a few are described briefly in terms of certain characteristics. Selections were made because the programs helped illustrate differences among programs. No attempt was made to rate programs as to excellence or to validate whether or not a given program actually does what it purports to do.

The number, size, and variety of programs grouped under a delivery system vary greatly and in an apparently uneven manner. This variety should be viewed as reflecting the present state of the art and, it is hoped, will help the reader more easily discern where new models may need to be developed.

Programs are presented according to the delivery system that is used. All programs have some degree of parent involvement, but some are delivered entirely within the home and are classified here as home based programs. While the mothers in these programs are generally viewed as the primary change agents, paraprofessionals or professionals in a few home based programs provide tutoring or direct teaching. Many home based programs, which begin with children ages 0 to 3, continue as center based programs after children are approximately 3 years old. Home based programs seem to lend themselves well to sparsely populated areas, to clusters of small towns, and to rural areas. This approach is also viable with parents who are initially reluctant to send their young children away from home or with parents from groups such as the Mexican and Indian cultures, which do not easily accept the absence of mother and child from the home.

Some programs may be classified as using a center and home approach. The children often attend a program primarily delivered at a center, but the parents may also be trained to deliver a program at home. Frequent staff visits to the homes and cooperative planning to coordinate school and home activities characterize these programs. Staff visits to the homes may involve parent conferences as well as the observation of parent-child interactions. Staff members may also model appropriate teaching techniques for parents during these visits. There is, therefore, a qualitative difference between programs that are center based and have limited involvement with parents at home and those that follow a center and home based model.

Another category is composed of center based programs. To reiterate, parental involvement is found in all classifications, but in this instance parent participation at the center itself is emphasized. While parents can learn to improve their teaching of their children in the home, the emphasis here is on parent teaching at the center. Carryover is encouraged, but in many instances only infrequent visits are made to homes by the staff. These programs tend to be for the older preschool child and/or the more severely handicapped child who can benefit from special equipment such as sound amplifiers or orthopedic equipment and from highly trained personnel such as physical and occupational therapists, psychiatrists, and special medical personnel.

Efforts to mainstream children can be found in several of the preceding delivery systems. Therefore, a section dealing with the concept provides selected highlights from these programs to help develop a broader view of the programs and their relationship to mainstreaming.

Several projects follow the technical assistance and consultative service delivery system. Programs in this category frequently rely on highly trained staff for identification and diagnosis of children as well as for inservice training of field staff and parents who will work directly with the handicapped children.

Two projects focus on young girls whose pregnancies are likely to produce handicapped children. These are categorized under the prenatal delivery system. The intent is to prepare these future mothers to cope with infants who may manifest developmental lags.

The last delivery system discussed is the intervention into higher level systems. It concentrates on developing attitudes, habits, and skills among administrators of agencies and public school systems.

Home Based Models: High Incidence and Cross Categorical

The Portage Project

A typical example of a home based approach for young handicapped children is located in the Portage (Wisconsin) Public Schools. The Portage Project serves handicapped children 0 to 6 years of age in a large rural area in southern Wisconsin. Its basic intent is to teach parents in the home how to use techniques of behavior modification to train their handicapped children. About two-thirds of the children live on farms while the remainder reside in or near small towns. The socioeconomic level varies from poverty to middle income. Approximately half of the children are considered mentally retarded, one-fourth have speech and language problems, and another one-fourth are physically handicapped. Also included among the handicapping conditions are behavioral problems, cultural deprivation, emotional disturbance, and hearing and vision impairment. No child is considered to be too severely handicapped to enter the project but a child must exhibit at least a 1 year lag in developmental age before he can be accepted.

Handicapping categories are not given particular emphasis; instead, the focus is placed on where a child is functioning and on plans to help him develop at a more rapid rate.

Children are referred to the program by physicians, local guidance clinics, hospitals, speech therapists, public school personnel, and county health nurses, as well as by friends, neighbors, and parents. Home teachers, who live in or near the districts served, typically contact the parents in the home. The child, however, is *not* labeled handicapped and the program is described as one for children who are of special concern. Initial enrollment may be on a trial basis, but after parental consent a standardized battery of tests is administered in the home by the home teacher and the results are reviewed by the project director.

The basic staff in the Portage Project consists of a director and professional and paraprofessional home teachers but also includes a training coordinator and a part time evaluation coordinator. A full time home teacher carries a case load of approximately 14 children and is involved in all phases of programing—recruitment, intervention, and followup.

Originally the project was funded primarily by BEH, but current funding is provided by local school districts and the State Department of Public Instruction.

The instructional program focuses directly on what a child can be expected to do without efforts to diagnose handicaps or to predict outcomes. Basic to the instructional program are a developmental sequence checklist and a set of 450 curriculum cards, which are included in the *Portage Guide to Early Education*. The checklist includes the areas of self help, cognition, socialization, language, and motor skills. The home teacher obtains baseline data on a given child and then uses the curriculum cards to design a program consistent with his needs. Both long term goals and precise weekly prescriptions are used to implement the program. During a typical week, the home visitor meets with the family and provides additional specific teaching cues. The parent is then observed working with the child to ensure that the prescribed behavior is being encouraged. The following week a similar procedure is followed, with baseline data again collected at the beginning of the session. Charts and records are maintained to show the child's growth.

Although the major emphasis of the project is the instructional program, the staff attempts to coordinate services for the children with other community agencies. Critical links have been established with physicians and clinics, county health nurses, welfare agencies, universities, parent organizations, and state departments.

A notable aspect of the Portage Project is the relatively limited amount of time spent by professional staff with a given child. Home teachers spend only 1½ hours per week with a child. In addition, parents are encouraged to spend at least 15 minutes every day working with their child.

Evaluation results of a pretest-posttest nature are based on the Developmental Profile and the Cattell Infant Intelligence Scale as well as on specific speech skills, on mother-child interaction, and on interaction and cooperation skills obtained through observation. Significant gains have been found in all of these areas. An important finding is that, although the project does not require heavy administrative support, it seems to have sufficient technical support and guidance to implement its program effectively. Strong inservice training is provided to maintain the quality of the program, an especially important feature because, although home teachers work autonomously, they do need a support system when problems arise.

The Telstar Project

Another home based program is the Telstar Project of the Alpena-Montmorency-Alcona Intermediate School District in Alpena, Michigan, in which the Department of Social Service and the public school system cooperate in the identification of the children and the supervision of the program. Children in this program tend to be moderately to severely handicapped and 0 to 6 years of age. The basic approach is to place one handicapped child with a "normal" child in a day care home, which provides for the care of both. There is, therefore, a model child for the handicapped child. The children are placed in satellite homes located near the child's usual place of residence. Each satellite worker agrees to take one nonhandicapped child in the home with the handicapped child and to participate in 90% of the required inservice training activities, which are based on the curriculum developed at the Meyer Children's Rehabilitation Institute of the University of Nebraska Medical Center. This curriculum, *Meyer Children's Rehabilitation Institute Teaching Program for Young Children,* emphasizes such areas as self care, body usage, and language development. Each child is evaluated on a bimonthly basis by project staff.

Programs Using Strategies Similar to the Portage Project

A number of home based programs rely on strategies similar to those employed in the Portage Project. The Preschool Handicapped Program sponsored by the Clinch-Powell Educational Cooperative at Harrogate, Tennessee, for example, serves children 0 to 6 years of age, many of whom are Appalachian culturally disadvantaged. Initially, child assessments are made in the areas of language, self help, socialization, and cognitive and motor skills. Parents are then trained to provide activities that remediate identified difficulties and prevent additional complications. This program offers service to children at home through a paraprofessional home visitor.

Another home based program has been developed in Wichita Falls, Texas, in the Region IX Education Service Center. Here, training is also provided parents so that they can implement the educational program with their children at home. Both professional and paraprofessional teachers receive preservice and inservice training, and parents may receive training to join the ranks of the paraprofessional teachers who visit homes on a weekly basis.

The Marshalltown (Iowa) Project is also similar to the Portage Project but places greater emphasis on development than on behavior modification. The project serves all handicapped children in a large rural area of Iowa. The children are served at home through parent and professional home advisor intervention. Home advisors visit homes weekly and train parents to write prescriptions that promote the learning of the handicapped child. A major aim is to develop an environment that is responsive to the child as well as to improve the quality of child-parent interactions.

The San Luis Valley Early Education and Home Intervention Project for the Handicapped at Alamosa, Colorado, is sponsored by the San Luis Valley Board of Cooperative Services and Adams State College. Children are served through biweekly home visitations, and intensive inservice training is provided the paraprofessionals who make these visits.

The Rural Infant Stimulation Environment Project (ages 0 to 3) at the University of Alabama at Tuscaloosa helps parents acquire improved skills in working with their handicapped children. There are provisions for comprehensive diagnosis and assessment, for the development of prescriptive plans, for family, ancillary, and volunteer training, for a support system for parents, and for systematic followup.

A similar program is conducted in Memphis, Tennessee, where a PEACH Project (Program for Early Attention to Children with Handicaps) is implemented. Children ages 0 to 3 participate in individually prescribed programs, which their parents or other family members are trained to implement.

Multiply handicapped children ages 18 months to 8 years are provided a program involving behavioral assessment and educational planning by the Early On Program in San Diego, California, under the sponsorship of San Diego State University. This project trains parents to be more effective in working with their handicapped children and upgrades the competencies of its professional staff through inservice training. The project emphasizes a linkage between community diagnostic services and educational programs, and its assessment procedures provide data for program planning.

Other Types of Parent Training Programs

The Parent Training Project in Morganton, North Carolina, offers a home program for moderately to severely mentally delayed children of 0 to 8 years of age. However, it approaches the training of parents in a different way. Parents are trained in groups established on the basis of the common developmental needs of the children, a technique that cuts across home background and socioeconomic level. Should a child participate in a day care program, his parents are still encouraged to become members of the project. Project staff includes the director, an evaluation coordinator, and eight parent trainers with undergraduate degrees in special education or related fields.

A critical factor in this program is the parents' willingness to learn to cope with the needs of their child. Indeed, the group meetings are designed to foster a sense of identification among the members as well as to present instructional content that is relevant to all. In general, the approach to training that is taught the parents involves an activity oriented approach to the child. All activities for the children are designed jointly by parents and the parent trainer, for it is hoped that parents will continue to follow program goals even after their children have graduated from the program.

In addition to group meetings, parent trainers also make occasional home visits to consult with individual parents concerning child progress. Some parents participate only in individual home visits because of transportation or other problems.

Another multifaceted approach to parental training is provided in the Comprehensive Training Program for Infant and Young Cerebral Palsied Children located at Milwaukee, Wisconsin. This program is designed to help cerebral palsied children develop to their fullest potential in the areas of speech and language development through direct intervention and intense parent participation. One of the emphases of the program is on prespeech development, which includes sucking, swallowing, and biting skills as well as overcoming feeding problems. In addition, emphasis is also placed on the experiential development of the child, since the opportunity for cerebral palsied children to learn by exploring their environment is limited. The age range of the children served is 0 to 3 at the time of admission.

As is to be expected, the program offers a broad family participation program, which begins with the completion of three questionnaires designed to survey parent knowledge about cerebral palsy as well as their needs and fears. The breadth of the program is illustrated by its six aspects, which include active participation in the child's therapy program, individual family counseling, group conferences, monthly evening meetings, Saturday morning meetings called "family affairs," and parent advisory subcommittees. The Saturday morning affair provides mothers, fathers, grandparents, siblings, and baby sitters an opportunity to learn about the program in an unstructured situation. The child is brought to this meeting so that therapists can demonstrate specific techniques as they discuss the child's problems and progress.

A noteworthy aspect of staff training is its focus on the sharing of knowledge and skills among the various disciplines in order to help each therapist become competent in treating "the whole child." This technique often makes it possible for only one professional to meet with a child in order to provide a total treatment program.

Early Identification Program

A typical offshoot of home based programs is an impetus for early identification and screening along with the heavy emphasis on programmatic interaction. Project Palatisha, the early education program for handicapped Indian children (ages 1 to 6) located at the Yakima Indian National Reservation, Toppenish, Washington, gives particular emphasis to the screening and identification of children who require special programing and services. Involvement of parents or surrogates through home visits and instruction, the training of local paraprofessionals who are Indians, and the coordination of services in the community are also major foci.

Home Program Using High School Students

Proyecto Casa or the Project for Children Acquiring Stimulation and Assistance is the homebound aspect of the Edgewood Schools's Early Childhood Education for the Handicapped Program in San Antonio, Texas. It serves Mexican-

American children from 6 months to 6 years of age. These children have a variety of handicaps and typically come from low income homes. A unique feature of this program is that its teaching staff consists of high school students who are trained and supervised by a homebound teacher. Typically, a pair of students goes into a home on a Monday, Wednesday, Friday schedule; one student acts as the teacher and the other as the observer. Once every 2 weeks the homebound teacher also observes the teen teacher working with the infant. These home teaching activities follow a 2 week intensive training program on how to work with children of this age, and additional inservice sessions on Tuesdays and Thursdays allow students to write lesson plans and to receive feedback about their successes and failures. The bilingual and cultural differences of Proyecto Casa place an extra premium on being sensitive to parental needs and values.

Home Cassette Tape Program

The Parent Tape Training Program of Ladson, South Carolina, provides a program for children 1 month to 5 years of age who are delayed in one or more areas of development. Trained home visitors visit the home weekly in order to consult with the parents and to provide them with cassette tape instructions about how to work with their child. Music provided by the music therapist provides background material as well as motivation for the enhancement of learning. A large library of materials permits the home visitor to select specific cassettes as teaching aids. During the home visit, parents observe the home visitor performing a given activity. Parents are then encouraged to repeat this activity and finally to carry it out when the home visitor is not present. The home visitor also collects basal and postbasal data on a weekly basis.

Early Stimulation as Prevention

A major trend among home based programs is the enrollment of high risk children at increasingly earlier ages. Further, the emphasis is on the prevention of problems rather than their cures. In Los Angeles, Infant Intervention in a Chicano Barrio for multiply handicapped infants 0 to 2 years old is designed to foster "bonding," or that responsiveness and awareness between infant and family which helps the handicapped child progress in the early sensory motor phase of development. The children are from low socioeconomic homes, and some of their parents are fearful of detection as aliens. Parent to parent support provided by an organized group of parents (EL ARCA Parent Group), and the services of community agencies are major components of the program. Parent meetings are held monthly.

The Dilenowisco Educational Cooperative in Norton, Virginia, sponsors an infant stimulation and parent involvement project that is preventive in nature. Parents are trained to be more effective change agents and high risk infants are grouped with low risk infants.

Home Based Models: Low Incidence

Project SKI*HI of Logan, Utah, serves hearing impaired children (0 to 5 years of age) in a home based program. The deployment of personnel is rather unusual, for the project parent advisor establishes a parent home program while a trained, part time language advisor living in the immediate geographic area makes weekly visits to the home. The full time parent advisor supervises the part time advisors and makes periodic home visits. The basic approach is auditory, although a total approach is used in homes where there are deaf parents. One rationale for the use of the auditory approach is that the earlier use of hearing aids permits much greater success in such programs than has been obtained previously.

Children are identified through a high risk checklist, which is attached to the birth certificate. A child shown to be at risk is registered and his parents are contacted by telephone when he is 6 months of age. The telephone call serves as a second screening, for parents of children at risk are instructed in how to conduct tests of frequency and intensity using materials found in the home. If parents feel there is no problem, they are asked to continue testing every few months and call if a problem is indicated. If parents feel the child has failed the hearing test, he is provided a professional audiological examination. If a hearing loss is noted on this evaluation, a hearing aid is obtained and the parent advisor helps the parent learn how to teach the child to accept the aid. Loaner aids are also maintained for emergency purposes.

Work with parents is based on a series of goals, which include parent advisor goals, parent goals, and child goals. The program helps the parent teach his child how to use his residual hearing. Teaching activities are conveyed through the parent visitor who visits the home 1 hour weekly. The basic home language program is an environmental one designed to use everyday activities within the home in ways that are linguistically meaningful to the hearing impaired child. The home language program is maintained as long as needed, typically once a week for a year and then biweekly for as long as necessary. Throughout the program, parents also receive the help of a child growth and development resource person, any necessary psychological services, periodic audiological testing, hearing aid mold fittings, hearing aid loan service, and other forms of professional assistance.

Young (0 to 2) multiply handicapped, high risk deaf infants and their parents are provided service through the Infant Stimulation Program for Multi-Handicapped and Deaf Children at the Boston University Horace Mann School for the Deaf (Allston, Massachusetts), which emphasizes a total (oral-aural and vision) approach. This program is implemented through intensive case finding, screening, testing, diagnosis, and prescriptive planning. The results of this testing are used to develop activities that are presented to parents during weekly home visits. Parents also receive counseling. Reevaluation of therapy, enrollment in other programs, and followup are important adjuncts to this program.

The Hearing and Speech Agency of Metropolitan Baltimore, Inc. (Baltimore, Maryland) provides a program for parents of hearing and/or language disordered children ages 0 to 3. Home based instruction is provided for parents or the caretakers of their children. In addition, certain topics are covered in group sessions held in the main offices.

Project Vision-Up of Gooding, Idaho, serves visually handicapped children (0 to 8 years of age) on an itinerant basis because of the low population density in the area served. Specially trained parent counselors and other itinerant teachers stationed throughout Idaho visit the homes of preschoolers, kindergarteners, and school children through the third grade in order to tutor and advise parents on how to help their children. They also make school visits during which they consult with teachers on how to help eligible children.

The Boston Center for Blind Children in Massachusetts offers a program which is available as a preschool model or as a community based or home teaching model. The staff has devised a Developmental Checklist, which assesses visually impaired, multiply handicapped infants and young children. It also has developed a file of activities related to the skills surveyed by the checklist, slide-tape programs, bibliographical materials, and a toy lending library.

The Access to Mainstream Project of Powellsville, North Carolina, is a home based program that serves the child from 0 to 3 years of age. Teacher counselors work with children and family members in the home at least once a week, and assistance is given to prepare children to move into higher level programs such as Head Start.

Home Followed by Center Models

Home based projects have also begun to develop sequential, interrelated programs. The next several programs to be described begin working with parents of children 0 to 3 years of age in the home and go on to help the parents enroll the child in a center based program as he becomes 2½ to 3½ years of age.

The Saginaw D.O.E.S. Care Program, sponsored by the public schools in Saginaw, Michigan, provides services for children who are 0 to 8 years of age and are trainable mentally retarded, educable mentally retarded, emotionally impaired, learning disabled, speech and language impaired, or physically or otherwise health impaired. Until the child is 3 years of age, he and his parents are served in the home by home trainers who work under the direction of the staff, which includes an occupational therapist, a physical therapist, a speech and language pathologist, a psychologist, and a nurse. Children who are 3 to 8 years of age typically attend classroom programs, which provide flexible groupings based on individual needs and learning styles. Parent involvement is secured through a number of approaches including observation, small and large group meetings, and individual conferences.

The Sewall Early Education Developmental Program (SEED) has been developed at the Sewall Rehabilitation Center in Denver, Colorado. The program serves handicapped children (ages 0 to 3 years) with developmental lags. There is a home based program for children 0 to 18 months and a center based program for those 18 to 24 months, which both parent and child attend once a week. When a child reaches 24 months and until the age of 3, he attends a program at the center. Parents participate in all levels of the program through counseling and training, group meetings, and direct teaching in the program.

The Hancock County Preschool Education Program in Sparta, Georgia, provides services similar to those found in many home based programs; however, considerable emphasis is placed on the assessment of children and on the development of a profile for each child. Parents are viewed as change agents for their children. Children 6 months through 3 years are served in the home while those 3 to 5 years are served in both the home and school setting.

The Early Childhood Education Program for handicapped children in Bismarck, North Dakota, works with children 0 to 8 years of age with a variety of handicapping conditions. The intervention begins as a home based program but older children (3 to 8 years) may be placed in classroom settings depending on their individual needs. Parents are heavily involved in the program at all levels.

Project KIDS in Decatur, Georgia, provides a broad program for children 0 to 5. Services to children 0 to 3 tend to be through identification, home visits, and parent center discussion groups. Children 3 to 5 years old are involved in center based programs, which feature a precision language based approach that is discussed in the following section.

HELP (Help Ease Learning Problems in Early Childhood), located in DeKalb, Illinois, provides services for noncategorically classified children from 0 to 3 years of age. Some children receive direct services in the form of weekly home visits from a certified teacher or a trained paraprofessional who works with the children and parents together. The teaching approach includes differential diagnosis and teaching based on developmental abilities and needs. Other children receive service through parent workshops, parent education, monitoring, and referrals. The program has also begun serving children who are integrated in licensed homes and day care centers.

Home and Center Based Model: High Incidence and Cross Categorical

Since a majority of the programs surveyed here rely on a combined home and center approach, four such programs will be considered in some detail in order to emphasize the likenesses and differences among them: the PEECH (Precise Early Education of Children with Handicaps) Project at the University of Illinois, Urbana-Champaign; the Chapel Hill Training Outreach Project in the public schools of Chapel Hill, North Carolina; the Preschool and Early Education Project at Mississippi State University, Starkville; and the Magnolia Preschool Handicapped Project in the public schools of Magnolia, Arkansas. Although these projects are now in the Outreach stage, each has an ongoing model demonstration program for young handicapped children.

The PEECH Project

The PEECH Project serves children who are mildly to moderately multiply handicapped. Deaf-blind, severely mentally and/or orthopedically handicapped are served in other programs in the community. Children are identified through a broad range screening procedure, CIP (Comprehensive Identification Process), designed to reach *all* handicapped children who need special programming. This screening process helps to insure that the hard to identify, mildly handicapped child is located as well as those who are moderately and severely handicapped. Children are drawn from 15 school districts serving the rural portions of one county in Illinois with 13,000 school age children. These school districts have a cooperative joint agreement with the University of Illinois, which is charged with coordinating and providing services to these young handicapped children.

The program is supported by local, state, and university funds. A major portion of the funding is derived from state reimbursement of personnel and transportation. The remainder of the costs is primarily borne by the local school districts with the university providing physical facilities and the salary of a coordinator. To be eligible for state reimbursement, personnel must meet state certification requirements and the program must adhere to specific rules and regulations regarding size of class, length of day, eligibility criteria, teacher-pupil ratio, and length of year. No child can be admitted to the program who has not reached 3 years of age. On the other hand, provision of educational programs and services to young handicapped children 3 and older is mandatory in Illinois, and thus there is a strong basis for the program.

Children are enrolled in eight classrooms, six at the Colonel Wolfe Center at the university, and two at distal sites in public schools in the joint agreement. Each class serves a maximum of 10 handicapped children plus 5 "normal" children who serve as models. In addition, a few children who would have to travel too far and/or have only mild problems are provided with a home based program.

Each classroom has one certified teacher and one paraprofessional for the 10 handicapped and 5 normal children. Two students in training in this specialized area are provided with practicum experiences. In addition to classroom personnel, psychologists, speech and language therapists, and social workers serve on the intervention team. There are interns in each of these areas as well as a practicum student in motor development.

The overriding belief of personnel in the PEECH Project is that a positive approach to programing for each child enhances the likelihood of his functioning at a higher level than would be true without special intervention. Since 70% to 80% of the handicapped children in the program have problems in the area of language, an instructional model derived from the Illinois Test of Psycholinguistic Abilities (ITPA) is used as a guide to curriculum development along with developmental guidelines.

A curriculum developed earlier for disadvantaged and normal children, GOAL (Game Oriented Activities for Learning), has been modified for use with these handicapped children. The children are involved in classroom activity for approximately 2½ hours each day during which they participate in large group, small group, and individual activities. A large percentage of the time is spent in small group activities carefully planned to meet individual needs. Behavioral objectives, criterion activities, and reinforcement followup lessons using a game format characterize these structured sessions. Careful daily observations of each child in critical areas of development help the teacher achieve a match between the child's stage of development and appropriate activities. A functional playground and indoor facilities promote gross and fine motor development concurrent with other facets of development such as language and social and emotional growth.

Input from ancillary team members—psychologist, language therapist, and social worker—helps to formulate appropriate procedures or to reverse ineffective procedures for achieving desirable objectives and goals. This input occurs during individual conferences, case staffings, and inservice training sessions.

An important component of the PEECH Project is parent involvement. Here again, a team approach is used. This aspect of the program can best be described as flexible in meeting the individual needs of parents. A variety of input is encouraged—large group meetings, small group meetings, individual conferences, classroom observation, direct teaching in the classroom and at home, use of parent library and toy lending library, assistance to ancillary personnel, assistance in preparation of parent newsletter, policy making on an advisory board, and assistance in screening of children. In general, parents reflect the community concern for the improved education of children and take a positive view of the program.

Children who leave the program typically enter the educational mainstream, although a few require resource class services and even fewer receive services in a special class. Careful plans are made to help the child make a smooth transition from the preschool to kindergarten or first grade, including detailed progress reports, staffings, and conferences with the child's next teacher.

The Chapel Hill Project

The second program to be discussed in the home and center based category is the Chapel Hill Training Outreach Project, developed by the public schools in Chapel Hill, North Carolina. Support for this program comes from the public schools, Community Action Agency, Junior Service Leagues, and Neighborhood Youth Corps. The instructional program is based on the Learning Accomplishment Profile (LAP), which was devised from developmental guidelines such as those used in the PEECH Project. A written curriculum (*A Planning Guide to the Preschool Curriculum: The Child, The Process, The Day*) has also been devised to work toward the behaviors specified in the LAP. During the remainder of the day, most children are enrolled in kindergarten, first grade classes, or day care programs.

Children are referred to the program though the public schools and by parents. No broad range screening program is used to identify subjects. Referred children are screened by special educators from the project and by family service coordinators; they are then informally evaluated by the classroom teacher using developmental guidelines. Children are accepted on a 3 to 4 week conditional basis to ensure that they are appropriately placed in the project.

Direct involvement of all parents is a major objective that is achieved through a variety of strategies—home visits, parent group meetings, and workshops. Specific behavioral objectives are established for individual parent-child interactions based on an observation of parent-child behavioral problems. The taking of baseline data, graphing, and systematic modification procedures are taught to parents. Role playing, videotaping, and observation are techniques used to train parents.

The Preschool and Early Education Project

The Preschool and Early Education Project (PEEP) located at Starkville, Mississippi, and sponsored by Mississippi State University in cooperation with Starkville Public Schools and the Mississippi State Department of Education, is the third project fitting the home and center based model. Children served by

PEEP are 4 to 7 years of age and are generally educable mentally retarded, although a few are more seriously handicapped. Some children have been rejected because they exhibited handicapping problems other than mental retardation. The children were recruited through individual community members and Head Start after contacts with physicians, churches, and local health and welfare agencies resulted in the identification of only a few individuals. Since the initial difficulties in recruiting children, there has been no shortage of referrals to fill the four classes of approximately 55 children.

Initial identification procedures include data on socioeconomic and educational status, social maturity, and intellectual functioning as measured by the Stanford-Binet Intelligence Scale, and supplemental data from tests such as the Frostig Developmental Test of Visual Perception or the Illinois Test of Psycholinguistic Abilities (ITPA). Occasionally children are enrolled in the program on a trial basis of 1 or 2 days. Home visits to gather initial data are also made by the social worker. Unique to this project is the fact that eligible children must also be approved by the state screening team, which consists of a psychologist, a physician, a speech pathologist, and an educator. A social worker and/or school administrator may also be included in this team.

The program for the children begins at 8:15 in the morning and continues until 2:30. During this time the children engage in both large and small group activities with emphasis placed on language development, structural arithmetic, music, art, Frostig activities, and ITPA remediation. In addition to the developmental curriculum, the program is supplemented with speech therapy activities. The speech therapist screens all children and provides twice a week instruction for 15 minute periods to those who need it.

The parent involvement program focuses on helping to provide home assistance to parents and on helping parents to develop a basic understanding of the school and its program. One of the outcomes of the program is a booklet entitled *Parents Can Teach, Too.* Social or health related information is also provided to parents. In addition, a weekly workshop is held for the approximately 10 mothers who can attend. Topics during these workshops include reinforcing behaviors at home, selecting safe toys, and parents' responsibility to the school. Transportation is provided to and from the workshops and to parent meetings. The greatest success was obtained when parent meetings were initially held in the home of a parent and subsequently transferred to the school.

Program evaluation is based on the readministration of the initial screening instruments in the fall and spring. Results suggest that two types of children are being served. One group shows quite significant gains in the program while the other group shows mixed gains. The first group is felt to be composed of children who were functioning in the mentally retarded level because of environmental deprivation and/or developmental delays, which were remediated during the program.

The Magnolia Preschool

The Magnolia Preschool Handicapped Project is located in a predominately rural portion of southwestern Arkansas and serves 30 children who are 5 years old and have a variety of handicapping conditions. These children with mental retardation, developmental retardation, speech and hearing problems, and emotional disturbances are served in two self contained classrooms using a diagnostic teaching procedure and behavior modification techniques.

During the first year of the project, children were sought throughout a two county area through direct approach to the public assisted by radio broadcasts and newspaper articles. Considerable effort was placed on public relations during the first year because parents were unaccustomed to the idea of 5 year olds attending school, and particularly 5 year old handicapped children. This resistance has decreased and recruitment is no longer a problem.

Initially, children are placed in one of the two classrooms for 5 hours a day according to their special needs as indicated by the results of the Illinois Test of Psycholinguistic Abilities and the Metropolitan Readiness Tests. As teachers gain an understanding of the children, however, they move into a more flexible program in which one teacher is primarily responsible for the art and music instruction while the other handles most visual and math instruction. Teaching is accomplished in small groups or individually with the aid of volunteers.

Project staff has developed a package of curriculum materials particularly geared to the rural Black child. Entitled *Curriculum Guidelines for Kindergarten Activities,* these materials focus on the areas of art, auditory perception, health, language development, mathematics, movement skills, music and rhythm, science, social studies, and visual perception. The curriculum includes original design activities as well as prepared commercial materials. At present these curriculum guides are considered to be "working guides."

In addition to the classroom program, special services are provided in the areas of speech therapy and language development, health, and social work. In contrast to the preceding three projects, the Magnolia Preschool has a half time registered nurse who helps during enrollment and provides some ongoing medical supervision in emergencies. The lack of immunization is one of her chief concerns. The quality of the morning snack and school lunch program is ensured through the services of a home economist provided by the school district on a half day a week basis. The social worker and an assistant director serve as family liaisons. Social workers often counsel families on matters both directly and indirectly related to the preschool child.

One of the notable aspects of the project is that it recruited teachers from local areas rather than from outside the area because of their immediate understanding of the community and its problems. As a result, there has been considerable need for both preservice and inservice training, since many people had to be retrained to perform their duties. Volunteers also play an important part in the program, providing the help needed to permit individual and small group work with children.

Program Similarities

As has been seen, many similarities exist among the preceding four projects because they are classroom based and public school affiliated, and they focus on the multiply handicapped child. Similarly, all tend to use the ITPA language model and to provide structured experiences for children whether in separate classrooms or integrated in some way with model or "pattern" children. Speech and language therapy are also important activities. Services to parents are uniformly considered to be important and occur both in the home and in the school. Work with parents can emphasize their problems, the relationship of the problems to the child, and/ or the parents' relationship with the child himself. Financial support is often derived directly through the school system. The lower age limit of the children served, whether it be 3 or 5, is determined by state laws. Some differences do occur among the projects, such as those related to developing a curriculum appropriate to the needs of rural Blacks as compared to small town children of both races. All programs, however, seem to be practical and productive in their area.

Other Home and Center Based Programs for the Multiply Handicapped

In addition to the four projects that have been described in detail, several projects throughout the country use similar approaches, but often emphasize one or more unique areas. PERSN (Preschool Education Reaches Special Needs) located in Mason City, Iowa, is designed to reach children 0 to 6 years of age. This project follows the general outline of the home and center based approach with possibly more emphasis given to mainstreaming than is generally found. The North Central Louisiana Model Preschool Program for Handicapped Children in Ruston, Louisiana, provides another clear example of the home and center approach, for children 3 to 5 years old.

The Ochlocknee Multi-Handicapped Outreach Project in Southwest Georgia provides a broad range comprehensive program for children 0 to 8 years of age who have two or more handicaps. Instructional programing includes cognitive development, language and communications skills, psychomotor development, social and emotional development, and self help skills. One aspect of the program is that it functions on a "zero reject" principle, either serving the child directly or referring him to other county agencies. The infant program is based on a classroom approach in which both children and mothers participate two or three times a week.

The Atypical Infant Development and Educational Systems Project (AIDES) of Napa, California, serves children with a wide variety of handicaps who are 0 to 5 years of age. Program duration is flexible, ranging from 2 hours a week to a maximum of 4 hours a day for 5 days a week, depending upon a child's needs. AIDES seems to be a rather typical home and center based program except for the developing program in the 0 to 3 age range and the fact that the classroom curricula has not yet been completely defined.

Preparing handicapped children for mainstreaming within the normal school population at the Circle Preschool was undertaken by the Alpha Plus Corporation of Piedmont, California. Activities include selective reinforcement of school adaptive behavior plus small group tutoring in language, cognitive, and motor skills, and mainstreaming the children into the normal school population. Parents are also trained to implement the program at home.

A program for language impaired children has been developed by the Easter Seal Society, Hazleton, Pennsylvania. Any child who has a 6 month or greater delay in language development is eligible for this program, which provides both home and center components.

A combined center and home program is found in the Las Palomitas Early Childhood Education for the Handicapped Project located in the New Mexico State University at Las Cruces, New Mexico. Some handicapped children (with various handicaps) and nonhandicapped children are enrolled in a classroom and receive instruction in the center. Others in sparsely settled communities receive services from their mothers who are trained to implement the program at home. Parents are required to spend half a day a week in the pilot school or in the home training program.

The major emphasis in the South Dakota Preschool Program for Handicapped Children, based at Pierre, South Dakota, is given to work with parents in the home based component of the program, but many children are brought into the center or classroom based component to receive additional reinforcement. These classroom sessions vary, but a child would minimally attend 2 sessions a week for at least 2 hours a day. As in many programs, parents often take an active part in classroom activities.

Norfolk State College, Norfolk, Virginia, has developed a center and home based program for children from different ethnic groups. It has an unusually large number of different ethnic groups represented in the program.

Children with a wide variety of handicaps are being served in a model program at the Children's Therapy Center in Sedalia, Missouri, which emphasizes individualized programing and parent involvement.

The Agency for Infant Development (AID) of Kentfield, California, provides services for children who are 0 to 3 years of age and who may be diagnosed as blind, partially sighted, Down's syndrome, or cerebral palsied but may also have suspected neurological deficits, delayed speech, and/or delayed development. Referrals tend to come from private physicians, clinics, and community agencies. A wide range of services is offered including individual visits, a mother and baby group (for mothers and their children who are usually under 1½ years of age), prenursery groups that meet 3 days a week for 3 hours a day, weekly parent discussion groups, and parent meetings of a general nature. The basic philosophy is based on a general developmental point of view with emphasis on the typical areas of classroom activities: personal and social skills, perceptual and fine motor skills, cognitive development, language development, and sensory motor skills. An attempt is made to apply learning theory in the process. However, as little is known about how 3 year olds learn as compared with older children, this tactic has created some problems in implementation of the project.

The Austin, Texas, Independent School District has developed A Comprehensive Service Delivery System for Preschool Multi-handicapped Children. The project emphasizes coordination of school, home, and community services.

Home and Center Programs for Children with Behavior Disorders

Most of the preceding programs were designed for multiply handicapped children, often with a particular emphasis on language handicaps. The next several programs, also relying on a combined home and center approach, focus on children who are basically behaviorally disordered and/or unprepared to participate in the usual school structure.

One such program is the Special Education in a Day Care System Project in Washington, D.C., which attempts to meet the needs of emotionally disturbed children 20 months to 6 years of age. Essentially all of the children are Black and from low income families. Efforts are made to identify the acting out child as well as the withdrawn child through the screening of a large number of day care centers in the central city. After a child has been identified, he is provided with prescriptive teaching for 20 to 30 minutes a day at his own center by an itinerant teacher. Sometimes he is taught with other children, and at other times he studies by himself in a quiet corner. Typically, the child is given a large number of reinforcement opportunities to help him develop feelings of confidence and self worth. Some children, of course, have perceptual handicaps and are provided with a curriculum tailored to that need. The basic curriculum is implemented through a typical nursery school setting with interest areas. Children in need of a highly specialized program may be bused to a central center for half day sessions and then returned to the home center. Work with parents is viewed as crucial in this program.

The Systems Network for Preschool Emotionally Disturbed Children in York, Pennsylvania, is also developing a model to serve emotionally disturbed children, both in the city and in rural poverty areas. The project has evolved a systematic and analytical assessment of structure, manpower, resources, linkages, and mechanisms necessary to provide for the emotionally disturbed preschool age child. Such assessments include those of the child, his family, and his environment in a total approach. Socioeconomic factors and related problems are among those considered in the systems analysis. Finally, the basic goal is to get the system operating to the point where the child is able to reenter regular school programing successfully.

Children enter the project on the basis of a child psychiatrist's examination and social worker data. A psychological examination is conducted only if and when necessary, and efforts are made to improve the behavior of the child without giving him a stigmatizing label. Initially, five emotionally disturbed children are identified and served by a central core staff who may work directly with the children as much as 3 hours a day and then integrate the children back into an adjacent child development center for the remainder of the day. The amount of time spent in the central core area is decreased and the amount of time in the day program increased as the child makes progress.

The development of the central core staff is basic to the project. This development began with the addition of a psychologist and a special education teacher (who work with the social service worker) and three teachers (two of whom are at the beginning teacher aide level). The information gained from training this central core staff to work with the children is then used to train staff members in the seven other child development centers. Central core staff work directly with the emotionally disturbed children served by the eight child development centers, either by bringing the child to the central core area and/ or working with the child in the satellite location.

Each of the child development centers relies on a "responsive environment approach," in which efforts are made to maintain consistency and limits and to establish structures that will help the child learn to use his own inner controls.

Parents are involved in the program at the planning and development stages and, through training and counseling with project personnel, in the provision of assistance within the neighborhood.

In many respects this program is similar to the basic home and center approach, although it is restricted to emotionally disturbed children. Further, there appears to be a movement away from special classroom placement and toward the integration of the emotionally handicapped child in the regular classroom program as soon as he is able to cope, even at a minimal level. In a sense, then, this program seems to be moving in the direction of the technical assistance or consultative services model, described later in this chapter.

Finally, considerable emphasis is given to staff development within the project. Since seven centers are involved, the capacity to train staff in the central core area and employ them in locations where they can work with emotionally disturbed children *in situ* is a strong organizational advantage.

Home and Center Programs with Integration and "Open Structure"

Another version of the home and center approach strongly emphasizes the integration of handicapped with nonhandicapped children. Typical is the program developed at the High/ Scope Demonstration Preschool in Ypsilanti, Michigan, which serves children 3 to 5 years old who have mild to moderate problems in mental, vision, or hearing development, who exhibit other health or physical problems, or who are considered to be emotionally disturbed. These handicapped or developmentally delayed children are placed in classrooms of 50% to 65% "normal" children. The classes meet 5 days a week for half day sessions.

Within the classroom, children follow the *High/ Scope Cognitive Preschool Curriculum: An Open Framework,* which provides teachers with an open framework for understanding and working with children. The "open framework" concept is considered to be important because the format provides teachers and child care workers with a structure on which to base the program while at the same time encouraging the initiation of new experiences and activities by both adults and children. Key areas within this curriculum are active learning, classification, representation, seriation, and temporal and spatial relations. Recently, most staff energies have been directed toward the classroom aspects of the program because not enough staff was available to fully maintain the parent aspects of the program. Nevertheless, the parent component is considered to be important.

The Schaumburg Early Education Center (Illinois) is unique because of the theoretical model it follows—the Piagetian model. Assessment procedures are based on developmental milestones in five areas, and this developmental profile is made by parents.

Another twist to the home and center approach is provided by the Resurrection Preschool Parent Cooperative Sheltered Classroom in Alexandria, Virginia. Since this is a cooperative preschool, parents are trained and used as paraprofessional classroom aides. One further difference is that the learning environment is "open" compared to the somewhat more structured approach used in other programs. The 8 handicapped children, with a variety of problems, are integrated into the total open school enrollment of 45 children. In addition to the open classroom experience for children, parents are helped to develop and use individualized curricula for their children at home.

Project PUSH (Parents Understanding Student Handicaps) located in Keyser, West Virginia, serves children 0 to 8 years of age with a wide variety of handicapping conditions. This rural Appalachian program is essentially eclectic in nature, implementing concepts from the developmental literature, from Piagetian theory, from the behavioral approach, and from prescriptive teaching. The result is a semistructured open classroom.

When the population to be served comes from a community as well as outlying rural areas, the home and center model must be modified. The Comprehensive Outreach Model Program (COMP), University Park, Pennsylvania, provides services to multiply handicapped infants and children 6 months to 5 years of age from low income families who live in the immediate college town or in selected rural county areas. Services to the community population are provided through a center based approach while those given in the rural area follow an *in situ* structure.

The child attending the rural Outreach program is involved in a series of activities that begin with his being observed in the home and/or day care center to determine his functioning in the motor, cognitive, adjustive, and communicative areas. The child is then brought to the university setting for additional observation and assessment. Based upon this data, objectives are determined and materials and methods selected. These materials and methods are tried out on the campus site, and parallel training is provided for both parents and rural staff to help them learn how to implement the prescriptive teaching program. After training, the child, rural staff, and parents return to the local site to implement the prescription. Representatives of the project team then visit the local setting to observe the implementation of the prescription and to obtain feedback that will ensure progress. Changes are made as indicated.

A similar approach is provided for those children who attend the University Park (Pennsylvania) Laboratory of Early Education Program, with the exception that they may be enrolled in classrooms based on one of three curricular models: cognitive developmental, Piagetian, and Precision Positive. The latter is based on modern learning theory and is presented in a prepared environment similar to the responsive environment classroom developed from the concepts of Nimmicht, McAfee, and Myer. Students are heavily involved in the implementation of this program, from the collection of data through the training of both themselves and parents in the program.

The Child Development Center, sponsored by United Cerebral Palsy of the Bluegrass, Inc., at Lexington, Kentucky, provides a home and center program for children who are 4 to 6 years of age. Children are identified through a series of screening clinics that work through public health and assistance organizations, school personnel, day care centers, and the media. Children attend a half day, 5 day a week program based on prescriptive teaching and therapy. Parent conferences and parent education classes are a part of the project. An interesting finding is the considerable drop in divorce rate among parents whose children enter the program. Another feature is the Lexington Computerized Tracking System, a computerized coding system for case records.

Use of Videotapes

Project MEMPHIS (Memphis Educational Model Providing Handicapped Infants Services) serves developmentally delayed children referred through the State Department of Public Welfare or Mental Health Services. Initially, children eligible for the project were 3 to 5 years of age but now are 0 to 3 years of age because of a new mandatory law that covers children 4 and 5 years of age. Project MEMPHIS relies on a developmental task analysis approach. Once a child is evaluated, lesson plans are selected, prepared, and implemented. The child and the parent are seen twice each week, once in the treatment center and once at home. Sessions are periodically videotaped to evaluate and document child progress. Discussions with the parents center around the training needs of the parent and modeling of new tasks by the teacher. Videotapes are used as part of a report to fathers during parent conferences held at night.

The Coordinated Early Education Program (CEEP) sponsored by the Eastern Nebraska Community Office of Retardation in Omaha has similarities to the previous program, but because of its major emphasis on behavior modification techniques, it is philosophically closer to the Seattle Model Preschool Center for Handicapped Children described in a following section. CEEP provides services to children 0 to 5 years of age through several related programs. The initial program is the infant stimulation program for children 0 to 2, which, with the help of the *Meyer Children's Rehabilitation Institute Teaching Program for Young Children,* demonstrates to parents how to select objectives and to train their child in sensory motor, language, motor, and adaptive behavior. A trainer visits the home for at least 1 hour a week in order to demonstrate to parents how to work with their child, to write prescriptions for the family, and to help them use a daily recording tool for documenting progress. The home trainer also monitors the child's growth and makes new recommendations to the family when necessary.

In addition, CEEP offers an infant day care program for children whose parents are out of the home because of work. Delayed infants in this program are integrated with nondelayed infants. A resource/consulting teacher assists the regular day care staff in providing for the delayed infant. Children who are 2 to 5 years of age are placed in a preschool program and, again, provided the services of a resource/consulting teacher. The emphasis is on the use of precision teaching techniques in the behavioral areas. Conceptual, language, self help, social, and motor skills are observed and charted. Similar procedures are used with nondelayed children to provide comparison data.

When a child enters the day care program, the resource/consulting teacher collects data during a 30 minute period of routine activities. The teacher notes such behaviors as sounds and words, interaction with staff and peers, and initiation of activities or interactions. These observations are evaluated and aims are established based on observations of normal children. Frequent increases in appropriate behavior are usually noted. Two weeks after the initiation of the program, a teaching team consisting of the child's parents, the resource/consulting teacher, and the preschool teacher meets to review the child's progress and to develop new goals. Others, of course, may also participate in these sessions. Of interest is the fact that 84% of all team meetings are attended by parents.

An unusual aspect of the program is that videotapes are made of the children in the school and reviewed at the team meetings. Such procedures were found to be quite beneficial to the meeting and to parents. Another unusual aspect is that staff training is competency based.

The Handicapped Children's Early Education Program (HCEEP) at the Dubnoff Center, North Hollywood, California, enrolls children who are at risk and are 0 to 5 years of age. Children eligible for the program are those who are developing under "handicapping conditions"; thus, a child may be essentially normal but nevertheless eligible if he is considered to be developing in a family where there are serious emotional or physical problems. One of the problems of the center is that of recruiting eligible children other than those with Down's syndrome or other conditions easily diagnosed at birth. The intake procedures in the program are notable because of the evaluative home visit and the play observation in the center. One of the more important aspects of the program is that parents are frequently visited in the home and concern for the development of the child is related to "whole family" development. Another important aspect of the program is the "expectation" held while working with the handicapped young child; that is, he is expected to change, grow, and develop.

Basically the children are divided into three groups: 0 to 18 months, 18 months to 3 years, and 3 to 5 years. The youngest group is brought to the center twice a week for 1 hour sessions. At times during the weekly session the infants play with each other while the mothers attend the parents' group meeting. In other sessions, the parents and children are grouped together with the teaching staff. The teacher also visits the home each week to discuss various problems with the mother.

The middle group (18 to 36 months) meets three times a week for 2 hour sessions. Parents are also visited at home each week and visit the center on a weekly basis. The 3 to 5 year old group meets 4 mornings and 1 evening each week. The evening session, from 4:00–7:00 p.m., is designed to allow fathers to attend. Home visits are made only as needed for this group. Activities in the preschool group are structured and unstructured, and teaching aids are used frequently. Infant sessions, on the other hand, focus specifically on particular problem areas.

Although stated objectives are used while working with parents and children, the atmosphere tends to be freer than one might usually anticipate. There is, nevertheless, a concern for the development of specific growth in children. One of the expressed needs of the project is for more transportation for those parents who need it.

A similar program has been developed for high risk infants (0 to 3) at the Suffolk Rehabilitation Center, Commack, New York. This project helps to meet the emotional needs of the family and extended family through individual and group counseling. A major component of the program is the diagnostic and therapeutic service offered in the home and at the center by a multidiscipline team—physician, infant teacher, rehabilitation therapist, speech pathologist, audiologist, psychologist, and social worker. The infant teacher visits the home weekly to work with the infant and the prime care giver.

Home and Center Programs Providing Bilingual Instruction

The Edgewood School's Early Childhood Education for the Handicapped Program of San Antonio, Texas, serves children 3 to 6 years of age from low income, Mexican American background. The children served tend to have all types of handicaps except severe orthopedic handicaps. In some ways this program is a typical home and center program, except that it provides bilingual instruction for children. On the other hand, it also provides special programs for the Spanish radio and television broadcasting network. The parent aspect of the program is called PINESA (Padres Interesados En Sus Angelitos). (Proyecto Casa, described earlier, is another program in the same school district.)

A Model for the Early Education of Handicapped Children and Their Families is an infant and family project located in the Department of Special Education at California State University, Los Angeles, California. It has as its major objective the design, implementation, evaluation, revision, and dissemination of a model for educating 0 to 3 year old handicapped children and their families. The parents are bilingual and the children are blind, deaf, deaf-blind, high risk, multiply handicapped, physically handicapped, mentally retarded, and emotionally disturbed. Although the intervention is both at home and in a center, cooperation with other agencies is also stressed.

Programs Using Electronic Information Systems

The Multi Agency Preschool Program for the Handicapped (MAPPS) at Utah State University, Logan, Utah, provides a unique home and center approach for children who are 6 months to 5 years of age. A computer monitors the packaged and sequenced curricula materials provided the children, who may be deficient in one or more of a variety of areas including cognitive-language and perceptual motor. Children are served either in the infant stimulation home based aspect of the program or integrated into regular preschool programs. A major purpose of this project is the economical dissemination of these materials to remote rural areas, where parents may be the only personnel available to provide the primary programing for handicapped children. Multiple agencies are involved in the implementation of this program.

Telecommunications of Educational Diagnosis and Prescription Regarding Pupils' Disorders has been developed at Ft. Lewis College, Durango, Colorado. This project features a home based educational preschool program for teaching the learning disordered child in conjunction with a school based program within the public schools. Through a teletypewriter system, educators have a response to their questions about a child's behavior within 4 hours. An analysis of objectives for the learner is made by the project team. Mini tests, demonstrations, and inservice materials help the learner to achieve the objectives.

Home and Center Based Model: Low Incidence

Several center and home based programs have been developed for children with low incidence handicaps. Reliance on a joint approach seems to stem from the fact that the home necessarily plays an important part in early learning, but at the same time center facilities are needed for special types of diagnosis and the modeling of desired behavior.

Deaf children 0 to 3 years of age are the focus of the Parent-Infant Program at the Central Institute for the Deaf in St. Louis, Missouri. The program provides "guided experiences" for the hearing, language, and multiply handicapped child and his parents in the Home Demonstration Center. The center contains two apartments, which resemble those of upper lower class homes. Teachers trained in the areas of the deaf, counseling, and behavior change assist parents by employing a variety of strategies such as modeling, directing, critiquing, and videotaping. These strategies are used while parents engage in typical daily tasks such as cooking and laundry. Parents are taught a variety of skills, which include talking at the child's eye level, checking comprehension, and rewarding vocalization. In addition to individual sessions, parents also attend two meetings per month. After a child is 24 months old, he is also enrolled in a class for 1½ to 2 hours per week. Parents also participate in these classroom activities. The basic goal of the program is to develop the parent as the designer, modeler, consultant, and authority figure who can maximize the development of his handicapped child.

The Infant Program for the Visually Impaired Child at Mason, Michigan, serves children 0 to school age, who are blind or visually impaired. Groups of six to seven children are brought into nursery school settings 4 half days per week. Younger children, 2 to 4 years of age, attend in the morning, and older children, 4 to 5 years of age, attend in the afternoon. The setting is a large house which provides a homelike atmosphere with a variety of areas—kitchen, dining room, living room, and play room. A teacher, two aides, and a volunteer aide work with the children. The teacher also conducts parent training activities and makes weekly visits during which he or she works with the parent and child on specific developmental tasks. A speech and language therapist provides part time service to the children and staff while the services of an occupational therapist, a physical therapist, and a clinical psychologist are also available.

Project TAPP (Technical Assistance to Preschool Programs) of Laramie, Wyoming, serves children with a variety of handicaps but especially those with communication disorders. Children served fall within the age range of 2 to 9 years and have performance IQ's of above 70. The project has two related programs. The first provides intensive training for parents who come with their children and live in university housing during the summer session. During the second or followup phase, which occurs during the winter, project staff travel to the home communities on a monthly basis to evaluate the child's progress, discuss problems, and redesign learning packets. During this followup phase, coordination with other professionals in the community is also sought to insure the optimal provision of services to the child.

One of the basic strengths of the program appears to be in the development of specific instructional objectives, which provide the parent with knowledge about the skill to be taught, criteria to judge progress, and a time limit recommended for the completion of the tasks by the child. Often objectives use materials designed specifically for the child, but commercial materials are also suggested or loaned for a period of time. Videotapes are made of the mother and child to help determine progress.

Since the intensive summer program would be too confining for mothers living in dormitory rooms, baby sitters are provided so that mothers can participate in a variety of evening programs especially designed for them. Exercise classes, arts and crafts groups, and other campus special events provide broadening experiences for the mother. Emphasis is also placed on bringing fathers and siblings to the center whenever possible.

The Hospital for Joint Diseases and Medical Center, New York, has established the First Chance Child Development Center where it conducts a program for children 0 to 3 with diagnosed problems of neuromuscular disease, such as cerebral palsy. Basic components of the program include (a) a training program for the child that is designed to help him cope effectively, both physically and socially, with a nonhandicapped world; (b) educational counseling for family members; (c) a program for early identification basically aimed at the medical community serving the children; and (d) consultation to educational programs such as Head Start that serve 3 to 5 year old children. Heavy emphasis is placed on physical development as well as on the development of intellectual and cognitive skills. Children are brought to the center for half day sessions up to 11 months of the year, and support and encouragement are provided parents as a part of the program.

The Vista Larga Therapeutic School Project in Albuquerque, New Mexico, serves children 0 to 7 years of age who have multiple problems in personal and social, language, intellectual, and emotional development. The basic approach appears to be to increase the attentiveness of the child, a goal consistent with the philosophy of the cooperative university and County Mental Health/Mental Retardation Center setting. One strength of the program is its flexibility, in that both short and long term therapeutic school experiences are provided the typical child for one or more years in classes that meet 4 half days per week.

The basic behaviorally oriented curriculum emphasizes the area of cognitive skills; interpersonal (object) relationships; language (communication) skills; self help skills; and fine and gross motor skills. As might be expected, the specification of target behaviors and skills, the development of strategies for modifying behavior and developing skills, and the establishment of long range goals and ancillary programing are part of the total approach. One focus of the program is to intervene in the total environment of the child, which of course includes his parents. Aspects of the parent program include initial contact, goal setting, feedback, classroom participation, individual and group therapy, parent association meetings, and other services.

Contributing to the training of project personnel are the Menninger Clinic in Kansas, the Julia Ann Singer Center in Los Angeles, and the League School in Brooklyn, since the Albuquerque center is part of a national network. Participating in the training aspects of the center are professionals, paraprofessionals, parents, and university students.

The Handicapped Children's Early Education Program of Tallahassee, Florida, uses the BKR educational approach and materials. It serves young children who are multiply handicapped, or severely or profoundly mentally retarded. The program is essentially center based with the children in the classroom 3 hours a day, 5 days a week. Children who live too far away to make transportation feasible or who have been rejected from classroom programs for one reason or another are provided with a home based program. Followup activities include assisting and supporting parents while recording developmental milestones, determining developmental tasks to be incorporated into the child's program, referring the child to various agencies, and enrolling him, when feasible, into a BKR based classroom.

One strength of the program is staff training that requires trainees to observe children, discuss behaviors, write objectives, participate in buzz sessions, read appropriate materials, use reinforcement techniques, formulate prescriptive programing for a child, participate in individual self evaluation conferences, and participate in rhythmics and intensive play. After teaching in parallel with an experienced staff member, trainees move on to solo teaching. Trainees come from a wide variety of public and private institutions and agencies.

Various assessment materials based on the BKR basic preschool curriculum have been devised at the center. In addition, the program is unique because of its focus on children whose etiology is unknown and/or profound retardation and/or unteachable.

Center Based Model: High Incidence and Cross Categorical

A fourth basic model that can be readily identified is one in which most of the activity occurs at a center: children are brought to the center for a variety of services; work with parents is conducted at the center; and training is held at the center. Still, a few activities may be conducted away from the center, such as parental reinforcement in the home of behaviors learned by the children at the center.

The Rutland Center

The center based program at the Rutland Center, Athens, Georgia, is distinct from other center based programs. It serves children who are 2 to 14 years of age and have severe emotional and/or developmental problems. The major goal of the center is to employ *Developmental Therapy,* a psychoeducational treatment process to reduce the social and emotional problems of children. Some understanding of how this program differs from the other center based programs previously discussed can be gained by noting the target areas: Behavior, Communication, Socialization, and Academics. Further, the Communication and Academic Skills areas are of greatest concern when they interact with the social and emotional development of the child. For example, one of the goals in the Communication area is to "use words to express onself in the *group*." Similarly, one of the goals in the Academic Skills area is to "successfully use signs and symbols in formalized school work and in *group experiences*." Thus, from the wording of the goals, it can be seen that the greatest importance is attached to communication and academic skills where they interact with the child's functioning in a social situation.

Eligible children are identified through a variety of sources; about half of the referrals come from parents, physicians, social workers, and agencies while the remainder come from local nursery schools or schools. Once a child has been accepted at the intake level and an initial interview has been conducted with the family, the child is tested and interviews are held with the child and teacher.

One assessment procedure is the Referral Form Check List (RFCL), a form congruent with the four target areas mentioned previously. Statements of behavioral problems are made, and each item is rated on a 5 point scale from "high priority problem" to "not a problem."

Data are collected by an educational diagnostician, a psychologist, and possibly a psychiatrist, and the results are reviewed along with the school contact report, RFCL profile, and parent interview results. All staff who have had or will have contact with the child discuss these findings, focusing on the needs of the child and family and on the help that the center might offer. If the child is accepted, an individual developmental therapy program is planned. Considered in the planning are the child's level of development (one of five levels in each of the four curricula areas), specific treatment objectives, length of treatment, and possible strategies for parent as well as school interventions. Subsequently, conferences are held between parents and staff during which specific test results are communicated to the parents in a manner designed to increase communication between the parents and the child's team monitor who serves as the liaison with the school. Similarly a conference is held with the regular school teacher to whom the child is likely to return.

Class attendance is relatively flexible in this program, and a child may attend classes for 1 to 2 hours a day, from 2 to 5 days a week. The length of time decreases as the child increases his attendance in a regular day care, nursery, or kindergarten program. Should a child be ineligible for one of these programs because the problem is not severe enough to warrant enrollment at the center, he might be enrolled in a "half way kindergarten," a center adaptation to local conditions. Since kindergartens are not compulsory in Georgia, small classes are provided for those children who are not old enough for first grade but whose problems are not severe enough to require placement in the center classes.

The program receives multiple funding, with monies coming from the State Department of Education, State Department of Human Resources, the Division of Mental Health, and the State Board of Education. Certain other funds are provided so that the center may act as a resource for a statewide comprehensive psychoeducational center network. In the past, eligible children have been selected from the local community and nearby areas; however, through the state-wide network, the program is becoming available to children throughout the state.

An important aspect of this program is its concern for integrating the child back into the regular program. Basically, it is held that a child may need to be taken out of the regular program for a period of time to learn new ways of functioning; however, total removal may prevent the development of the generalized behaviors required to be successful in a regular program. Therefore, the intent is to keep the child out of the regular classroom programs only long enough for him to learn new behaviors. It is hoped that he will soon be placed in a situation where he can practice these new behaviors. Another strength is the follow-through provision. The center teacher visits the regular classroom each week and exchanges information with the regular classroom teacher. Emergencies, consultation, and occasional support after the child leaves the center program are also provided as needed.

The Rutland Center is staffed by approximately 60 people from diverse backgrounds, including special education, social work, psychology, and evaluation. Much of the work is done on a team basis, a team being composed of a lead teacher, a support teacher, and a monitor working with eight children. In addition to the work of the lead teacher and the support teacher who is expected to complement the lead teacher, the monitor observes the class daily and feeds this information back to the center teachers as well as to the child's regular teacher. The parent monitor duties include planning and carrying out parent conferences and contacts, providing immediate feedback to the teaching team on group processes, and recording individual children's responses and teachers' techniques. Team roles are often rotated among staff members so that the lead teacher on one team becomes the monitor on another team.

Three instruments are used to evaluate the program: the RFCL mentioned earlier, the Developmental Therapy Objectives Rating Form (DTORF), and the Systematic Who-to-Whom Analysis Notation (SWAN), all of which appear in *The Rutland Center Model for Treating Emotionally Disturbed Children*. The DTORF contains 144 objectives and is completed for each child every 5 weeks by treatment team members. This form provides a graphic summary of the child's current developmental stage and rate of progress (see Figure 20 of Chapter 5, "Record Keeping"). The SWAN instrument is also based on representative objectives and measures the child's interaction in the classroom with other children, with the team, and with materials. The appraisal of service to parents is based on frequency counts and on unobtrusive measures such as information shared, parental acceptance, and degree of involvement.

Of the graduates of the program 65% were placed in regular elementary classes; the remainder went to nurseries, kindergartens, or special classes.

In summary, the Rutland Center represents a unique approach for several reasons. First, its focus on children with emotional problems is atypical. Further, it enjoys close cooperation with the mental health agencies of the state and functions on an area basis rather than within the boundaries of a particular school district. Finally, its emphasis on what is termed "developmental therapy" is unique.

The Mini Community for Disturbed Children

A center based program designed to reach a more restricted population is the Mini Community for Disturbed Children, sponsored by the Educational Alliance, Inc., in New York City. The project serves 3 to 7 year old disturbed children from low income Puerto Rican, Black, and Chinese families. It attempts to develop a mini community of parents and young peers within a community center and is based on systems theory, child development principles, the psychology of learning, and special education techniques. One criterion for eligibility is that the child's behavior be deviant enough to prevent placement in a typical day care and/or Head Start program.

Following an intake procedure, children are placed in small groups with a higher staff-pupil ratio than in the regular program, a ratio that is maintained through the use of paraprofessionals. Cognitive as well as social development is emphasized in these groups. The curriculum emphasizes the development of a positive self image, perceptual motor functioning, concepts of time and space, and language skills through activities based on arts and crafts, music, storytelling, science, dramatic play, block building and cooking. Length of placement in the program ranges from 3 to 11 months. Once a child has developed basic skills in the special program, he is placed in a regular program with a trained paraprofessional available to assist him during the transition period. Backup, of course, is provided for temporary regressions. A similar procedure is used when the child moves from a day care program to the regular school program. Ongoing diagnosis is part of the program.

Parents are involved in the program in a variety of roles, especially in advocacy for their child, in evaluation and assessment, in policy making, and in teaching other parents new roles.

Other Special Class Programs

The Los Angeles Unified School District, Special Education Division, sponsors the Dual Educational Approach to Learning (DEAL) for children ages 3 to 10 with a wide range of handicapping conditions. The project offers an open structured classroom environment called the *option* program and a teacher selected plan of instruction called the *formal* program. The open structured program is designed to help the child develop a positive self concept, and the formal program should increase achievement in basic skill areas. In this program, handicapped children are integrated with nonhandicapped children.

Project RHISE (Rockford Handicapped Infant Services Expansion) at Rockford, Illinois, serves children 0 to 3 who are handicapped or at risk. The Rockford School of Medicine is assisting in the identification and diagnosis of the children and in the analysis of the results. Delivery of services is through a medical clinic, residential organization, a classroom center, or a new mobile van. Children needing service attend classes twice a week.

The Early Education for Speech and Hearing Handicapped Project of the five county area near Lancaster, South Carolina, serves children who are 3 to 8 years of age. The development and implementation of remedial prescriptions during therapy classes (2 to 4 days weekly) are a major thrust of this project. Parents, teachers, speech clinicians, and volunteers are involved in these activities. The project provides services to the children in a five county area and also involves the services of an interagency team of existing specialists.

The Comprehensive Support Program for Handicapped Children in Day Care Settings has been developed at the Mile High Child Care Association of Denver, Colorado. Project personnel train day care personnel and special education aides to provide support and educational assistance to parents who are working with their handicapped children. This training takes place in the special classes provided the handicapped children. Inservice training is also provided for the staff of the project, including the teachers of the special classes.

Mainstreaming Programs

The basic thrust of the preceding programs has been individual or special class placements. The next several programs serve the handicapped child while he is in a mainstream program or in transition to a mainstream program.

The Child Care and Development Services of Los Angeles, California, sponsors the Handicapped Early Childhood Assistance Program, which has as its objectives the identification of emotionally handicapped children (ages 2 to 6) from low income homes and their integration with nonhandicapped children in a day care setting. The program offers an educational and therapeutic program, which promotes the "maximum acquisition of skills." Parents and volunteers are trained in concepts of child development and techniques for educating young children.

The program at the Liberty County Preschool in Bristol, Florida, provides another example of a center based integration program. Here, handicapped and economically disadvantaged children ages 3 to 5 are provided a common early education program with normal children. Included in the program is a resource classroom with intensive, individualized instruction for kindergarten age children with special needs.

In Saginaw, Michigan, Project PAR has been developed to prepare mentally retarded 4 and 5 year old children for public school placement through attendance in a quality day care program.

In the Learning Center of Federal City College, Washington, D.C., handicapped children, ages 2 to 6, are integrated into open classroom experiences with normal children. Weekly training sessions for staff are open to parents and concentrate on helping teachers meet the special needs of handicapped children.

The Demonstration Diagnostic Intervention Model for Early Childhood at Houston, Texas, attempts to serve handicapped children in classroom settings that vary from Head Start to kindergarten programs. Initially, children are screened in the areas of hearing, distant vision, fine and gross motor coordination, language, learning skills, and social interaction. Children are provided diagnostic services through individualized programs provided at model kindergarten learning centers (KLC's). A highly skilled diagnostic team operates the KLC's within regular kindergarten classes and parent training programs.

The Diagnostic Resource Unit of the Martin Luther King, Jr., Child Development Center, in Atlanta, Georgia, is working toward the goal of integrating handicapped children into regular programs. The initial plan integrates three handicapped children into each of six local programs. Center staff help local staff with diagnostic and resource assistance. Project Maine Stream, located in Cumberland Center, Maine, also reaches out to consult with nursery school teachers who have handicapped children integrated into their classrooms as does the Integration Model at Framingham State College, Framingham, Massachusetts.

The Behavioral Sciences Institute, Carmel, California, has developed an Accountable Re-entry Model (ARM) for handicapped children ages 4 to 8. The major objective of this project is to demonstrate that handicapped children can be assisted to reenter the mainstream using procedures that are systematic and programed to improve the handicapped child's academic, social, and motor skills. Children attend both a special class and a regular class until they demonstrate the skills needed to attend the regular class only. Parents and aides work directly with the children in the special classroom.

Project GOOD START located within the Washington, D.C., school system is concerned with developing the skills of 4 to 7 year old handicapped children so that they can enter regular classroom programs. Children eligible for the project are those who have never been in school or who have been in school but now need additional help before full placement in a regular program can again be achieved. The program is provided half days, 5 days a week.

Other Programs

Various programs spread about the country also deserve mention. The Responsive Environment Early Education Program (REEEP) developed in the public schools at Clovis, New Mexico, is designed to help 3 to 5 year old high risk children acquire language in English and Spanish and improve their cognitive and affective development. An Early Childhood Education for the Handicapped Project has been established by the Department of Education in Hato Rey, Puerto Rico. This service centered program serves children with moderate to severe handicapping conditions in the areas of speech and hearing, mental retardation, and emotional disturbance. The Catawba County Children's Center of Conover, North Carolina, is a center based project that serves children 3 to 7 years of age who have a variety of handicaps. One unique aspect is that children who need to come earlier or stay later than the established hours for the educational component may also take advantage of cooperating day care facilities. The North Shore University Hospital at Manhasset, New York, sponsors a program for preschool children (ages 3 to 5) with primary language disorders. This program stresses the development and use of methods for effective training.

The Seattle Model Preschool Center

The Model Preschool Center for Handicapped Children is part of the Experimental Education Unit of the College of Education and the Child Development and Mental Retardation Center at the University of Washington, Seattle. This center based program each year serves approximately 200 children from 0 to 6 years of age, who have a wide variety of handicapping conditions of both high and low incidence.

The Center offers several types of programs:

1. Infant learning programs. There are two different programs for infants from 0 to 18 months. One is for Down's syndrome children; the other is for "at risk" infants exhibiting a variety of handicapping conditions at, or shortly after, birth.
2. Programs for children with communication disorders. Children from 2 to 6 years of age having a variety of different types of lags in communication, but who may have other handicapping conditions as well, are served in four classes in this program. The children are grouped by age and are taught by teachers and communication disorders specialists using a team approach within the classroom setting.
3. Integrated preschool. This program integrates handicapped children with nonhandicapped peers who serve as "models" for normal patterns of speech and behavior. The program usually serves about 12 handicapped children and 6 nonhandicapped models.
4. Programs for Down's syndrome children. In addition to the infant learning program for Down's syndrome children, the early preschool serves Down's children from 19 months to 3 years of age. The intermediate program serves children 3 to 4 years of age, and the advanced preschool serves Down's children who are 4 to 5 years old. The Down's kindergarten class serves children from 5 to 6 years of age.
5. Preschool programs for severely handicapped children. The Model Preschool Center has two classes for severely handicapped children. One is a diagnostic class where program staff determine the functional level(s) of children and develop prescriptive programs for children who will be entering school programs. The other class enrolls severely handicapped children for a longer period of time.

Staff in the Model Preschool also provide a wide variety of assistance through outreach and technical assistance, working with local, state, regional, and national networks.

Children are referred to the Center by a variety of sources: various professionals within the community (e.g., pediatricians, nurses, and developmental therapists), clinics, hospital personnel, 40 school districts within the Puget Sound region, agencies within the community, family friends, and the families of handicapped children themselves. Program eligibility is *sometimes* based on certain external factors such as training and research needs—the Center is part of a university based training and research facility—but it is most often based on classroom space, the availability of other appropriate programs within the community, and the needs of the child. However, because the Center is engaged in a long term study of home reared Down's syndrome children, infants and children with this genetic anomaly have been without exception admitted to the program.

All applications for admission to the Model Preschool Center are processed through the Experimental Education Unit Admissions Officer, and the applications for those children who are considered for placement in one of the Center's programs are reviewed by the Consultant Advisory Committee. In addition, wherever possible baseline data are collected on the child's performance and reviewed in order to determine the most appropriate placement for the child, whether at the Center or in another program. Frequently, children are accepted for short term diagnostic placements, after which they are returned to appropriate programs within their communities.

When children are admitted to the Model Preschool Center, they are placed in a Center program that best meets their needs and that is appropriate for their age, developmental readiness, and the severity or kind of handicapping condition(s) they exhibit. Although the specific program emphases vary from class to class to meet these different needs, there are some basic procedures and program orientations that are common to all classes in the Center. First, the programs are developmental. A major goal is to help each child approximate as nearly as possible normal patterns of development in motor, cognitive, communication, social, and self help skills. Second, the staff in all classes are aware that the children will return to appropriate placements within their home communities after their stay at the Center and seek to make that transition as smooth as possible. Third, instruction in the Model Preschool Center provides opportunities for large group experiences, small group activities, and individualized instruction to further gross and fine motor, communication, social, cognitive, and self help skills for each child in any given program. Individualized instruction for children is based on initial and ongoing assessment and performance data.

Parents and staff together establish behavioral objectives for the children and continuously review the children's progress toward these objectives, with a view to changing the program whenever necessary. Teachers rely on positive reinforcement as part of the instructional technology used to help each child reach his or her behavioral objectives. Finally, parent training and involvement are major program components. The staff recognize the immensely important teaching that parents can contribute to their children's development and work with the parents in strengthening the continuity between center and home.

The Center staff is relatively large and varied in terms of experience and background. Because of the program's responsibilities to training, research, service, outreach, and technical assistance, a number of different disciplines are involved in different aspects of the programs. Adult-child ratios vary depending on the age of the children served and the severity of their handicapping conditions. Many of the classroom assistants are students in training or parents who regularly participate in classroom activities under the supervision of the Head Teacher.

Project funding is broad based and includes federal, state, and private monies depending on the function(s) served and the nature of the individual programs. Two of the programs in the Model Preschool Center have been validated by the USOE's National Review and Dissemination Panel. Work with Head Start is funded through the OCD Regional Resource Access Project.

Center Based Model: Low Incidence

The preceding center based programs serve children with a broad range of handicaps and/or a higher incidence. The following discussion will include center based programs that serve restricted types of populations of low incidence.

The UNISTAPS Project

UNISTAPS of St. Paul, Minnesota, provides a program for hearing impaired children (0 to 6 years of age). Over half of these children are described as profoundly deaf. Although the basic referral problem is hearing impairment, some children, of course, have other handicaps such as learning disabilities, crippling conditions, visual impairment, and emotional problems. About three-fourths of the children are provided with binaural amplification through UNISTAPS or public school funds. The students are drawn from the Minneapolis–St. Paul area, and a few travel as far as 50 miles to participate in the program. Referral to the program is typically from a physician or the audiology clinic.

Unlike most other projects, this program has multiple funding, which is reflected in its name: UNI for University of Minnesota, STA for State Department of Education, and PS for Minneapolis Public Schools. In addition to funds, each institution provides some input in terms of personnel and training assistance. Considerable emphasis has been given to developing a strong working relationship within and throughout the system.

A program strength is found in its provision of multiple options for working with parents and children. These options include an infant program (for children 0 to 3½ years of age), a parent-child nursery, and a primary program for children 3½ to 6 years of age. The primary program is broken down into half day nurseries, regular nurseries, full day and half day kindergartens, a half day hearing impairment kindergarten, a readiness program, and an integrated program.

When a child is in the infant program, he is helped to develop cognitive, aural/oral communication, and social skills as well as the dynamic use of his residual hearing. At the same time, his parents are helped to accept their feelings and attitudes about his hearing loss as well as to gain an understanding and acceptance of it. While in the program, both parents and child meet with the tutor counselor for a weekly one hour session, which takes place in a homelike setting. Initially, the counselor demonstrates an activity for the parent with the child. Later, the parent begins to assume a lead role and, with the help of the tutor counselor, provides the child with language stimulation in the daily living situation.

When the child has gained a level of functional use of his residual hearing and has acquired certain language and social skills, both he and the parent are graduated to one of the other programs. One of the basic options is the parent-child nursery for those children who have been identified late and need considerable basic help. Parents and children participate in nursery classes three mornings a week and spend one hour weekly in individual auditory and language stimulation activities. Graduation from this program typically leads to one of the preprimary programs. In the half day nursery, children are provided with intensive auditory training and attend individual speech and language periods. When a certain skill level has been attained, children advance to a regular nursery school program where, with the full time use of hearing aids, they are able to function with normally hearing children.

Parent counselors and social workers help locate suitable schools which must meet certain state licensing, curriculum, and staff requirements. If necessary, additional help for the parent and child may be continued through the UNI-STAPS tutoring. If the placement proves to be unsatisfactory, routine reviews disclose the problem and arrangements are made to place the child in another setting.

Some children, of course, do not develop as rapidly in linguistic and auditory skills as others and are enrolled in full day kindergarten programs that emphasize language reinforcement, speech activities, and auditory training. Children with a slightly different constellation of problems might be placed in a half day regular kindergarten and a half day hearing impaired program. The child's development is enhanced by participation with normally hearing children for a portion of the day while the specialized speech, language, and auditory training is under the supervision of a trained teacher of the deaf.

Finally, before the hearing impaired child is placed in a regular classroom, he is given additional help in the area of reading readiness through a basic preprimer series. Children who go through this program tend to end up in the middle academic group by the end of the first grade and finally enter integrated programs.

The Langley Porter Project

The Langley Porter Neuropsychiatric Institute in San Francisco, California, has a project that centers on the problems of the preschool deaf child with emotional/behavioral problems. The thrust of this project is to determine constructive ways in which classroom teachers of the preschool deaf can cope with behavioral problems. The basic need for the project stems from the high incidence of emotional problems among deaf children. At times, these problems are so severe that children of less than 3 years of age are removed from "regular" school programs.

In addition to providing mental health consultation for teachers of preschool deaf children, the project also conducts psychotherapy for preschool deaf children and their parents. Videotape documentation of these activities is used in other educational areas. Typically, a child is scheduled for a weekly appointment for play therapy while his parents are also given a weekly appointment with the same or a different therapist. Teachers are helped in the integration of the child into the classroom program, but where the classroom situation cannot be modified, home teaching is arranged as a last resort.

The UCLA Program

The UCLA Intervention Program for Developmentally Handicapped Infants and Children, located at the UCLA School of Medicine, enrolls about 12 children, 18 months to 3 years of age, who attend a 3½ hour session for 5 days a week. Most of the children are cerebral palsied but a few have autistic, emotional, behavioral, or rubella generated problems. Such a heterogeneous set of problems can prove to be useful because the more advanced children act as models for the others. The major emphasis of the program is learning through play under the supervision and direction of two teachers and two therapists who function as a unit. Most recently a built-in modification called Thera-Play or the fun house has been used (see Figure 20 of Chapter 8, "Physical Facilities and Environments"). This structure, which is about 12 feet in diameter and hexagonal in shape, is lined with a number of resilient materials such as burlap and Naugahyde. The inside of the structure is designed to provide the child with a variety of stimulation regarding shape, size, and texture.

Considerable attention is given to the involvement of the parents in the project through their assistance in the school program and through monthly parent meetings. Some parents find the prenursery a place of hope and encouragement while others look at it as a source of frustration and threat. Efforts are made to help all parents through the involvement of a large staff of medically trained individuals; social workers; teachers; psychologists; and physical, occupational, and speech therapists.

Since the program is located in a university setting, many experimental evaluations have been conducted within the program including an evaluation of the effect of confining children in a group to a smaller space than typical.

The Jessie Stanton Developmental Playground of the New York City University Medical Center provides another unique planned environment for children with handicaps. The playground has been particularly developed for children with some form of neurological insult. (See Chapter 8, "Physical Facilities and Environments," pp. 189–191.)

Programs for the Physically Handicapped

Another area of low incidence is the physically handicapped child. The Infant Education for Multihandicapped Children Project at the University of Virginia Medical Center, Charlottesville, is one such program that focuses strictly on the physically handicapped infant. Children typically enter the program as soon as they are discharged from the hospital after birth. Each child is supported educationally with weekly sessions and 6 weeks of developmental assessments. In addition, children receive comprehensive multidisciplinary medical care through the medical center. Social work support is provided to both children and families. This program differs from others because of its emphasis on the physically handicapped child and because of the early age at which intervention begins.

In the Casa Colina Hospital for Rehabilitation Medicare, in Pomona, California, children 18 months to 6 years of age who are orthopedically and/or neurologically involved attend a therapeutic preschool. Some have emotional problems. Parents are trained to be the primary therapists of their children who are placed in a center based program. The goal is to help the child move into the most normal type of educational program possible for him.

Programs for the Multiply Handicapped

The Early Education for Institutionalized Multi-Handicapped Young Children Project implemented at Kent State University in cooperation with the Hattie

Larlham Foundation at Mantua, Ohio, emphasizes working with institutionalized children who are profoundly involved in one or more ways. Behavior modification is a distinguishing characteristic of the program, which is designed to stimulate vocalization, language, gross and fine motor development, and socialization. The use of the Minnesota Child Development Inventory and the Bayley Child Development Scale also provides a different character to this program since they are used to help select program sequences and establish criteria for progress.

Severely and multiply handicapped infants are being served indirectly in the Early Identification and Comprehensive Rehabilitation Outreach Project developed by the Home for Crippled Children in Pittsburgh, Pennsylvania. Specifically, the target populations served by the project staff are personnel on the staffs of various institutions and community agencies serving young handicapped children and parents of handicapped infants.

Early Education for Multi Handicapped Children, a program that coordinates medical and nursing care services with educational, therapeutic, and social and recreation services, has been developed in Clinton, South Carolina, at Whitten Village, a division of the South Carolina Department of Mental Retardation. This program is designed for multiply handicapped children who are prone to be bedfast and dependent. The goal is to foster the development of these handicapped children so that they will be able to attend school programs on the grounds of the institution.

In Anchorage, Alaska, the Alaska Head Start Special Services Project has undertaken to serve handicapped and other high risk children. The project is sponsored by three groups: the Easter Seal Society for Alaska Crippled Children and Adults, the Special Services Delivery System, and Head Start. Native paraprofessionals are trained to work with teachers and parents of the handicapped in the regular Head Start program. The largest groups of children being served are vision and hearing impaired. The project covers an area one-third the size of the 48 contiguous states of the United States and includes Eskimos, Indians, Aleuts, and nonnative populations.

Mainstreaming

The integration of handicapped children with nonhandicapped children is generally referred to as mainstreaming. Multiple reasons may be given for mainstreaming including having the nonhandicapped children model for the handicapped children, providing sets of children with the opportunity and problems associated with learning how to get along with others, and keeping each from becoming resistive and nonaccepting of individual differences in others.

In the previous sections, programs have been identified that mainstream children, and it seems fruitful to reiterate some of these programs to help clarify the breadth of this activity. The first delivery system—the home based model— would appear to offer limited opportunity to mainstream because service is typically provided one child and one parent in the home. Nevertheless, the Telstar Project (Alpena, Michigan) is established to place a handicapped child in a day care home with a nonhandicapped child. Thus, there is a mainstreaming effect for children in this home based system. The Access to Mainstream Project of

Powellsville, North Carolina, has a different approach. The focus of this project is to work with children 0 to 3 years of age and their parents in the home with the goal of preparing the child to enter the mainstream. Thus, although the actual service does not involve actual integration, the goal of the program is integration.

The home followed by the center model offers a greater opportunity to mainstream children than does the home based model. For example, the Saginaw (Michigan) D.O.E.S. Care Program works with children in the home until they reach 3 years of age. When a child is 3 to 8 years of age, he is typically enrolled in a classroom program that provides flexible groupings based on individual needs and learning styles. Another program is HELP (Help Ease Learning Problems in Early Childhood), located in DeKalb, Illinois. This project serves noncategorically classified children who are 0 to 3 years of age. One aspect of the program, however, is to serve children who are integrated into licensed homes and day care centers, a mainstreaming approach.

The home and center based model provides even greater opportunity for mainstreaming through the center based aspects of each program. In the PEECH Project at the University of Illinois (Urbana-Champaign), mainstreaming is accomplished by integrating 8 to 10 handicapped children with 4 to 6 nonhandicapped children. In the Las Palomitas Early Childhood Education for the Handicapped Project in Las Cruces, New Mexico, some of the handicapped children are enrolled in classrooms with nonhandicapped children who are also receiving service in the center. In some of the sparsely settled communities, on the other hand, the mother and handicapped child receive services in the home. The Systems Network for Preschool Emotionally Disturbed Children in York, Pennsylvania, which serves emotionally disturbed children, appears to be a project that is moving from the special classroom approach to the integrated or mainstreaming approach. These are only a few of the home and center based programs that mainstream children.

The center based model is one that appears to have the highest potential for mainstreaming, yet one where other factors may play an important part. Many of the center based programs are located in high density areas to serve categorically identified children. Lack of space and pressure to serve the handicapped child may inhibit the recruitment and involvement of the nonhandicapped child. Nevertheless, some programs are mainstreaming in one way or another. The Seattle Model Preschool Center at the University of Washington, for example, provides many different types of programs. In one component, less severely handicapped children are integrated with normal "model" children. The Rutland Center of Athens, Georgia, provides a flexible program for handicapped children. Flexibility occurs in at least two dimensions: (a) the amount of time per week that is spent in the program and (b) the type of program in which the handicapped child is enrolled. Regular day care, nursery, kindergarten, and half day kindergarten are settings in which the handicapped children are enrolled.

Briefly, then, mainstreaming is a viable concept in the development of programs for young handicapped children. Its use is not limited to any one type of delivery system but may be used as an integral part of any of these types of programs.

Technical Assistance or Consultative Services Model

Delivery of services is more indirect in technical assistance and consultative programs than in the four major systems already discussed. This is because the technical services are generally provided to staff members in existing projects rather than to the young handicapped children themselves. Such a model is exemplified by Project Prevent in Hanover, New Hampshire. This program is designed to work with existing programs by helping to identify the target population, by assisting in the development of remedial solutions either in the field program directly or though a project based class, and by referring handicapped children to the program or agency that is best able to meet their needs.

Project Prevent began through liaison and consultation with school and Head Start programs for children 5 to 8 years of age. Initial emphasis was placed on the younger children through the introduction of screening programs for 5 year olds. The identified population was then referred to the project where a preschool education specialist gathered further data through parent conferences, classroom observations, and other agencies. Conferences were then held and plans made to serve a given child either in his present setting or by referral to another program, according to the consensus of all involved. A prescriptive plan was developed as a part of these recommendations and a followup procedure was established. Teachers in whose classes these children were placed could request aid as needed. Occasionally, the basic plan of gathering data through classroom observation was supplemented by placing a child in a diagnostic class on a half day, 4 day a week schedule. During this period the child usually remained in his regular program for the other half day.

After the first year, resource rooms were established within local school systems to provide both diagnostic and/or short and long term treatment of those children who could not be served in a regular program. These classrooms also helped to build credibility among teachers and helped them to accept prescriptive teaching as a methodology.

Project Prevent has recently extended downward the age range of the population served and currently includes children 3 to 5 years old. Nevertheless, most referrals continue to come from classroom programs and only a few from pediatricians or other direct referral resources. Children who are referred directly are diagnosed and placed in preschool programs through agency and teacher cooperation.

Finally, it is important to note that most of the services provided by this project are consultative, although some classrooms are maintained, and to that extent Project Prevent resembles center based as well as assistance and consultative models.

Another variation of the consultative model is found in the Putnam City Early Childhood Prevention Program (PEPP) of Oklahoma City, Oklahoma. The handicapped children (kindergarten through second grade) remain in the regular classroom, and project staff direct inservice meetings with staff, aides, and parents and develop curricula to meet the individual needs of handicapped children.

A more highly technical version of the consultative model can be seen in the Normalization Programming for Young Children Project in Athens, Ohio, which serves handicapped children in a three county, rural, poverty area. Through this project children are evaluated and individually planned programs are developed for each child in the physical, social, language, and cognitive areas. Additional services to the child are provided through parent education, retraining and further training of regular and special teachers, provision for child care workers in normalized day care settings, and training of home visitors. A program strength is its transdisciplinary teaming. The program attempts to cross train each specialist on the team, a procedure that requires from 3 to 5 months but ultimately enables each specialist to provide therapeutic services based on concepts derived from the other disciplines.

The INREAL (Inclass Reactive Language Therapy) Project of Boulder, Colorado, uses a reactive language therapy technique in an open education classroom setting. The focus of this program is on children 2½ to 6 years of age who have been diagnosed as language impaired and/or potentially learning disabled. Language therapists serve preschools and public school kindergartens on a half day basis, 5 days a week. Parents are also served through working in the classroom with the INREAL therapist and by attending inservice workshops to learn the INREAL approach. INREAL therapy emphasizes the establishment of an empathic relationship with the child, the use of play therapy, and the use of the psycholinguistic techniques of self talk, parallel talk, verbal monitoring, expansion, and modeling.

Technical Assistance for Center Based Programs

Technical assistance for center based programs is also being developed. The Bill Wilkerson Hearing and Speech Center in Nashville, Tennessee, is concerned about providing and improving the audiologic and educational services for children (0 to 6) with hearing, speech, and language impairments. A wide variety of individuals—hearing and speech experts, special and mainstream educators, medical practitioners, public policy makers, and paraprofessionals—are involved in this activity. The unique aspect of the project is its development of materials, techniques, and procedures for the preservice and inservice training of staff. The varied methods include verbal presentations, audiovisual programs, printed materials, and group discussion guides. The center also has developed a variety of slides, tapes, and black and white videotape and color video cassette productions, which can be used in training programs.

Similarly, SPOT (Special Preschool Outreach and Training Program) of Gary, Indiana, is developing a variety of self instructional multimedia modules, observation systems of interaction in the classroom, and classroom instruction evaluation modules. In some ways, SPOT is similar to other programs in the Outreach phase of the BEH funding; yet, the focus of its efforts seems to place the program closer to the technical assistance end of a continuum than many of the other model programs.

The CEEP Project (Comprehensive Early Education Program) of Birmingham, Alabama, is developing an approach that combines certain aspects of the center based model with those of the technical assistance and consultative models. Children ages 0 to 2 can be served, but more typically served are those who are 3 to 7 and enrolled in classroom programs such as Head Start, day care, or public schools. At the time the children enter the program, the classroom teacher and three other trained teachers from the project administer to the children a series of developmentally based activities in the areas of auditory comprehension, verbal communication, gross and fine motor, adaptive behavior, creativity, cognitive numbers, and cognitive reading. The results are recorded on optical scanning sheets, scored, and reported on a computer printout form that describes each child's developmental level and the functioning of the group or class in which the child is located. Project personnel then consult with teachers and other personnel about programs and activities that will meet the needs identified during the procedure. Project personnel and teachers can select from over 800 learning units that are keyed to the test results. The test activities can be readministered to help evaluate progress and develop future plans as needed.

Programs for the Gifted and Talented Handicapped

Two unique programs being developed to help enhance the development of gifted and talented children who are handicapped seem to fit into this model. The RAPYTH Project (Retrieval and Acceleration of Promising Young Talented and Handicapped) at the University of Illinois will serve young children (3 to 5 years old) who have one or more handicaps and show evidence of potential for unusual development in the intellectual, academic, creative, performing arts, social, or physical areas. Initially, children will be located through CIP (Comprehensive Identification Process), which helps locate, screen, and evaluate children with handicaps who need additional training and experience before they enter the regular school programs. Also, children being served in a PEECH (Precise Early Education of Children with Handicaps) type program will be observed and the information used to delineate those children who have made excellent progress and may be ready for even higher level activities.

All data will be considered and children will be placed in either an Open Ed or a Guilford "Structure of the Intellect" (SI) based classroom. Based on experience gained in these classrooms, procedures, materials, and training packages are to be modified from the GOAL curriculum and SI model materials for dissemination to other programs. Data on teacher behavior and teacher-pupil interaction as well as information on the children and parents will be made available so that interested individuals may make informed decisions about the model classroom they want to implement, as well as the materials needed to support their choices. In addition, guidelines will be developed to help match pupils and teachers with program models to maximize growth enhancing interactions.

In Chapel Hill, North Carolina, the Chapel Hill Training Gifted Project is being developed to identify and serve young children who exhibit unusual abilities despite emotional, physiological, or cultural handicaps. Eligible children will be 3 to 8 years of age and enrolled in a program such as the state schools for blind, deaf, and cerebral palsied or Head Start. The basic approach will be to identify the children using the Learning Accomplishment Profile (LAP) and new norms developed to delineate this population. Additional screening activities will be developed to tap intellectual processes that cannot be evaluated with the present materials. The curriculum will be adapted from that presently used in the project. Additional activities will be designed to enhance creativity, inquiry, and convergent and evaluative thinking.

The project will also involve a network of programs in North Carolina that are presently using the basic curriculum. Observation of activities by visitors will be conducted in a university affiliated facility.

Prenatal Model

The prenatal model focuses on prevention more than any other model. FEED (Facilitative Environments Encouraging Development), being developed at the Institute for Child Study, Indiana University, Bloomington, focuses on promoting parenting attitudes, knowledge, skills, and interaction patterns in preparents (high risk potential parents) who are enrolled in junior high schools (ages 12 to 15). An additional goal is to encourage among these teenagers a responsiveness to the social and emotional, cognitive, and physical needs of the handicapped.

The project population is drawn from areas where teenage pregnancy is high and where existing environmental factors are significantly associated with high risk birth. The rationale for the project is essentially that the high risk child is the product of the high risk mother and that this mother is usually a teenager. A large percentage of these mothers have negative attitudes toward the unborn child, have inadequate medical care, lack male support, come from homes that are characterized by serious social and emotional problems, and often have premature babies who are frequently handicapped.

These teenagers enroll in an elective course, which focuses on child development and parent-child interaction principles. The curriculum design uses a stimulus sampling approach to develop a course with high relevance to local needs. The content draws heavily from psychology, special education, and health education, and the instruction relies on conflict management strategy. Project personnel believe that use during teacher training will enhance the implementation of conflict management.

Three teachers are responsible for the supervision of the program: the health educator, who is responsible largely for hospital field experiences; the First Chance educator, who is responsible for field experiences with the handicapped child; and the classroom educator who is responsible for the experiences in the junior high school class. All three assist in the implementation of the conflict management strategy. Classes of teenagers range in size from 20 to 25, and cooperative planning among the team at each site is imperative.

Teenagers in this program work as aides in a model preschool handicapped class. This experience, it is felt, will help them develop positive attitudes toward the handicapped and to discover and understand the special needs of these children. Another practice site is at a community oriented hospital. This experience is designed to promote a more positive attitude toward hospitals among the teenagers so that there will be a willingness to seek help for prenatal and postnatal care and delivery of their babies.

It is the contention of the project staff that FEED's conflict management program promotes learning among teenagers that is not only relevant to their current life conditions but also to their future status as parents. It is hoped that through the experiences provided in the project fewer children born to these high risk mothers will have handicapping conditions because these young women will have the knowledge, skills, and attitudes to facilitate the growth of their children from the time of birth.

The Developmental Education, Birth through Two (DEBT) Project of Lubbock, Texas, has a variety of goals. One of these is to develop and present a program for pregnant students. Additional goals include the identification of young children with a variety of problems, instructional programs for parents, the provision of play and water therapy, and a followup of all the babies born to the students. The program is generally broad based and attempts to reach all of the needs of the high risk infant—physical, social, emotional, mental, educational, and medical.

Intervention into Higher Level Systems Model

Identification and intervention activities with the 0 to 3 year old population are becoming of increasing interest. United Cerebral Palsy of Northwestern Illinois and the Peoria Association for Retarded Children (Peoria, Illinois) sponsor a project designed to help other agencies develop their services to this young population. This effort attempts to involve medical schools and state universities in the presentation of selected concepts concerning this young population. The intent is to have these concepts presented as a part of the regular curriculum at the university level.

The Baltimore Early Childhood Learning Continuum of the Baltimore City (Maryland) Public Schools emphasizes mainstreaming but attempts to work through the higher levels of organizations in each school. The children served are those with relatively mild to moderate handicaps of all types—sensory, learning, and behavioral. A systems approach is used to assess the strengths and weaknesses of a school for a school year. A plan is evolved that emphasizes (a) programs and communication, (b) development of instructional alternatives, and (c) extensive inservice training. A mainstreaming program is then developed at each participating school, a process that requires a full year to implement.

The Las Palomitas Early Childhood Education for the Handicapped Project in Las Cruces, New Mexico, offers a program for multiply handicapped children 0 to 5 years of age. The project has produced a guide for helping teachers determine what level a given handicapped child might eventually be expected to attain. The guide is broken down into the basic areas of communication, psychomotor, social, and self help with suggested activities for each. Such an approach should prove useful in achieving successful and realistic mainstreaming.

SUMMARY AND CONCLUSION

Some 120 First Chance projects have been briefly reviewed in this chapter to identify different delivery systems and to provide a range of examples for each. Although many programs have unique characteristics, they generally fall into seven delivery system categories:

1. Home.
2. Home followed by center.
3. Center and home.
4. Center.
5. Technical assistance and consultative services.
6. Prenatal.
7. Intervention into higher level systems.

In most of the above categories, programs have been further classified as to whether they serve high incidence and cross categorical populations or low incidence populations. Programs have been included that serve rural, small urban, and inner city populations as well as a variety of ethnic groups. Finally, programs have been included that rely on interventions that vary from the highly structured to open education and are delivered by professionals, paraprofessionals, teenagers, parents, and volunteers.

Prevention is a key word among many projects, especially in high risk and prenatal programs. Some projects emphasize the direct provision of service to the parent or child while others attempt to intervene with universities who are training the professionals who will one day work in those projects

Funding agencies also vary greatly, but many projects have sought multiple funding. Projects are sponsored by public schools, public agencies, private agencies, universities, and special interest groups. Although most of the data is maintained by hand, several projects are computer based.

It can be concluded that First Chance programs offer an exciting variety of approaches for educating young handicapped children. For the reader who wishes to obtain more detailed information about projects, a directory of all First Chance projects may be found in Appendix A.

RESOURCES

Comprehensive Identification Process (CIP). PEECH Project, Urbana-Champaign, Illinois, 1975. (Available from Scholastic Testing Service, Inc., 480 Meyer Road, Bensenville IL 60106. $54.50.)

Comprehensive Services for Atypical Infants and Their Families—An Overview (film). A Nationally Organized Collaborative Project to Provide Comprehensive Services for Atypical Infants and Their Families, New York, New York. 1976. (Available from United Cerebral Palsy, Inc., 66 E. 34th Street, New York NY 10016. $65; rental, $10 for three days.)

Curriculum Guidelines for Kindergarten Activities. Magnolia Preschool Handicapped Project, Magnolia, Arkansas. 1973. (Available from West Side Preschool Program, P.O. Box 428, Magnolia AR 71753. $3.00.)

Developmental Checklist. Boston Center for Blind Children, Boston, Massachusetts. (Available from the center, 147 South Huntington Avenue, Boston MA 02115. $5.00.)

Developmental Therapy: A Textbook for Teachers as Therapists for Emotionally Disturbed Young Children. Rutland Center, Athens, Georgia. 1975. (Available from University Park Press, Baltimore MD 21202. $9.75.)

GOAL (Game Oriented Activities for Learning). PEECH Project, Urbana-Champaign, Illinois. 1972, language; 1973, mathematical concepts. (Available from Milton Bradley Co., Springfield MA. $125 each.)

High/Scope Cognitive Preschool Curriculum: An Open Framework. High/Scope Demonstration Preschool Project, Ypsilanti, Michigan. 1974. (Available from ERIC Document Reproduction Service, P.O. Box 190, Arlington VA 22210, ED 069 383; and from High/Scope Educational Research Foundation, 600 North River, Ypsilanti MI 48197. $.75.)

Learning Accomplishment Profile (LAP). Chapel Hill Training Outreach Project, Chapel Hill, North Carolina. (Available from the project, Lincoln Center, Merritt Mill Road, Chapel Hill NC 27514. $2.00.)

Lexington Computerized Tracking System. United Cerebral Palsy of the Bluegrass, Inc., Lexington, Kentucky. (Available from UCPB Child Development Program, 465 Springhill Drive, Lexington KY 40503.)

Meyer Children's Rehabilitation Institute Teaching Program for Young Children. Meyer Children's Rehabilitation Institute, Omaha, Nebraska, 1974. (Available from The Council for Exceptional Children, 1920 Association Drive, Reston VA 22091. Order no. 88. $4.25.)

Parents Can Teach, Too. Preschool and Early Education Project, Starkville, Mississippi. (In *Selected Readings in Early Education of Handicapped Children.* Available from The Council for Exceptional Children, 1920 Association Drive, Reston VA 22091. Order no. 85. $4.25.)

PEECH Learning Playground (Sample Lesson Plans). PEECH Project, Urbana-Champaign, Illinois. (Available from the project, 403 E. Healey, Champaign IL 61820. Free.)

A Planning Guide to the Preschool Curriculum: The Child, The Process, The Day. Chapel Hill Training Outreach Project, Chapel Hill, North Carolina. (Available from ERIC Document Reproduction Service, P.O. Box 190, Arlington VA 22210. ED 097 968.)

Portage Guide to Early Education. The Portage Project, Portage, Wisconsin. 1972, revised 1976. (Available from the project, 412 E. Slifer, Box 564, Portage WI 53901. $32 per set plus shipping.)

Portage Project "Book of Readings." The Portage Project, Portage, Wisconsin. 1976. (Available from the project, 412 E. Slifer, Box 564, Portage WI 53901. Free.)

The Rutland Center Model for Treating Emotionally Disturbed Children. Rutland Center, Athens, Georgia. 1972. (Available from ERIC Document Reproduction Service, P.O. Box 190, Arlington VA 22210, ED 087 703; and from Technical Assistance Office, Rutland Center, 698 N. Pope Street, Athens GA 30601. $5.00.)

4 IDENTIFICATION, SCREENING, AND ASSESSMENT

Alice H. Hayden
Eugene B. Edgar

☐ If the national goal to provide programs for all handicapped children by 1980 is to be attained, there is an urgent need for parents and personnel from many different disciplines to work together in an effort to screen, assess, and identify children with handicapping conditions. As any student in special education knows, "experts" are not always entirely in agreement on definitions of handicapping conditions. There are some variations, too, in the classifications or categories of exceptional children and youth. Problems involved in arriving at a nationally accepted definition of learning/language disabilities illustrate the differing points of view on this one exceptionality.

The fact that there are wide differences within the realm of "normal" is generally recognized and accepted, but society must recognize too that there are also wide differences in any population of handicapped children and adults. Yet some seem to think of *the* handicapped as a single population having characteristics that clearly set that population apart. There is still a great need for continued education of the public about handicapping conditions even though substantial strides have been made in this area within the past few decades. The incidence of handicapping or potentially handicapping conditions is so great that few families can completely escape contact with this reality.

A COMPLEX PROBLEM

The authors of this chapter believe that professionals in different disciplines can and will come to agreement on functional definitions of handicapping conditions; but the problem of reaching agreement on procedures for screening, assessment, and identification of handicapping conditions is more complex. A cursory review of the literature indicates that there is an abundance of publications on the identification, screening, assessment, or evaluation of handicapped children. Many checklists, inventories, instruments, and devices have been developed and used by specialists in different disciplines. Some are for different age levels; some are for different types of handicapping conditions.

Although the term *evaluation* is frequently used in relation to handicapped children, *assessment* is the term preferred in this chapter.

Evaluation has many different meanings and certain connotations that may be more misleading than helpful. The purpose of any attempt to screen, assess, or identify handicapped individuals is not to label or to set apart any individual as being different from other individuals. Rather, the purpose is to determine those who may need special services so that deficits that may limit the attainment of their full potential can be prevented or remediated as fully as possible.

There are many causes of handicapping conditions—some known, some unknown—but knowledge about the etiology is not always useful even in preventing the condition from occurring in other individuals, although much research effort is being directed to this end. Until preventive measures are found, society must cope as effectively and as efficiently as possible in helping handicapped individuals and their families to understand and to work with the problems that a handicapping condition may impose.

Many handicapped individuals have far more potential than is commonly realized. The contributions of many handicapped people to various fields and aspects of life have been documented again and again in history and literature. *Biographical Sagas of Will Power* (Baker, 1970) discusses the contributions of such well known handicapped people as Helen Keller, Franklin Roosevelt, Louis Braille, and Thomas Edison. Who knows how much the world might profit from the contributions of other handicapped people if all were provided needed programs and services to help them attain their fullest potential? Who knows how much heartache the handicapped and their families might be spared and how much more effectively and efficiently these individuals might perform if needed services and effective programs were provided?

Certainly society does not help handicapped individuals and their families though pity and overprotection. Society helps people with handicapping conditions through remediating those conditions that can be treated and by providing programs that enable these individuals to become as independent as possible.

But the handicapped must first be identified—a task that is not always simple, for there are many subtle types of handicapping conditions that may escape early detection because they cannot be readily observed. Thus, the general public is usually aware of the more readily observable handicapping conditions but frequently shows no awareness of more subtle problems. Although public awareness of the obvious handicapping condition often results in stares of amazement and in embarrassment of the handicapped person, the public is often responsive about providing services for an obviously handicapped individual. Those with more subtle forms of handicap tend to suffer less from public stigmatization— but suffer instead from a lack of appropriate programs.

Identification, screening, and assessment may be complicated by many factors: The age of the child and severity of the handicapping condition(s) may make accurate assessment difficult; resources and personnel to conduct early screening and assessment may vary widely from one community to another; environmental conditions affecting health and health habits may vary considerably; differences in nutritional intake and eating habits or lack of sufficient nourishment may cause problems; and certain cultural, religious, and language differences pose difficulties in assessment unless those who are screening and assessing are thoroughly acquainted with the populations with whom they are working. Basically, children from backgrounds other than the White middle class should not be classified or labeled with instruments that were standardized on White middle class children. The authors feel that no children should be classified or labeled with such instruments; however, there are additional considerations (including legal ones) when dealing with children from different ethnic backgrounds.

IDENTIFICATION

The first stage in identifying a handicapping condition can be defined as establishing an awareness that a problem exists. For children with certain kinds of handicapping conditions, identification can occur at birth. For instance, children with physical anomalies such as microcephaly or deformities such as cleft palate, children with severe cerebral damage, most Down's syndrome children, and children with extremely low Apgar ratings (Shipe, Vandenberg, & Williams, 1968) or very low birth weight are usually identified within the first five minutes following birth. Other indices of handicapping conditions may be noticed during the first few days following birth. Behaviors and characteristics that normal infants do not exhibit such as coma, severe lethargy, constant crying, convulsions, recurrent apnea, bulging fontanelle, rapidly increasing head size, unequal size of eye pupils, absent corneal reflexes, and paralysis of any extremity, facial muscle, or eye muscle serve as indicators that the child is at high risk and needs further extensive assessment (Parmelee & Michaelis, 1971).

There are, however, many handicapping conditions that go unnoticed for some time. Children suffering from these conditions evidence subtle developmental lags that may not be identified until later in life. Often the parent is the first person to suspect a problem. Fellendorf and Harrow (1970) reported that 70% of children with hearing problems are first identified by their parents. The fact that parents are often the first to suspect a problem is due to the lack of formal procedures to screen children between the newborn nursery and school (Kakalik, Brewer, Dougharty, Fleischauer, Genensky, & Wallen, 1974) and to pediatricians' lack of time or the techniques to notice developmental problems (Oppenheimer, 1965; Fellendorf & Harrow, 1970).

Too often the doctor's suggestion that a handicap is probably not serious and should be ignored leads to a delay in providing appropriate services: "A wait-and-see attitude prevails, to the detriment of the child. Physicians still say, 'He'll grow out of it.'" (Richardson, 1973, p. 8). Even if techniques for screening were routinely used, many young children, especially those from lower socioeconomic families, would not have access to them because they do not receive continuous health care and their problems often go undetected until they enter school (American Academy of Pediatrics, 1971). The time span during which handicapping conditions remain undetected needs to be shortened, and formal screening is one method for reducing this time.

SCREENING

Screening can be defined as the testing of a large population in order to identify those individuals who are most likely to manifest a handicap. It is a formal procedure for identifying people with *suspected* handicapping conditions. Screening is not—or should not be—used to label an individual; nor is it used to prepare *specific* objectives for intervention. A more intensive and complete assessment must follow for those individuals identified through the screening process. However, screening is an essential first step, an "early warning" signal that more intensive, precision assessment of a child's strengths and deficits is required in order that remedial—or, ideally, preventive—activities can be initiated.

There are instances of established screening techniques that are in common practice today. One example is the screening for PKU (phenylketonuria), which is mandated by law in many states. This relatively simple procedure of taking a urine sample for analysis during the first few days following birth has proven to be an effective device for identifying children with PKU.

Early Screening Devices

Considerable work has been done to develop other infant screening devices (Barnard & Collar, 1973; Knoblock, Pasamanick, & Sherard, 1966) that can be used by pediatricians and other medical personnel to identify young high risk children. Most of these scales are based on the Gesell Behavior Examination (Gesell & Amatruda, 1969). A good rationale for this type of scale is presented by Ames (1967). DiLeo (1967) has pointed out that data from this type of scale represent the here and now and must be used with caution when predicting future behavior.

The Developmental Screening Inventory (DSI) (Knoblock et al., 1966) is a checklist of normal neurological, motor, and intellectual behaviors from 1 month through 18 months of age. The DSI was designed for use by pediatricians as a quick method for noting developmental lags in children.

Oppenheimer (1965) has prepared a much more simple checklist of developmental milestones for use by pediatricians as a rough screening device for young children. Some items on this checklist are: sitting delayed beyond 9 months; lack of initiative at 1 year of age; walking delayed past 18 months; marked lack of interest in usual toys; and delayed verbal identification of objects.

The Developmental Profile (Alpern & Boll, 1972) is an inventory that measures developmental growth from 0 to 12 years in the areas of physical development, self help behaviors, social skills, academic behaviors, and communication skills.

The Denver Developmental Screening Test (DDST) (Frankenburg, Dodds, & Fandal, 1970) is a screening device that pediatricians can use to determine whether a child has developmental deviations. The DDST measures child growth in the areas of gross motor skills, language skills, fine motor adaptive skills, and personal-social skills.

Broussard and Hartner (1971) have developed a Neonatal Perception Inventory that uses parental ratings of the average infant and their own infant as a means of detecting "at risk" infants. Barnard and Douglas (1974) are attempting to develop a method of screening infants that combines parental reporting, examining child behaviors indicating high risk (birth complications, low Apgar ratings, low Bayley scores, etc.), parent conditions suggesting high risk (low educational level of the mother), and child-parent interaction data. Additionally, these procedures will be packaged so that the screening device can be used in conjunction with typical infant contact programs, such as immunization, which routinely reach a large proportion of the infant population.

Hearing and Vision Screening

A recent study by the Rand Corporation (Kakalik et al., 1974) has reviewed screening techniques to detect hearing and vision impairments. Although numerous devices are used at present for screening infants (Goldstein & Tait, 1971) and preschoolers (Bordley & Hardy, 1972) for possible hearing loss, researchers do not agree on which techniques are the most efficient. The screening for visual problems is more difficult than that for hearing (Lin-Fu, 1971), and most vision screening devices are only satisfactory for acuity. Disorders such as unilateral amblyopia (lazy eye) are often missed with current screening procedures (Gallagher & Bradley, 1972).

Because of the inadequacies of both vision and hearing screening, the Rand report (Kakalik et al., 1974) does *not* recommend comprehensive mass screening of preschool children for hearing and vision problems until the screening devices are more thoroughly evaluated. Instead, it recommends that high risk infants be mandatorily followed up and that physicians, teachers, and others who regularly see preschool children over time be trained in the early detection of hearing and visual problems.

Screening for Emotional Problems

The identification of emotional problems through screening has not been well documented. Rogolsky (1968) has made several recommendations for screening for emotional disturbance—all of which depend on teacher observation of child behavior. Rimland (1964) has developed a parental checklist of child behaviors that may indicate autism for children between the ages of 3 and 5 years of age. This type of checklist has been used by pediatricians to refer children to the Regional Intervention Project (RIP) in Nashville, Tennessee (Ray, 1974).

As Rutter (1970) stated, the behaviors of very young infants are not valid predictors of emotional growth. Not until the child is at least 6 months old can behavioral observations on emotional problems or behavior disorders be considered valid. Therefore, in the case of infants under 6 months of age it is important that followup assessment of those with suspected behavior problems include an assessment of the settings in which the behavior occurs. The problem may derive from the setting and not the child.

Screening for Learning Problems

In screening for potential learning problems, there has been a recent onslaught of "tests" proposed to identify potentially learning disabled children. As Gallagher and Bradley (1972) have noted, to date these measures have failed to meet the standards of formal tests set by the American Psychological Association (French & Michael, 1966). Teacher identification of learning disabled children appears to be the best screening method at present (Haring & Ridgway, 1967). The use of language assessment scales such as the Sequenced Inventory of Communication Development (SICD), developed by Hedrick, Prather, and Tobin (1975), holds promise for identifying children who have difficulties with language and communication and who *might* be potentially learning disabled. However, as mentioned in the Cohen (1972) evaluation of the Illinois DIAL Project, until an operational definition of learning/language disabilities is derived, screening for the learning disabled child may be counterproductive by leading to the stigma of a negative label.

Difficulties of Screening

Gallagher and Bradley (1972) have reviewed the effectiveness of early childhood screening devices. The large numbers of false positives (those children who are identified as having a handicap when in reality none exists) and false negatives (those children who are identified as having no handicap when in reality one does exist) that result from these scales make their widespread use problematic. Although false positives can be eliminated during extensive followup assessment (at a large cost in both money and manpower), the false negatives remain undetected.

Kakalik and colleagues (1974) have listed six problems with current screening procedures:

1. A large number of children with handicaps remain undetected.
2. Many children are misidentified.
3. Many identified children are labeled and are thus stigmatized.
4. There are inadequate followup services for children identified as having a suspected handicap.
5. There are insufficient trained personnel to work with these children.
6. There has been a failure to create, use, and exploit technology.

If the goal of screening for handicapping conditions is reducing the time that elapses before intervention begins, then adequate screening procedures must be developed. Since many formalized screening procedures are of questionable validity (Gallagher & Bradley, 1972; Kakalik et al., 1974), alternative screening procedures need to be considered. At the very least, screening batteries should be used to increase the predictive validity (Meier, 1975). Zehrbach (1975) has proposed a Comprehensive Identification Process (CIP) for locating and screening children for a preschool handicapped classroom and for insuring appropriate followup services to the children identified as in need of additional services. Especially noteworthy in Zehrbach's approach is the identification of mildly handicapped children who are often overlooked by the traditional screening approaches.

Some experts believe that despite the difficulties with existing screening devices, and despite the need to go on working to develop better alternative methods of screening, there is no doubt that almost any kind of screening now in widespread use is better than *no* screening effort. For those children who are identified as needing further assessment, they insist, screening is the beginning of possible "salvation." Without it, a child may wait months or years before assessment and intervention begin, and these investigators say that each such delay is undoubtedly harmful in its augmenting effects on a handicap.

One effort now under way to provide services to children who might otherwise be denied them resulted from the 1967 Early and Periodic Screening, Diagnosis, and Treatment (EPSDT) amendment to Title 19 of the Social Security Act. The

Department of Health, Education, and Welfare called for the screening of Medicaid children under 21 throughout the country to begin in February 1972. The American Academy of Pediatrics, with funding from the Office of Child Development, is involved in this extensive screening effort. A volume related to this effort provides an excellent discussion of medical screening procedures: *A Guide to Screening for the Early and Periodic Screening, Diagnosis, and Treatment Program (EPSDT) under Medicaid* (Frankenburg & North, 1974). A companion volume, *A Guide to Dental Care for the Early and Periodic Screening, Diagnosis, and Treatment Program (EPSDT) under Medicaid* (Lindahl & Young, 1974), acknowledges the different purposes of medical and dental screening and focuses more specifically on delivery of dental care.

ASSESSMENT

Assessment is usually considered to be the complete and exhaustive pinpointing of an individual's skills and deficits. Assessment is indicated for all children who are identified as potentially handicapped. These procedures should include taking multiple data in natural settings and searching for and evaluating possible secondary handicaps. The results of assessment should not be used to label individuals but to prepare appropriate intervention techniques. Because accurate assessment becomes more difficult as the severity of a problem increases, for children with severe handicaps even more data points may be needed than for their less handicapped peers in order to produce adequate assessment.

Assessment techniques must be matched to the individual child. Some procedures may use rather gross measures of skill development, which may be appropriate for the mildly handicapped child while the more severely handicapped child needs to be assessed on minute skill increments.

Yet *complete* assessment is not always indicated. In the not too distant past, 20 to 30 years ago, a teacher who noted what seemed to be abnormal behaviors might ask for "a complete workup" on a given child. A complete workup or assessment in a clinic takes a tremendous amount of time and involves considerable cost. There were, therefore, long waiting lists at most clinics, and teachers and parents were frustrated because of the delays.

Availability of Resources for Assessment

Now, however, most teachers can pinpoint their concerns about whether a child has a hearing loss, a vision problem, or some particular condition that needs to be checked by a professional in a specific area. Thus, services are available much more readily and the assessment team generally has information about the child's behavior that has led to the referral. There are, however, some problems that are indeed difficult to pinpoint, and clinics or physicians are not infrequently asked by parents, "Is something wrong with my child?" These parents may have observed a particular child's behaviors and may have made comparisons with other siblings or with neighbors' children that prompted their concerns. A few well chosen questions may help the physician get to the parents' specific concern.

Indications for Assessment

Children themselves may sometimes ask questions that call attention to a problem. For example, one child asked her teacher, "Do you think I am dumb?" The astute teacher said, "Of course I don't think you are dumb. Why do you ask that?" To which the child replied, "My family thinks I am dumb." The teacher knew that the child came from a brilliant family—the father was a lawyer; the mother a pediatrician. The teacher had known the other siblings, one whose IQ score was about 170; another 160. A check of the records showed that the child who asked the question had an IQ score of 135. The teacher shared the child's concern with the mother, who immediately began to change some patterns in the home to give the child the individual recognition she deserved.

But children seldom have any basis for comparison. How does a child know whether he sees as other children see? How does he know if he hears as other children hear? Children's behaviors can, however, alert parents and teachers to potential problems if parents and teachers observe these carefully enough.

Data Based Assessment

Assessment should be based on objective data; the person doing the assessment must be careful in interpreting data. Predictions based on incomplete data almost always prove to be incorrect. A number of years ago, parents of a visually impaired child were told that they should not expect the child to be able to keep up with her class because of her impairment. The person who conveyed this "information" apparently did not know that the child was the youngest in her class and seemed to have no difficulty in school tasks or peer relationships. Fortunately, the parents decided that they would not worry about the child's inability to keep up with her class until the class caught up to her—which it never did. One wonders what might have happened if this "information" or interpretation had been communicated to her.

Types of Assessment Procedures: Need for Interdisciplinary Effort

Since assessment can be defined as "the critical observation and analysis of behavior from which the treatment needs are determined and the procedures and goals are determined" (Banus, 1971, p. 31), assessment needs to be a team effort, calling on the expertise of many professionals (Haring, Hayden, & Beck, 1976).

Medical personnel may need to be consulted to determine if medical interventions are possible. Otologists (for auditory assessment), ophthalmologists (for visual assessment), neurologists (for neurological assessments), pediatricians (for general physical examinations), and nutrition specialists (for workups) may all be included in the formal assessment of handicapped children.

Others should also be included in assessment procedures: audiologists (to determine the exact nature of hearing loss), optometrists (to determine the possible use of corrective lenses), physical therapists or occupational therapists (to intervene when motor impairments are suspected), psychologists (to determine cognitive and socioemotional functioning), and communication disorders specialists (to perform language and speech assessment).

These specialists may provide valuable information that can be used in establishing effective educational programs for handicapped children. Additionally, they serve to verify that indeed a handicap exists. Mendelson (1967), in discussing a collaborative project, made a good case for the use of interdisciplinary teamwork: "Without this cross-exchange of information, the tendency to produce spurious results because of a lack of integration of the findings of two or more disciplines engaged in a particular research task is undoubtedly increased" (p. 37).

The Role of the Teacher in Assessment

As noted by Hayden (1974), more and more children are being served in various types of preschool programs, and teachers and others who work daily with preschool children are in a unique position to collect in depth assessment data on handicapped children. Because of their daily association with children in familiar settings, teachers are able to observe children's natural performance for extended periods of time. By comparing the children's daily performance to their test performance, the teacher can often validate or question the formal test results. In fact, one of the teacher's major responsibilities should be to collect *ongoing* assessment data in order to update current educational objectives and educational programing.

Additionally, day care and preschool staff must be trained to detect behaviors that may be indicators of potentially handicapping conditions. Following the procedures outlined by Allen, Rieke, Dmitriev, and Hayden (1972), these professionals and paraprofessionals are in an excellent position to identify those children who may need more formal assessment. By systematically observing and recording specific child behaviors that occur excessively, that occur instead of appropriate behaviors, or that interfere with the child's acquisition of appropriate skills, the teacher is in an excellent position to identify potentially handicapped children.

The Teacher Observation Form

By systematically observing child performance, the teacher may note many behaviors suggesting that in depth assessment by other professionals is warranted. The Teacher Observation Form for Identifying Children Who May Require Additional Services was developed by staff in the Clinical Training Unit and the Model Preschool Center for Handicapped Children at the Experimental Education Unit, Child Development and Mental Retardation Center, University of Washington (Seattle). This rather short device pinpoints behaviors that may indicate that the child should be referred to an appropriate specialist.

The Teacher Observation Form covers the following areas: learning, motor, social, visual, and hearing skills; general health; and language. The form, shown in Figure 1, is a sample of the kind of important data teachers can collect.

Figure 1

Teacher Observation Form
for Identifying Children Who
May Require Additional Services
Model Preschool Center for Handicapped Children
(Seattle, Washington)

Child's Name: _____ Birth Date: _____

Date: _____ Teacher's Name: _____

	LANGUAGE	YES	NO	SOMETIMES
1.	Does the child use two- and three-word phrases to ask for what he wants?			
2.	Does the child complete sentences to tell you what happened?			
*3.	When the child is asked to describe something, does he use at least two or more sentences to talk about it?			
4.	Does the child ask questions?			
5.	Does the child seem to have difficulty following directions?			
6.	Does the child respond to questions with the right answers?			
7.	Does the child seem to talk too softly or too loudly?			
8.	Are you able to understand the child?			

	LEARNING	YES	NO	SOMETIMES
9.	Does the child seem to take at least twice as long as do the other children to learn pre-academic concepts?			
10.	Does the child seem to take half the time needed by other children to learn pre-academic concepts?			
11.	Does the child have difficulty attending to group activities for more than five minutes at a time?			
12.	Does the child appear extremely shy in group activities; for instance, not volunteering answers or answering questions he is asked, even though you think he knows the answers?			

	MOTOR	YES	NO	SOMETIMES
13.	Does the child continuously switch a crayon back and forth from one hand to the other when he is coloring?			
14.	Do the child's hands appear clumsy or shaky when he is using them?			
15.	When the child is coloring with a crayon, does the hand that he is *not* using appear tense (for instance, clenched into a fist)?			

* Question applies if child is four years or older.

Figure 1 Continued

MOTOR (continued)	YES	NO	SOMETIMES

16. When the child walks or runs, does one side of his body seem to move differently from the other side? For instance, does the child seem to have better control of the leg and arm on one side than on the other? Does he lean or tilt to one side when he is walking or running?
17. Does the child seem to fear or not be able to use stairs, climbing equipment, or tricycles?
18. Does the child stumble often or appear awkward when he moves?
*19. Is the child capable of dressing himself except for tying his shoes?

SOCIAL	YES	NO	SOMETIMES

20. Does the child engage in at least two disruptive behaviors a day (tantrums, fighting, screaming, etc.)?
21. Does the child appear withdrawn from the outside world (fiddling with pieces of string, staring into space, rocking his body, banging his head, talking to himself, etc.)?
22. Does the child play alone and seldom talk to the other children?
23. Does the child spend most of the time trying to get attention from the adults?
24. Does the child have toileting problems at least once a week (wet or soiled)?

VISUAL OR HEARING	YES	NO	SOMETIMES

25. Do the child's eye movements appear jerky or not coordinated?
26. Does the child seem to have difficulty seeing objects? For instance, does he:
    tilt his head to look at things?
    hold objects close to his eyes?
    squint?
    show sensitivity to bright lights?
    have uncontrolled eye-rolling?
    complain that his eyes hurt?
27. Does the child appear awkward in tasks requiring eye-hand coordination such as pegs, puzzles, coloring, etc.?

* Question applies if child is four years or older.

(Continued on next page)

Figure 1 Continued

VISUAL OR HEARING (continued)	YES	NO	SOMETIMES

28. Does the child seem to have difficulty hearing? For instance, does he:

    consistently favor one ear by turning the same side of his head in the direction of the sound?

    ignore, confuse, or not follow directions?

    complain of head noises or dizziness?

    have a very high or very low or monotonous tone of voice?

GENERAL HEALTH	YES	NO	SOMETIMES

29. Does the child seem to have an excessive number of colds?
30. Does he have frequent absences because of illness?
31. Do his eyes water?
32. Does he have discharge from:

    his eyes?

    his ears?

33. Does the child have sores on his body or head?
34. Does the child have periods of unusual movements (like rapid eye blinking) or "blank spells" which seem to appear and disappear without relationship to the social situation?
35. Does he have hives or rashes?

    Does he wheeze?

36. Does he have a persistent cough?
37. Is he excessively thirsty?

    Ravenously hungry?

38. Have you noticed any of the following conditions:

    constant fatigue?

    irritability?

    restlessness?

    tenseness?

    feverish cheeks or forehead?

39. Is the child overweight?
40. Is he physically or mentally lethargic?
41. Has he lost weight without being on a diet?

It should be noted that the first four questions in the language section of this form are used to direct the teacher toward collecting two kinds of data: data about the environment in which communication is occurring (or not occurring); and data concerning age appropriate language. For example, in question 3: If the answer is "No, he does not describe things," then the teacher should collect class-room data (and ask the parents to provide data from the home) to find out whether expectations for the child's performance are too low and whether there are insufficient opportunities for him to describe things. If, however, the child does describe things, the topic is specific age appropriate language. For instance, if a 4 year old child is not describing things in 2 to 3 word phrases, there may in fact be a language delay. Children who are identified as having suspected language delay are then assessed with the Sequenced Inventory of Communication Development (Hedrick, Prather, & Tobin, 1975). The data from the assessment are used to formulate individual programs for the children (Rieke, 1974).

The Preschool Profile

Another communication assessment device for use by classroom teachers is included in the Preschool Profile (Figure 2), also developed by staff at the Seattle Model Preschool Center for Handicapped Children. This profile lists expectations for children's oral language development under "asks," "tells," and "answers," which are communication categories that yield useful information concerning developmentally appropriate performance and that are correlated with other aspects of the child's development.

Teachers must be cautious in interpreting observational information. Labeling and "instant diagnosis" can only serve to stigmatize children and *not* to enhance their educational opportunities. In all cases observations should continue over time to eliminate the possibility of one or two "bad days." Additionally, characteristics of the setting must always be observed and analyzed to ensure that the environment is not eliciting the inappropriate behavior (Caldwell, 1967).

Uses of Ongoing Assessment Information

The primary role of the preschool teacher is to efficiently analyze educational activities in order to enable all children to acquire appropriate skills. But this analysis will not be efficient, much less effective, if it is based only on hunches, intuition, or past experience. The teacher needs objective data. By collecting ongoing data on child performance, the teacher can know exactly what skills each child has mastered, what skills the child is currently engaged in learning, and whether the child is in fact acquiring new skills. By using explicit behavioral objectives and measuring child performance in relation to them, the teacher has a daily record to tell him which programs are not facilitating child growth. When this occurs, he can use his collected data to alter the educational activity appropriately in order to individualize instruction for improved child performance.

As has been noted, many different assessment tools have been developed for use with different age levels and different populations. Some groups may rightfully question the use of "standard, White, middle class measures" in culturally different populations. Valid, culture free tests are difficult to develop although there have been many attempts to do this.

Combinations of Assessment Measures

Most assessment teams prefer to use a combination of assessment measures as a check and double check to arrive at what would seem to them to be the best

Figure 2

Preschool Profile*, Model Preschool Center for Handicapped Children (Seattle, Washington)

	GROSS MOTOR SKILLS	FINE MOTOR SKILLS	PRE-ACADEMIC SKILLS	SELF-HELP SKILLS
0-12 months	SITS WITHOUT SUPPORT. PULLS SELF TO STANDING. CRAWLS. IMITATES ARM MOVEMENTS: e.g., SHAKES RATTLE, CRUMPLES PAPER.	REACHES FOR OBJECTS. PICKS THINGS UP WITH THUMB AND ONE FINGER (PINCER GRASP). TRANSFERS CUBE FROM ONE HAND TO OTHER HAND.	LOOKS DIRECTLY AT ADULT'S FACE. IMITATES GESTURES: e.g., PAT-A-CAKE, PEEK-A-BOO, BYE-BYE. TRACKS OBJECTS (FOLLOWS THEM SMOOTHLY WITH EYES).	FEEDS SELF CRACKER, MUNCHING, NOT SUCKING.
12-24 months	WALKS ALONE. WALKS BACKWARD. BEGINS TO RUN. PULLS TOY. SEATS SELF IN CHILD'S CHAIR. WALKS UP AND DOWN STAIRS, HAND HELD. RUNS 50 FT. WITHOUT FALLING. KICKS LARGE BALL.	RELEASES CUBE INTENTIONALLY. BUILDS TOWER OF 5 CUBES. SCRIBBLES (NOT NECESSARILY LOOKING AT PAPER). DOES NOT DROOL. PUTS CUBE IN, TAKES CUBE OUT OF CONTAINER.	FOLLOWS ONE DIRECTION INVOLVING FAMILIAR ACTIONS AND OBJECTS: e.g., GIVE ME (TOY). SHOW ME (BODY PART). GET A (FAMILIAR OBJECT).	USES SPOON, SPILLING LITTLE. DRINKS FROM CUP. CHEWS FOOD. PASSIVELY COOPERATES IN DRESSING. REMOVES GARMENT.
24-36 months	GOES UP AND DOWN STAIRS, ONE FOOT LEADING. JUMPS IN PLACE, TWO FEET TOGETHER. PEDALS TRIKE. PUSHES AND STEERS WHEELED TOY.	SCRIBBLES AND LOOKS AT PAPER WHILE SCRIBBLING. IMITATES CIRCULAR, VERTICAL, HORIZONTAL STROKES. MAKES SMALL MARKS. TURNS PAGES SINGLY. SNIPS WITH SCISSORS. HOLDS CRAYON WITH THUMB AND FINGERS, NOT FIST.	UNDERSTANDS ANOTHER: e.g., GIVES ANOTHER OBJECT ON REQUEST. MATCHES FAMILIAR OBJECTS. MATCHES/SORTS OBJECTS BY COLOR. MATCHES/SORTS OBJECTS BY SHAPE. MATCHES/SORTS OBJECTS BY SIZE.	OPENS DOOR BY TURNING HANDLE. PUTS COAT ON/OFF. USES SPOON, NO SPILLING. GETS DRINK UNASSISTED. WASHES/DRIES HANDS WITH ASSISTANCE. VERBALIZES TOILET NEEDS.

36-48 months	WALKS ON A LINE. BALANCES ON ONE FOOT 5 SECS. HOPS IN PLACE. USES SLIDE WITHOUT ASSISTANCE. GALLOPS. RIDES (i.e. STEERS AND PEDALS) TRIKE. JUMPS OVER 6" OBJECT, LANDING ON BOTH FEET TOGETHER. THROWS BALL OVER HEAD. CATCHES BALL BOUNCED TO HIM. COPIES CIRCLE. IMITATES CROSS. TRACES DIAMOND. PLACES SMALL PEGS IN PEGBOARD. DRIVES NAILS AND PEGS ALREADY SET IN PLACE.	POINTS TO 6 BASIC COLORS. ROTE COUNTS TO 3. COUNTS 2 OBJECTS, AND TELLS HOW MANY. DOES 7 PC. PUZZLE. POINTS TO SHAPES.	POURS WELL FROM PITCHER. SPREADS WITH KNIFE. BUTTONS/UNBUTTONS. WASHES HANDS UNASSISTED. PULLS ON SHOES. FOLLOWS CLASSROOM ROUTINE WITH MINIMUM TEACHER ASSISTANCE. KNOWS OWN SEX. KNOWS OWN AGE. KNOWS OWN LAST NAME. USES TOILET INDEPENDENTLY.
48-60 months	WALKS BACKWARD HEEL-TOE. RUNS ON TIPTOE. BENDS FROM WAIST W/KNEES EXTENDED TO PICK THINGS UP. WALKS UP/DOWN STEPS ALONE, ALTERNATING FEET. TRACES TRIANGLE. COPIES CROSS. COPIES SQUARE. PRINTS A FEW CAPITAL LETTERS. CUTS ON A LINE CONTINUOUSLY.	NAMES 6 BASIC COLORS. NAMES SHAPES. ROTE COUNTS TO 10. COUNTS 1-4 OBJECTS AND TELLS HOW MANY. MATCHES/SORTS OBJECTS BY TEXTURE. RECOGNIZES OWN PRINTED NAME.	CUTS FOOD WITH A KNIFE: e.g. SANDWICH, CELERY. LACES SHOES. KNOWS OWN CITY/STREET. FOLLOWS INSTRUCTIONS GIVEN TO GROUP.
60-72 months	WALKS A BALANCE BEAM. CAN COVER 2-3 YARDS, HOPPING. TURNS SOMERSAULT. SKIPS. JUMPS ROPE. JUMPS FROM 12", LANDING ON TOES. COPIES TRIANGLE. COPIES FIRST NAME. PRINTS SOME NUMBERS. CUTS OUT SIMPLE SHAPES. CHILD'S HANDEDNESS IS WELL ESTABLISHED. (i.e. CHILD IS LEFT OR RIGHT HANDED.)	NAMES SOME LETTERS. NAMES SOME NUMERALS. NAMES PENNY, NICKEL, DIME, QUARTER. COUNTS 6 OBJECTS AND TELLS HOW MANY. CAN TELL WHAT NUMBER COMES NEXT. COPIES BLOCK DESIGN. LEARNS TO DISTINGUISH LEFT FROM RIGHT.	

This profile is a working draft only and was prepared by the Communication Program staff: Communication Disorders Specialists Linda Lynch, Jane Riske, and Sue Soltman, and Teachers Donna Hardman and Mary O'Conor. The authors would appreciate feedback on the usefulness of this profile which is in the process of revision.

(Continued on next page)

Figure 2 Continued

	MUSIC/ART/STORY	SOCIAL SKILLS AND PLAY SKILLS	UNDERSTANDING LANGUAGE	ORAL LANGUAGE
0-12 months		SMILES SPONTANEOUSLY. IS SHY WITH STRANGERS. PAYS ATTENTION TO OWN NAME.	LOOKS AT PEOPLE WHO TALK TO HIM. RESPONDS DIFFERENTIALLY TO VARIETY OF SOUNDS: e.g., PHONE, VACUUM, CLOSING DOORS, ETC. RESPONDS TO SIMPLE DIRECTIONS ACCOMPANIED BY GESTURES: e.g., COME, GIVE, GET.	MAKES DIFFERENT VOWEL SOUNDS. MAKES DIFFERENT CONSONANT-VOWEL COMBINATIONS. VOCALIZES TO THE PERSON WHO HAS TALKED TO HIM. USES INTONATION PATTERNS THAT SOUND LIKE PHRASES: e.g., INTONATIONS THAT SOUND LIKE SCOLDING, ASKING, TELLING.
12-24 months	MOVES TO MUSIC, NOT NECESSARILY IN TIME. FINDS FAMILIAR OBJECT IN PICTURE ON REQUEST. LOOKS AT PICTURES IN BOOK, PATTING, POINTING TO, OR NAMING OBJECTS OR PEOPLE. PAINTS WITH WHOLE ARM MOVEMENT. SATISFIED WITH ONE COLOR IN PAINTING.	PLAYS BY SELF. WATCHES OTHERS. CLAIMS AND DEFENDS POSSESSION. IMITATES HOUSEWORK. CARRIES, DUMPS, POURS.	RESPONDS TO SPECIFIC WORDS BY SHOWING WHAT WAS NAMED: e.g., TOYS, FAMILY MEMBERS, CLOTHING, BODY PARTS. RESPONDS TO SIMPLE DIRECTIONS GIVEN WITHOUT GESTURES: e.g., GO, SIT, FIND, RUN, WALK.	ASKS FOR ITEMS BY NAME. ANSWERS WHAT'S THAT? WITH NAME OF OBJECT. TELLS ABOUT OBJECTS OR EXPERIENCES WITH WORDS USED TOGETHER (2-3 WORDS): e.g., MORE JUICE.
24-36 months	PARTICIPATES IN MUSIC GROUP: e.g., SINGS, CLAPS, DANCES, DANCES WITH GROUP. MOVES IN TIME TO MUSIC. PAINTING: USES SOME WRIST ACTION: SCRUBS; PAINTS DOTS AND LINES; NO REGARD FOR COLOR OR PRODUCT. PATS OR POKES CLAY MATERIAL.	PLAYS NEAR OTHERS, NOT NECESSARILY IN SAME ACTIVITY. PLAYS WITH WATER AND SAND. BUILDS WITH BLOCKS IN SIMPLE LINES. NAMES SIMPLE BLOCK STRUCTURES: e.g., BED, BRIDGE, ETC. PUSHES LOADED VEHICLE. ENJOYS ROCKING TOYS. INITIATES DOMESTIC PLAY WITH DOLL, HAS TEA PARTIES.	RESPONDS TO PUT IT IN AND PUT IT ON. RESPONDS BY SELECTING CORRECT ITEM: BIG VS. LITTLE OBJECTS. ONE VS. ONE MORE OBJECT. IDENTIFIES OBJECTS BY THEIR USE: SHOW ME WHAT MOTHER COOKS ON BY SHOWING STOVE, OR SHOW ME WHAT YOU WEAR ON YOUR FEET BY SHOWING SHOE.	ASKS QUESTIONS. ANSWERS WHERE IS IT? WITH PREPOSITIONAL PHRASES: e.g., IN THE BOX, ON THE TABLE. ANSWERS WHAT DO YOU DO WITH A BALL? e.g., THROW, CATCH. TELLS ABOUT SOMETHING WITH FUNCTIONAL SENTENCES WHICH CARRY MEANING: e.g., ME GO STORE OR MY HUNGRY NOW.

36-48 months	KNOWS PHRASES OF SONGS.
	LISTENS TO SHORT SIMPLE STORIES.
	MAKES RELEVANT COMMENTS ABOUT STORIES.
	'READS' FROM PICTURES (i.e. TELLS STORY.)
	NAMES OWN PICTURE. NOT ALWAYS RECOGNIZABLE.
	MANIPULATES CLAY MATERIALS:
	  e.g., ROLLS BALLS, SNAKES, COOKIES, ETC.
		PLAYS IN SAME ACTIVITY WITH OTHER CHILDREN. NOT NECESSARILY INTERACTING.
		BEGINS TO INTERACT IN PLAY.
		HELPS PUT THINGS AWAY.
		BEGINS TO TAKE TURNS/SHARE.
		BEGINS DRAMATIC PLAY:
		  e.g., TRAVELLING, PLAYING HOUSE, PRETENDING TO BE ANIMALS.
		COMBINES BLOCKS AND CARS.
			RESPONDS TO PUT IT BESIDE AND PUT IT UNDER.
			RESPONDS TO COMMANDS INVOLVING 2 OBJECTS:
			  e.g., GIVE ME THE BALL AND THE SHOE.
			RESPONDS TO COMMANDS INVOLVING 2 ACTIONS:
			  e.g., GIVE ME THE CUP AND PUT THE SHOE ON THE FLOOR.
			RESPONDS BY SELECTING CORRECT ITEM:
			  e.g., HARD OBJECTS VS. SOFT OBJECTS.
			RESPONDS TO WALK FAST BY INCREASED PACE, AND TO WALK SLOWLY BY DECREASED PACE.
				ANSWERS WHICH ONE DO YOU WANT? BY NAMING IT.
				ANSWERS IF...WHAT & WHAT... WHEN QUESTIONS:
				  e.g., IF YOU HAD A PENNY, WHAT WOULD YOU DO?
				  WHAT DO YOU DO WHEN YOU'RE HUNGRY?
				ANSWERS QUESTIONS ABOUT FUNCTION:
				  e.g., WHAT ARE BOOKS FOR?
				ASKS FOR OR TELLS ABOUT WITH GRAMMATICALLY CORRECT SENTENCES:
				  e.g., CAN I GO TO THE STORE?
				  I WANT A BIG COOKIE.

48-60 months	DRAMATIZES SONGS.
	ATTENDS TO LONGER, MORE COMPLEX STORIES.
	REMEMBERS STORY LINE.
	PAINTING:
	  MAKES AND NAMES RECOGNIZABLE PICTURES.
	DRAWS A MAN WITH 2 PARTS.
		PLAYS AND INTERACTS WITH OTHER CHILDREN.
		UNDERSTANDS SHARING/TAKING TURNS.
		PLAYS DRESS-UP.
		COMBINES BLOCKS, FURNITURE, PROPS FOR DRAMATIC PLAY.
			RESPONDS BY SHOWING PENNY-NICKEL-DIME.
			RESPONDS TO COMMAND INVOLVING 3 ACTIONS:
			  e.g., GIVE ME THE CUP, PUT THE SHOE ON THE FLOOR, AND HOLD THE PENCIL IN YOUR HAND.
			
			ABOVE ITEMS ARE SELECTED FROM THE SEQUENCED INVENTORY OF COMMUNICATION DEVELOPMENT. UNIVERSITY PRESS, UNIVERSITY OF WASHINGTON, 1975
				ASKS HOW QUESTIONS.
				ANSWERS VERBALLY TO HI AND HOW ARE YOU?
				TELLS ABOUT SOMETHING USING PAST TENSE AND FUTURE TENSE.
				TELLS ABOUT SOMETHING USING CONJUNCTIONS TO STRING WORDS AND PHRASES TOGETHER:
				  e.g., I HAVE A CAT AND A DOG AND A FISH.

60-72 months	RECOGNIZES RHYME. CAN RETELL STORY. DRAMATIZES STORY. SHOWS INTEREST IN CLOCKS, CALENDAR. PASTES AND GLUES APPROPRIATELY. MODELS OBJECTS WITH CLAY. COLORS WITHIN LINES.	CHOOSES OWN FRIEND(S). PLAYS COMPETITIVE GAMES. ENGAGES IN COOPERATIVE PLAY WITH OTHER CHILDREN, USING PROPS. PLANS DETAILED BLOCK CONSTRUCTION. USES CONSTRUCTION TOYS: e.g., LEGOS, RIG-A-JIG. PLAYS SIMPLE TABLE GAMES.	SEE PRE-ACADEMIC SKILLS	CHILD WILL HAVE ACQUIRED BASIC GRAMMATICAL STRUCTURES INCLUDING PLURALS, VERB TENSES, AND CONJUNCTIONS. FOLLOWING THIS DEVELOPMENTAL ABILITY, THE CHILD PRACTICES WITH INCREASINGLY COMPLEX DESCRIPTIONS AND CONVERSATIONS.

The Communication Program was funded initially as part of the Model Preschool Center for Handicapped Children. Experimental Education Unit (WJ-10), Child Development and Mental Retardation Center, University of Washington, Seattle, Washington, 98195 by Grant No. OEG-0-72-5371, U.S. Office of Education, Program Development Branch, BEH, Washington, D.C. Dr. Alice H. Hayden is Project Director.

"package" for the population or populations being assessed. Most educators realize that there are merits and limitations inherent in most assessment instruments and prefer to use several different measures to attempt to assess a child's assets and deficits. A single measure must be topflight if decisions are to be made on the results of the measure. Recognition must also be given to the differences in skills and time needed to use certain assessment measures.

It is for this reason that many programs have attempted to assemble their own assessment packages—packages that the program staff have reason to believe are best suited to their particular population and situation, taking into account the particular skills of program staff. Some of the different packages that have been developed for use in certain of the exemplary preschool programs are listed in a later section of this chapter. For the most part, they represent a composite designed to provide systematic assessment basic for the study of preschool age children.

There has been no attempt to evaluate these assessment packages here, for the acid test of their effectiveness lies in how well they serve the particular population and program for which they were designed. However, several "rules of thumb" for evaluating assessment devices include the following considerations. Assessment devices should provide for the *direct measurement* of child behavior. These measurements need to include *multiple data points,* especially for the more severely handicapped. In order to obtain the most accurate results, assessment is best performed in a *natural setting.* The assessment materials should include *objective developmental behaviors* that are *skill level* appropriate for the children to be assessed. The information obtained from the assessment should be easily transformed to either *educational plans* or specific referrals for in depth assessment of possible *secondary handicaps.*

The assessment devices currently in use in the various preschool programs are program specific but do have many commonalities. The process of assessment usually involves teachers looking directly and frequently at specific child behaviors. The assessment materials contain procedures for measuring objective, sequenced developmental behaviors in the skill areas of gross motor, fine motor (or cognitive), communication, and social/self help behaviors. Although the format of the materials varies, the various procedures facilitate data collection and decision making by the *teacher.*

Common Assessment Procedures

In general those assessment devices and procedures assembled by the preschools have proven to be very successful for the personnel who devised the procedures. However, the diversity of the assessment procedures results in an incompatibility of data between preschool programs. This lack of similarity makes program evaluations difficult, masks the relative effectiveness of various program strategies, and limits the development of appropriate instructional sequences for handicapped children.

The Battelle Columbus Laboratories has been contracted by the Bureau of Education for the Handicapped to develop a common assessment procedure for early education for the handicapped programs. Currently in an experimental edition, the Children's Early Education Developmental Inventory (CEEDI) (Newborg, Wnek, Stock, Schenck, & McFadden, in press) is an attempt to develop a standardized procedure for measuring child progress. When developed, CEEDI, or an equivalent procedure, will enable special educators to systematically isolate the most effective intervention procedures for young handicapped children.

Another common assessment project has been under way for several years at the Experimental Education Unit, University of Washington, Seattle. This project, the Uniform Performance Assessment System (UPAS), is based on several years of research on classroom assessment procedures, the SICD (Hedrick, Prather, & Tobin, 1975), and the Developmental Pinpoints (Cohen, Gross, & Haring, in press). Information gathered from these sources has been combined into a common format which, when completed, will provide basic assessment information on handicapped children and youth from 0 to age 21. Currently UPAS is being used with children who developmentally range from 0 to 6 years of age. Initial assessment information as well as information for developing sequenced instructional programs for children may be obtained from the UPAS data. However, the most critical aspect of UPAS is the generation of common ongoing evaluation data across school programs.

ASSESSMENT PACKAGES, CHECKLISTS, INVENTORIES, PROFILES

The list of assessment packages in this section is not intended to be a comprehensive one. Other instruments are being developed in ongoing projects, but the following projects have developed some of the more widely used packages.

Comprehensive Children's Services for Rural and Non-Urban Areas (Fargo, North Dakota) has developed A Pre-School Screening Program by Parents for Children. This material includes screening devices for auditory acuity; visual acuity (far and near point, fusion, depth perception, and color blindness); motor, visual, auditory, and language skills; self concept; parents' assessment of their child; and school readiness.

The Center for Preschool Services in Special Education (Philadelphia, Pennsylvania) has a preschool rating scale for coordination (gross and fine motor), verbal expression, auditory understanding, orientation, social relations, and psychiatric behaviors.

The Marshalltown Project (Marshalltown, Iowa) has developed the Behavioral Developmental Profile, which measures development in the areas of communication, social, and motor skills. Home advisors in the home based model Marshalltown Project are also taught to use the Developmental Profile (Alpern & Bell, 1972). Following diagnosis of the child's developmental deficits using these two instruments, the home advisor writes a weekly behavioral prescription for children from 0 to 6 years of age. Instructions given in the prescription are to be carried out by the parent or caregiver during the week.

The New Haven Preschool Program for Handicapped Children (New Haven, Connecticut) has edited a Developmental Screen—Preschool Level in language-cognition, visual motor conceptualization, visual discrimination, motor coordination, numbers, and digit span. Additionally, a Preschool "Follow-up Questionnaire" has been devised. The experimental Developmental Screen— Infant Level is a chronologically downward extension of the Beers Developmental Screening Device containing items similar to those in the preschool screening survey.

The Infant Program for the Visually Impaired Child (Mason, Michigan) has adopted a Receptive-Expressive Language Assessment for use with blind children.

Project MEMPHIS (Memphis Educational Model Providing Handicapped Infants Services, Memphis, Tennessee) is a demonstration training program serving handicapped children from 0 to 5 years and their foster parents. The project employs a three step assessment, program planning, and continuous evaluation approach using the MEMPHIS Model of Individual Program Planning and Evaluation, which is contained in *Enhancing Developmental Progress in Preschool Exceptional Children*. The assessment portion of the developmental task analysis is the MEMPHIS Comprehensive Developmental Scale, which is included in the project's *Instruments for Individual Program Planning and Evaluation*. It is administered by the teacher and covers five developmental areas: personal-social skills, fine motor skills, gross motor skills, language skills, and perceptual-cognitive skills. In addition to the three steps of assessment, program planning, and continuous evaluation, a curriculum guide, *Lesson Plans for Enhancing Preschool Developmental Progress,* has been developed, which specifies behavioral objectives and presents skill sequences in small steps.

Program Development for Preschool Handicapped Indian Children (Tucson, Arizona) has developed the Harris Articulation Test; a Developmental Screening Questionnaire for Preschool Children (used to identify children who may have mental, speech, sensory, emotional, physical, or developmental learning problems); and a device, Assessment by Behavior Rating, for use after initial screening.

The Rutland Center (Athens, Georgia) has developed referral and intake procedures that facilitate the analysis of varied assessment data. The Rutland Center has also developed a curriculum, *Developmental Therapy: A Textbook for Teachers as Therapists for Emotionally Disturbed Young Children,* to coordinate with the assessment analyses and thereby to promote instructional programing geared to the individual child's special needs.

The Boston Center for Blind Children (Boston, Massachusetts) has devised a Developmental Checklist for self help skills, expressive language, receptive language, gross motor performance, fine motor performance, social skills, and orientation and mobility.

The Schaumburg Early Education Center (Schaumburg, Illinois) has developed a checklist of Developmental Milestones in self help skills, intellectual development, socioemotional development, language, and motor skills.

The Chapel Hill Training Outreach Project (Chapel Hill, North Carolina) has developed a Learning Accomplishment Profile (LAP) for gross motor skills, fine motor skills, social skills, self help skills, cognition, and language. Coordinated curricula to facilitate individually appropriate programing for children are included with the LAP.

The Early Childhood Learning Center (El Paso, Texas) has adopted a Developmental Screening Scale for use with children between the ages of 36 and 72 months. Areas included in the scale are self help; social; gross motor; fine motor; verbal, cognitive, and linguistic; and perceptual motor.

The Magnolia Preschool Handicapped Project (Magnolia, Arkansas) has developed rating scales for social skills and motor skills.

The Alaska Head Start Special Services Project (Anchorage, Alaska) has developed a visual-auditory screening test.

Pamela Gross, Marilyn Cohen, and Norris G. Haring of the Experimental Education Unit at the University of Washington (Seattle) have developed a collection of Developmental Pinpoints designed particularly for assessing and programing for severely handicapped children. The checklist adapts and compiles the descriptors of skills found in a variety of standard, commonly available developmental inventories or profiles by making these descriptors of performance specific and unambiguous enough to be readily measurable. It also arranges them in a format that tracks each separate skill area (e.g., fine motor, communication) over time rather than listing *all* skills appearing in a child's performance at a given age. Such a format is a practical one for a teacher working in a classroom, since usually a teacher works with one skill at a time. In the standard developmental scales, the teacher would have to scan long lists of behaviors in order to find the next step in the sequence of a particular skill area. The Developmental Pinpoints provide sequential steps for the following areas: fine motor, gross motor, receptive language, expressive language, prereading, premath, music, self help skills, self-other discrimination, social, reinforcement, memory, and general behavior.

The Portage Project (Wisconsin) has developed the *Portage Guide to Early Education,* divided into a developmental sequence checklist and a set of curriculum cards. The checklist encompasses 450 separate behaviors arranged sequentially in relation to cognitive, language, self help, motor, and socialization skills for children from 0 to 5 years of age. Each of the curriculum cards matches a skill in the checklist and prescribes procedures and materials for teaching each of the behaviorally defined skills. Using both parts of the *Portage Guide,* staff and parents in this home based program can identify a child's present skill level and plan short and long range curriculum objectives for him.

The Technical Assistance Resource Center in Early Childhood Education for the Handicapped at the Meyer Children's Rehabilitation Institute (Omaha, Nebraska) has developed a three volume prescriptive teaching package, entitled *Meyer Children's Rehabilitation Institute Teaching Program for Young Children.* The first volume includes a skill sequence checklist covering language (receptive and expressive), self help (fine motor and self help), motor (gross motor and upright posture), preacademic (memory and general information), and emotional and social (body awareness and general social interaction) skills as well as prescriptive teaching cards for these skills. The second volume suggests ways of integrating the prescriptions into regular classroom activities. The final volume is called *Equipment and Materials for Use in Nursery Schools for Handicapped Children.* In addition, the Center has produced a 16 mm film showing how to adapt the techniques used in the Educational Evaluation of Preschool Children to make educational diagnoses and prescriptions for handicapped children aged 2 to 6.

The United Cerebral Palsy of the Bluegrass, Inc. (Lexington, Kentucky) has developed the Lexington Developmental Scale. This scale can be used to identify specific instructional objectives for children, pinpoint the children's developmental levels, and portray their developmental progress. The scale covers motor, language, personal, social, cognitive, and emotional development.

To reiterate, this list is by no means inclusive. There are many other materials that have been developed by programs and centers throughout the country, including, for instance, the Judge Baker Foundation in Boston, the state of Michigan's vision screening program in Mason, the primary program for hearing impaired children in St. Paul, Minnesota, the early identification and home intervention program in Coeur d'Alene, Idaho, and the Outreach project sponsored by the Bill Wilkerson Hearing and Speech Center in Nashville, Tennessee.

For a more detailed list of various assessment devices, see the *Evaluation Bibliography* (Technical Assistance Development System, 1974) and Appendix B of this handbook. See Friedlander, Sterritt, and Kirk (1975) for a more detailed discussion of specific assessment procedures. Also, the test collection of the Educational Testing Service has a special Head Start collection that can be found in the test collection *Bulletin,* available from the Educational Testing Service, Princeton, New Jersey 08540.

APPROPRIATE SPECIAL SERVICES AND EDUCATIONAL PROGRAMS

Screening and assessing handicapped children are virtually meaningless endeavors unless adequate services are provided for these children (Hobbs, 1975). Too often children who have been identified as "at risk" simply become statistics due to the lack of a coordinated effort between agencies or individuals. The Rand report (Kakalik et al., 1974) noted that, although the goal of screening and assessment procedures is to shorten the time between identifying a problem and delivering treatment for that problem, the lack of treatment opportunities often makes the goal unattainable.

After initial screening, any children who have been identified as at risk should be followed until they receive appropriate services or the suspected handicapping conditions are found not to be present. The immediate followup service for children potentially at risk varies according to the suspected problem. Children identified as at risk on visual or aural screening devices are often retested in an attempt to further eliminate false positives. However, *all* children identified as at risk at any time should be followed to determine whether there really is a problem. Those children who are identified as definitely at risk need to be referred for a complete assessment by competent specialists. The assessment data must be recorded and the child referred to the appropriate service agency. Screening without referral of children at risk is dangerous not only because the child will be denied needed services, but also because it results in labeling and parental anxiety. Assessment without referral takes these dangers one step further. Thus, appropriate referral is the critical sequel to both screening and assessment.

Referring children assessed as handicapped should serve at least two major needs. First, corrective medical services and prosthetic aids should be fully explored. Second, handicapped children need to be referred at the earliest possible date to appropriate educational programs.

In the child's educational program, assessment data need to be collected continually, because child performance data serve to evaluate the effectiveness of the educational programs. These data enable teachers to make appropriate program modifications for the children. Additionally, the teachers' observations can pinpoint various behaviors that indicate the need for additional, finer focus assessment. This process of data collection by teachers in essence completes the information loop. Screening data are used to refer children for complete assessment. Assessment data are used to refer the child to appropriate intervention services. The data collected while the child is receiving educational services are used to validate the assessment data, to further screen the child for other possible handicaps, and to provide the basis for programing the most appropriate and effective education possible. As long as these information loops remain open and appropriate referrals are made, the handicapped child will be ensured of receiving the services that he needs and that each individual has the right to receive.

REFERENCES

Allen, K. E., Rieke, J., Dmitriev, V., & Hayden, A. H. Early warning: Observation as a tool for recognizing potential handicaps in young children. *Educational Horizons,* 1972, *50*(2), 43–55.

Alpern, C. D., & Boll, T. J. *Developmental profile.* Indianapolis: Psychological Development Publications, 1972.

American Academy of Pediatrics. *Lengthening shadows: A report of the Council on Pediatric Practice on the delivery of health care, 1970.* Evanston IL: Author, 1971.

Ames, L. B. Predictive value of infant behavior examinations. In J. Hellmuth (Ed.), *Exceptional infant* (Vol. 1). New York: Brunner/Mazel, 1967.

Baker, H. J., *Biographical sagas of will power.* New York: Vantage Press, 1970.

Banus, B. S. *The developmental therapist.* Thorofare NJ: Charles B. Slack, 1971.

Barnard, K., & Collar, B. S. Early diagnosis, interpretation and intervention: A commentary on the nurse's role. *Annals of New York Academy of Science,* 1973, *205,* 373–382.

Barnard, K., & Douglas, H. G. (Eds.). *Child health assessment part 1: Literature review.* Washington DC: Health Resources Administration Division of Nursing, US Department of Health, Education and Welfare, December 1974. (DHEW Publication No. [HRA] 75–30, US Government Printing Office)

Bordley, J. E., & Hardy, J. B. A hearing survey on preschool children. *American Academy of Ophthalmology and Otolaryngology,* 1972, *76,* 349–353.

Broussard, E. R., & Hartner, M. S. S. Further considerations regarding maternal perception of the first born. In J. Hellmuth (Ed.), *Exceptional infant* (Vol. 2). New York: Brunner/Mazel, 1971.

Caldwell, B. M. Descriptive evaluations of child development and of developmental settings. *Pediatrics,* 1967, *40,* 46–54.

Cohen, M. A., Gross, P., & Haring, N. G. Developmental pinpoints. In N. G. Haring & L. Brown (Eds.), *Teaching the severely handicapped: A yearly publication of the Ameri-*

can *Association for the Education of the Severely/Profoundly Handicapped* (Vol. 1). New York: Grune & Stratton, in press.

Cohen, M. A. Evaluation report on DIAL submitted to the Office of Superintendent of Public Instruction, State of Illinois. In C. D. Mardell & D. S. Goldenberg (Eds.), *Learning disabilities/early childhood research project: Annual report.* Springfield IL: State of Illinois, The Office of the Superintendent of Public Instruction, 1972.

DiLeo, J. H. Developmental evaluations of very young infants. In J. Hellmuth (Ed.), *Exceptional infant* (Vol. 1). New York: Brunner/Mazel, 1967.

Fellendorf, G., & Harrow, I. Parent counseling, 1961–1968. *Volta Review,* 1970, *72,* 51–57.

Frankenburg, W. K., Dodds, J. B., & Fandal, A. W. *Denver developmental screening test.* Denver: University of Colorado Medical Center, 1970.

Frankenburg, W. K., & North, A. F. *A guide to screening for the Early and Period Screening, Diagnosis, and Treatment Program (EPSDT) under Medicaid.* Washington DC: American Academy of Pediatrics and the Social and Rehabilitation Service, US Department of Health, Education, and Welfare, 1974 (Document No. [SRS] 74–24516)

French, J. W., & Michael, W. B. *Standards for educational and psychological test manuals.* Washington DC: American Psychological Association, 1966.

Friedlander, B. Z., Sterritt, G. M., & Kirk, G. E. (Eds.). *The exceptional infant* (Vol. 3). New York: Brunner/Mazel, 1975.

Gallagher, J. J., & Bradley, R. H. In I. J. Gordon (Ed.), *Early childhood education. The seventy-first yearbook of the National Society for Education.* Chicago: The University of Chicago Press, 1972.

Gessell, R., & Amatruda, C. *Developmental diagnosis.* New York: Harper & Row, 1969.

Goldstein, R., & Tait, C. Critique of neonatal hearing evaluation. *Journal of Speech and Hearing Disorders,* 1971, *36,* 3–18.

Haring, N. G., Hayden, A. H., & Beck, G. R. General principles and guidelines in "programming" for severely handicapped children and young adults. *Focus on Exceptional Children,* 1976, *8*(2), 1–14.

Haring, N. G., & Ridgway, R. Early identification of children with learning disabilities. *Exceptional Children,* 1967, *33,* 387–395.

Hayden, A. H. Perspectives of early childhood education in special education. In N. G. Haring (Ed.), *Behavior of exceptional children: An introduction to special education.* Columbus OH: Charles E. Merrill, 1974.

Hedrick, D., & Prather, E. M. A behavioral system for assessing language development. In R. L. Schiefelbusch (Ed.), *Language of the mentally retarded.* Baltimore MD: University Park Press, 1971.

Hedrick, D., Prather, E. M., & Tobin, A. *The sequenced inventory of communication development.* Seattle: University of Washington Press, 1975.

Hobbs, N. *The futures of children.* San Francisco: Jossey-Bass, 1975.

Kakalik, J. S., Brewer, G. D., Dougharty, L. A., Fleischauer, P. D., Genensky, S. M., & Wallen, L. M. *Improving services to handicapped children.* Santa Monica CA: The Rand Corporation, 1974.

Knoblock, H., Pasamanick, B., & Sherard, E. S. A developmental screening inventory for infants. *Pediatrics,* 1966, *38,* 1095–1108. (Supplement)

Lindahl, R. L., & Young, W. O. *A guide to dental care for the Early and Periodic Screening, Diagnosis, and Treatment Program (EPSDT) under Medicaid.* Washington DC: American Society of Dentistry for Children, American Academy of Pedodontics, and the Social and Rehabilitation Service, US Department of Health, Education, and Welfare, 1974. (Document No. [SRS] 74–24515)

Lin-Fu, J. S. *Vision screening of children.* Washington DC: US Department of Health, Education, and Welfare, Health Services and Mental Health Administration, Maternal and Child Health Service, 1971.

Meier, J. H. Screening, assessment, and intervention for young children at developmental risk. In N. Hobbs (Ed.), *Issues in the classification of children* (Vol. 2). San Francisco: Jossey-Bass, 1975.

Mendelson, M. A. Interdisciplinary approach to the study of the exceptional infant: A large scale research project. In J. Hellmuth (Ed.), *Exceptional infant* (Vol. 1). New York: Brunner/Mazel, 1967.

Newborg, J., Wnek, L., Stock, J. R., Schenck, E. A., & McFadden, D. *The CEEDI: Children's early education developmental inventory.* Columbus OH: Battelle Columbus Laboratories, in press.

Oppenheimer, S. Early identification of mildly retarded children. *American Journal of Orthopsychiatry,* 1965, *35,* 845–851.

Parmelee, A. H., & Michaelis, R. Neurological examination of the newborn. In J. Hellmuth (Ed.), *Exceptional infant* (Vol. 2). New York: Brunner/Mazel, 1971.

Ray, J. Personal communication, August 18, 1974.

Richardson, S. O. Neglect of children with language and learning disabilities. *Hearing and Speech News,* 1973, *41*(5), 8–9, 24–27.

Rieke, J. Communication in early education. In N. G. Haring (Ed.), *Behavior of exceptional children: An introduction to special education.* Columbus OH: Charles E. Merrill, 1974.

Rimland, B. *Infantile autism.* New York: Appleton-Century-Crofts, 1964.

Rogolsky, M. Screening kindergarten children: A review and recommendation. *Journal of School Psychology,* 1968, *7,* 18–27.

Rutter, M. Psychological development: Predictions for infancy. *Journal of Child Psychology and Psychiatry,* 1970, *11,* 49–62.

Shipe, D., Vandenberg, S., & Williams, R. D. Neonatal Apgar ratings as related to intelligence and behavior in preschool children. *Child Development,* 1968, *39,* 861–866.

Technical Assistance Development System. *Evaluation bibliography* (Tadscript #2). Chapel Hill NC: University of North Carolina, 1973.

Zehrbach, R. R. Determining a preschool handicapped population. *Exceptional Children,* 1975, *42,* 76–83.

RESOURCES

Assessment by Behavior Rating. Program Development for Preschool Handicapped Indian Children, Tucson, Arizona. 1973. (Available from Elizabeth Y. Sharp, Department of Special Education, College of Education, University of Arizona, Tucson AZ 85721. $.50 plus postage.)

Assessment by Behavior Rating Manual. Program Development for Preschool Handicapped Indian Children, Tucson, Arizona. 1975. (Available from Elizabeth Y. Sharp, Department of Special Education, College of Education, University of Arizona, Tucson AZ 85721. $2.50.)

Behavioral Developmental Profile. The Marshalltown Project, Marshalltown, Iowa. (Available from ERIC Document Reproduction Service, P.O. Box 190, Arlington VA 22210. ED 079 917.)

Comprehensive Identification Process (CIP). PEECH Project, Urbana-Champaign, Illinois. 1975. (Available from Scholastic Testing Service, Inc., 480 Meyer Road, Bensenville IL 60106. $54.50.)

Developmental Checklist. Boston Center for Blind Children, Boston, Massachusetts. (Available from the center, 147 South Huntington Avenue, Boston MA 02115. $5.00.)

Developmental Milestones—Miniwheel and Maxiwheel. Schaumburg Early Education Center, Schaumburg, Illinois. 1976. (Available from SEEC Communications, 804 W. Bode Road, Schaumburg IL 60193. $5.00 for samples and observational guidelines.)

Developmental Screen—Infant Level (experimental). New Haven Preschool Program for Handicapped Children, New Haven, Connecticut. (Available from the project, 400 Canner Street, New Haven CT 06511. $.50)

Developmental Screen—Preschool Level (1974 revision). New Haven Preschool Program for Handicapped Children, New Haven, Connecticut. (Available from the project, 400 Canner Street, New Haven CT 06511. $2.50.)

Developmental Screening Questionnaire for Preschool Children (revised). Program Development for Preschool Handicapped Indian Children, Tucson, Arizona. 1974. (Available from Elizabeth Y. Sharp, Department of Special Education, College of Education, University of Arizona, Tucson AZ 85721. $.25 plus postage.)

Developmental Screening Scale. Early Childhood Learning Center, El Paso, Texas. 1972. (Available from the center, P.O. Box 10716, Early Childhood Division, El Paso TX 79997. Free.)

Developmental Therapy: A Textbook for Teachers as Therapists for Emotionally Disturbed Young Children. Rutland Center, Athens, Georgia. 1975. (Available from University Park Press, Baltimore MD 21202. $9.75.)

Enhancing Developmental Progress in Preschool Exceptional Children. Project MEMPHIS, Memphis, Tennessee. 1974. (Available from Fearon Publishers, 6 Davis Drive, Belmont CA 94002. $4.00 to individuals; $3.00 to schools.)

Gross Motor Capabilities. Alaska Head Start Special Services Project, Anchorage, Alaska. 1975. (Available from Easter Seal Society, 726 E Street, Anchorage AK 99501. $3.50.)

Harris Articulation Test. Program Development for Preschool Handicapped Indian Children, Tucson, Arizona. 1973. (Available from Elizabeth Y. Sharp, Department of Special Education, College of Education, University of Arizona, Tucson AZ 85721. $1.25 plus postage.)

Infant Evaluation Scale. Comprehensive Children's Services for Rural and Non-Urban Areas, Fargo, North Dakota. (Available from Southeast Mental Health and Retardation Center, 700 First Avenue South, Fargo ND 58102. $19.50.)

Instruments for Individual Program Planning and Evaluation. Project MEMPHIS, Memphis, Tennessee. 1974. (Available from Fearon Publishers, 6 Davis Drive, Belmont CA 94002. Single copy, $1.50; 25 for $11.00.)

Learning Accomplishment Profile (LAP). Chapel Hill Training Outreach Project, Chapel Hill, North Carolina. (Available from the project, Lincoln Center, Merritt Mill Road, Chapel Hill NC 27514. $2.00.)

Lesson Plans for Enhancing Preschool Developmental Progress. Project MEMPHIS, Memphis, Tennessee. 1973. (Available from Kendall/Hunt Publishing Co., 2460 Kerper Boulevard, Dubuque IA 52001. $13.95.)

Lexington Developmental Scale— Long Form and Screening Form. United Cerebral Palsy of the Bluegrass, Inc., Lexington, Kentucky. 1973. (Available from ERIC Document Reproduction Service, P.O. Box 190, Arlington VA 22210, ED 103 455; and from UCPB Child Development Program, 465 Springhill Drive, Lexington KY 40503. Long Form Manual, $5.00; Screening Form Manual, $1.50. Charts for each manual available separately.)

Magic Kingdom of OZ Preschool Screening Manual. Comprehensive Children's Services for Rural and Non-Urban Areas, Fargo, North Dakota. (Available from Southeast Mental Health and Retardation Center, 700 First Avenue South, Fargo ND 58102. $5.00.)

Magic Kingdom of OZ Screening Program. Comprehensive Children's Services for Rural and Non-Urban Areas, Fargo, North Dakota. (Available from Southeast Mental Health and Retardation Center, 700 First Avenue South, Fargo ND 58102. $3.50.)

Meyer Children's Rehabilitation Institute Teaching Program for Young Children. Meyer Children's Rehabilitation Institute, Omaha, Nebraska. 1974. (Available from The Council for Exceptional Children, 1920 Association Drive, Reston VA 22091. Order no. 88. $4.25.)

Portage Guide to Early Education. The Portage Project, Portage, Wisconsin. 1972, revised 1976. (Available from the project, 412 E. Slifer, Box 564, Portage WI 53901. $32 per set plus shipping.)

Preschool "Follow-up" Questionnaire. New Haven Preschool Program for Handicapped Children, New Haven, Connecticut. (Available from the project, 400 Canner Street, New Haven CT 06511. $.25.)

Receptive-Expressive Language Assessment (experimental II). Infant Program for the Visually Impaired Child, Mason, Michigan. 1975. (Available upon request and approval of Gloria M. Anderson, Ingham Intermediate School District, 2630 West Howell Road, Mason MI 48854.)

The Way a Child Grows—Developmental Testing. Alaska Head Start Special Services Project, Anchorage, Alaska. (Available from Easter Seal Society, 726 E Street, Anchorage AK 99501. Pamphlet, $1.00; slides/audio cassette, $40.00.)

5
RECORD KEEPING

H. D. (Bud) Fredericks
Victor L. Baldwin
David N. Grove
William G. Moore

□Children's records include many things—medical records, diagnostic and screening results, and progress records. Because of the comprehensiveness of the term the question must logically be asked, What kind of records must be maintained for children in early childhood programs? In answer to this question, this chapter focuses on records and record keeping systems used by the First Chance Network projects.

BASES FOR FIRST CHANCE PROJECT RECORDS

There are no federal requirements for First Chance Network projects to maintain specific administrative records, and thus local requirements dictate. Each parent organization or sponsoring organization of a model project, a school district, a nonprofit corporation, or a university has peculiar requirements for administrative records, and the First Chance Network wisely has not imposed additional record keeping on the projects. Therefore, administrative records are a local option.

First Chance Network projects are required, however, to maintain rather complete records on children's progress, and this requirement stems from two sources:

First, records must be considered to be the basis for decision making about an individual child's program. Hayden and Edgar (Chapter 4, "Identification, Screening, and Assessment") make the point that assessment instruments provide the basis for the type of program formulated for the child. Thus, these instruments provide baseline data against which future progress and future decisions about the child's programs can be made.

Types of data that programs maintain are either continuous data, periodic probe data, or pretest-posttest data, all of which contribute, based on the frequency of data, to decisions about a child's educational program. In fact, the frequency of educational decisions is usually in direct relationship to the frequency of data gathering, but that will be discussed in more detail later. The immediate point is that records are essential for individual programing for children since these records contain a list of the competencies children have acquired and those they need to acquire, and since programs to aid children in acquiring these competencies must be initiated.

The second requirement for maintaining records on children's progress stems inherently from the First Chance model program concept. During the first 3 years of the life of a project, it must demonstrate that its model components are making changes in the lives of the children it serves. Without such evidence, other potential projects would not be convinced to emulate this project, and this emulation or replication is an essential underlying concept of the First Chance Network.

Thus, the keeping of records of children's progress is necessary for at least two reasons: (a) The records or data are the basis for decisions about the child's programs; and (b) data which demonstrate effectiveness regarding children's progress are necessary to influence others to replicate. In addition, of course, each project finds a number of other reasons for keeping records—reporting to parents, reporting to local school districts, reporting to local funding agencies.

OPEN RECORDS AND CONFIDENTIALITY

An important concern of all the First Chance projects is the relationship of open records and confidentiality. These seem on the surface to be conflicting terms, but in actual practice they should not be. All records of a particular child must be open to that child and to his or her parents or guardians. These records must be available for examination at any time, and staff of the project must be available to explain them to the parents or the guardians.

However, these records are confidential in that they are not open and not available to anyone other than parents, guardians, or professional staff who must deal with that child. All projects must be aware that individual child records cannot be made available to persons other than the parents, guardians, or professional staff. Thus, there are requirements for storage and for security, of which projects must be aware. One of the most important things new projects should do is to obtain permission from parents to reveal the data about their child, if not by name, at least anonymously. Unless this anonymous permission is granted, it will be difficult to reveal data to projects that desire to replicate the program.

The problem of open records and confidentiality is a legal one, and consequently, if there is any doubt on the part of any program about what it is allowed and required to reveal, legal assistance should be obtained. One of the better approaches is to have legal representatives on the program's advisory board, who would be available to give opinions about this important current topic.

TYPES OF PROJECT RECORDS

Just as there is a wide diversity of types of model projects, there is also a variety in the assessment procedures used for tracking the progress of children. Some projects use standardized instruments, whereas others have developed their own instruments, finding the standardized instruments not to be suitable for their population or for their curriculum. Still others use a combination of standardized instruments and their own instruments.

Another dimension of the assessment diversity is the frequency with which assessments are made. A number of projects, primarily those that are behaviorally oriented, focus on a continuous data system, requiring the recording of data on a daily basis. Other projects use a probe system, which periodically reassesses the progress of the child. Some use a pretest-posttest paradigm. And finally, some projects use combinations of these.

A lengthy monograph could be written on the various instruments and procedures used for child assessment by First Chance model projects. The sampling contained in this chapter only points up the necessity for systematically gathering the assessment procedures used by these model projects, evaluating their effectiveness, and publishing them in a format that helps others establish programs for the early education of handicapped children. The sample of projects listed in the following sections illustrates a variety of assessment models, and the descriptions are, of necessity, brief. For further information about the procedures, contact persons are listed in Appendix A.

SAMPLES OF CONTINUOUS OR DAILY DATA KEEPING

The sample of projects presented in this section focuses on the day to day or periodic assessment of children's progress. Hayden and Edgar (Chapter 4) have reviewed the initial assessment instruments available throughout the First Chance Network. Frequently these initial assessment instruments will have implications for the kinds of data projects will maintain because it is incumbent upon a project to be able to compare the progress of a child vis-à-vis the initial child assessment. Frequently, therefore, the types of data will closely parallel the measurements contained in those initial assessments.

On the other hand, projects will often use those initial assessments as baseline data which indicate that children do in fact need the service of the First Chance Network and then give further assessment to the child based upon their own curriculum or their particular methods of instruction. The projects selected here are believed not only to have exemplary features but also to represent a wide variety of the types of assessment procedures available.

Teaching Research Infant and Child Center

Among the projects using a continuous data keeping system is the Teaching Research Infant and Child Center in Monmouth, Oregon, which conducts a program for both multiply handicapped children and children in a normal day care setting. The latter children frequently come from deprived backgrounds, and many are bilingual. Both settings use continuous data keeping systems, which have as their basis comprehensive curricula with learning tasks broken down into minute behaviors so that the progress of the child can be precisely measured.

The philosophy of the settings is to provide efficient individual programing. The teacher must be able to measure accurately the skills and capabilities the student possesses in all curriculum areas and must further be able to track the student's progress through the curriculum areas.

Implied in this tracking is the necessity to respond to data collected. For instance, if the data being gathered about the child's progress indicate that no progress has been made for the past 3 or 4 days, the teacher is required to modify that child's program by either reducing the complexity of the task, increasing the power of the reinforcer, or modifying the way in which the materials are presented to the child. On the other hand, if the student is moving through the steps of a sequence at a rapid rate with few incorrect responses, the teacher should probe ahead to determine whether or not the child possesses more advanced skills that would allow him to move through that sequence more rapidly or to skip portions of the instructional sequences. Thus, in both instances the data are telling the teacher to alter the child's program. For the Teaching Research Infant and Child Center this ability to respond to the data and to modify programs accordingly is the essence of individual programing.

Data Keeping for the Handicapped

Data on self help and motor skills. The administrative procedures used in daily data keeping in the classroom for the multiply handicapped might best be illustrated by examining an example of a child who has been placed in a self help skill program for feeding himself. This child is just beginning to learn to eat with a spoon. The steps that the child will go through are as follows:

1. Move hand to mouth from dish.
2. Release hand 1 inch from mouth.
3. Release hand 3 inches from mouth.
4. Release hand 5 inches from mouth.
5. Release hand 7 inches from mouth.
6. Release hand 10 inches from mouth.
7. Release hand 13 inches from mouth (add any additional steps required).
8. Release hand immediately above plate.
9. Release hand as food is scooped.
10. Child scoops food himself. (Fredericks et al., 1976, pp. 44–45)

The program is to be conducted each day with the child and described on a program cover sheet (see Figure 1). In setting up these programs for the child this cover sheet would appear on a clipboard followed by the sequence of steps and the data forms. (Partially completed data forms are shown in Figures 2 and 3.) This data form is used for all data recording in the preschool, except toilet training and behavior problems. In the left hand margin there is a space for the date. The next column shows the reinforcer used. The next two columns show the phase and step of the curriculum sequence to be taught. Then follow 10 columns for recording the results of each trial or attempt by the child to perform the behavior. The final column is labeled "Comments" and allows room for the volunteer or teacher to make notes about the child's performance. The type of data recorded in the trial boxes is standardized. A slash or vertical line indicates that the child has performed the step correctly; a circle indicates that he performed it incorrectly or did not do it.

Figure 2 gives the data for a child (S) on a walking program. An examination of the data on October 12 (10/12), October 13, and October 14 indicates that the child is having difficulty progressing beyond step 2 of phase IV of Independent Movement—Grasping Reflex. Notice that the reinforcer being used up to this point is social reinforcement. Previous data indicate that the child's favorite reinforcer is sugar coated cereal. The teacher instructs the volunteer working with S during the following day (October 15) to use the sugar coated cereal. This information is transmitted to the volunteer by merely writing the reinforcer into the appropriate place on the data form. The child's performance improved considerably with the added power of the reinforcer.

Figure 3 provides examples of two other situations that require reactions from a teacher examining the data. W was a cerebral palsied child, 3 years old, placed on a program to learn to eat with a spoon. The data indicate that, on October 3, W was on step 2 of the program and achieved success. However, the volunteer noted in the comment column that the child failed to close his mouth after putting food in his mouth. Since the teacher believed that it was senseless to continue the motor aspects of the program until the child learned to close his mouth after removing the spoon, she inserted an additional step in the program. She cued the

Figure 1

Program Cover Sheet, Teaching Research Infant and Child Center (Monmouth, Oregon)

Name: W

Task Objective: _Eating with a spoon or fork._

Date Started: _3/3_

Date Completed: _____

Materials and Setting: _Dish with food; spoon or fork; place removed from rest of family._

Pretest: _Child could hold spoon but did not know how to use it to eat._

Treatment:

I. Cue or Instructions:

1. Verbal: _Eat, W._

2. Nonverbal: _____

3. Incorrect Response: _____

II. Reinforcement:

1. Verbal: _Good eating, good, etc._

2. Nonverbal: _Favorite food._

3. Incorrect Response: _Assist_

Criterion Level of Acceptable Behavior: _Three consecutive correct responses._

Posttest: _____

Figure 2

Data on S on Walking Program
Teaching Research Infant and Child Center
(Monmouth, Oregon)

Child's Name ___5___
Phase Behavior IV—Independent
Movement—Grasping

/ = Correct response
0 = Incorrect response
∅ = Correct response with assistance

Date	Reinforcer Used	Phase	Step	Trials										Comments
				1	2	3	4	5	6	7	8	9	10	
10/11/73	Social	IV	1	0	0	0	0	0	/	0	/	/	0	
10/12/73	Social	IV	1	0	0	/	0	/	/	/	/	/		Was getting tired toward the end.
10/12/73	Social	IV	2	0	0	0	0	/	0	0	0	0	0	
10/13/73	Social	IV	2	0	0	0	0	0	/	0	/	0	0	
10/14/73	Social	IV	2	0	/	0	0	0	0	0	/	0	0	
10/15/73	Social/sugar coated cereal	IV	2	0	0	/	0	/	/	/				

Figure 3

Data on W Feeding Program
Teaching Research Infant and Child Center
(Monmouth, Oregon)

Child's Name W

/ = Correct response
0 = Incorrect response
Ø = Correct response with assistance

Date	Reinforcer Used	Phase	Step	Trials										Comments
				1	2	3	4	5	6	7	8	9	10	
10/3/72	Pudding/social	V	2	/	/	/								Child does not close mouth
10/4/72	Pudding/social	V	2a	0	0	/	/	0	/	0	0	/	/	Adult closes mouth
10/4/72	Pudding/social	V	2a	0	0	0	0	0	0	0	0	0	0	
10/5/72	Pudding/social	V	2a	0	0	0	0	0	/	/	0	0	/	
10/5/72	Pudding/social	V	2a	/	/	/								
10/9/72	Pudding/social	V	3	/	0	/	/	0	0	/	/	0	/	
10/9/72	Pudding/social	V	3	/	/	/								
10/10/72	Pudding/social	V	4	/	/	/								Probe ahead to step 9 tomorrow
10/11/72	Pudding/social	V	9	/	/	/								
10/11/72	Pudding/social	V	10	0	0	0	0	/	0	0	0	/	0	
10/12/72	Pudding/social	V	10	/	/	0	0	/	/	0	/	/	0	
ABSENT 10/26/72	Pudding/social	V	10	0	0	0	0	0	/	/	0	/	/	
10/26/72	Pudding/social	V	10	/	/	/								

volunteer the next day to be aware of that change by writing "2a" in the step column on the next line, dated October 4. This entry cued the volunteer to refer to the sequence on the clipboard where 2a had been penciled in by the teacher. Step 2a required the adult to assist the child in closing his mouth.

Thus, the data informed the teacher that an additional step in the sequence was necessary. In this case, that additional step was necessary because of the idiosyncratic behavior of the child. In other instances, the teacher may be faced with a situation where the child's performance is quite poor, and despite the use of the most powerful reinforcers, the performance does not improve. Additional steps may then have to be added to the sequence to make the task easier for the child.

Figure 3 also provides another example of the way in which a teacher may react to the data gathered. Notice that on October 9 and 10 the child moved through steps 3 and 4 of the program without an error. Based on these data, the teacher suspected that the child could move through the steps more rapidly, and so the teacher added to the comment section on October 10, "probe ahead to step 9 tomorrow." On October 11 that probe was conducted; the child performed correctly and continued on the program to successfully complete it.

Thus, these two data records indicate the uses to which the data can be put: (a) modifying the program so as to overcome a difficult area where the child is not progressing as fast or as accurately as desired and (b) revising the program so that the child can move more rapidly through it when it is apparent that progress is good.

Data on toilet training. Toilet training at the Teaching Research Infant and Child Center also requires daily data keeping. The format on which toilet training data are kept is shown in Figure 4, a partially completed toilet training form. Notice that across the top of the form are numbers from 1 to 15. These represent the days of the month. In the left hand column, the hours of the waking day are divided into half hour increments. Three basic symbols are used: a circle indicates urination; a triangle indicates bowel movements; and an *X* indicates potty. These can be combined. For instance an *X* in the circle or triangle indicates that the urination or bowel movement was completed on the potty. A circle and a triangle combined indicates that both a urination and a bowel movement occurred. An *X* standing alone indicates that the child was placed on the potty but neither urinated nor defecated. (A complete description of this data system is contained in Fredericks, Baldwin, Grove, & Moore, 1975.)

Data on social behaviors. A third kind of data is that associated with social behaviors. Baseline data are gathered during the initial assessment period. Once it is determined that a program for inappropriate social behavior is necessary, that program is initiated and data maintained usually in graph form. For instance, the data in Figure 5 show that two treatment strategies were tried with *L*, a 2½ year old who habitually threw tantrums. In Program 1, *L* was ignored; there was little improvement in her behavior. In Program 2, *L* was placed in a chair outside the room; *L* showed a decided improvement by a reduction of the number of tantrums and the length of time she cried. Graphs are maintained for each child for which a social behavior program is considered necessary.

Figure 4

Toilet Training Chart
Teaching Research Infant and Child Center
(Monmouth, Oregon)

TOILET TRAINING CHART

⨻ = Bowel Movement in Toilet   ⊗ = Urination in Toilet
△ = Bowel Movement   O = Urination
X = Child on Potty; No results

	1	2	3	4	5	6	7	8	9	10	11	12	13	14	15
7:00 - 7:30	O	O	O	O	O	O	O	O	O△	O	O	O	O△	O	O
7:31 - 8:00				△	X	⨻	X	⨻		⨻	X	X		⨻	X
8:01 - 8:30	O	⨻	⨻				⨻		O		⨻	⨻	O	X	
8:31 - 9:00	△				X	O				O				X	O
9:01 - 9:30				△				O	△		O	O	O		
9:31 - 10:00		O		⊗	O										
10:01 - 10:30	O							O	O	⊗		△		O	X
10:31 - 11:00		O		O											
11:01 - 11:30															
11:31 - 12:00				O				O			O	⊗	⨻	X	X
12:01 - 12:30		△	⊗		△	O△	⊗⨻	X	X	⊗⨻	X	X		△⨻	⨻
12:31 - 1:00		⊗						⨻	X				O		O
1:01 - 1:30	O△							O				O		O	
1:31 - 2:00				O				O		O	O				
2:01 - 2:30					O		O						O		O
2:31 - 3:00		O	O	△							O	O		O	
3:01 - 3:30				O				O	⨻	⨻	X	⊗	X	X	⨻
3:31 - 4:00	O△	△	⨻		⨻	⊗⨻	X	X	O		⨻		⨻	⨻	O
4:01 - 4:30		O		O			O	⊗		O		O	X		
4:31 - 5:00					O	O	△		O		O		X	O	
5:01 - 5:30	O		O					O					O		
5:31 - 6:00				O			O			O					
6:01 - 6:30		O	△	⨻	X				⨻	X	X	⨻	X	⊗⨻	X
6:31 - 7:00					⨻		O	O	O		⨻	O	O		
7:01 - 7:30	O△			O	O	⊗		△		O					O
7:31 - 8:00															

Necessity of data keeping. Although the amount of data being gathered in the preschool may seem a burden and an unnecessary chore to the novice teacher of the moderately and severely handicapped, the Teaching Research Infant and

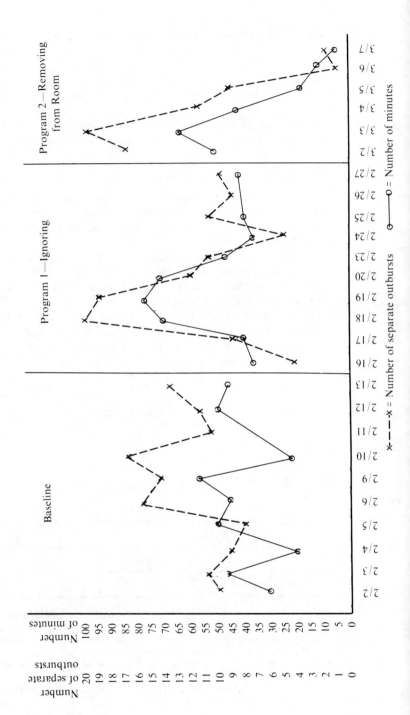

Figure 5

Record of L Crying
Teaching Research Infant and Child Center
(Monmouth, Oregon)

Child Center emphasizes the principle reasons why those data are necessary. The data certainly can be used to evaluate the effectiveness of a program. But, more important, they are the basis for all the children's programs and alterations of programs conducted in the preschool. With the data, children who by the very nature of their handicaps will be retarded in their education will be moved at the optimum pace through an educational program. Their time will not be wasted, nor will they be asked to do more than their present capabilities allow. Moreover, the data will assist the teacher in making the most efficient use of teaching time.

Data Keeping for the Disadvantaged

The previous sections describe the type of continuous data system used for the moderately and severely handicapped in the Teaching Research Infant and Child Center. That center also has a program for disadvantaged children, which uses a different type of continuous data.

Each major area of the curriculum has a grid, which contains a space for each of the skills in that major area along the top and spaces for each pupil in the classroom along the left side. In the example shown in Figure 6, Joe, Sara, and Lupe were pretested in April on skills A through H. Joe met criterion on skills A and B, but did not on skills C through H. Sara met criterion on A through D and F, but did not on E, G, and H. Lupe met A and B, but did not meet C through H. The teacher will now place the three children on the appropriate programs

Figure 6

Major Area Grid
Teaching Research Infant and Child Center
(Monmouth, Oregon)

Pre-Reading Skills Objectives:

	A	B	C	D	E	F	G	H
Joe	4/15	4/15						
Sara	4/12	4/13	4/13	4/13		4/13		
Lupe	4/15	4/15						

Note: The capital letters correspond to skills objectives as follows. Examples of some of these are:
   A. Child matches circle, square, triangle, rectangle, with three distractors.
   B. Child finds circle, square, triangle, rectangle, with three distractors.
   C. Child volunteers name of circle, square, triangle, rectangle, with three distractors.
   D. Child matches colors red, yellow, blue, green, orange, purple, black, white and brown, with three distractors.

designed to teach the first skill that they could not meet. Therefore, Joe and Lupe will begin working on skill *C* and Sara on skill *E*. The shaded areas on each skill indicate a pretest date, with no instruction having been received in the classroom.

Also, each skill has an inventory sheet (see Figure 7) that lists the component phases and steps (task analysis) of the skill, in much the same way as the major area grid listed the component skills of reading. The system of dating and shading are identical to that of the major area skills grid.

Figure 7 shows that on skill *C* (child volunteers name of circle, square, etc.) Joe had difficulties with square and rectangle and Lupe had difficulties only with the circle. Sara is not listed because she met criterion on skill *C*. A volunteer will be running the skill *C* program and will need detailed information as to which step and phase each child is working on. The volunteer will also need to record whether or not each child met criterion on that particular phase and step so that the teacher (and other volunteers) will know whether or not to move the child to the next step. Another form, the daily data sheet, fulfills these functions (see Figure 8).

The phase and step numbers are entered in the bottom half of each divided rectangle on the daily data sheet. The date a session is conducted is entered on the top half. If the child meets criterion on the phase/step, the numbers are circled and the child moved to the next appropriate phase/step. If the child does not meet criterion, the number is not circled and the child stays on that phase/step for the next session. If the child stays on the same phase/step for a certain number of sessions, the teacher will write a branching step or change reinforcers.

When a child completes a phase or step, that date is entered in the appropriate

Figure 7

Inventory Sheet for Reading Skills, Naming Shapes
Teaching Research Infant and Child Center
(Monmouth, Oregon)

	PHASE I				PHASE II				PHASE III				PHASE IV			
	1	2	3	4	1	2	3	4	1	2	3	4	1	2	3	4
Joe	4/15	4/15	4/15	4/15	4/15	4/15		4/15	4/15	4/15	4/15					
Lupe	4/15	4/15			4/15	4/15	4/15	4/15	4/15	4/15	4/15	4/15	4/15	4/15	4/15	4/15

In this example, the phases and steps are as follows:

Phase I—Child volunteers name of circle. Step 1—No distractors
Phase II—Child volunteers name of square. Step 2—One distractor.
Phase III—Child volunteers name of triangle. Step 3—Two distractors.
Phase IV—Child volunteers name of rectangle. Step 4—Three distractors.

Figure 8

Daily Data Sheet, Skill C, Naming Shapes
Teaching Research Infant and Child Center
(Monmouth, Oregon)

Skill *C* (Names Shapes) Daily Data Sheet

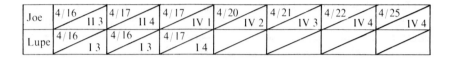

Joe	4/16	4/17	4/17	4/20	4/21	4/22	4/25
	II 3	II 4	IV 1	IV 2	IV 3	IV 4	IV 4
Lupe	4/16	4/16	4/17				
	I 3	I 3	I 4				

column of the inventory sheet. When the child completes the skill, the data are entered on the major area grid.

In summary, therefore, three documents are used to track progress through the academic curriculum:

1. The major area grid lists each skill in a curriculum area and shows progress of all children in a class across an entire curriculum area. This grid is useful for yearly progress reports.
2. The skills inventory sheet lists each phase/step in one skill and shows smaller bits of progress. The sheet is useful for showing short term progress, and also, volunteers use it to move the child to the next appropriate phase/step.
3. The daily data sheet gives the volunteer detailed information necessary to present the program to the child and also shows the teacher whether branching or reinforcer changes are necessary.

The Portage Project

Another First Chance project that uses a system of continuous recording is the Portage Project, sponsored by the Cooperative Education Service in Portage, Wisconsin. This project is basically a home teaching program.

To facilitate planning for individual children, the project staff devised the *Portage Guide to Early Education,* an early childhood curriculum guide in two parts.

1. A developmental sequence checklist, which lists sequential behaviors from birth to 5 years of age in five developmental areas—cognitive, language, self help, motor, and socialization. (See Figure 9 for a sample of part of the cognition sequenced checklist.)
2. A set of curriculum cards to match each of the 450 behaviors stated on the checklist, using behavioral objectives to describe the skill and suggesting materials and curriculum ideas to teach each of the 450 behaviors. (See Figure 5 of Chapter 6, "Curriculum and Instruction," for a sample curriculum card.)

The checklist is used to pinpoint the behaviors the child already exhibits in five developmental areas. This is considered initial baseline behavior. Based on this

Figure 9

Sample of Checklist
Cooperative Educational Service Agency #12
(Portage, Wisconsin)

COGNITION   Name _____

Age Level	Card No.	Behavior	Entry Behavior	Date Achieved
0-1	1	Visually follows object past midline		
	2	Follows light with eyes, turning head		
	3	Responds to sound		
	4	Follows bell/sound		
	5	Reaches for rattle		
	6	Eyes follow half circle		
	7	Grabs at ring		
	8	Grasps rattle		
	9	Retains rattle		
	10	Puts ring in mouth		
	11	Grasps a rubber block or toy		
	12	Reaches, grasps, puts in mouth		
	13	Removes block from cup		
	14	Places block in cup with aid		
	15	Puts block in cup without aid		
	16	Dangles a toy		
	17	Puts 3 blocks into cup, empties cup		
	18	Shakes a bell		
	19	Transfers toy from one hand to the other		
	20	Drops and picks up toy		
	21	Finds block hidden under cup		
	22	Pushes 3 blocks train style		
	23	Retains 2 blocks in one hand		
	24	Pincher grasp		

behavior, the home teacher can then prescribe the next behavior on the checklist, often dividing the behavior, which is called a long term goal, into smaller segments. Thus, the child is assigned a goal he will achieve within one week regardless of the severity of the handicap.

As baseline data are collected on each new prescription, the task is demonstrated to the parent as the home teacher works with the child. The home teacher then observes the parent working with the child on the prescription, often providing the parent with additional teaching information.

An activity chart for each prescription is left with the parent (see Figure 10). This chart describes in behavioral terms what goal is to be accomplished, how often the skill is to be practiced, what behavior is to be reinforced, and how it is to be reinforced. The directions are specific and the parent has the activity chart to refer to during the week. The parent is instructed to record on the activity chart the child's behavior each day on each prescription. The Portage Project reports that recording proves to be reinforcing to the parents because they can see the daily changes in their child's rate of appropriate responses. When the home teacher returns the following week, he records postbaseline data on the previous week's activities. This helps the home teacher validate the accuracy of the parent's recording.

If the parent has not been able to work effectively with the child during the week, the home teacher might need to modify the prescriptions (perhaps there were too many) or give the parent additional reinforcers for the child.

A log is kept on each child listing each behavior prescribed, the date the curriculum was initiated, the date the behavior was achieved, and the developmental area under which the behavior was assumed, that is, self help, language, cognitive, socialization, or motor. This log provides information concerning the specific behaviors each child has learned, the date he learned them, and the duration of each prescription. In addition, it provides data concerning the percentages of success on task.

The National Children's Center

The National Children's Center, Inc., in Washington, D.C., is developing a model organizational system, entitled Curriculum Evaluation Feedback Model, which permits individualization of instruction in an integrated classroom setting. This project uses some standard behavior modification techniques such as defining behavior objectives, pinpointing behaviors, establishing baseline data, determining the criteria for success, and establishing a reinforcing hierarchy. In addition, an instructional sequence using extensive task analysis has been developed.

The record keeping part of the program centers around the evaluation of the techniques used. Figure 11 shows the baseline data form for recording how the child does on a daily basis. This is known as the "Level 1 Data Sheet."

A daily summary of progress for each lesson area is maintained by cumulative records. (See Figure 12 for an ongoing example of such a record.) These records are used in planning and decision making in programing.

Another interesting aspect of this program is the research design that has been

Figure 10

Sample Activity Chart
Cooperative Educational Service Agency #12
(Portage, Wisconsin)

EARLY EDUCATION PROJECT

Child's Name _B_   1/71

Home Teacher's Name _____

ACTIVITY CHART

Week of _9/13/71_

BEHAVIOR: _Language_
B will say the sound
'wa' as in 'water' with aid
3 trials, 3 times/day

NUMBER OF
times B
Says 'wa'

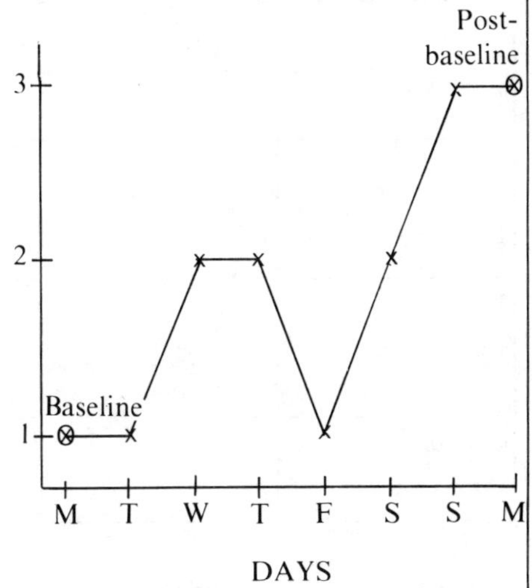

Post-baseline

Baseline

M T W T F S S M

DAYS

DIRECTIONS: _Record 1st 3 trials each day- Practice 3 times_
each day
Sit B in front of you. Make the 'wa' sound several times
and have B watch you as you do this. Then use
the mirror and encourage B to watch you by looking
into the mirror. Use your fingers to gently guide B's
mouth into position and ask her to repeat 'wa' after you
and encourage her to look at herself in the mirror as she
does this. Praise B for each attempt and as B begins
to consistently repeat the 'wa' sound reduce the
pressure on the mouth. Continue praising success.

Figure 11

Level 1 Data Sheet
National Children's Center
(Washington, D.C.)

Instructor: _____			
Criterion: _____		Date: _____	
	1	2	3
Child's Name	Content Area: Book #: Lesson #:	Content Area: Book #: Lesson #:	Content Area: Book #: Lesson #:
1.			
2.			
3.			
4.			
5.			
6.			
Comments			

built into the program. The program uses a multiple baseline design, wherein the effectiveness of reinforcers can be measured by using reinforcers for one of the behaviors for which the child is being taught and withholding those reinforcers from the other behaviors and then at a periodic time adding those reinforcers. In Figure 13 the multiple baseline design shows three programs: perceptual motor, greeting, and verbal imitation. Reinforcers for perceptual motor were delivered starting on day 2, and the behavior immediately achieved 100% appropriate responses.

On day 6 verbal imitation came under the influence of reinforcers, and appropriate responses immediately increased to approximately 90%. At day 10 greetings came under the control of reinforcers and they too increased to between 90% and 100%. Thus, all three behaviors from the period day 10 to day 12 were functioning at 90% to 100% appropriate responses. This technique of using the multiple baseline design to demonstrate the power of reinforcers has potential for both teacher training and parent training.

Figure 12

Daily Summary of Progress
National Children's Center
(Washington, D.C.)

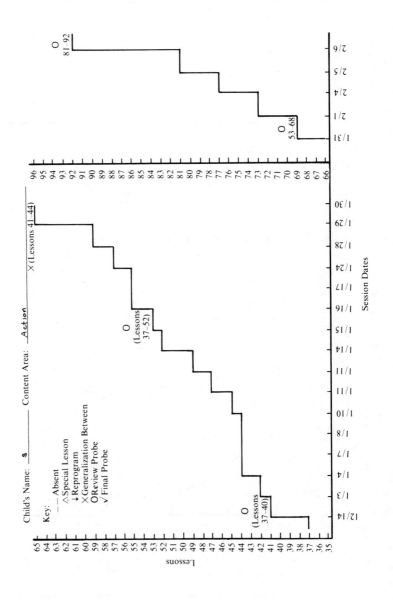

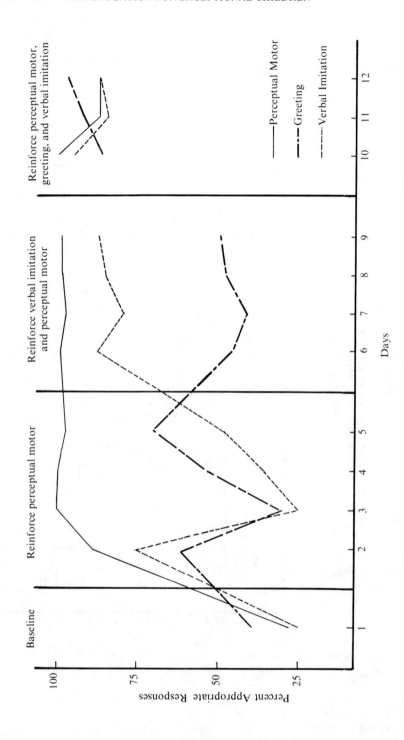

Figure 13

Multiple Baseline Design
The National Children's Center
(Washington, D.C.)

SAMPLES OF DATA SYSTEMS USING PROBES

A number of the First Chance Network projects use a system known as probing, that is, taking recordings of children's progress at periodic intervals in lieu of daily recordings. These intervals and the type of probes vary considerably from project to project.

The Medford Preschool

The Medford Preschool in Medford, Oregon, has a system that employs screening data, daily data, probes, and parent reporting.

In the area of screening, the child is given two pretests to determine if he qualifies for the preschool program. These tests are the Engelmann Basic Concept Inventory and the Peabody Picture Vocabulary Test. To qualify for entrance into the preschool, the child must have a total of 50 or more on the Basic Concept Inventory or must score with a mental age of 1 year below chronological age on the Peabody Picture Vocabulary Test. While the child is being tested to determine his qualification for preschool, the head teacher interviews the parent or parents in order to learn about any health or physical problems, behavior problems such as tantrums, and any siblings in the family who have had learning or behavior problems.

After acceptance, the child is given a baseline test on all areas of the curriculum. Every test is dated on the day the test is administered. If the child can answer or perform a task, a cross is put in the appropriate sequence task box and the child may skip that sequence or series of sequences during the remaining year. See Figure 14 for an example of a completed sequence task box. As can be noted, baseline data indicated that the child could perform behaviors 1 and 3. Behavior 2 would be blank at that time.

The dates shown in Figure 14 would be entered as follows: After the initial baseline is recorded and teaching has begun, the child must have three dates in each task box to show that he has accomplished the task and can cope with or retain the task designated. Two of the dates may be recorded by the teacher but the third date must be obtained by the paid teacher aide, who is the prober. The teacher aide dates her probe data in a different color ink. The prober takes the children individually out of the immediate classroom to perform all probes. Three dates were used because it was found that children generally retained a task after having responded three times, rather than two or less. After more than three correct responses, many children seemed to be bored with the task and would not respond correctly.

Probes in the language area are taken once every month. Probes for math are taken every 2 weeks. All of the prereading and reading skills except name recognition and name writing are taken every 2 weeks.

All of the motor tasks are recorded by the immediate teacher. However, sit-ups and push-ups are recorded on a graph instead of a regular sequence task box. See Figure 15 for an example of a sit-up graph.

Oral counting is also recorded on a graph. Every child is encouraged to count

Figure 14

Example of Recording of Baseline and Probes
Medford Preschool
(Medford, Oregon)

Polars

Given an auditory cue, the child will verbally respond with the correct polar.
Baseline 9/5/73

	1	2	3
	+	10/12/73 10/26/73 11/19/73	+

1. If it is not long, it is *short.*
2. If it is not full, it is *empty.*
3. If it is not big, it is *little.*

---

to 100. However, this counting must be done 3 days in consecutive order before the child is ready for a probe.

Daily individual programs are planned on the basis of these data. Since data are maintained in language, prereading skills, math, and motor activities, each of these programs can be evaluated and modified daily.

In addition to data being maintained on academic progress through a combination of probes and continuous data gathering, special programs must be established for some children to improve their social behavior. Most of these programs focus on inappropriate behavior or behavior problems. With each pinpointed behavior problem, baseline data are taken, a program established, and continuous data maintained to provide information to modify the program as necessary.

Another form of daily data is parent reporting. An underlying philosophical tenet of the preschool is that parents should be involved in the education of their children. Home programs have been useful not only to provide this involvement but also to enhance the progress of children. A sample of a home program and the data obtained from that program is shown in Figure 16.

The San Felipe Del Rio Project

In the San Felipe Del Rio Consolidated Independent School District (Del Rio, Texas) a probing system is used in which probing is planned for a group. The children's names are listed separately to allow for individual differences. Age levels and performance levels of the group may be used.

Figure 15

Example of Perceptual Motor Sit-Up Graph
Medford Preschool
(Medford, Oregon)

Baseline: 9/5/73 - Given a verbal cue, the child will do 25 sit-ups.

Sequences:
  A. Raising head and shoulders only
  B. With arms extended
  C. With hands behind head
Criterion: Three consecutive times.

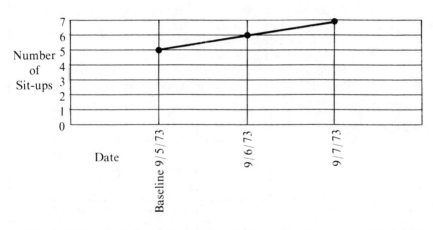

Sequence C

Figure 17 shows the recording probe sheet used by the project. The initial probe column is used for baseline data. There is room for three additional probes, which need not be taken on subsequent days. The fourth probe, however, should be the column for posttreatment information. Dates must be placed in all probe columns. A completed probe sheet of the initial probe for three children is shown. The data sheet can be used for a number of children and the teacher can record these during the course of the instruction.

The Access to Success Project

The Access to Success Project in Ankeny, Iowa, uses an informal readiness test for a preschool inventory. This is a nonstandardized instrument that allows more latitude, according to the project, than a standardized test. It is used in conjunction with, not in lieu of, the more objective types of tests. The Informal Readiness Assessment, which was developed by Allen R. Frank and Joan Zynda, Division

Figure 16

Example of Home Program
Medford Preschool
(Medford, Oregon)

Child: __Jane Smith__   Teacher: ___Mary Jones___

Content: __Sound Writing__   Date Initiated: __1/7/74__

Goal: Given a verbal cue, my child will respond correctly to "write this letter, *a, c, d.*"

Procedure: 1. *Every day* at same time, work for 10 minutes.
2. Ask your child to write the *a, c, d,* presenting him the letters in random order.
3. *Record* the number of correct and incorrect answers below.
   + = Correct   0 = Incorrect
4. *Help* your child practice the letter he missed.
5. *Praise your child generously.*

Reward: (Agreed upon by teacher and parent)
Example: Have a friend over for overnight.

Sample for Recording:

Cards	Jan. 8	
a	+	
c	0	
d	+	

---

of Special Education, University of Iowa, includes the following subtests: classroom behavior, visual discrimination, auditory discrimination, visual motor perception, direction following, reading readiness skills, and math readiness skills. The inventory is not administered at one time but is given at frequent intervals in order to get a complete perception of the child's capabilities. Based upon this inventory, programs are developed for the child.

The Magnolia Preschool Handicapped Project

The Magnolia Preschool Handicapped Project in Magnolia, Arkansas, has designed a form (Figure 18) for summarizing the skills possessed by each child in

Figure 17

Probe Sheet
San Felipe Del Rio Consolidated Independent School District
(Del Rio, Texas)

Group: C.A., R.M. and J.L.	Age Range	6 years	

Area _____ Performance Level ____ 4 - 5 ____

Objective: ____ The children will demonstrate competency with pronouns (*he, him,*

she, her, they, them) by using them correctly in sequence story.

	INITIAL PROBE	2ND PROBE	3RD PROBE	4TH PROBE
Children	Date: 3/21/72	Date:	Date:	Date:
	he him she her they them			
C A	✓ x x ✓ x x			
R M	✓ x x ✓ x x			
J L	✓ x x ✓ x x			

Those who succeed here go to enrichment area.

Activity:
Learn Pronouns: *he, him, she, her, they, them*
Techniques:
1. Pretest use sequence stories from sequence story activity. Record each child's responses.
2. Structure picture sentence in slotted sentence. Substitute written word for picture in who slot (put it on top). "Read" sentence using target word.
3. Use pronouns in each child's individual "sentence book."
4. Set up structured group situations to use target pronouns.
Materials:
DLM Sequence Cards
Magazine picture
Individual picture books

Figure 18

Skill Summary Form
Magnolia Preschool Handicapped Project
(Magnolia, Arkansas)

ANALYSIS OF SKILLS

Date _____

CHILD'S NAME	ROTE COUNTS	RATIONAL COUNTS	WRITES NUMERALS	RECOGNIZES NUMERALS	IDENTIFIES COINS							IDENTIFIES SHAPES							UNDERSTANDS SPATIAL RELATIONS								WRITES NAME (NOTE ANY MISTAKE)	HANDEDNESS	IDENTIFIES LETTERS		
					Penny	Nickle	Dime	Quarter	Half Dollar	Dollar		Circle	Square	Triangle	Diamond	Rectangle	Oval	On	In	Beside	Behind	Under	Front	Between				Few	Most	None

Figure 18 (continued)

ANALYSIS OF SKILLS

CHILD'S NAME	VISUAL			KNOWS COLORS								CLOTHING SKILLS					KNOWS TELEPHONE	KNOWS ADDRESS	KNOWS FULL NAME	KNOWS BIRTHDAY	LANGUAGE SKILLS			AUDITORY		
	Likeness & Difference	Sequence Memory	Left right	Red	Orange	Yellow	Green	Blue	Black	Purple	Tie	Buckle	Snap	Zip	Button					Names	Ability to Communicate	Describe	Identifies Familiar Sounds	Association	Sequence and Memory

a group. The form has the advantage of presenting information on a large number of specific behavioral objectives for as many as 19 children at a time. By the addition of more lines, the same form could accommodate more children. The form requires, of course, a curriculum with established criterion levels for each of the skill objectives.

The Rutland Center

The Rutland Center in Athens, Georgia, has developed a document known as the Developmental Therapy Objectives Rating Form (DTORF). In addition, a Systematic Who-to-Whom Analysis Notation (SWAN) has been devised to determine the behavioral activities of the child. These behavioral activities include a wide spectrum of behaviors—verbalizations and various physical activities ranging from physical contact to waiting in turn. An observation methodology has been developed, for which training programs are available by contacting the Rutland Center and specifically William W. Swan, Outreach Project Director.

Description of DTORF

Because of space limitations the SWAN will not be discussed herein, but a description of the DTORF follows: The objectives of the *Developmental Therapy* curriculum (*Developmental Therapy: A Textbook for Teachers as Therapists for Emotionally Disturbed Young Children*, Wood, 1975) are 144 general statements outlining a series of sequential, developmental milestones in the four curriculum areas of behavior, communication, socialization, and preacademics. These statements are intended to be used as treatment objectives to guide the teacher in planning appropriate sequences of experiences for the disturbed young child. Thus, they serve as the curriculum basis for the treatment model and provide the framework for implementing therapeutic growth and progress toward a foundation for normal development. In addition, they function as the basis for a criterion referenced program evaluation system.

The DTORF contains abbreviated statements for each of these objectives. The DTORF is used by the teachers for rating the child's mastery of developmental objectives and recording specific objectives that the child has not mastered. These unmet objectives become the major therapy emphasis for each child.

The child's treatment team (lead teacher, support teacher, and parent worker) rates the child on the series of objectives in each of the four curriculum areas. These selected objectives serve to delineate the major focus of treatment for the child during each 10 week treatment period. At least one, and no more than four, major focus objectives are used in each of the curriculum areas.

The objectives are rated sequentially, with mastery of previous objectives being necessary before new objectives are initiated.

Purposes of DTORF

The DTORF is used for three major purposes: The first is to aid in the grouping of children for treatment. Children are grouped in therapy classes according to their major focus objectives, as indicated by the DTORF. In this way, classes are composed of children at similar developmental stages. A child's modal stage of development in each of the four curriculum areas determines his group placement. Children are regrouped at the end of each 10 week treatment period on the basis of current DTORF ratings. Current DTORF data are required for a child to be changed from one group to another during a 10 week treatment period.

The second major purpose of the *Developmental Therapy* objectives involves planning a child's treatment program. By delineating a child's level of developmental mastery according to the objectives and by determining where developmental skills are not mastered, the point of intervention is established. The treatment team can then select activities and plan strategies to provide a child with experiences appropriate for furthering his development. Where developmental lags have been identified plans can also be made to provide intensive attention in order to strengthen a child in the areas of weakness.

In addition to providing a focus for individualizing a program, the *Developmental Therapy* objectives aid in planning for a total class group. By determining which objectives are of major focus for all children in a group, experiences, materials, and strategies can be selected for the benefit of the entire group. It should be noted that since the treatment objectives are representative, they do not include everything that might be included in a treatment program. They are intended to guide the teachers in planning.

The third purpose of the DTORF is to document the progress of a child during treatment. The DTORF is completed for the first time after the child has participated in the program for 8 class days. It is subsequently completed on each child at the middle (5 weeks) and end (10 weeks) of each treatment period. Used in this manner, the DTORF reflects a child's developmental baseline at time of enrollment, the most current level of functioning, and changes that occur over time. These changes in mastery of developmental objectives are summarized in a growth profile (DTORF summary) each 10 weeks and are further summarized in a short DTORF summary, which reports percentages of objectives mastered.

DTORF Procedures

The procedures used for completing the DTORF are as follows: Those staff members who have had direct contact with the child, his family, and his school during the referral and intake process are asked to give a general consensus rating of the child's stage of development in each of the *Developmental Therapy* curriculum areas. Only the overall stages of development, not specific objectives, are considered at this point. The general goals for each developmental stage are used by the staff to make this first determination. The information for making this initial decision of a child's level of functioning in each of the four curriculum areas is obtained from individual testing and parent and school conference information during the intake process. The staff consensus concerning stage of development determines the group (stage of *Developmental Therapy)* at which the child will enter the program.

These initial judgments, based on intake information, occasionally prove inaccurate. Children frequently react quite differently in an individual testing situation and do not exhibit the problems or behaviors for which they were referred. This is particularly true in cases where the problem area involves group socialization skills.

To aid in overcoming the difficulties involved in placement based on intake information and to establish the initial focus for treatment, the treatment team completes a DTORF baseline after each child has been in the program for a period of 8 class days. (See Figure 19 for a partial baseline DTORF.) Since most children feel comfortable in the classroom setting and begin to show their typical, individual responses after a period of a few days, it is felt that such a baseline gives an accurate assessment of a child's current level of functioning. If major discrepancies occur between the initial placement at the time of acceptance and the DTORF 8th day baseline, it is then possible to change the child's group placement.

As previously mentioned, each child is rated on the *Developmental Therapy* objectives by his treatment team at the end of 5 weeks and again at the end of the 10 week treatment period. This 10th week rating (see Figure 20) provides the basis for determining placement for the child during the next treatment period and gives the next treatment team valuable treatment information (major focus objectives) for work with the child during the subsequent 5 week treatment period.

The DTORF must be done by consensus of the three members that constitute the treatment team. It is completed without consulting any previous DTORF data. Since both subjective and observational data from home, school, and center are the basis for rating, each team member's opinions must be considered, and no one member should be allowed to dominate or overly influence the rating process. It is also helpful to include the opinions and observations of any other staff members who may work with the child in the treatment program, such as a recreation teacher or an art or music therapist.

When rating a child, the treatment team must consider each *Developmental Therapy* objective and decide whether or not a child (a) has achieved mastery of the objective, (b) needs further work and support toward mastery of the objective, or (c) is not yet ready to work on the objective.

It is necessary to have one person on the treatment team designated to be responsible for making sure that a DTORF is completed on each child in a group on the determined date. Usually the lead teacher for the group assumes this responsibility.

Figure 19

Baseline DTORF 3 areas in Stage 1
(Full form in Figure 20)
Rutland Center
(Athens, Georgia)

DTORF

REV. 8/74
E009

Developmental Therapy Objectives Rating Form

Child's Name _Johnnie 0000l_ Class Stage _I_ Raters: _Team ↑_

Date _7/28/73_ Type Rating (Check One)—Baseline _X_, 5th Week ___, 10th Week ___

STAGE I

BEHAVIOR

- X 1. respond by attending
- X 2. respond by sust. attend.
- X 3. single mot. response
- X 4. complex mot. response
- NR 5. assist in self-help
- 6. respond indep. play mat.
- 7. respond w/recall/routine

COMMUNICATION

- X 1. attend/speaker
- X 2. resp./motor beh.
- X 3. resp./verbal approx.
- X 4. init./vb. approx.
- NR 5. recog. word/to adult
- 6. recog. word/to child
- 7. word sequence

SOCIALIZATION

- X 1. aware/adult
- X 2. attend/adult beh.
- X 3. resp. to name
- X 4. imitat. acts/adult
- NR 5. solit. play
- 6. resp. request/come
- 7. resp. single request
- 8. same as C5
- 9. same as C6
- 10. same as C7
- 11. exhibit emerg./self
- 12. seek contact/adult

Note. From "Developmental Therapy Curriculum Objectives" by C. Combs, in M. M. Wood (Ed.), *Developmental Therapy: A Textbook for Teachers as Therapists for Emotionally Disturbed Young Children*, University Park Press, Baltimore MD, 1975. Copyright 1975 by University Park Press. Reprinted by permission.

Figure 20

10th Week DTORF for Johnnie
Rutland Center
(Athens, Georgia)

DTORF   REV. 8/74
Developmental Therapy Objectives Rating Form   E009

Child's Name JOHNNIE   00001   Class Stage I   Raters: TEAM #1
Date 12/2/75 Type Rating (Check One)-Baseline ___, 5th Week ___, 10th Week X

===

	BEHAVIOR	COMMUNICATION	SOCIALIZATION
STAGE I	✓ 1. respond by attending	✓ 1. attend/speaker	✓ 1. aware/adult
	✓ 2. respond by sust. attend.	✓ 2. resp./motor beh.	✓ 2. attend/adult beh.
	✓ 3. single mot. response	✓ 3. resp./verbal approx.	✓ 3. resp. to name
	✓ 4. complex mot. response	✓ 4. init./vb. approx.	X 4. imitat. acts/adult
	✓ 5. assist in self-help	✓ 5. recog. word/to adult	✓ 5. solit. play
	✓ 6. respond indep. play mat.	✓ 6. recog. word/to child	✓ 6. resp. request/come
	✓ 7. respond w/recall/routine	X 7. word sequence	✓ 7. resp. single request
			✓ 8. same as C5
			✓ 9. same as C6
			X 10. same as C7
			X 11. exhibit emerg./self
			X 12. seek contact/adult
STAGE 2	△ 8. use play mat./appro.	X 8. answer/recog/word	NR 13. paral. play/spon.
	NR 9. /no interven.	X 9. recept. vocab.	___ 14. same as B9
	___ 10. partic. work time/ no intervention	NR 10. label feel./pict.	___ 15. init. min. move./child
	___ 11. partic. play time/ no intervention	___ 11. command activity/ simple wrd. seq.	___ 16. partic./sharing
	___ 12. spon. partic.	___ 12. use words ex. min. info./adult	___ 17. coop. act/child at play
		___ 13. use words ex. min. info./child	___ 18. coop. act./child in organ. activ.
STAGE 3	___ 13. vb. recall rules/proc.	___ 14. accept praise	___ 19. turns w/o remi.
	___ 14. contri. to gp. expect.	___ 15. same as B13	___ 20. share/min. rem.
	___ 15. vb. conseq./expect.	___ 16. spon. describe work	___ 21. sug. to teacher
	___ 16. vb. reasons/expect.	___ 17. same as B14	___ 22. partic/act. sugges. child
	___ 17. vb. other ways beh./ indiv.	___ 18. same as B15	
	___ 18. refrain when others	___ 19. pride/words/gestures	___ 23. pref./child
	___ 19. main. contr. & comply	___ 20. vb./feeling/resp.	___ 24. desc. char. of others
		___ 21. same as B16	
STAGE 4	___ 20. resp. appro./l'der choice	___ 22. vb. recog. feel/oth.	___ 25. suggest. act/grp.
	___ 21. spon. partic./activ. prev. avoid	___ 23. vb. recog. feel/self	___ 26. same as B20
	___ 22. implem. alter. beh.	___ 24. verb. praise/oths.	___ 27. same as B21
	___ 23. vb. exp. cause & ef.	___ 25. non vb./expre./ feel./art, music	___ 28. diff./char./others
	___ 24. resp./provocation/ control	___ 26. spon. expre. own feel./words	___ 29. phys./vb. support/ others
	___ 25. resp. appro./ new sugges.	___ 27. express others feel.	___ 30. partic. gp. plng. & pb. solv.
		___ 28. vb. expre. exper./ feel./art, music	
		___ 29. same as B23	
STAGE 5	↓ 26. construc. suggest.	↓ 30. maintain posit. relats. verb.	↓ 31. init. & main./ interp. & gp. rel.

Figure 20 (continued)

(PRE)ACADEMICS

STAGE 1		STAGE 3	
✓ 1. same as B1		N̸R 32. recog. gps. to 10	
✓ 2. same as B2		⊥ 33. left-right visual orien.	
✓ 3. same as B3		⊥ 34. recog. writ. names for	
✓ 4. same as B4		color words	
✓ 5. resp. fine/motor/24 mo.		⊥ 35. recog. written labels	
✓ 6. imitate wds./acts of		⊥ 36. recog. & write numerals for	
adults		groups/1–10	
✓ 7. resp. by simple		⊥ 37. write first/last name/date	
discrim. of obj.		with sample	
✓ 8. same as C3		⊥ 38. eye-hand coord./6 yr. level	
✓ 9. same as C4		⊥ 39. body-coord./6 tr. level	
✓ 10. short-term memory/		⊥ 40. recog. & write numerals for	
obj. & people		groups/11–20	
✓ 11. resp. w/classif./simil.		⊥ 41. write alpha./simple words	
obj. w/diff. attri.		⊥ 42. add-subtract/0–10	
✓ 12. short term memory/vb.		⊥ 43. use ordinal/concepts verbally	
expressions		⊥ 44. lstn. to story & resp. appro.	
✓ 13. body coord./3–4 yr.		⊥ 45. read prim. vocab./sentences	
level		⊥ 46. add-subtract above 10	
X 14. match similar pictures		⊥ 47. write basic words/memory	
X 15. recog. color names		or dictation	
X 16. eye-hand cord./4 yr. level		⊥ 48. part. group. act./write,	
N̸R 17. recog. body parts		tell, mural	

STAGE 2		STAGE 4	
⊥ 18. recog. use of obj.		⊥ 49. write name, ad., date/memory	
⊥ 19. recog. detail in pictures		⊥ 50. read, write/sentences	
⊥ 20. rote count to 10		⊥ 51. read, write quant. words	
⊥ 21. count to 5 (1 to 1)		⊥ 52. contribute gp. project/	
⊥ 22. name colors		expressive skills	
⊥ 23. count to 10 (1 to 1)		⊥ 53. write indiv. exper. stories	
⊥ 24. eye-hand cord./5 yr. level			
⊥ 25. recog. diff./shapes, symbols,			
numerals, words			
⊥ 26. categorize diff. items/		STAGE 5	
similar char.		⊥ 54. write for comm.	
⊥ 27. write recog. approx. of		⊥ 55. read/pleas. & info.	
first name w/o asst.		⊥ 56. write of feel., attit.	
⊥ 28. discrim. differences		↧ 57. read/info. feel. & beh.	
(up-down, etc.)		of others	
⊥ 29. body cord./5 yr. level			
⊥ 30. recog. gps. to 5			
↧ 31. listen to story telling			

PROGRESS NOTES

Symbols used to record information on the DTORF and their definitions are as follows:

✓—Indicates mastery of an objective. The child does this 9 out of 10 times at the center and away and will need only minimum reinforcement to retain the behavior.

X—Indicates a major focus objective. The child is ready to begin or needs to continue intensive work on this objective. At least one, but no more than four, major focus objectives should be marked for each child in each curriculum area.

R—Indicates a secondary objective. This is an objective where a child has nearly attained mastery but still needs further work and support. A rating of R may be used in two ways: (a) to indicate that a child needs further work on an objective that has been previously marked as a major focus but that he no longer needs intensive attention to this objective or (b) to indicate that a child needs to work on an objective with the idea that he will attain mastery without the objective ever having to become a major focus objective. The one instance where an R rating is inappropriate is as a precursor to a major focus objective. In other words, it should not be used to indicate gradual movement toward major focus on an objective. An R is counted as an X toward the maximum of four major focus objectives in a curriculum area.

NR—Indicates that a child is not yet ready to begin work on an objective. After four R or X marks have been recorded in a particular curriculum area the remaining objectives are automatically marked NR.

It is important that each representative objective on the DTORF be marked in one of these four ways and that no blank spaces occur. The treatment team member designated to be responsible for completion of the DTORF data should check to make sure that every objective is marked so that there are no blank spaces. Later it is difficult to determine reasons for blank spaces, and such omissions make evaluation data invalid.

Each objective should be rated in the sequence presented. If several objectives in a curriculum area are identified as needing treatment focus for a particular child, ordinarily the objectives should be selected in the order in which they occur on the rating form. These objectives would then continue to be major focus objectives until they are marked as secondary objectives or mastered.

Exceptions to selecting objectives in sequence will occur, however. When these exceptions do occur and an objective is selected out of sequence, the treatment team should write a brief explanation on the rating form for the benefit of the evaluation staff in charge of collecting DTORF data.

The United Cerebral Palsy Project

Some projects have developed rather unique ways of keeping track of progress. One such methodology has been developed by United Cerebral Palsy of New

York City, Inc. In an article entitled "When Words Are Not Enough—
Videotape" (Marinoff, 1973), use of the videotape is described by the project as
follows:

> The human eye is limited. This fact became clear to the teachers and special-
> ists of the Early Education Project of United Cerebral Palsy of New York
> City, Inc., who work with exceptional children in a total range of intellectual
> ability from profoundly retarded to the gifted. All of the children have neu-
> rological impairments and motor problems and enter the program at the
> earliest time of identification of a problem through six years of age. The
> video education specialist, in close cooperation with the project director and
> the program evaluator, developed a multiuse videotape program to help an-
> swer many of the "it is difficult to understand" problems brain damaged
> children present.
>
> But don't be misled. Don't expect the end product to be a Hollywood pro-
> duction. It won't be and it shouldn't be. The intimacy of this videotape re-
> cording program comes from its flexibility and informality. Imagine captur-
> ing the spontaneity of a child's movement, or zooming in to find the nuances
> of his fine motor control, and then having it permanently recorded for eval-
> uation and review. This is where the human eye is helped, for videotaping of
> classroom activities provides an instant replay, a stopping and starting pro-
> cess to see what exactly the child is doing, and thus helps to design strategies
> with goals. When words are not enough, the videotape recording provides
> visual insights toward much needed answers.
>
> Videotape recording is used as a tool where other media do not work as
> well. The equipment includes a Sony portable camera and videotape rec-
> order (Sony Video Rover II, AV/AVC 3400 Rover) with an extended bat-
> tery for outdoor use. Also included are two monitors, one for small groups
> and one for large audiences. The videotapes are not used as a new found
> gimmick where audiotape or film would be preferable; however, they do
> work easily and comfortably in many aspects of the total education struc-
> ture, particularly:
>
> 1. As a means of immediate feedback for teachers in the area of self-evalu-
>   ation and increased understanding of children.
> 2. As an evaluation measure in cases where standardized tests fail to
>   indicate growth which has occurred.
> 3. As an ongoing source of relevant teaching material for teachers, stu-
>   dents, and supportive staff.
> 4. As a way to bring parents to a realistic comprehension of their own chil-
>   dren.
>
> In each category or classification of use for videotape, the completed tape
> itself is only important as a stimulus for thinking and meaningful discussion.

Of primary concern are the dynamics involved in the process of people sitting together and viewing these tapes and with the exciting exchange of ideas and observations which always results at such times. (pp. 66–67)

USE OF STANDARDIZED TESTS AS PRETEST-POSTTEST MEASURES

Not yet mentioned is the use of standardized tests, although they are in wide use throughout the First Chance Network. The project sponsored by the Panhandle Child Development Association in Coeur d'Alene, Idaho, is a good example of one that uses the Illinois Test of Psycholinguistic Abilities as a pretest-posttest measure for progress of children in language development. The Medford Preschool (Oregon) uses the Basic Concept Inventory and the Peabody Picture Vocabulary Test. See Appendix B for a sample of the standardized pretest-posttest measures used by some projects throughout the Network.

CONCLUDING COMMENTS

Keeping track of a child's progress can be done in a number of ways. Those projects that keep continuous data do so in order to make daily modifications to the teaching methodology or the child's program. These projects are mostly behavioristically oriented. Other projects use probes—periodic assessments of the child's performance. Still others use pretest-posttest data. The formats in which these data are maintained vary considerably. This chapter has attempted to give a small sample of the different systems.

Which data system, if any, in the long run produces the best results with children can only be determined through long range analysis of the children's progress. This type of analysis has yet to be accomplished.

REFERENCES

Fredericks, H. D., Baldwin, V., Grove, D. N., & Moore, W. G. *Toilet training the handicapped child.* Monmouth OR: Instructional Development Corp., 1975.

Fredericks, H. D., Riggs, C., Furey, V., Grove, D., Moore, W., McDowell, J., Jordan, E., Hanson, W., Baldwin, V., & Wadlow, M. *Teaching research curriculum for moderately and severely handicapped.* Springfield IL: Charles C Thomas, 1976.

Marinoff, S. L. When words are not enough—Videotape. *TEACHING Exceptional Children,* 1973, *5,* 66–73.

Wood, M. M. (Ed.) *Developmental therapy: A textbook for teachers as therapists for emotionally disturbed young children.* Baltimore MD: University Park Press, 1975.

RESOURCES

Developmental Therapy: A Textbook for Teachers as Therapists for Emotionally Disturbed Young Children. Rutland Center, Athens, Georgia. 1975. (Available from University Park Press, Baltimore MD 21202. $9.75.)

Informal Readiness Assessment. Access to Success Project, Ankeny, Iowa. 1971. (Available from Heartland Education Agency, 1932 Ordnance Road, Ankeny IA 50021. Free.)

Portage Guide to Early Education. The Portage Project, Portage, Wisconsin. 1972, revised 1976. (Available from the project, 412 E. Slifer, Box 564, Portage WI 53901. $32 per set plus shipping.)

The Portage Guide to Home Teaching. The Portage Project, Portage, Wisconsin. 1975. (Available from the project, 412 E. Slifer, Box 564, Portage WI 53901. $3.95 plus $1.00 postage and handling.)

Systematic Who-to-Whom Analysis Notation (SWAN). Rutland Center, Athens, Georgia. (In *The Rutland Center Model for Treating Emotionally Disturbed Children.* Available from ERIC Document Reproduction Service, P.O. Box 190, Arlington VA 22210, ED 087 703; and from Technical Assistance Office, Rutland Center, 698 N. Pope Street, Athens GA 30601. $5.00.)

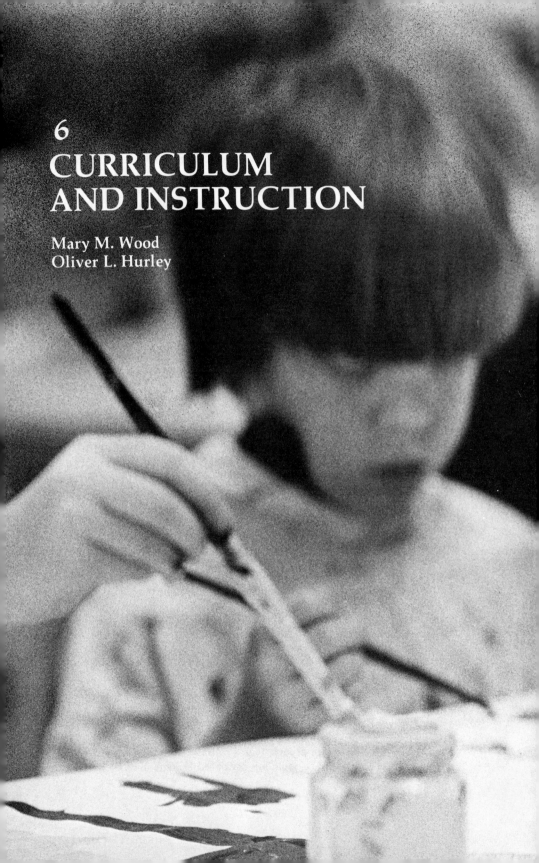

6
CURRICULUM
AND INSTRUCTION

Mary M. Wood
Oliver L. Hurley

□"Children learn what they are taught." How often is this simple idea expressed! Yet, is its full impact felt in designs for curriculum strategies for handicapped young children? Introspection would suggest at this point, "Sure, a good teacher can find a way to help a handicapped child learn almost anything." But what is it, precisely, that this good teacher wants her handicapped children to learn? To answer this question is to be on the road to curriculum development.

The projects in the First Chance Network have asked the same question, and information for this chapter is based upon in depth review of the written curricula provided by 20 First Chance projects. The projects followed different routes to curriculum development; yet, each has arrived at a curriculum that seems to suit its own goals. In developing its curriculum, each project identified the conditions under which its particular group of youngsters could make optimum progress. In order to do this, the projects had to recognize the individual differences of the children and consider the values and goals of each child's family.

Next, each project selected its particular curriculum rationale and organized the content areas. Then, the project determined the extent to which the rationale was to be extended into the organization of the curriculum content, objectives, techniques, teaching materials, and activities. Such internal consistency between rationale, goals, objectives, procedures, materials, methods, and evaluation is an essential element in any curriculum (Mayer, 1971, p. 286). To adequately complete the task of curriculum planning, each of the projects also had to explore the point of juncture between the project, the educational community's expectations, and the project's relevance to the broader expectations of society. All of these are necessary considerations when planning a curriculum for any young child (Bronfenbrenner, 1971; Cronbach, 1969; Deutsch, 1966, p. 16).

ORGANIZING A CURRICULUM AROUND A RATIONALE

Any curriculum should contain a rationale statement that expresses a point of view of what education of young handicapped children is all about, with special focus on the youngsters for whom the curriculum is intended. The rationale is a synthesis of a philosophy of education and a view of the needs and development of young handicapped children. It is the *raison d'être* of the document called "curriculum." As such, it should include statements of purpose, guiding principles, and significance, as well as content areas and long range overall goals and objectives.

First Chance curricula were organized in five basic ways:

1. The *amelioration of deficits* approach begins with children's specific problems. Curricula designed from this point of view might be described by the terms *remedial, compensatory, rehabilitative, prescriptive,* or *behavioral analysis.* When building a curriculum from this rationale the content areas emerge from assessment of a child's problems and are directed toward correcting specific deficits (Karnes, 1969).
2. The *basic skill areas* approach begins with the skills children use in the process of learning. Curricula are organized around skills such as lan-

guage, attention, sensory motor processes, social skills, perception, auditory processes, gross and fine motor facility, self help skills, and memory. A frequently cited model for this rationale among the First Chance projects is the Illinois Test of Psycholinguistic Abilities (ITPA). With this approach to organizing a curriculum, the content areas can be identified as "skill" or "process" areas (Camp, 1973, pp. 187–198; Staats, 1968, pp. 397–469).

3. The *developmental tasks* approach begins with sequences of normal development. Curricula provide hierarchical sequences of tasks, skills, or content that are derived either from normative information about the ways children develop or from developmental analysis of task complexity, usually related to chronological age or sequence of skills. Content areas selected in this approach tend to be broad categories of child development that are subsequently sequenced into objectives representing hierarchical steps in maturation or in task analysis (Evans, 1971, pp. 311–313; Spodek, 1973, p. 84 ff).

4. The *psychological constructs* approach begins with concepts from psychological theory. A curriculum organized around this rationale will generally be constructed from a number of the following content areas: self concept, locus of control, divergent thinking (creativity), convergent thinking, primary mental abilities, motivation, identity, sexuality (sex role), need gratification, and cognition. While these areas represent processes, in a sense, the primary substantiation for their importance to curriculum has come from theoretical work attempting to explain many complex facets of personality and intellect (Evans, 1971, pp. 313–319; Ojemann, 1967, pp. 195–204).

5. The *educational content areas* approach begins with areas of academic content. This approach, perhaps the closest to curriculum used in regular preschool programs, defines areas of learning on the basis of (pre)academic content to be learned. The areas most frequently included are: prereading, number (conservation), music, art, dance (body movement), play, story telling, social studies (people), and nature (Bereiter & Engelmann, 1966).

It is clearly evident that a curriculum can be constructed around a combination of these basic rationale types. Particularly, the first and second types are used effectively together (a deficits in basic skills approach). The second and third types are occasionally combined (basic skills sequenced developmentally). To a lesser degree, there are combinations of the fifth rationale with the first and second types (deficits in educational content or educational content defined in terms of basic skills). Rarely is curriculum developed around psychological constructs entirely. However, in combination with other approaches, several psychological constructs may be scattered throughout a curriculum (particularly self concept and cognition).

Occasionally, upon close study of the actual curriculum material, one will find that an impressive rationale has not been consistently extended throughout the

Figure 1

The Range in Curriculum Content Areas Included by 20 First Chance Projects in 1974

Content Areas	1	2	3	4	5	6	7	8	9	10	11	12	13	14	15	16	17	18	19	20	Total
Art			x	x	x																3
Auditory perception (processing discrimination)	x		x		x				x					x		x	x				7
Behavior												x							x		2
Behavior modification						x															1
Body awareness			x																		1
Cognition (conceptualizing intellectual development)			x	x			x	x	x	x	x	x	x	x	x				x		11
Creativity						x			x												2
Discipline				x																	1
Expressive language (also, storytelling finger play)				x						x					x	x	x			x	6
Fine motor	x						x	x		x				x			x				6
Gross motor	x				x		x	x		x				x	x		x	x			9
Health, mental (emotional)									x										x		2
Health, physical					x				x												2
Home activities				x		x							x			x					4
Independence									x												1

Language (communication; speech)	x	x	x	x	x	x	x	x	x	x	x	x	x	x				x	14
Math				x															1
Motor skills (physical activities; locomotion)				x			x		x		x					x	x		6
Music				x	x														2
Perception		x					x				x								3
Personal-social							x						x						1
Preacademics ("tools for learning")								x		x							x		2
Receptive language										x	x	x	x				x		5
Science					x				x										2
Self concept (self image)		x		x					x										3
Self help				x			x		x	x	x		x				x		7
Sensory motor					x														1
Social-emotional							x		x	x	x		x						4
Socialization				x			x		x	x	x	x	x			x			6
Social studies (people/holidays/field trips)				x	x				x										3
Toys					x														1
Visual perception (processing; discrimination)	x	x		x							x		x				x		5

Note: An x indicates the area is included in the curriculum.

curriculum. Or a rationale statement may be missing because it was thought to be implicit in the materials or because such a statement was never considered necessary.

SELECTING THE CONTENT AREAS

Another major consideration in curriculum development is: What should be included (and what should be omitted)? Such decisions should be founded upon the rationale and should result in content areas that represent logical selections, clearly expressing the rationale.

The range of curriculum content areas was reviewed in 1974 and is summarized in Figure 1. This summary indicates that of 32 content areas language and cognition are the only areas included consistently in at least half of the reviewed curricula. Auditory and visual perception, when considered as one area, were also represented in half of the curricula. The full effectiveness of any one curriculum cannot be determined by merely identifying the selected areas. More important is the logical consistency with which the areas relate to each other, comprising a total package for expression of the overall curriculum goal, or rationale.

PUTTING THE CONTENT TOGETHER

Because each content area draws heavily from other content areas, organization of the curriculum is a critical aspect. The content should be organized to link identification, assessment, objectives, and evaluation procedures in logical and consistent ways. While few First Chance curricula actually report the ways the areas of content are organized, one usually can identify the organization by examining the description of procedures for using the curriculum.

There are three fairly common styles for organizing curriculum content: parallel, crossover, and spiral. Figure 2 illustrates these three arrangements schematically. Unfortunately, one may occasionally find a curriculum with little organization in its content areas. Figure 3 illustrates schematically how a curriculum without organization might appear.

Organizing content into parallel units is a fairly widespread practice. With this system, each content area generally is sequenced independently. There are advantages and disadvantages to the parallel arrangement. Adaptations for an individual child can be easily made so that the rate of learning in an area of greatest disability will not hold back his progress in another area. Unfortunately, there seem to be skills needed in one area as preliminary building blocks for accomplishments at a later phase in another area. For this reason, some curricula combine the parallel content organization with the crossover concept.

In organizing content to cross over into other content areas, specific objectives usually are identified as significant to different areas within different sequences. This is seen most often in some forms of unit teaching, in open classroom modules, or in a few developmental curricula that cross reference key milestones. The advantages of an arrangement that cross references objectives and content

Figure 2

*Schematic Illustrations of
Three Styles for Organizing
Curriculum Content*

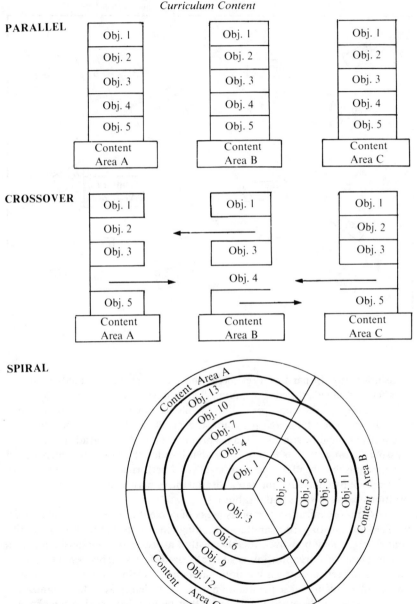

Figure 3

*Schematic Illustration of a
Curriculum with No Organization*

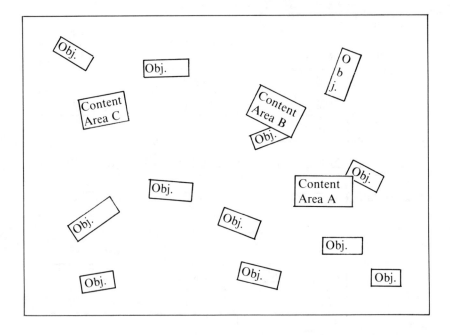

areas are many. In particular, elements that have a significant contribution to another area are identified. For example, a child who fears adults may have significant delay in communication skills. While he may make some progress in a carefully designed language program, the problem of his relationships with adults also should be considered in his program plan. A second advantage of the crossover arrangement is that of somewhat limiting the extent to which a child might be pushed ahead in one area far beyond performance in another area. In the very young child such interarea discrepancies may lead to unjustified exaggerations between skills and disabilities.

The spiral organization combines areas of content into sequences of interdependent units, with particular units preceding other units. In this way four or five content areas may be woven together within a system of prerequisite units. In unit teaching this organization is generally used. It is a highly complex system but certainly reflects the assumption that a child's various areas of functioning are interdependent and sequential in nature. A difficulty with this organization for a severely handicapped youngster is that he may have such discrepancy in functioning within some content areas that the system may need to be modified.

Figure 4

Representative Examples of
Types of Curriculum Organization

	Parallel	Crossover	Spiral
Deficit-Amelioration	Detroit MI	*	New Haven CT
Basic Skills	Sacaton AZ Starkville MS Schaumburg IL	*	St. Paul MN (3–6)
Developmental	Memphis TN Rochester NY Chapel Hill NC	Athens GA Portage WI	St. Paul MN (0–3)
Psychological Constructs	Marshalltown IO	*	*
Educational Content	El Paso TX Magnolia AR	*	*

* Among the materials reviewed, none was found to illustrate these organizational styles.

EXAMPLES OF CURRICULUM ORGANIZATION

The ways curriculum philosophy is actually expressed through rationale and content organization are illustrated in Figure 4. This grid is not intended to be an exhaustive summary of all First Chance curricula, but rather a sample of a variety of approaches to curriculum organization.

The Detroit Preschool

As can be seen from Figure 4, the Detroit (Michigan) Preschool Technical Assistance Resource and Training Center is viewed as having primarily a deficit amelioration orientation organized in parallel fashion. This project lists three major curriculum objectives: (a) to identify strengths and weaknesses, (b) to remediate the weaknesses, and (c) to conduct systematic periodic reevaluation of multiply handicapped preschool children. The curriculum covers five areas: gross motor functioning, fine motor functioning, visual perception and discrimination, auditory discrimination, and language functioning.

The children are taught individually as well as in groups. The project uses its own Preschool Developmental Assessment Scale to obtain profiles of each child in the five areas mentioned as well as for the group as a whole. This information is then used to plan group and individual activities for the children aimed at remediating deficiencies.

The curriculum discusses the five areas separately—in a parallel fashion. The text of the materials available for review was descriptive of the implementation of the project—how the profiles were used for group and individual planning. The substance of the curriculum itself was not available to the reviewers.

The Gila River Indian Community

The *Speech Correction Curriculum* of the Gila River Indian Community Handicapped Children's Early Education Program (Sacaton, Arizona) is an example of a basic skills curriculum developed in a parallel mode. The curriculum focuses entirely on speech development. Because of this it would parallel any other curricula the project uses. The curriculum guide contains five major sections. The first chapter gives activities for manipulation of the muscles and organs used in speaking. Chapter 2 gives listening activities. Chapter 3 contains suggestions for helping children with speech difficulties in the form of principles that should govern therapy, suggestions and principles for ear training, and suggestions and principles for teaching the sounds /s/, /z/, /k/, /g/, /l/, /sh/, /f/, /v/, /r/, /ch/, /p/, /b/, /t/, and /d/. Chapter 4 deals with the sequence and principles of practice. Chapter 5 contains sample lesson plans. In the way the guide is written, coordination of speech correction with other areas of instruction is not stressed.

The Preschool and Early Education Project

Curriculum Planning and Curriculum Materials: Preschool and Primary Level is the curriculum developed by the Preschool and Early Education Project at Mississippi State University (Starkville). This is another example of a basic skill curriculum developed in a parallel mode. The basic skill is language development since overall objectives are stated in terms of psycholinguistic ability. The curriculum is organized into "mini units," each with its own set of objectives.

There are units on body awareness (body parts and functions, cleanliness, and management), auditory perception, and visual perception; and sections on peg board activities, number concepts, expression of ideas, scheduling, and instructional sequences and checklists for handwriting and beginning arithmetic.

The curriculum is intended for children between the ages of 4 and 9 years, who are described as disadvantaged, with developmental handicaps in language or perception.

The Schaumburg Early Education Center

The curriculum described in the Schaumburg (Illinois) Early Education Center (SEEC) project proposal begins with a checklist of developmental milestones. Directions for facilitation of a child's development are targeted, developmental goals developed, activities planned, and ongoing evaluation carried out. The curriculum thus becomes individual for each child. The basic curriculum materials are *Developmental Milestones—Miniwheel and Maxiwheel* and *Action Experiences.* The curriculum content is organized around the child. The staff reacts to the child and uses the developmental milestones as a frame of reference in the five areas of (a) intellectual development, (b) language development, (c) motor skills development, (d) social-emotional development, and (e) self help skills. Each area is treated parallel to the others, even though it is likely that in day to day operations crossover and spiraling occur.

Thus, the Schaumburg Project is seen as an example of a primary basic skills and developmental task orientation in a parallel mode intended for children between 3 to 6 years of age.

Project MEMPHIS

The curriculum, *Lesson Plans for Enhancing Preschool Developmental Progress,* designed by Project MEMPHIS (Memphis, Tennessee), is an example of a curriculum with a developmental orientation. Its five content areas are presented in a parallel fashion.

The project gives two training programs, one for foster children and one for foster parents. The curriculum is for children whose developmental ages range between 0 and 60 months. The curriculum guide provides a developmental evaluation form for educational programing, the MEMPHIS Comprehensive Developmental Scale (included in the project's *Instruments for Individual Program Planning and Evaluation).* This scale is essentially a checklist used to evaluate deficiencies and abilities and, in effect, constitutes the curriculum in the areas of personal-social, gross motor, fine motor, language, and perceptual-cognitive skills. Within each area the skills are arranged in hierarchical fashion.

Unlike most other curricula, the MEMPHIS guide does not contain the usual listing of educational activities within the areas covered. Instead, the guide discusses fully the development of specific, observable, behavioral objectives based on the developmental evaluation and provides examples of general goals, more specific objectives, and very specific objectives for both child and parent training programs. The discussion of educational treatment is in terms of broad principles with examples of lesson plans for each of the five content areas.

Chapter 5 of this curriculum guide provides a good example of the expression of the linkages of rationale, assessment, objectives, and evaluation.

The Rochester Project

The Rochester (New York) Preschool Special Education Project has developed the *Preschool Special Education Habilitative Program for Inner City Youngsters and Their Families,* which is an example of a developmental orientation in a parallel mode with evident attempts at crossover. The curriculum, for children with developmental ages between 2 and 36 months, covers six areas: social-emotional, speech and language, gross motor, fine motor, self help, and cognitive skills. Crossover is most evident in the last two areas, which are heavily cross indexed to the other four. The activities and skills within each area are presented in a developmental hierarchy. The curriculum presents a good explication of the linkages between philosophy, rationale, referral, assessment, curriculum objectives, evaluation, and general principles of instruction.

The Chapel Hill Project

The Chapel Hill (North Carolina) Training Outreach Project provides three volumes, the Learning Accomplishment Profile (LAP), an Infant LAP, and *A Planning Guide to the Preschool Curriculum: The Child, The Process, The Day*. The LAP has three sections, an evaluation checklist, a task level profile of skills, and 44 instructional units. The checklist is developmental, from 0 to 6 years of age, and is used to identify a child's abilities and weaknesses from which curriculum objectives for each child are derived. The LAP covers the areas of gross and fine motor skills, language development, cognitive development, social skills, and self help skills. The second section, the task level profile, describes different activities in terms of levels of functioning. It serves as both a checklist and a guide for what to teach and the sequence in which to teach it. These are easily translated into behavioral objectives. The third section presents 44 units broken down into isolated concepts and arranged in a hierarchy of responses.

These 44 units are repeated in more detail and elaboration in *A Planning Guide*. The *Guide* also contains good discussions of curriculum development, instructional objectives, task analysis, the unit approach, error free learning, correct reinforcement, and principles for teacher made materials, art activities, and homework/parent work.

The sections in the LAP and the *Guide* are essentially presented in a parallel mode. While in practice there is probably a good deal of crossover and spiraling, no instructions are given for dovetailing the evaluation with the task level analysis and the units. For this reason, the Chapel Hill curriculum is presented here as an example of a developmental orientation in a parallel mode.

The Marshalltown Project

The curriculum, *Home Stimulation of Handicapped Children: Professional Guide,* from the Marshalltown (Iowa) Project, was the only project of the 20 reviewed for this chapter that selected content areas primarily with a psychological orientation.

It is a script for conducting 12 parent training sessions on eight topics: orientation to the home stimulation project, creation of a responsive environment, toys as learning tools, creativity, self concept, discipline (behavior modification), language, and sensory motor development. Each session is scheduled and timed to last 1½ hours. The guide also contains techniques for monitoring changes in parent behaviors. The topics are not interrelated for instructional purposes and are therefore classified as parallel in organization.

Early Childhood Learning Center

The Early Childhood Learning Center of El Paso, Texas, has a curriculum entitled *Curriculum Guide: Early Learning Center for Exceptional Children*. It is an example of an educational content orientation with a slight mixture of basic skills. The curriculum contains chapters on the following: social worker's role, language program, speech therapy at home, story telling and finger play, holidays, art activities, field trips, cooking, self help and socialization, music, physical activities, conceptual skills, and playground activities. Units and/or activities are presented within each chapter. The program is intended for multiply handicapped children 3 to 5 years of age. Each area is developed primarily independently of the others—a parallel mode.

A companion volume, *Structured Experiences for Developmental Learning,* is developed from the ITPA model, for kindergarten and first grade children. Each page contains a goal, objective, method, and criterion for performance. Cross coding has not been accomplished, making this second volume a parallel mode with a basic skills orientation.

The Magnolia Preschool

The curriculum of the Magnolia (Arkansas) Preschool Handicapped Project, *Curriculum Guidelines for Kindergarten Activities,* is organized into sections on auditory perception, language development, visual perception, social studies, science, mathematics, health, gross motor skills, music, and art. It is mainly a listing of activities within each area and subtopic. Detailed lesson samples are given for math. This guide is an example of an educational content orientation (with some basic skills added) in a parallel mode.

The Rutland Center

The curriculum of the Rutland Center in Athens, Georgia, *Developmental Therapy: A Textbook for Teachers as Therapists for Emotionally Disturbed Young Children,* is one of two examples of a developmental orientation in a crossover mode. This curriculum is developed for children ages 3 to 14 years who are seriously emotionally disturbed or behaviorally disordered.

Close linkage of the rationale, assessment process, treatment/educational process, and evaluation is carefully explicated. The four basic curriculum areas are behavior, communication, socialization, and (pre)academics. By using a developmental rating form in each of these four areas a child's program is planned. The developmental milestones in each area are cross listed in such a way that, for example, those milestones in behavior that are also significant in other areas are identified. This is one way in which crossover is accomplished. From the rating form a profile of the child's functioning in various areas is obtained. This profile determines the objectives for that child in accord with certain principles and guidelines discussed in the curriculum. The second way that crossover is accomplished is through the use of *Developmental Therapy* stages:

- Stage 1—Responding and trusting.
- Stage 2—Learning individual skills.
- Stage 3—Applying individual skills to group procedures.
- Stage 4—Investing in group processes (valuing one's group).
- Stage 5—Applying individual/group skills in new situations (generalizing and valuing).

Each stage's different emphasis, techniques, materials, and experiences are reflected in the rating forms just mentioned and in the comprehensive detailed list of objectives for each area of the curriculum. This seems to amount to a "double crossover" arrangement.

Examples of activities are given, but lists of specified activities and units are not provided. The emphasis in the curriculum description is on the process of mastering objectives by stages. Therapeutic principles for the teacher, for the selection of activities, for child-adult interaction, and for managing behavior are discussed.

The Portage Project

The *Portage Guide to Early Education,* developed by the Portage (Wisconsin) Project, is another example of a curriculum with a developmental orientation in a crossover mode. The curriculum is basically composed of a card file that is accompanied by the Portage Project Checklist. The curriculum is intended for children 0 to 5 years of age. The checklist is used to identify the behaviors the child is not exhibiting and is organized in such a way as to provide a continuous record of the child's entry behavior, the behaviors he has learned, the date achieved, and the specific curriculum taught. Each behavior on the checklist has a number which corresponds to a particular card in the card file (see Figure 5). The behaviors are grouped into five areas: cognition, self help, motor, language, and socialization. The cards are color coded by area and contain behavioral descriptions of the behavior, the expected age level of attainment of the behavior, suggested activities for teaching, and a criterion of successful attainment. Many cards are cross coded both within and across the five areas (crossover). Thus, the teacher or parent can target a behavior, find suggestions for teaching it, and identify necessary prior behaviors.

The five areas mentioned also represent a basic skills approach, within which the skills are listed developmentally and somewhat hierarchically. This curriculum package includes parallel elements (between areas), crossover elements (among cards within and among areas), and spiraling elements (by cross referencing to earlier skill cards).

The New Haven Preschool

Generally, spiraling is most evident in those curricula dealing with motor skills. This is probably a reflection of the state of knowledge in the field regarding the sequences of motor development.

The New Haven Gross Motor Curriculum from the New Haven (Connecticut) Preschool Program for Handicapped Children is discussed here as an example of a curriculum with a deficit amelioration orientation with some spiraling. It should be noted that this is a single area (gross motor) curriculum and not a total description of the New Haven curriculum.

This curriculum is intended for 3 and 4 year old cerebral palsied, mentally retarded, or neurologically impaired children. It covers the following tasks:

Figure 5

Sample Curriculum Card
Cooperative Educational Service Agency 12
(Portage, Wisconsin)

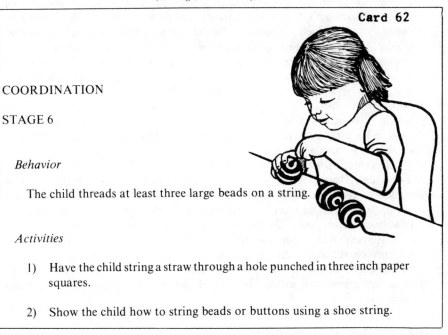

Card 62

COORDINATION

STAGE 6

Behavior

The child threads at least three large beads on a string.

Activities

1) Have the child string a straw through a hole punched in three inch paper squares.

2) Show the child how to string beads or buttons using a shoe string.

Note. From *Portage Guide to Early Education,* by S. Bluma, M. Shearer, J. Hilliard, and A. Frohman, Portage WI: Portage Project, 1976.

walking, running, maintaining balance, climbing up and down stairs, jumping, hopping, skipping, throwing, catching, kicking, climbing, pushing, and pulling. Within each skill area there is a sequence of skills. Common faults and representative activities are identified for each skill area.

The spiral features are evident in the sequences within each skill. For example, balancing at the lowest level is the ability to stand on the floor without falling; at the highest level it is the ability to stand on a balance beam without falling. All of this is predicated on a certain level of "walking" ability. Hence, many activities reappear at succeeding levels of the hierarchy of skills but in complex fashion.

The UNISTAPS Project

The UNISTAPS Project (St. Paul, Minnesota) publishes two curriculum guides. One is for hearing impaired children, 0 to 3 years of age, and their parents. This project is a family oriented, home based program. The second guide is for hearing impaired children, 3 to 6 years of age, in a primarily center based program.

The curriculum, *Curriculum Guide for Preprimary Hearing Impaired Children, 3-6 Years of Age,* lists goals in 10 areas: physical health, mental health, independence, self image, socialization, intellectual development, preacademics ("tools of learning"), language, creativity, and motor. However, the curriculum has chapters in which the sequential stages are presented on social studies and science, language, reading, mathematics, speech, and auditory training. The curriculum focuses most on language and cognitive development. Other content areas (e.g., social studies and science) are treated as vehicles through which the goals can be achieved, language can be developed, and cognition can be improved. Within the model presented in this chapter, the curriculum is a combination of basic skill with educational content, within a developmental framework in both spiral and parallel modes. Spiraling occurs within areas but the curriculum is parallel across areas.

The guide, *Curriculum Guide: Hearing Impaired Children, Birth to Three Years, and Their Parents,* is comprehensive. It includes chapters dealing with guidelines for developing many aspects of an infant program: language and vocabulary, stages of receptive and expressive language, evaluation, goals and objectives, developmental patterns, home centered activities, sample phrases, suggested experiential activities for successive age levels, individual teaching, experience charts, and auditory training. The focus is on what parents can do to facilitate the development of their children. This curriculum has a developmental orientation with some implied spiraling, but primarily in a parallel mode.

THE COMPLETE CURRICULUM

Perhaps the most confusing aspect of any curriculum occurs when the written materials do not make a clear distinction between the *project description* and the *instructional curriculum.* Separation of these two aspects of a project makes it easier to determine which curriculum is complete and which components are suitable for adaptation to other programs.

In addition to a clearly identified rationale and a logical organization discussed previously, there are a number of other aspects to consider in a complete curriculum.

Child Population

The child population for which the curriculum was originally developed should be reported, including at least handicapping condition(s), cultural and ethnic groups, and chronological age. (A few projects report child population according to developmental status rather than by handicapping condition.)

Among the curricula reviewed there were no particular age categories standardly used. Several programs target on the 5 year old specifically. Other programs include 0 to 3, 0 to 5 (or 6), 3 to 5 (or 6), 4 to 9, and 3 to 4 year olds. A few curricula do not report either chronological or developmental age.

Among the programs, curricula are available for a wide variety of handicapping conditions, including speech and language delays, hearing impairment, orthopedic problems, neuromuscular disorders, visual problems, mental retardation, Down's syndrome, perceptual problems, and emotional disturbance. While one can find a curriculum specifically designed for each of these handicapping conditions, the predominant approach is a curriculum applicable to a number of handicapping conditions. In such instances, the handicapping condition is reported to be "mixed." In these mixed programs, the degree of severity of the various handicapping conditions is generally not reported and in most instances no reference is made to highly specialized techniques or equipment needed for specific, severely handicapping conditions. One might safely conclude, therefore, that curricula identified for a mixed handicapped population are, in general, applicable for children with mild to moderately severe disabilities.

A few curricula are designed with ethnic cultures in mind, in particular Indian, Mexican American, and Alaskan. A number of curricula are used with handicapped Black children but with no particular emphasis reported on Black culture. For a discussion of curricula for various ethnic groups, see Chapter 7, "Special Program Needs of the Culturally Diverse Child."

Objectives

Objectives are at the heart of any curriculum. Whether they are stated in behavioral terms, are defined as general performance goals, or are implicit in the details of an activity, it is through objectives that the rationale is expressed and the program moves forward.

Just as the First Chance projects represent many different rationales for curriculum selection and organization, their curriculum objectives also are stated in ways reflecting these many different approaches. Several programs have linked child assessment procedures directly into curriculum objectives. In many programs, assessment items are actually used as curriculum objectives. In one program the objectives are the product of a careful task analysis of skills and processes within content areas. A variation of this occurs in two projects using videotape analysis procedures for assessment. From such procedures individual child objectives are stated in behavioral terms.

The extent to which criterion (mastery) behavior is provided varies greatly. A number of programs with carefully explicated objectives leave decisions about mastery to the judgment of the teacher, probably assuming that the criterion is implicit in the objective statement. A few programs have specific detailed performance criteria including frequency with which the desired behaviors should occur.

Perhaps the most frequently used criterion is a reference to expected age norms; that is, how the "average" child will perform on an item at a particular chronological age. Age norms are seldom referenced to particular research studies, and there is an implicit assumption of a universally accepted age standard for certain performance. Such an assumption is not always valid since (a) a particular disability may make it impossible for a normal age referenced criterion behavior to occur and (b) there has been little research examining the sequence in which handicapped children follow or do not follow normal patterns of development.

Activities and Materials

When specific materials are suggested they should be appropriate to the rationale, objectives, and specific child population for which they are intended. If a curriculum provides principles for selecting materials, these may be extremely helpful. Such principles can be used in adapting a curriculum for other programs and staffs.

Among the First Chance curricula excellent suggestions for activities can be found for a variety of settings (home, school, and center), for children with all types of handicapping conditions, and for children of all ages. Suggested activities are generally incorporated into the body of the curriculum, but it is not unusual to find them in appendices or in separate packages. There are numerous examples of highly creative and useful instructional material of this sort, in particular:

- A handbook of ideas for body movement, music and songs, and an art curriculum, *Art for Young Children*, from the Preschool and Early Education Project at Mississippi State University (Starkville).
- *Nutrition Instruction and the School Lunch—Ideas for Nutrition Instruction* from the Magnolia (Arkansas) Preschool Handicapped Project.
- A *Priceless Playground for Exceptional Children* from the El Paso (Texas) Early Childhood Learning Center.
- *Developmental Levels of Waterbug Swimming Skills* from the Alaska Resource Center in Anchorage.
- *Stimulation for Infants and Toddlers* from the Nisonger Center in Columbus, Ohio.
- Auditory training exercises included in the appendix of the UNISTAPS (St. Paul, Minnesota) *Curriculum Guide for Preprimary Hearing Impaired Children, 3-6 Years of Age.*
- The Chapel Hill (North Carolina) *Planning Guide to the Preschool Curriculum*—a compendium of suggestions, organized around unit activities. The appendix of that publication contains two useful bibliographies: *Suggested Books for Young Children* and a *Music Bibliography*.
- An excellent description of language development, in time blocks from 0 to 3 years of age, provided in the appendix of the UNISTAPS *Curriculum Guide: Hearing Impaired Children, Birth to Three Years, and Their Parents*. This volume also contains activities for individualized teaching and for using experience charts.

Assessment of Progress

Each objective, activity, and procedure should offer some standard of mastery, telling the teacher when a child is ready to progress and giving direction for what should come next. These success criteria may be observable or judgmental but, in any case, should be clearly specified.

The Chapel Hill (North Carolina) curriculum provides general descriptions of the way a child should perform each task on the LAP. The Rutland Center (Athens, Georgia) *Developmental Therapy* objectives offer examples of mastery and specify that a child must meet the objective 90% of the time at home, nursery, and center. In *Language Related Activities: Curriculum Assistance for Teachers of Normal and Language Disabled Preschoolers,* the Rockville (Maryland) Project specifies a criterion behavior for each instructional goal, primarily referenced to chronological age performance standards. The Portage (Wisconsin) Project provides a behavioral description of how a child is expected to perform on each specified objective in the entire card file.

A number of projects use a summary profile procedure to document the progress of an individual child as he progresses through a curriculum. Such a procedure lends itself to a growth profile, pinpointing components of growth and lag.

Physical Setting and Schedules

A description of the physical setting, schedule of activities, time, and any special furnishings should be included in a complete curriculum. If the curriculum requires no special arrangements, that fact should be stated also.

A wide variety of settings are included among the First Chance curricula. The Portage (Wisconsin) Project and the Marshalltown (Iowa) Project curricula are designed for parents to conduct in the home setting. The UNISTAPS (St. Paul, Minnesota) Project for hearing impaired children, 0 to 3 years, is designed primarily for home use by parents but may be conducted by others in a variety of settings such as a demonstration room or an integrated nursery school.

The special center setting is probably used most often in projects serving a particular type of disability, such as the Rutland Center for emotionally disturbed (Athens, Georgia), the Montgomery County Society for Crippled Children and Adults, Inc. (Rockville, Maryland), the Child Development and Mental Retardation Center at the University of Washington (Seattle), and the Nisonger Center at The Ohio State University (Columbus).

Another frequently used setting is the integrated nursery, Head Start, or day care center. Examples of projects operating primarily in this mode include those located in Chapel Hill, North Carolina; Rochester, New York; Anchorage, Alaska; and Starkville, Mississippi (Mississippi State University).

Several projects use both a specialized setting such as a diagnostic nursery and regular nursery programs. Examples of this approach are the Rochester, UNISTAPS, and MEMPHIS Projects.

Format

Curriculum should be prepared in a format that is efficient and clear for the people who will be using it. Generally, the simpler the format, the easier it will be to implement the content.

The loose leaf or bound mimeographed format is used most often in First Chance curriculum guides. Index cards, sometimes color coded, are also used. Both ways of presenting the material can be useful if the organization of the content has been carefully prepared.

Curricula that are more difficult to manage are often separated into a series of loosely stapled pages, lacking protective covers, with assessment scales in one series, instructions for use in another package, and specific lesson plans and activities in still another series. However, many of the difficulties inherent in using a curriculum in such a format can be overcome if the relationship among the packages has been clearly identified and procedures are carefully outlined.

Perhaps a major contribution to preschool curriculum and instruction has been made by the First Chance projects through the creative use of audiovisual formats. An extensive array of materials has been developed on a variety of instructional topics. There are films, slide tapes, and videotape presentations (a) providing orientations to early intervention, (b) discussing identification, (c) discussing assessment, and (d) describing programs.

Users

Each curriculum should define its user groups: teachers, parents, teacher aides, administrators, and children. With adaptations, materials developed for any one of these groups may be useful to the other groups.

The majority of the curricula have been developed for use by teachers and teacher aides. A few programs specify that the curriculum material was prepared for use by speech therapists, and a number of curricula have portions specified for use by parents. There are few curricula, however, that are designed solely for implementation by parents. Parent materials are characteristically of three types: those that teach basic behavior modification techniques, including observation, recording, and reinforcement systems; those that specify steps for language stimulation; and those that are intended to assist parents in improving their own effectiveness in teaching self help skills or in parent-child relationships.

Similarly, few curriculum materials among the First Chance programs have been developed for children as the primary users. A few notable exceptions are the sign language dictionary and the handbook *Eyeglasses* developed by the Alaska Head Start Special Services Project. The lack of materials designed specifically for the child to use may be a reflection of the existence of a significant number of curriculum materials already available through commercial avenues or the fact that teachers are relying on their own materials, made specifically for individual children.

Curriculum Verification

The curriculum should report evaluation procedures or other documentation concerning curriculum verification and progress of children. The curriculum may look good, but does it work? And under what conditions? With which children? Often such results are reported in research journals and are difficult to locate for particular curricula. In any case, some report of child characteristics and process or outcome information are necessary.

In addition, there should be information reporting at least planning processes or criteria for selecting the curriculum. Field testing procedures have been provided by the Rockville (Maryland) experimental curriculum. The Rutland Center (Athens, Georgia) provides five standards for curriculum development which reflect the basic rationale behind *Developmental Therapy*. The Rochester (New York) and MEMPHIS (Tennessee) Projects provide a rationale for each content area and discussions of the salient processes involved.

The introductory chapter of the Chapel Hill (North Carolina) *Planning Guide* reviews concepts of curriculum task analysis and evaluation and offers eight specific steps used in curriculum planning with an individual child. Perhaps the greatest number of projects implicitly rely upon achievement of objectives by children as the means to verify curriculum.

If a curriculum does not include documentation of its effectiveness or development, but does provide a system which seems useful in a new program, it may still be appropriate, particularly if verification is included as one of the new program's objectives.

CONCLUDING COMMENTS

When reviewing existing curricula, one should consider the approach to which he or she is personally and professionally inclined (Weikart, 1971). For example, if a teacher is committed to the idea that the learning process must be a series of steps appropriate to a child's individual sequence of maturation, that teacher will want a developmentally based curriculum. Or if a teacher has received training in a prescriptive teaching approach, that teacher may be most effective using a curriculum designed around an amelioration philosophy. Or if it is necessary to conduct the program in children's homes, the curriculum should facilitate home based efforts.

Perhaps a curriculum will need to be applicable to a group of children with unique characteristics for which no curriculum is specifically designed. This might require adaptation from a curriculum which seems fairly applicable in other respects. Or, perhaps the children represent a much broader range of characteristics than reported in any curricula, and thus it may be appropriate to combine aspects of several curricula.

Many effective curricula present each goal or objective in a separate package complete with activity, materials, specific techniques for conducting the activity, and the criterion for mastery. Such units often specify when it should be used, what should have occurred before, and suggestions for parallel or supplementary procedures, often cross referenced with other objectives.

Perhaps the most important aspect to examine in a curriculum is the relationship of the specific objectives to the overall rationale. There should be clear, logical links between what the curriculum is attempting to do (rationale), how it is organized to accomplish the specific aspects of its effort (content and objectives), and how accomplishment can be determined (evaluation).

REFERENCES

Bereiter, C., & Engelmann, S. *Teaching the disadvantaged child in the preschool.* Englewood Cliffs NJ: Prentice-Hall, 1966.

Bronfenbrenner, U. Who cares for America's children? *Young Children,* 1971, *26,* 157–163.

Camp, J. C. A skill development curriculum for 3-, 4-, and 5-year-old disadvantaged children. In B. Spodek (Ed.), *Early childhood education.* Englewood Cliffs NJ: Prentice-Hall, 1973.

Cronbach, L. J. Heredity, environment, and educational policy. *Harvard Educational Review,* 1969, *39,* 338–347.

Deutsch, M. Early social environment: Its influence on school adaptation. In F. M. Hechinger (Ed.), *Preschool Education Today.* New York: Doubleday, 1966.

Evans, E. D. *Contemporary influences in early childhood education.* New York: Holt, Rinehart, & Winston, 1971.

Karnes, M. *Investigations of classroom and at-home interventions, Research and Development Program on Preschool Disadvantaged Children* (Final Report, Vol. 1). Urbana: University of Illinois, Institute of Research for Exceptional Children, May, 1969.

Mayer, R. S. A comparative analysis of preschool curriculum models. In R. H. Anderson & H. G. Shane (Eds.), *As the twig is bent.* Boston: Houghton Mifflin, 1971.

Ojemann, R. H. Incorporating psychological concepts in the school curriculum. *Journal of School Psychology,* 1967, *3,* 195–204.

Spodek, B. *Early childhood education.* Englewood Cliffs NJ: Prentice-Hall, 1973.

Staats, A. W. *Learning language and cognition.* New York: Holt, Rinehart, & Winston, 1968.

Weikart, D. P., Rogers, L., Adcock, C., & McClelland, P. *The cognitively oriented curriculum: A framework for preschool teachers.* Washington DC: National Association for Education of Young Children, 1971.

RESOURCES

Action Experiences. Schaumburg Early Education Center, Schaumburg, Illinois. 1976. (Available from SEEC Communications, 804 W. Bode Road, Schaumburg IL 60193. $3.00.)

Art for Young Children. Preschool and Early Education Project, Starkville, Mississippi. (For availability information contact Ernestine W. Rainey, Preschool and Early Education Resource Center, Drawer EP, Starkville MS 39206.)

Calendar of Developmental Activities for Preschoolers: A Resource Book for Teachers. Technical Assistance Resource Center in Early Childhood Education for the Handicapped, Omaha, Nebraska. 1975. (Available from Meyer Children's Rehabilitation Institute, University of Nebraska Medical Center, 444 S. 44th Street, Omaha NB 68131. $2.50.)

Cerebral Palsy and Related Developmental Disabilities—Prevention and Early Care: An Annotated Bibliography (Volumes I–IV). A Nationally Organized Collaborative Project to Provide Comprehensive Services for Atypical Infants and Their Families, New York, New York. (Available from Ohio State University Press, 2070 Neil Avenue, Columbus OH 43210. Volumes I-III, $9.50; Volume IV, $2.50. Also available from ERIC Document Reproduction Service, P. O. Box 190, Arlington VA 22210. Volume I, ED 111 160; Volume II, ED 111 161; Volume III, ED 111 162.)

Curriculum Guide: Early Learning Center for Exceptional Children. Early Childhood Learning Center, El Paso, Texas. 1974. (Available from the project, P. O. Box 10716, El Paso TX 79997. $4.50.)

Curriculum Guide: Hearing Impaired Children, Birth to Three Years, and Their Parents. UNISTAPS Project, St. Paul, Minnesota. 1976. (Available from ERIC Document Reproduction Service, P. O. Box 190, Arlington VA 22210, ED 057 527; and from Alexander Graham Bell Association for the Deaf, 3417 Volta Place, N.W., Washington DC 20007, $7.00.)

Curriculum Guidelines for Kindergarten Activities. Magnolia Preschool Handicapped Project, Magnolia, Arkansas. 1973. (Available from West Side Preschool Program, P. O. Box 428, Magnolia AR 71753. $3.00.)

Curriculum Guide for Preprimary Hearing Impaired Children, 3–6 Years of Age. UNISTAPS Project, St. Paul, Minnesota. (Available from ERIC Document Reproduction Service, P. O. Box 190, Arlington VA 22210, Ed 064 812; and from Minnesota Department of Education, Document Section, Room 140, Centennial Building, St. Paul MN 55101, $2.50.)

Curriculum for "Teaching Young Children with Special Needs." Alaska Head Start Special Services Project, Anchorage, Alaska. (Available from Easter Seal Society, 726 E Street, Anchorage AK 99501.)

Curriculum Planning and Curriculum Materials: Preschool and Primary Level. Preschool and Early Education Project, Starkville, Mississippi. 1974. (For availability information contact Ernestine W. Rainey, Preschool and Early Education Resource Center, Drawer EP, Starkville MS 39206.)

Developmental Levels of Waterbug Swimming Skills. Alaska Head Start Special Services Project, Anchorage, Alaska. 1973. (Available from Easter Seal Society, 726 E Street, Anchorage AK 99501. $1.00.)

Developmental Milestones—Miniwheel and Maxiwheel. Schaumburg Early Education Center, Schaumburg, Illinois. 1976. (Available from SEEC Communications, 804 W. Bode Road, Schaumburg IL 60193. $5.00 for samples and observational guidelines.)

Developmental Therapy: A Textbook for Teachers as Therapists for Emotionally Disturbed Young Children. Rutland Center, Athens, Georgia. 1975. (Available from University Park Press, Baltimore MD 21202. $9.75.)

Eyeglasses. Alaska Head Start Special Services Project, Anchorage, Alaska. 1973. (Available from Easter Seal Society, 726 E Street, Anchorage AK 99501. $.50.)

Family Education Program for Preschool Hearing Impaired Children. Alaska Head Start Special Services Project, Anchorage, Alaska. 1973. (Available from Easter Seal Society, 726 E Street, Anchorage AK 99501. $3.50.)

Getting a Head Start on Social Emotional Growth: A Guide for Preschool Teachers. Technical Assistance Resource Center in Early Childhood Education for the Handicapped, Omaha, Nebraska. 1976. (Available from Meyer Children's Rehabilitation Institute, University of Nebraska Medical Center, 444 S. 44th Street, Omaha NB 68131. $2.00.)

Getting a Head Start on Speech and Language Problems: A Guide for Preschool Teachers. Technical Assistance Resource Center in Early Childhood Education for the Handicapped, Omaha, Nebraska. 1974. (Available from Meyer Children's Rehabilitation Institute, University of Nebraska Medical Center, 444 S. 44th Street, Omaha NB 68131. $1.25.)

Home Stimulation of Handicapped Children: Professional Guide. The Marshalltown Project, Marshalltown, Iowa. Revised 1975. (Available from ERIC Document Reproduction Service, P. O. Box 190, Arlington VA 22210. ED 079 922.)

Idea Sheets for Language Development. Alaska Head Start Special Services Project, Anchorage, Alaska. (Available from Easter Seal Society, 726 E Street, Anchorage AK 99501. $3.00.)

An Individualized Curriculum Guide. Early Childhood Education for the Handicapped Program, San Antonio, Texas. (Available in limited quantity from José Cardenaz Early Childhood Center, 3300 Ruiz, San Antonio TX 78228, Attn: Barbara Schmidt. $6.00.)

Infant LAP (Learning Accomplishment Profile). Chapel Hill Training Outreach Project, Chapel Hill, North Carolina. (Available from the project, Lincoln Center, Merritt Mill Road, Chapel Hill NC 27514. $3.00.)

Instruments for Individual Program Planning and Evaluation. Project MEMPHIS, Memphis, Tennessee. 1974. (Available from Fearon Publishers, 6 Davis Drive, Belmont CA 94002. Single copy, $1.50; 25 for $11.00.)

Language Development for the Young Child: A Language Skill Workbook for Teaching Preschool Children. Ernestine W. Rainey. Preschool and Early Education Project, Starkville, Mississippi. (Available from Humanics Associates, 881 Peachtree Street, N.E., Suite 112, Atlanta GA 30309. $6.00.)

Language Related Activities: Curriculum Assistance for Teachers of Normal and Language Disabled Preschoolers. A Remedial Program for Children with Language and Speech Disabilities, Rockville, Maryland. 1973. (Available from Montgomery County Society for Crippled Children and Adults, Inc., 1000 Twinbrook Parkway, Rockville MD 20851. $3.00.)

Learning Accomplishment Profile (LAP). Chapel Hill Training Outreach Project, Chapel Hill, North Carolina. (Available from the project, Lincoln Center, Merritt Hill Road, Chapel Hill NC 27514. $2.00.)

Lesson Plans for Enhancing Preschool Developmental Progress. Project MEMPHIS, Memphis Tennessee. 1973. (Available from Kendall/Hunt Publishing Co., 2460 Kerper Boulevard, Dubuque IA 52001. $13.95.)

Methods and Materials in Education of the Hearing Impaired. Alaska Head Start Special Services Project, Anchorage, Alaska. 1973. (Available from Easter Seal Society, 726 E Street, Anchorage AK 99501. $4.00.)

The New Haven Gross Motor Curriculum. New Haven Preschool Program for Handicapped Children, New Haven, Connecticut. (Available from the program, 400 Canner Street, New Haven CT 06511.)

Nutrition Instruction and the School Lunch—Ideas for Nutrition Instruction. Magnolia Preschool Handicapped Project, Magnolia, Arkansas. 1974. (Available from West Side Preschool Program, P. O. Box 428, Magnolia AR 71753. $2.50.)

A Planning Guide to the Preschool Curriculum: The Child, The Process, The Day. Chapel Hill Training Outreach Project, Chapel Hill, North Carolina. (Available from ERIC Document Reproduction Service, P. O. Box 190, Arlington VA 22210. ED 097 968.)

Portage Guide to Early Education. The Portage Project, Portage, Wisconsin. 1972, revised 1976. (Available from the project, 412 E. Slifer, Box 564, Portage WI 53901. $32 per set plus shipping.)

Pre-School Curriculum Guide. EACH Project, DeKalb, Illinois. (Available from DeKalb County Special Education Association, Early Childhood Division, 405 Gurler Road, DeKalb IL 60115. $3.00.)

A Priceless Playground for Exceptional Children. Early Childhood Learning Center, El Paso, Texas. 1973. (Available from Learning Resources Press, 609 La Cruz, El Paso TX 79902. $1.75.)

Sexual Development and Sex Education for the Mentally Retarded. Comprehensive Children's Services for Rural and Non-Urban Areas, Fargo, North Dakota. (Available from Southeast Mental Health and Retardation Center, 700 First Avenue South, Fargo ND 58102. $4.00.)

Speech Correction Curriculum (Indian). Gila River Indian Community Handicapped Children's Early Education Program, Sacaton, Arizona. (Unpublished. For availability information contact Gila River Indian Community Program, P. O. Box A, Sacaton AZ 85247.)

Stimulation for Infants and Toddlers. Developmentally Delayed Infant Education Project, Columbus, Ohio. (Available from the Nisonger Center, Ohio State University, 1580 Cannon Drive, Columbus OH 43210.)

Structured Experiences for Developmental Learning. Early Childhood Learning Center, El Paso, Texas. 1973. (Available from Learning Resources Press, 609 La Cruz, El Paso TX 79902. $6.00.)

Teaching Young Children with Special Needs. Alaska Head Start Special Services Project, Anchorage, Alaska. 1973. (Available from Easter Seal Society, 726 E Street, Anchorage AK 99501. $6.50.)

Total Communication Handbook and Lessons. Alaska Head Start Special Services Project, Anchorage, Alaska. (Available from Easter Seal Society, 726 E Street, Anchorage AK 99501. Handbook, $6.00; lessons, $1.00.)

Total Communication Video Lessons (tapes). Alaska Head Start Special Services Project, Anchorage, Alaska. (Available from Easter Seal Society, 726 E Street, Anchorage AK 99501. Rental, $20.00 plus insurance and one way postage.)

Why a Registry. Alaska Head Start Special Services Project, Anchorage, Alaska. (Available from Easter Seal Society, 726 E Street, Anchorage AK 99501. Slides/audio, $35.00; rental, $10.00.)

Working wih Children. The Ochlocknee Multi-Handicapped Outreach Project, Ochlocknee, Georgia. (Available from S. W. Georgia Program for Exceptional Children, P. O. Box 110–A, Ochlocknee GA 31773. $2.00.)

7 SPECIAL PROGRAM NEEDS OF THE CULTURALLY DIVERSE CHILD

Jasper
Harvey

▢This chapter is concerned with children who are linguistically and culturally different from mainstream middle class America. There are special program needs for these children who are different and whose parents are different from those who formulate and effect social and educational policy.

DEFICIT MODELS OF CULTURAL DIVERSITY

Abrahams and Troike (1972) indicated that much of the writing and research dealing with cultural diversity and the disadvantaged has been ethnocentric in that *diversity* or *disadvantaged* was defined in terms of differences from urban middle class linguistic and cultural characteristics. Further, the assumption has been that difference is deprivation, and various programs have been planned and operated on a deficit model. Such a model views the child as having no culture of his own and as being deficient in terms of middle class modes, which are assumed to represent "real" culture.

The basic assumption of the deficit model (i.e., the "cultural deprivation model") is that children live in conditions that seriously limit and impair growth and development of verbal facility. Baratz and Baratz (1970) viewed this theory as "unrealistic in terms of current linguistic and anthropological data and, at worst, ethnocentric and racist" (p. 30).

Bronfenbrenner (1972) discussed the need for all parents from all cultures to reunite with their children:

> It is not only children from disadvantaged families who show signs of progressive neglect. An analysis of child rearing practices in the United States over a twenty-five year period reveals a decrease in all spheres of interaction between parents and children. Cross cultural studies comparing American and European (East and West) parents reach the same conclusions. (p. 11)

In an earlier statement, Norris (1967) noted that an unsatisfactory parent-child relationship may have a direct effect on play or exploratory behavior, which in turn may affect social development in later life. An infant's social play, directed initially toward the parents and then toward the peer group, is a critical step developmentally (p. 139). Lack of fulfilling social play may result in an individual who finds the environment so distressing and frightening that he reverts to repetitive stereotypes (p. 142).

DEVELOPMENT OF SOCIAL ADEQUACY

The most pervasive program need for the culturally diverse child is a developmentally planned program which provides strategies that allow development of social adequacy. In the early 1960's Harvey, McMillan, and Ebersole (1964) discussed 11 areas of curriculum from a developmental context that they indicated were necessary for attainment of personal, social, and vocational competence. The development of social adequacy was seen as a developmental process, beginning with early childhood skills and progressing through the school years toward suitable vocational placement.

In a similar context, Vance (1973) stated, "There is a general agreement that a multitude of diverse variables interact to produce a competent or disabled adult" (p. 501). She suggested that traditional models concerning the interrelations which produce the environment-pathology relationship have been inadequate for refining or developing theories to account for "the complexity of the developmental relationships or provide for all relevant classes of environmental and individual variables" (p. 501). There seems to be evidence that symptom or deficit evolution, over time, involves a process which is hierarchical, complex, and dynamic and which is not explainable in terms of simple learning principles.

Vance indicated that a model for social disability should give specific attention to the intrinsic individual differences among children and adults. She suggested the need for a genetic model that facilitates "generation of hypotheses that can specify complex interactions and relevant properties of the environment in potentiating and shaping individual differences" (p. 502). Vance pointed out that phenotypic behaviors even under the most careful genetic control are the product of a genotype in an environment. Further, developmental potential or phenotypic reaction ranges "appear to vary differently with genotype, with kind of behavior, and especially with different environments" (p. 502).

Vance (1973) suggested that an ecological model allows for the study of the development of social disability in terms of "interdependency and interaction between organism *and* environment as these influence the development of a hierarchy of human functions" (p. 502). Equally important, an ecological model provides for environmental variables of a noncultural and nonstructural type, which frequently are attendant with conditions such as deprivation and poverty.

Barker (1960, 1963, 1965) and Wohlwill (1970) have considered the scope of contextual variables to be included in the most viable model of social disability. Such a model should allow for emergent interactional phenomena where both the organism and the environment are changed in the process. These phenomena include variables such as order, rhythmicity, under- and overstimulation, density, saliency, and responsiveness.

Zigler and Phillips (1963) took the position that all variations of deviance are the result of a unitary phenomenon and that syndromes include differences in degrees in developmental lag in behavioral systems which underlie the continuum of social competence. White (1959) defined competence in its broadest biological sense as the organism's capacity to interact effectively with its environment. So defined, competence becomes an interactional term that must include both individual and environmental aspects.

Inkeles (1966, 1968) emphasized the structure of social processes and culturally defined interaction as the primary determinants for development of competencies or for the failure to develop them. Competence is manifested in specific social contexts that provide information for determining role behaviors which must be learned.

Thomas, Chess, and Birch (1968) and Phillips and Zigler (1961) have pointed out that when social and/or environmental conditions are such that they prevent development of higher cognitive processes, the symptoms of deviancy are manifested in acting out or impulse control and ultimately as disability in cognition and reality functions.

TEN SPECIAL NEEDS IN PROGRAMS
FOR CULTURALLY DIVERSE CHILDREN

Many of the First Chance programs are dealing with culturally diverse children. Reviews of their published materials do not always indicate the depth of understanding of diversity which may be observed firsthand in a given project. As one example, the special program needs of the culturally diverse child was a continuing concern of Gotts and Harvey at The University of Texas at Austin. They developed a Program for Staff Training of Exemplary Early Childhood Centers for Handicapped Children and, on a continuing basis, graduate programs in Early Education for Handicapped Children over the 1969–1976 period.

There are a minimum of 10 recurring needs in programing for culturally diverse children. Each of these needs is presented with discussions from various sources, including data from BEH First Chance programs.

Understanding the Life Styles of the Culturally Diverse

Program staffs need to be concerned with analyzing and understanding the life styles of Americans who are linguistically and culturally different from mainstream middle class America. In discussing this area of need, Diggs (1974) stated,

> Under the guidance of well sensitized professional personnel, culturally different children can be given the background experiences necessary for them to grow at their own rate and in accordance with their own developmental and cultural characteristics. (p. 578)

The critical implication is that the child be afforded an individualized program on a developmental basis and with significant regard for his or her own culture's expectations.

A meaningful explanation of some cultural variables was given by Dil (1974), who compared the positive and negative forces with which a child must cope during development. The nonhandicapped middle class American child is progressing or developing in a milieu that presents essentially positive forces (see Figure 1). This child has minimal negative aspects that must be overcome to progress within the preschool program with adults from the dominant culture.

However, the young handicapped child who is from a culture other than the dominant one must overcome or learn to cope with a myriad of forces that the new dominant culture imposes (see Figure 2). As these forces meet in the early childhood program, the child begins to deal with them on a daily basis. As the sensitized professional guides the child's development, there is a molding and softening of forces insofar as the child's parents are "carried along" so that their home expectations are "in tune" with the child's total development. At best, the analogy is that of white water on the river at the rapids. It is hoped that school, professionals, home, and family can come together to help the child stay in an uncapsized boat and negotiate the rapids. The alternatives are obvious.

Figure 1

*Developmental Milieu of the
Nonhandicapped Middle Class Child*

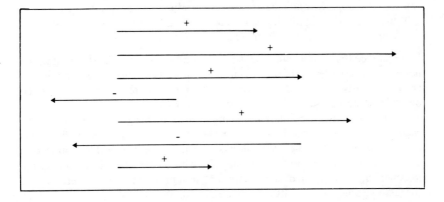

Sarason (1973) contrasted the life styles of the Jew and the Black in coping with the dominant middle class culture:

> Jews and blacks share the characteristic "this is a hostile world." . . . Two historically rooted attitudes contradict each other: "This is a hostile world" and "this is a society free of prejudice." . . . This aspect of blackishness (in white society) is historically rooted and will be immune to change except over a long, long period of time. Blacks, of course, are absolutely correct when they say that an equally long period of time will be required for whites to overcome *their* historically rooted attitudes toward blacks. (p. 968)

Figure 2

*Developmental Milieu of the
Handicapped Culturally Diverse Child*

S = Early Childhood Program (School)

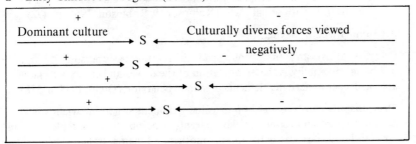

Sarason continued,

> What is there in man's history and in the corpus of social science knowledge which contradicts the statement that few things are as immune to quick changes as the historically rooted, psychological core of ethnic and racial groups? Jewishness and blackishness are products . . . of social and cultural history, and their psychological cores will successfully resist short-term efforts aimed at changing them. (pp. 969–970)

He explained that "discrimination is a wound-producing act, the effects of which never heal in the lifetime of the victim" and further that "historically rooted discrimination [its causes and consequences] is immune to change by efforts based on our accustomed short-time perspective" (p. 970).

Professionals who are intimately involved with programs for the handicapped, and who as individuals have lived in diverse cultures, seem to be underscoring the need for sensitization of personnel as well as the need for a long term effort to program meaningfully for the child who is a member of another culture in America. Simply stated, short term, one shot programs have low probability for lasting gains for the culturally diverse child.

Becoming Aware of the Cultural Diversity of Lower Class Whites

Middle class educators need to become aware that lower social and economic Whites, because of their ethnic and linguistic closeness to middle class America, have become an "invisible minority." They have stable and well organized cultural patterns which are different from and frequently strongly opposed to those of the middle class.

Hurlock (1972) identified three basic cultural systems in America: the general American culture, social class cultures, and ethnic group cultures. In each of these, a child is given the opportunity to learn those tasks and values considered appropriate within that culture and he is thwarted in the development of skills and values considered inappropriate. Diggs (1974, p. 578) cited Robinson and Robinson (1965) as stating,

> Of all the child's subcultural identifications, probably none is more important to the ultimate behavioral patterns he will acquire than his social class membership. Aims and purposes, abilities and achievements, all tend to vary significantly with social class. (Robinson & Robinson, 1965, p. 472)

Diggs summarized by saying,

> Every social class and ethnic group produces a certain basic personality, and this basic personality is the organization of the drives and emotions which are the deeper underlying elements of mental behavior. (Diggs, 1974, p. 578)

Project staffs can be caught up in value judgment situations when working with lower social and economic class parents. One poignant example from an early childhood class was Betty and her mother and their externally visible relationship. For more than a year members of the staff had been deeply critical of the mother's "disinterest and unconcern" with every aspect of Betty's program. She made no effort to transport her at any time nor to do any of the middle class valued mothering tasks expected of her.

During the second year of the program it became necessary for Betty to undergo surgery. This was arranged for: The caseworker gave the mother funds to cover the bus trip to a medical center, cab fare to and from the hospital, and subsistence while Betty was hospitalized. On arrival in the strange city, the mother asked directions to the medical center, was told generally the direction to go to get there, and was advised to take a cab. With Betty in tow, a younger sibling on her hip, the mother walked the more than 10 miles to the medical complex. When Betty was checked in that evening, the mother was told that she could come in by 8:00 a.m. the next morning so as to be there when Betty returned from surgery. Later, when the nurse checked by the room, the mother and younger sibling were asleep on the floor. Fortunately, the hospital staff was sensitive to her needs and there she stayed, day and night, until Betty was released from the hospital. The mother walked with Betty and her sibling to the bus station.

Later that year, during a parent session, Betty's mother told about that experience as a matter of fact occurrence. When asked why she had not taken a cab, she said she did not know how to get one and that no buses went directly from town to the medical center, so she "just walked." Needless to say, the staff's prior judgments of "disinterest and unconcern" on the part of Betty's mother changed drastically. It was difficult for many of those involved to conceptualize how narrow and circumscribed the mother's world had been and to understand how threatening the strange city, the transportation difficulties, the medical center, and Betty's surgery must have been.

Focusing Program Content on Various Cultures

Program content, that is, curriculum in its broadest sense, needs to focus on the many cultures that exist in this country. Valnez's (1972) statement at the Norfolk State College Conference on Cultural Diversity—Focus on Minorities indicated how critical the teacher's behavior can be:

> Teacher behavior is probably the most important variable in assuring the success or failure of any student. The classroom teacher is generally responsible for the selection of programs as well as the daily interactions with students in the application of these programs. (p. 8)

The University of Arizona Project

The staff of Program Development for Preschool Handicapped Indian Children at the University of Arizona (Tucson) have developed units and monthly curricula that attend specifically to Papago and Yaqui cultures.

One of these, the *Communication Unit Based on "Coyote Imitates Skunk,"* uses a Papago legend as the base of information for children to do specific tasks related to visual discrimination, visual memory, visual closure, motor imitation, visual reception, visual association, manual expression, auditory discrimination, auditory memory, auditory closure, verbal imitation, auditory reception, auditory association, and verbal expression. Items used for specific tasks are ones familiar to Indian children: desert scenes, basket designs, shakers, baskets, pottery, cacti, round houses, coyotes, and skunks.

Another unit, the *Communication Unit Based on "The Frog,"* uses a Yaqui Indian legend as an information base for children to do specific tasks related to auditory discrimination, auditory memory, auditory closure, verbal imitation, auditory reception, verbal expression, auditory association, visual discrimination, visual memory, visual closure, motor imitation, visual reception, visual association, and manual expression. Items and words used in teaching the various tasks are familiar to Indian children. Among those items are a Yaqui, a saguaro, a frog, a dog, a bear, a watermelon, squash, corn, Indian masks (Pascola and Chateyka masks), a gourd, a picture of a Yaqui woman, and a picture of a mesquite tree.

The September and November curricula from *A Bicultural Curriculum for Preschool Indian Children* give more specific emphasis to the importance of cultural diversity than any other First Chance project materials reviewed. They stress the importance of being Indian and pride in the heritage, language, and culture of the tribe or nation.

The September curriculum gives specific consideration to the closeness of the Indian family and community and to the apprehensiveness of children coming to school for the first time. The need for bringing the child's environment into the classroom and ways this can be accomplished are discussed.

In social studies, stress is given to the importance of being Indian, the security derived from belonging to the tribe or nation, and pride in the heritage, language, and culture of the tribe. These are accomplished through use of special events on the Indian calendar; attendance at fiestas and celebrations; use of Indian clothing and other objects in teaching; trips to the reservations during a feast to see preparations, hear the language, and see where the people live; visits to places that are important to the religious beliefs of the tribe; learning of and participation in songs and dances of the tribe; use of pictures of members of the tribe in bulletin boards and in teaching; dramatization of family and community situations using Indian language; and use of Indian music with musicians where possible.

Parallel teaching is used for foods, health, mathematics, art, and music. This allows comparison of Indian and American concepts and values.

The curriculum for November describes in some detail the room environment, which uses Indian materials and cultural items. Indian stones are used for the language arts base. Holidays such as November 2, the Day of the Dead, are celebrated as the Papago culture prescribes. Activities are planned around making wreaths and placing the wreaths on graves in the reservation cemetery. Other November days celebrated are November 3, the feast day of St. Martin de Porres, and November 25, the feast of Christ the King, parton saint of Pascua Pueblo. Field trips and activities are planned around these days.

The social studies curriculum uses the structure of the Papago family. Personal relations are learned and discussed in relation to Papago cultural values. The same format is used for the Yaqui culture.

The Alaska Project

One of the initial projects in the First Chance Network was the Alaska Head Start Special Services Project (Anchorage). To surmount the problems posed by the vast land mass and sparce population, the Alaska Resource Center worked in tandem with native Head Start and Community Action Programs. Hearing impairment was chosen as the targeted disability due to its appreciably higher incidence in Alaska than in the "lower 48" and Hawaii.

As a direct result of initial development on that early First Chance project, a subsequent cooperative Bureau of Education for the Handicapped and Office of Child Development grant enabled the Alaskan group to develop some 23 different media packages for handicapped children, their parents, and teachers and paraprofessionals who work with them. These media packages consist of teaching manuals, pictorial pamphlets, model programs, teaching syllabi, videotapes, radio scripts, and filmstrips.

Training to Eliminate Negative Stereotypes

Teachers and other personnel need to receive preservice and inservice training that eliminates or greatly diminishes the negative stereotype of different cultural and linguistic patterns. Abrahams and Troike (1972) discussed the fact that teachers "who have been raised and trained with a negative stereotype of . . . cultural and linguistic patterns will find . . . change in viewpoint difficult" (p. 2). They stated further that the minority group child is seen "as having no true culture of his own, but as simply being deficient in middle class modes of speech, behavior, and cognition" (p. 3). The middle class modes "are tacitly taken as representing the only 'real' culture" (p. 3). A critical point made by Abrahams and Troike was that

> until we are able to carry into the cross-cultural encounter the expectation of other equally valid forms of cultural organization, we will never be able to understand these others, let alone "help" them (p. 3.)

Some of the work done by Tait (1972) with blind children seems applicable to the child reared in a culture other than White middle class. Mastery of the environment, which also may be a source of trouble for the child in a minority group, is obtained through spontaneous exploration of the environment. As the more subtle kinds of behavior exhibited by the preschool teacher are interpreted by the child in terms of his own culture, the end product can approximate rejection. Rejection in turn results in antiexploratory behavior that prevents "the utilization of behavior which would ordinarily lead to mastery of the environment and a reduction of the fear of the unknown" (p. 149).

One of the most damaging stereotypes has centered around the concept of intelligence as reflected by the IQ score alone. In discussing some factors to consider, Barnes (1971) indicated that when an intelligence test is administered by a White examiner or when a Black child anticipates that test results will be used to compare him with White peers, it is

> hypothesized that anticipation of failure elicits feelings of being victimized and covert hostility toward the tester. Since overt expression of hostility toward white authority is fraught with danger, the impulse is suppressed and elicits emotional responses disruptive to the subject's test performance. (p. 16)

According to Barnes, the greatest potential for harm lies in interpreting a child's IQ score as though it reflected "some absolute factor, process, etc., regardless of the condition of measurement or of the group being observed" (p. 20). He stated that

> in interpreting test results of disadvantaged minority group children considerable caution and knowledge of group background factors—social and cultural—are necessary, on the part of the examiner, in assessing the probable effect of these factors on test results. (p. 21)

Each examiner must be aware that the "test results he elicits, and their interpretations may result in actions, opinions, beliefs having far reaching consequences for disadvantaged minority group members as well as for society as a whole" (p. 28).

Diggs (1974), in discussing the teaching-learning process, indicated that it requires continuing focus on

> (a) development of cross cultural skills for professionals and paraprofessionals working with culturally different children, (b) development of competency based field experiences for professionals concerned with multicultural education, (c) development of cooperative education centers which eliminate barriers among educational authorities and respond to needs of unique multicultural areas, and (d) inservice and preservice training for teachers on the new concepts of multicultural education. (p. 583)

Recognizing the Exclusion of the Racially Different

Professionals need to recognize that peoples whose skin colors are different have been more rigidly excluded—politically, socially, economically, and educationally—than any other groups.

Abrahams and Troike (1972) indicated that, while European groups were able to "pass" within one native born generation, peoples whose skin color was different have remained culturally distinct.

> They continued to speak their accustomed language and to follow their different life-ways though their cultural practices, attitudes, and values were inevitably affected by their being excluded and kept in a subordinate status. (p. 4)

Many subordinate and stigmatized groups are saying "no" to new programs that have been developed in an attempt to accomplish the assimilation that other groups went through years ago. These various groups are finding an integrity in their own cultures and in their own ways. Abrahams and Troike (1972) pointed out,

> If we expect to be able to teach students from such groups effectively, we must learn wherein their culture differences lie and we must capitalize upon them as a resouce, rather than doing what we have always done and disregarding the differences or placing the students in the category of "non-communicative," thereby denigrating both the differences and the students. (p. 5)

In this same context Diggs (1974) noted that culturally different children have varied backgrounds that result in different behavioral styles and interests. These behavioral styles include linguistic differences and differences in standards of performance, rules of play, and family life styles, which may precipitate value differences between teacher and student. Power becomes an issue in such a situation. The teacher is in the power position and most frequently the child loses. The result is that, more often than not, the child and his family view the teacher's attempts to change him in a negative context and view the teacher's inability to accept the child as a reflection on their culture.

Understanding Personal and Public Attitudes

Professionals need to learn to investigate and to understand what it is in their own public and shared attitudes that has made it difficult to teach the culturally diverse child. Abrahams and Troike (1972) have posited the need to learn

> what is it about our own cultural mechanisms which, in the face of the threat posed by a person we do not understand, results in our resorting to the most overt and highly structured dimensions of our own ordering system—rules and regulations. (p. 6)

Barnes (1971) discussed the position held by "a small fraternity of American psychologists" who assert that "black and other oppressed minority children, as a group, achieve below whites because of their genetic inferiority to whites" (p. 3). Barnes noted further that whatever one's position is regarding such an explanation, these psychologists "cannot be ignored because they are a part of the fabric of American History . . . and have considerable potential influence on those at powerful policy making levels" (p. 3). Such a position provides for no "form of external or post-natal manipulation to prevent academic retardation and to increase individual achievement" (p. 3).

An investigation and understanding of public and shared attitudes, according to Abrahams and Troike (1972),

> attempts to do only one thing—to humanize students by opening the eyes and ears of educators to the possible alternative systems which the young may bring into class. (p. 6)

Educators have tried various strategies, many of which have failed. For young handicapped children who are from a diverse culture there seems to be no other way "than to provide them with a sense of dignity in themselves" (p. 6). An example of this is a program that considered the need for self dignity. The data are from hearings of the Senate Select Committee on Nutrition and Human Needs. On Thursday, January 23, 1969, Superintendent of Schools Taylor (1970) of San Diego, Texas, described a program begun in 1959 in response to pervasive problems in nutrition, health, the dropout rate, and daily attendance. Initially a lunch program was begun; later, with federal assistance, a breakfast program was added.

Also, a program for 5 year old children was started to provide them a 13 month program prior to entering first grade. Over the first 3 years of operation, attendance climbed some 15% with overall average daily attendance increasing to 95% or greater. All of this preceded Head Start and Title I of the Elementary and Secondary Education Act (ESEA, Public Law 89–10).

Taylor was questioned about the close family ties of the Mexican American family and the fact that small children were allowed to leave the family. The point was made that the teachers had to be convinced of the children's needs. When families saw teacher and staff demonstrate their interest by coming to work at 7 a.m. and leaving late in the afternoon, the program sold itself.

Allowing the Child to Find Integrity and Identity

The culturally diverse child needs to be allowed the "life space" to find an integrity and an identity in his own culture and in his own way.

In a discussion of cultural diversity in relation to Black children, Harris (1972) indicated that some

students are much better prepared to succeed in school than others—not simply in "natural intelligence" but in broad experience in acquaintance with the tools of learning and in the knowledge of schools and their purposes. (p. 20)

In this same vein, Diggs (1974) noted that

culturally different children tend to grow up with identifiable behavioral patterns and interests resulting from the influence of their subcultural groups, and these patterns may enhance or diminish motivation. (pp. 578–579)

In certain instances, the coping behaviors of children are viewed negatively within the dominant White middle class classroom. Yet, if these behaviors are completely extinguished for all settings, the child may be left defenseless in his peer group in later life. Stated another way, behavior that is deviant in one setting is quite appropriate in another setting. As Mayer (1973) pointed out,

What is acceptable and what is not acceptable in behavior varies from culture to culture, family to family, and even person to person. We all have our own ideas as to what is acceptable behavior and what is not. These differences can be very confusing to a child. (p. 3)

Continuing Assessment

Continuing assessment of all children and especially those from diverse cultures should be broadly based.

Factors Influencing Test Results

Barnes (1971) discussed factors influencing current test results on the basis of (a) the concept of intelligence, (b) test reliability and disadvantaged minority groups, (c) examiner-examinee interaction, (d) failure barriers built into assessment techniques, and (e) the single determinant concept.

Concept of intelligence. The test maker's concept of intelligence influences the kinds of behaviors tapped by various items on the test. Intelligence tests "typically . . . place emphasis on what the testee can do rather than on what he can learn" (p. 14). Such an assumption implies that the child "has had opportunities to learn equal to others with whom he is compared" (p. 14). Barnes stated,

> Given the nature of life conditions of the black child, perhaps IQ tests based on ability to learn rather than on what he can do at a given time would have greater predictive value for him. (p. 14)

Test reliability and disadvantaged minority groups. Barnes noted that "little attention has been given to . . . the possible contingency of test reliability upon the group's position and status in the social structure" (p. 14). Children from minority groups have a smaller spread of scores than children from the middle class. As a result, reliability coefficients computed for a middle class sample, when used with a disadvantaged Black sample, may well make the test ineffective in differentiating within a group. This is due to the minority group's more restricted range of scores, which differ from the normative group on which instrument reliability was determined.

Examiner-examinee interaction and the single determinant concept. These factors were discussed earlier in relation to the need to eliminate negative stereotypes.

Failure barriers built into assessment technique. Barnes stated that attempts to develop culture free and culture fair tests have proven unsuccessful. He suggested that a culture specific intelligence test for Black children would enable educators to make the kinds of predictions that current tests now make possible for White children. Such predictions would relate primarily to the child's potential and the type of teaching or training that would facilitate his development.

First Chance Project Measurement Instruments

Special Education in a Day Care System sponsored by the National Child Day Care Association (NCDCA) in Washington, D.C., uses the "developmental team" approach for screening, diagnosis, and treatment. Screening is done with an instrument designed and developed for this program by the Kingsbury Remedial Center. The intent is to identify children of 4 years or older who may be expected to have learning problems, especially in areas pertinent to reading. The test includes visual, auditory, kinesthetic, verbal, and gross motor areas. The instrument was developed prior to BEH funding due to the need for early identification of children who might develop problems after school entry. First screenings were administered during 1971 and 1972 to 125 children. Only one teacher was available to work with the identified high risk children in NCDCA's 15 preschool centers. That teacher went from center to center to work on a one to one basis with high risk children. The program for each child was prescriptive in that the Kingsbury instrument yields a profile for prescriptive teaching.

With BEH funding, two additional developmental teachers are working with additional high risk children. Diagnosis is made through use of the developmental test developed under HEW's Early and Periodic Screening Diagnosis and Treatment Program (EPSDT). Data obtained from the test and a "getting to know the child" approach are used prior to beginning treatment. Treatment or training consists of curriculum suggestions for the child's teacher in addition to daily 20 minute tutoring sessions with each child who has been identified as having severe or multiple developmental lags.

The Alaska Head Start Special Services Project has developed, as previously noted, a group of media packages. The *Understanding Young Children Series* includes critical developmental areas and uses short informational sentences accompanied by stick drawings to illustrate concepts presented. Activities and checklists are included in each manual. The five booklets in the series are *The Handicapped Child in the Normal Preschool Class,* which includes visual disabilities, hearing disabilities, and motor disabilities; *Emotional and Behavioral Development and Disabilities; Learning Development and Disabilities; Language Development and Disabilities;* and *Intellectual Development and Disabilities.*

The San Felipe Del Rio (Texas) Project has developed The Del Rio Language Screening Test (English/Spanish), which measures oral language development. It includes five subtests for ages 3-0 to 6-1 years which assess memory for single words, sentences, commands, and stories. The format is as follows:
1. Receptive Vocabulary. (The child points to one of three pictures.)
2. Sentence Repetition. (The sentence length varies, but there is similar linguistic complexity.)
3. Sentence Repetition. (There is increasing grammatical complexity but similar length of sentences is maintained.)
4. Oral Commands. (The child performs tasks serially in response to simple commands, which range from 1 to 4 in number.)
5. Story Comprehension. (There is an increase in length and complexity of sto-

ries. These are read to the child, who then is questioned on content of the story.)

Regarding overall assessment in the Del Rio Project, Hanna (1973) stated

Observation of behavior and the recording of behavior is an integral part of planning and ongoing evaluation. Specificity in description of behaviors and the changes occurring in behavior are part of individualization. (p. 18)

To assist in objectifying observations, probe sheets and behavior evaluation sheets, which list specific goals with dates of initiation and dates of accomplishment, have been developed.

The concept of continuing assessment implies daily attention to the development of each individual child. Daniel (1972) outlined the need for infant stimulation when he stated,

The major objective of infant stimulation is enrichment of the child's environment and shaping development using whatever potential he may have. (p. 3)

It is at this earliest level that developmental lag begins. The kinds and amounts of infant stimulation vary greatly across cultures. In this same context, Sarason (1973) noted,

The nature and force of the process of cultural transmission never skip generations, particularly when their ways have been finely honed over the centuries. They will not be quickly blunted. (p. 971)

He went on to say that the

one thing we can say with assurance is that our concepts of intelligence are value laden, culture and time bound, and deficient in cross cultural validity. (p. 971)

When considering test results, Diggs (1974) stressed that the critical aspect is that they be used to improve instruction for culturally diverse children, not for placement or exclusion.

Realizing Commonalities and Diversities Across Cultures

There are commonalities across all cultures. It is the areas of diversity that are critical, and these areas change from group to group—Alaskan native, Black, Mexican American, American Indian, Chinese, and lower social and economic class White.

The Black Child

While some children come to school with a rich background of experience and a vocabulary of thousands of words, Harris (1972) pointed out that other children have had little "experience beyond the rooms in which they live and the streets on which they play" (pp. 20–21). She indicated that frequently their primary contact with parents has been for punishment. When thrust into a school setting with children who have broad experiential backgrounds and large vocabularies and a teacher who "speaks familiarly of things which they have never heard nor seen" (p. 21), what are they to make of it? Some of the children overcome the deficits (as seen by the school's and teacher's standards) and manage to catch up; others become lost in the educational process. Harris (1972) discussed the following special needs among Black children:

1. The school must recognize the special needs among students and go to the source of those needs.
2. Student problems can be helped through a teaching process that recognizes where the children are, begins where they are, and incorporates what is known about the nature of learning, the learner, presentation of what is to be learned, and assessment of outcome.
3. The child needs to learn what he needs to know, to learn what he is expected to know, and to overcome fear of adults. "The child generally has not had experience with friendly, helpful adults" (p. 22).
4. The schoolroom and its varied equipment must become familiar. Things are learned for their use and through use comes self expression and the expansion of a child's world.
5. Each child deserves—and must have—respect to function as he can function. Perhaps initially it will be only with much individual attention but, with time, he will function in a group.
6. The teacher should provide a learning setting that encourages inquiry and creativity, that allows for and rewards individual differences, that provides flexibility of procedures, and that provides for both individual and group participation and achievement. Many of these special needs which Harris attributed to Black children also have applicability to a greater or lesser extent to other cultures.

Harris (1972) indicated that the history of Black people and the resultant cultural diversity have created "social, political and economical inequality for Black people" (p. 23). Those who work in educational settings that include Black children must recognize the problems inherent in the child's first entrance to school and must work toward the elimination of these problems.

Diggs (1974) discussed some implications for motivation, which include the school and home environment and teacher attitudes. Diggs made the following observations concerning the influences of the school and home environment:

1. The emotional climate in the classroom and the interaction between the teacher and the culturally different child are important in the stimulation process.
2. Also important is the child's position in social groupings, first within the family in terms of role expectancy and development of initial skills in interpersonal relations.
3. Observation of the culturally different child in terms of behavior is useful only insofar as evaluation is made in terms of the child's own purposes or goals.

4. "It is important to focus attention on the child's subjective reactions to events occurring about him; his perceptions determine his behavior more than so called 'reality' " (p. 579).
5. "All behavior may be seen in a social context, and motivation can be greatly influenced by a social setting" (p. 579).

In regard to teacher attitudes, Diggs suggested that "educators must be free of prejudices if their classrooms are to provide an environment conducive to interaction and learning" (p. 579).

The Indian Child

Graves (1972), who is a Red Lake Band Chippewa, stated,

Ethnically speaking, American Indians are many different peoples, but each group possesses a rich tradition and a set of values. To cite a few examples: Pueblo and Hopi communities of New Mexico and Arizona and the Navajo are perhaps best known, but Indian communities are found as well in other parts of the country . . . there are Eastern Cherokees of North Carolina; the Chippewas of Red Lake, Minnesota; the Saulk and Fox of Iowa; the Hidatsa, Mandan, Arikawa and several divisions of Teton Sioux in the Dakotas; the Blackfeet and Cheyennes in Montana. Other states in which Indian groups survive include Oklahoma, California, Nebraska, Kansas, Wyoming, Idaho and Washington. (pp. 25–26)

Indian communities vary in size from the Navajo's 90,000 or greater population in Arizona and New Mexico to the few hundred Saulk and Fox in Iowa. There is great diversity in culture among the tribes, and "Indians still tend to identify themselves first as Navajos, Sioux, or Chippewas and secondarily as Indians" (p. 26).

Graves' plea is "that these people be permitted to make their own patterns within the greater pattern of present-day American society and that they not be required to deracialize in order to become more 'Americanized' " (p. 26). He pointed out that the "simple way of life is often a profoundly knowing way" and that some of the "primitive patterns are patterns of survival, and patterns of successful accommodation to nature" and further are "an area of knowledge which science today is grappling to rediscover" (p. 26).

Graves noted that "matters of policy, services and teaching will be most effective if the diversity of Indian groups is considered and it is remembered that American Indians constitute very heterogeneous groups of people" (p. 26). He pointed out that the Indian child, of whatever tribe or band, should not have to identify with non-Indian values and life styles at the expense of his own ethnic group identity. Graves noted that

Indians have been making accommodations and adjustments to society and economy from early times . . . and should be given the opportunity to select the best from both cultures, or better yet, all of the cultures of America. (p. 28)

The Chinese Child

Chang (1972) indicated that concern with cultural diversity recognizes "ethnic factors as an integral part of the child's learning processes" (p. 37). In the past, many educators have believed that immigrants of whatever background would give up their own ethnic heritage and assimilate into the American dominant culture. Chang noted that today "it is more realistic to use multi-ethnic group models to analyze American society" (p. 37).

Chang (1972) stated that some of the problems Chinese children face in the early school years can be "analyzed in terms of the accommodation model rather than the assimilation model" due to the fact that their families have "not formed a functional part of the American culture" (p. 39). Because of the language barrier, Chinese people are not joiners, they speak Chinese at home, read Chinese newspapers, and visit one another among relatives and friends. In citing reasons for cultural conflict, Chang indicated that most Chinese children still are taught traditional behavior patterns and the predominant values of filial piety, good manners, silence before adults, and patience and moderation in all things. He pointed out that these "traditional Chinese values are in direct conflict with American values such as self-independence, self-assertion, and spirit of competition" (p. 39).

Because of the social isolation in which Chinese children develop during the preschool years, they may be passive in classrooms, sometimes smiling rather than answering a teacher's question, and may have feelings of inadequacy when given the opportunity to interrelate with their peers.

They cannot generalize what they have learned at home to the larger world. . . . It must be a very painful experience for the children who have to find a way of coexistence between the two worlds without guidance. (p. 41)

Chang (1972) made three suggestions regarding the crucial roles teachers play in the personality development of Chinese children:

1. Be patient and understanding, especially with the Chinese children's reticence to talk, for a "vocal person is not appreciated among Chinese people" (p. 41). Once Chinese children feel the teacher is a friend, "they tend to overcome the traditional shyness" (p. 41).
2. Assist children to make friends with their peer group. These friends will help bridge the gulf between the Chinese children's home world and the larger society in which they are schooled. Since many Chinese parents are involved in business most of their waking hours, they may not be able to help. Further, the home culture may be so different that parents "feel inadequate to tell their children what to do beyond their home world" (p. 42).
3. Give positive support to their ethnic heritage. Since the inner well being of the child is dependent on his pride in his own ethnic identity, failure to appreciate his Chinese identity tends to hinder or negate his development of a non-Chinese identity.

The Mexican American Child

Eiler (1972) noted that the term *Mexican American* is more accurately used when referring to people of Mexican descent who were born in the United States. Four dimensions must be considered in relation to the Mexican American culture: (a) traditional customs and beliefs, (b) religion, (c) language, and (d) socioeconomic status. The traditional custom regarding home life places the father as the dominant figure and the mother as a child bearer, "uniquely protective of her children" (p. 44). Eiler noted that education is not stressed in the Mexican American culture for several reasons:

1. Education poses a threat to the father-son image, or machismo.
2. Education for girls is thought to make them too aggressive, domineering, and independent.
3. Parents understand the child's frustration in and with school and do not wish to add more pressure.
4. It is feared that education will influence children to disregard folk culture.
5. Parents ridicule or prohibit children speaking English at home.
6. Greater emphasis is placed on values of patience and cooperation than on education.
7. There may be little initiative to acquire material gain because of reliance on fate.

Eiler (1972) indicated that when considering special program needs, the Mexican American child needs to be helped to understand customs and cultures other than his own and to begin to appreciate others' values and judgments. Among the child-teacher barriers may be the inability to communicate in English. According to Eiler, teacher education and training should provide teachers with the ability to teach bilingually, to understand and appreciate cultural differences, and to view these differences as assets.

Including the Parents

A critical program need for the culturally diverse child is inclusion of his parents as an integral part of his program.

Street (1974) noted that work with parents is a primary function in the Special Education Center of the National Child Day Care Association (NCDCA) in Washington, D.C. Parents are involved in the program through work in the classroom with teachers, individual counseling, and group meetings. Basic to this aspect of the program is the concept that parents are partners with the teaching teams.

Training is another important component of the NCDCA's program. This is a broadly based aspect, which focuses on parents, classroom teachers in day care centers who have disturbed children in their classrooms, classroom teachers in centers who work with the developmental teams, and the therapeutic associate teacher. The training of parents is classroom centered in that they learn basic child development and therapeutic methods while actually working with chil-

dren in the classroom. In addition, counseling and group sessions give reinforcement to classroom involvement.

In a discussion of parent and community involvement, Diggs (1974) stressed,

Parents should be included in the total programing process and should participate in training programs designed to support their children in their
learning process in the home as well as to make them employable as aides in
the classroom. (p. 583)

She emphasized further that the

family molds the child's future life and is a part of him for all time. As he
encounters an ever-widening circle of people . . . the family may be a source
of wisdom, strength, and comfort or a source of confusion or insecurity.
(p. 583)

Hess, Shipman, Brophy, and Dear (1968) studied the cognitive environments
of urban preschool children. A correlation was found between the child's intellectual performance and the mother's language abstraction. Conceptualization
at the abstract level was found to be related to maternal language style.

Wachs, Uzgiris, and Hunt (1971) investigated the cognitive development of
infants from different environmental backgrounds. Their findings indicated that
opportunity to hear the verbal symbols for specific objects, actions, and relationships and the intensity of stimulation accompanied with a variety of situations or
circumstances appeared to be most consistently related to psychological development. Their findings suggested that certain rearing patterns hampered psychological development, for example, stimulus bombardment from which the child
cannot escape accompanied by involuntary exposure to excessive varieties of circumstances.

Tulkin and Kagan (1972) indicated that mothers' attitudes toward their children are not independent of social and economic conditions. Those attempting
to change mothers' behaviors must consider the relation of those behaviors to
other aspects of the social system.

CONCLUDING STATEMENT

When social and/or environmental conditions are such that they prevent or
hinder development of higher cognitive processes, the symptoms of deviancy are
manifested in acting out or failure in control and ultimately as disability in cognition and reality functions (Thomas, Chess, & Birch, 1968; Phillips & Zigler,
1961). The most critical factor becomes the way one views the child. It has far-
reaching implications for the kinds of intervention strategies employed in curricula devised for children.

Gotts' (1974) definition of a handicap gives full cognizance to this critical factor:

A handicap refers to the personal and social consequences of innate or
adventitious conditions or injuries which result in impairments, disorders,
dysfunctions, or disabilities in sensory, perceptual, integrative, psychomo-

tor, communicative and/or conceptual functioning so as to interfere with the child's normal development through his interaction with human and physical environments.

This way of viewing an exceptional child recognizes that the incidental condition of cultural diversity, as it interferes with a child's development through appropriate interaction with human and physical environments, can be the most pervasive and damaging of any impairment, disorder, dysfunction, or disability.

REFERENCES

Abrahams, R., & Troike, R. (Eds.). *Language and cultural diversity in American education.* Englewood Cliffs NJ: Prentice-Hall, 1972.

Baratz, S., & Baratz, N. Early childhood intervention: The social science base of institutional racism. *Harvard Educational Review,* 1970, *40* (1), 29–50.

Barker, R. Ecology and motivation. In M.R. Jones (Ed.), *Nebraska Symposium on Motivation.* Lincoln: University of Nebraska Press, 1960.

Barker, R. On the nature of the environment. *Journal of Social Issues,* 1963, *19,* 17–38.

Barker, R. Explorations in ecological psychology. *American Psychologist,* 1965, *20,* 1–14.

Barnes, E. *Intellectual assessment of black folks: Perspectives on misconceptions, shortcomings, and consequences.* Paper presented at the National Leadership Institute Conference on Early Childhood Development and Special Education, Washington, D.C., October 14–15, 1971.

Bronfenbrenner, U. Reunification with our children. *Inequality in Education.* 1972, No. 12, 10–20.

Chang, P. New approaches to early education of Chinese children with special needs. In R. Diggs (Ed.), *Conference proceedings: Cultural diversity—Focus on minorities.* Norfolk VA: Norfolk State College, Early Education Assistance Act Project, 1972.

Daniel, C. Infant stimulation. In R. Diggs (Ed.), *Conference proceedings: Cultural diversity—Focus on minorities.* Norfolk VA: Norfolk State College, Early Education Assistance Act Project, 1972.

Diggs, R. W. Education across cultures. *Exceptional Children,* 1974, *40,* 578–583.

Dil, N. Personal discussions with a professional who came into the United States as an adult, 1974.

Eiler, R. Cultural diversity as related to educational problems of Mexican-American children. In R. Diggs (Ed.), *Conference proceedings: Cultural diversity—Focus on minorities.* Norfolk VA: Norfolk State College, Early Education Assistance Act Project, 1972.

Gotts, E. *Perspectives on early education programs for exceptional infants and preschoolers.* Paper presented at National Conference on Early Intervention with High Risk Infants and Young Children, Chapel Hill, North Carolina, May 1974. (From original paper)

Graves, B. Techniques in meeting the special needs of Indian and other minorities in a multicultural society. In R. Diggs (Ed.), *Conference proceedings: Cultural diversity—Focus on minorities.* Norfolk VA: Norfolk State College, Early Education Assistance Act Project, 1972.

Harris, Y. Cultural diversity as related to the Black American. In R. Diggs (Ed.), *Conference proceedings: Cultural diversity—Focus on minorities.* Norfolk VA: Norfolk State College, Early Education Assistance Act Project, 1972.

Harvey, J., McMillan, F., & Ebersole, L. *Special class curriculum and environment and vocational rehabilitation of mentally retarded young adults.* University: University of Alabama, Department of Special Education (RD–842), 1964.

Hess, R., Shipman, V., Brophy, J., & Dear, R. *The cognitive environments of urban pre-school children*. Chicago: University of Chicago, Graduate School of Education, 1968.

Hurlock, E. *Child development*. New York: McGraw-Hill, 1972.

Inkeles, A. Social structure and the socialization of competence. *Harvard Education Review*, 1966, *36*, 265–283.

Inkeles, A. Society, social structure, and child socialization. In J. Clansen (Ed.), *Socialization and society*. Boston: Little, Brown, 1968.

Mayer, C. *Development and learning*. Anchorage AK: Early Childhood Education Project, Alaska Treatment Center for Crippled Children and Adults, 1973.

Norris, D. *The naked ape*. New York: McGraw-Hill, 1967.

Phillips, L., & Zigler, E. Social competence: The action-thought parameter and vicariousness in normal and pathological behaviors. *Journal of Abnormal and Social Psychology*, 1961, *63*, 137–146.

Robinson, H., & Robinson, N. *The mentally retarded child: A psychological approach*. New York: McGraw-Hill, 1965.

Sarason, S. Jewishness, Blackishness and the nature-nurture controversy. *American Psychologist*, 1973, *28*, 962–971.

Staz, P., Rardin, D., & Ross, J. An evaluation of a theory of specific developmental dyslexia. *Child Development*, 1971, *42*, 2009–2021.

Street, V. Director, Special Education in a Day Care System, National Child Day Care Association, Special Education Center, Washington, D.C. 20002. Personal correspondence, June 1974.

Tait, P. The effect of circumstantial rejection on infant behavior. *New Outlook*, 1972, *66*, 139–151.

Taylor, B. Getting them ready to be taught. *IRCD Bulletin*, 1970, *6*, 5–6; 14.

Thomas, A., Chess, S., & Birch. H. *Temperament and behavior disorders in children*. New York: New York University Press, 1968.

Tulkin, S., & Kagan, J. Mother-child interaction in the first year of life. *Child Development*, 1972, *43*, 31–41.

Valnez, E. Mainstreaming: Past-present-future. In R. Diggs (Ed.), *Conference proceedings: Cultural diversity—Focus on minorities*. Norfolk VA: Norfolk State College, Early Education Assistance Act Project, 1972.

Vance, E. Social disability. *American Psychologist*, 1973, *28*, 498–511.

Wachs, T., Uzgiris, I., & Hunt, J. Cognitive development in infants of different age levels and from different environmental backgrounds: An exploratory investigation. *Merrill-Palmer Quarterly*, 1971, *71*, 283–317.

White, R. Motivation reconsidered: The concept of competence. *Psychological Review*, 1959, *66*, 297–333.

Wohlwill, J. The emerging discipline of environmental psychology. *American Psychologist*, 1970, *25*, 303–312.

Zigler, E., & Phillips, L. Social effectivenesss and symptomatic behaviors. *Journal of Abnormal and Social Psychology*, 1960, *61*, 231–233.

Zigler, E., & Phillips, L. Social competence and the process-reactive distinction in psychopathology. *Journal of Abnormal and Social Psychology*, 1963, *65*, 215–222.

RESOURCES

Accident Hazards and Measures for Prevention. Alaska Head Start Special Services Project, Anchorage, Alaska. (Available from Easter Seal Society, 726 E Street, Anchorage AK 99501. $2.00.)

A Bicultural Curriculum for Preschool Indian Children. Program Development for Preschool Handicapped Indian Children, Tucson, Arizona. 1973. (Available from Elizabeth Y. Sharp, Department of Special Education, College of Education, University of Arizona, Tucson AZ 85721. Divided by months; each month costs $3.00 to $3.50 plus postage.)

Communication Unit Based on "Coyote Imitates Skunk": A Papago Legend. Program Development for Preschool Handicapped Indian Children, Tucson, Arizona. 1974. (Available from Elizabeth Y. Sharp, Department of Special Education, College of Education, University of Arizona, Tucson AZ 85721. $1.00 plus postage.)

Communication Unit Based on "The Frog": A Yaqui Indian Legend. Program Development for Preschool Handicapped Indian Children, Tucson, Arizona. 1974. (Available from Elizabeth Y. Sharp, Department of Special Education, College of Education, University of Arizona, Tucson AZ 85721. $1.00 plus postage.)

The Del Rio Language Screening Test (English/Spanish). San Felipe Del Rio Consolidated Independent School District, Del Rio, Texas. (Available from National Laboratory Publishers, Inc., P. O. Box 10003, Austin TX 78840.)

Double Trouble. Alaska Head Start Special Services Project, Anchorage, Alaska. 1974. (Available from Easter Seal Society, 726 E Street, Anchorage AK 99501. Booklet, $2.00; slides/audio cassette, $55.00; filmstrip, $15.00; rental, $10.00.)

Isaac Iron. Alaska Head Start Special Services Project, Anchorage, Alaska. 1974. (Available from Easter Seal Society, 726 E Street, Anchorage AK 99501. Booklet, $1.50; filmstrip/audio cassette, $10.00; rental, $5.00.)

The Staff Training Prototype Series. Program for Staff Training of Exemplary Early Childhood Centers for Handicapped Children, The University of Texas, Austin. (Available from ERIC, LEASCO Information Products, Inc., P. O. Drawer O, Bethesda MD 20114.)

The Understanding Young Children Series. Alaska Head Start Special Services Project, Anchorage, Alaska. (Available from Easter Seal Society, 726 E Street, Anchorage AK 99501. $7.00.)

This chapter was written by Jasper Harvey prior to his joining the Bureau of Education for the Handicapped. No official support or endorsement by the Bureau of Education for the Handicapped is intended or should be inferred.

8
PHYSICAL
FACILITIES AND
ENVIRONMENTS

Margaret H. Jones

□Handicapped children often experience difficulties in making contact with their environment, and social interaction is frequently limited. It is necessary, therefore, to develop an environment in which interaction between adult and child and between child and child can flow freely. Play is the natural medium for social interaction, especially when the facility promotes group activity, that is, when the environment is adapted to the special needs of the children and families to be served.

The physical facility should be as flexible as possible to provide for changing and novel stimulation and yet be safe for very young children. The physical facility provides the first step in the therapeutic process since everything the child sees or experiences facilitates sensory motor learning and emotional rehabilitation (Swan, 1974). The facility should present an inviting, comfortable appearance. A dreary, dark, poorly maintained facility is depressing for staff as well as for parents and children already faced with discouraging and difficult problems. Fortunately, with imagination, color planning, and improvised equipment, much can be accomplished without great cost, as can be seen from the facilities of the BEH First Chance projects and other programs described in this chapter.

PROGRAM OBJECTIVES

Before developing the space available it is essential to define the objectives of the program. Among the questions to be asked are the following:

1. What are the ages and problems of the children to be served?
2. What programs are to be carried out with the children?
3. How are parents, volunteers, students, and others to be involved?

INDOOR FACILITIES

The interior space should provide for a variety of special areas:

1. A reception area, which should be attractive and should include appropriate informational material regarding the program and type(s) of children enrolled.
2. Administrative office space.
3. Classroom(s). The classroom should have movable cupboards, which allow for division and redivision of the room as program needs change; low open shelves, which invite children to select materials; and doors on cabinets, which allow storage of things not needed and make for a less cluttered appearance. Also, if displays set up by the teacher are changed from time to time, even very young children tend to be increasingly observant of the environment. At snack time or lunch a circular table with chairs adapted for each child promotes interaction. Also important is provision for privacy away from intervention, an area where the child can play alone.
4. Bathroom. Since this is an important area for one to one interaction of teacher or therapy staff and child, it should be adjacent to the therapy area and to the classroom. In order to provide opportunity for development of

independence it should include stairs for walking up to the wash bowl; potty chairs, with arms, low on the floor; a table for changing diapers; and space for children's clothes (clean and soiled).
5. Therapy area. This could be a single room serving speech, occupational, and physical therapy. It should be located adjacent to the classroom to permit free interchange of staff and children between the two areas. Since the therapists, especially for the very young children, serve as consultants for teaching staff and parents in addition to providing individualized evaluation and therapy, they often work in the classroom and outdoor areas.
6. Observation room or area. A one way window and an intercom are desirable but a simple muslin curtain over a window will suffice for viewing classroom, therapy, and bathroom areas.
7. Individual rooms to provide privacy for medical, psychological, or other testing, and counseling or conference sessions.
8. Staff work areas.
9. Storage areas.
10. Conference room suitable for informal gatherings of parents, staff conferences, and other group meetings.

Figure 1 is a suggested plan to permit observation of activities in the classroom, bathroom, therapy area, and testing rooms from a single viewing area. Ingress into each room is from outside the unit except for the bathroom, which is open to both classroom and therapy areas. Easy flow between classroom and therapy area is provided.

Figure 2 (from Berkeley, 1969) illustrates subdivisions that have proven satisfactory for a nursery school program in which only one room is available. According to Berkeley,

> The whole approach is to treat the handicapped children as much as possible as if they were normal. Thus, the open shelves along the window wall, with a grab rail at the near edge, encourage the children to get their own toys. The single large table in the center of the room encourages interaction; its height is adjustable, and its edge is notched so that wheelchairs can come in close to the work surface. The housekeeping corner, a standard part of any nursery school, has its small sinks angled toward the rear, to minimize water splashing out onto wheelchairs and metal braces. Water play and sand play are also traditional; here, the two specially designed tables are notched and shallow to permit play from a wheelchair. The easel is another unique design—it can be lowered to the floor for use by children who have no arms and paint with their feet. The aim, throughout, is to give each child as much room for development as possible, despite his disability. (pp. 68–69)

This specialized physical environment was planned to facilitate the educational experiences of the multiply handicapped preschoolers and to avoid continuous adjustments in the physical environment, such as constant manipulation of materials, furniture, and accessories. Easy access to materials is more important to the handicapped child than it is to the nonhandicapped preschooler.

Figure 1

Suggested Floor Plan for Indoor/Outdoor Unit for Prenursery Program

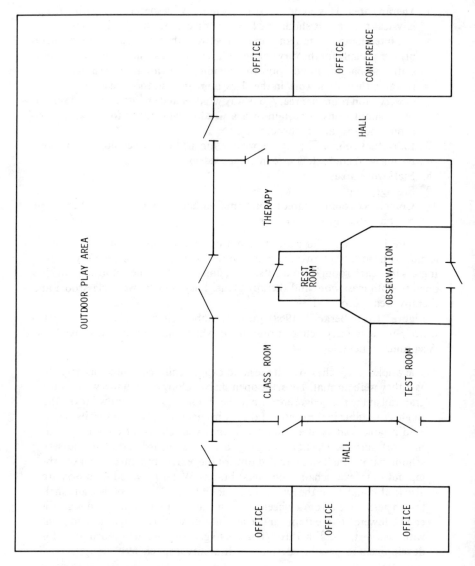

At the UCLA Intervention Program for Developmentally Handicapped Infants and Children (Los Angeles, California), the Pre-School Nursery for Multi-handicapped Children aims toward an "extended home" situation, with varied multisensory experience and encouragement of independence and self care. Theirs is "an invitation for a day of living and growing." Equipment and

Figure 2

Floor Plan for Nursery Program

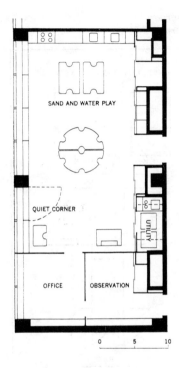

The Katherine Lilly Conroy Preschool Learning Laboratory, in the Research Rehabilitation Wing of the Institute of Rehabilitation Medicine, 400 East 34th Street, New York, New York. Owner: New York University Medical Center. Architects: Skidmore, Owings & Merrill; Jack G. Dunbar, interior designer. Building area: 882 square feet.

Note. From "Pioneering Nursery School" by E. P. Berkeley, *Architectural Forum,* March–April 1969, p. 69. Copyright 1969 by Billboard Publications, Inc. Reprinted by permission.

materials produce an environment that meets the play needs of the child as well as the daily experience of eating, toileting, dressing, and sleeping. Materials become a part of the environmental curriculum.

Quiet areas can be arranged in many ways. For example, "a small alcove with a lowered ceiling, cushions on the floor and soft lighting provides the children with opportunity for privacy" (Rafael, 1973). Another approach is to find a large (5 × 6 foot) discarded packing carton. The top can be open or partially open and doors and windows can be cut in the sides. This offers a retreat as well as an invitation to explore.

Adapted equipment (some homemade and some commercially available at moderate cost) should be selected on the basis of the problems of the children to be served. For example, bean bag chairs not only can serve as seats but also afford opportunity for balance and coordination training as children climb over them. The individualized prone standing boards shown in Figure 3 make it possible for severely handicapped children to be upright and play around a table.

Figure 3

Prone Standing and Kneeling Boards
for Children Aged 1 ½ to 3 Years
UCLA Pre-School Nursery
(Los Angeles, California)

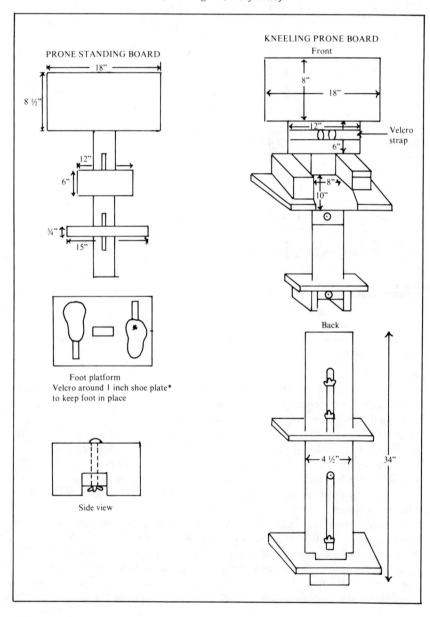

Figure 4

Sawhorse Chair for Children Aged 2 ½ to 3 Years
UCLA Pre-School Nursery
(Los Angeles, California)

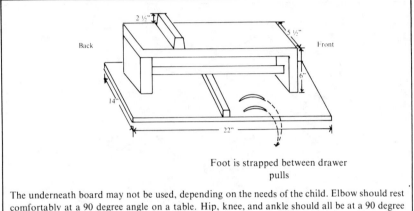

Foot is strapped between drawer
pulls

The underneath board may not be used, depending on the needs of the child. Elbow should rest comfortably at a 90 degree angle on a table. Hip, knee, and ankle should all be at a 90 degree angle. Abdomen should touch the table when sitting.

The foot board can be elevated and padded so that the child can kneel instead of stand. To promote balance in sitting, a sawhorse chair (see Figure 4) can be used with a regular table or a cut out table if needed for side to side balance. Parents have devised special equipment for side lying by severely physically handicapped children (see Figure 5).

For the emotionally disturbed, guidelines are given in a script and slide show entitled *The Physical Plant* from the Rutland Center in Athens, Georgia. For such children Schiffer (1969) called attention to the size of the classroom, indicating that too large a room reduces the opportunity for interaction. He suggested an optimal size of 50 square feet per person and an irregularly shaped floor area instead of one that is geometrically uniform.

Play facilities and equipment for retarded children were discussed by Cratty (1974), who emphasized the need for rest and quiet areas as well as for activity areas.

OUTDOOR PLAY AREAS

Because the handicapped child often does not have the opportunity to explore natural environments, the outdoor play area should be concerned with providing grass, trees, water, and other normal outdoor environmental settings.

This can be done even in a rooftop outdoor playground, as illustrated by the Jessie Stanton Developmental Playground for Pre-School Handicapped Children at the Institute of Rehabilitation Medicine, New York University Medical Center. Figure 6 shows the playground's four areas, each with potential for offering varied experiences with natural materials:

Figure 5

Side Lyer
UCLA Pre-School Nursery
(Los Angeles, California)

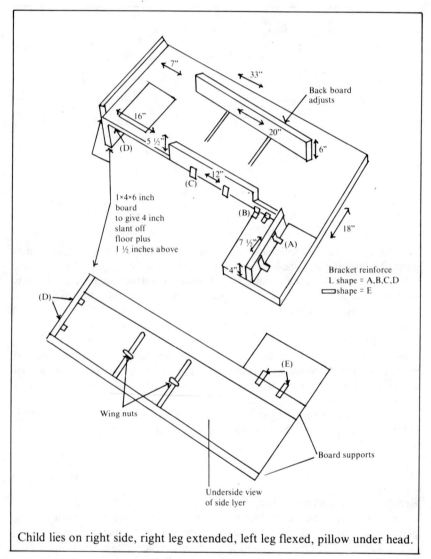

Child lies on right side, right leg extended, left leg flexed, pillow under head.

Figure 6

*Jessie Stanton Developmental Playground for Pre-School Handicapped Children
Institute of Rehabilitation Medicine
New York University Medical Center
(New York, New York)*

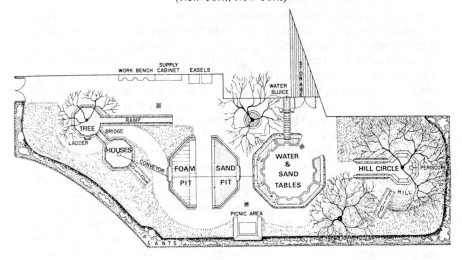

1. The bridge tree house.
2. Foam and sand pits at ground level for those unable to sit or walk.
3. Sand and water tables (fed by an artificial waterfall).
4. Hill and hill circle with embedded slide and periscope in the fence.

Custom designed by the New York University Medical Center (funded by BEH), this playground gives primary consideration to children using several different types of locomotion. There is space for two wheelchairs to pass side by side, surface configurations that allow for wheelchair movement, and multilevel viewing for children in wheelchairs.

Figure 7 shows portions of the Garden Training Area at the UCLA Cerebral Palsy Pre-School Nursery. The ground level play area, specially designed for young handicapped children, emphasizes a peaceful, uncluttered atmosphere, with an uneven grassy center, a walkway around the circumference, plantings of various kinds mainly peripheral to the walkway, and areas of special activity including a sand area at ground level, swings, and a playhouse (modified Japanese tea house) with low-rise steps and handrails.

The PEECH Playground

The PEECH Learning Playground shown in Figure 8 is a model learning playground developed at the University of Illinois. It was designed by a landscape architect working closely with a specialist in the motor development of pre-school handicapped children. The needs of the children in the PEECH program and the kinds of activities that would promote their total development were the primary concerns which determined the design of the playground. Also important was the requirement that the playground be low in cost and easy to replicate at other sites around the nation.

The playground is a total learning environment made up of interconnecting and interrelated structures situated around a large open area. There are several climbing structures, with platforms, ladders, a sliding pole, a slide, and a tunnel (Figures 9 and 10); a winding tricycle path (Figures 11 and 12); an outdoor class-room area; a set of tire swings (Figure 13); and a system of water troughs emptying into a wading pool, surrounded by a sand-play area (Figures 14 and 15). All the structures were made from inexpensive materials such as old tires, railroad ties, and telephone poles. The help of staff, parents, and volunteers kept the total cost of the entire playground to about $2,000.

The PEECH Learning Playground was designed to promote the language, cognitive, and social development as well as the motor development of pre-school handicapped children. Varieties of texture, color, shape, and size in the structures and the landscaped environment of the playground, in addition to the various kinds of activities the playground allows, are all conducive to the modeling of language. Shapes and colors strategically placed on the structures help the teachers reinforce concepts taught in the classroom. Areas suited to individual or group play, such as tunnels, wide platforms on the climbers, and the very wide slide, are included on the playground to promote social development. In addition, the structures are designed so that children can practice all the basic motor skills, such as walking, jumping, or climbing, at all levels of development. For example, opportunities for walking on a balance beam range from using the wide railroad ties around the sand-play area all the way to walking on a narrow beam several feet above the ground.

The PEECH teachers use this Learning Playground in two ways. Informally, in periods of supervised free play, children are encouraged to practice basic motor skills as they interact with the playground environment. Concepts (up-down, slow-fast) and language modeling are introduced naturally by the teachers as opportunities arise. However, the motor development of preschool handicapped children is too important to be left totally to chance, so the PEECH teachers also write lesson plans for use on the playground. These lesson plans, which include behavioral objectives and criterion activities to help evaluate the children's progress, use a game format to encourage each child to practice the basic motor skills at his own level of development. The games are used to motivate the children to practice such skills as climbing, jumping, and throwing, and also promote the development of language and cognitive and social skills.

INSIDE OR OUTSIDE FACILITIES AND EQUIPMENT

Some equipment may be placed inside or outside, for example, the playhouse shown in Figure 16. Activities in this playhouse made of slats can be observed unobtrusively.

Figure 7

UCLA Pre-School Nursery Playground
(Los Angeles, California)

Modified Japanese tea house, rocks, and trees

Sand area and climbing bars

Figure 8

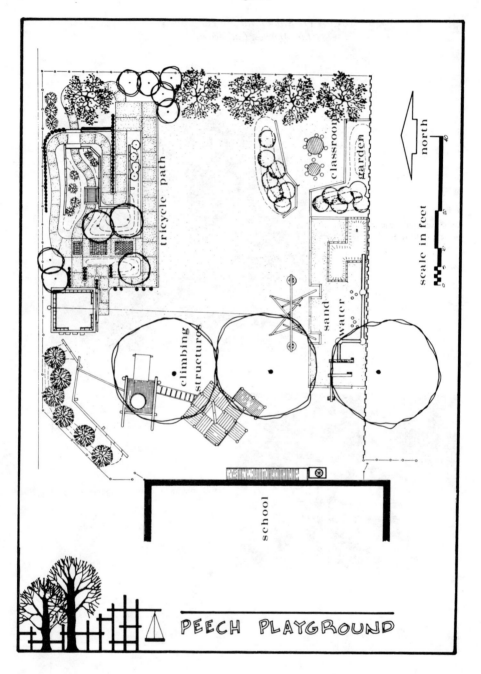

Figure 9

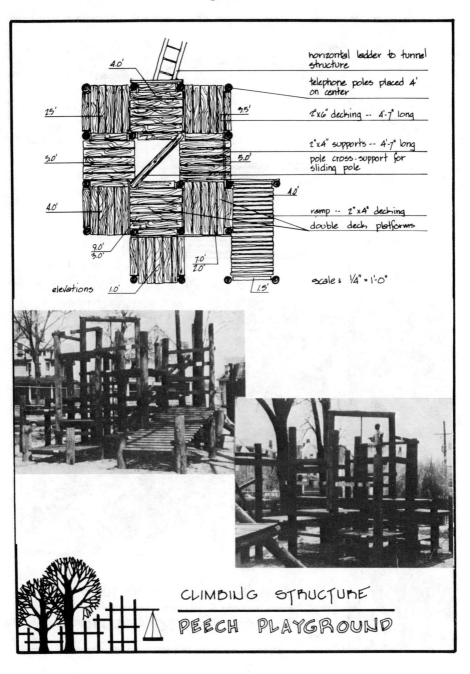

horizontal ladder to tunnel structure

telephone poles placed 4' on center

2"x6" decking -- 4'-7" long

2"x4" supports -- 4'-7" long

pole cross-support for sliding pole

ramp -- 2"x4" decking

double deck platforms

scale: ¼" = 1'-0"

elevations

CLIMBING STRUCTURE

PEECH PLAYGROUND

Figure 10

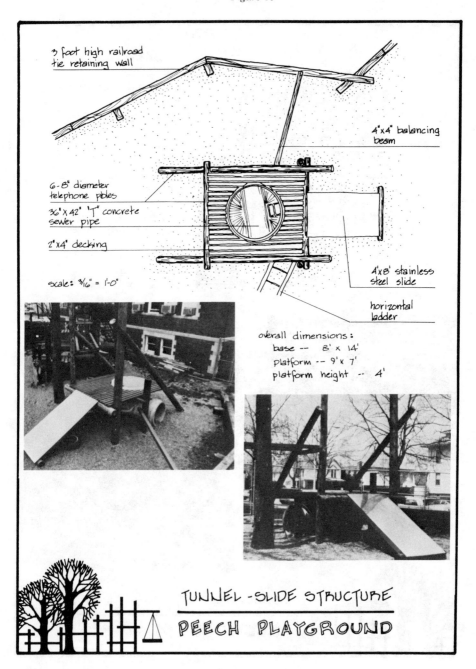

3 foot high railroad tie retaining wall

4"x4" balancing beam

6-8" diameter telephone poles

36'x 42' "T" concrete sewer pipe

2'x4' decking

scale: 3/16" = 1'-0"

4'x8' stainless steel slide

horizontal ladder

overall dimensions:
base -- 8'x 14'
platform -- 9'x 7'
platform height -- 4'

TUNNEL-SLIDE STRUCTURE

PEECH PLAYGROUND

Figure 11

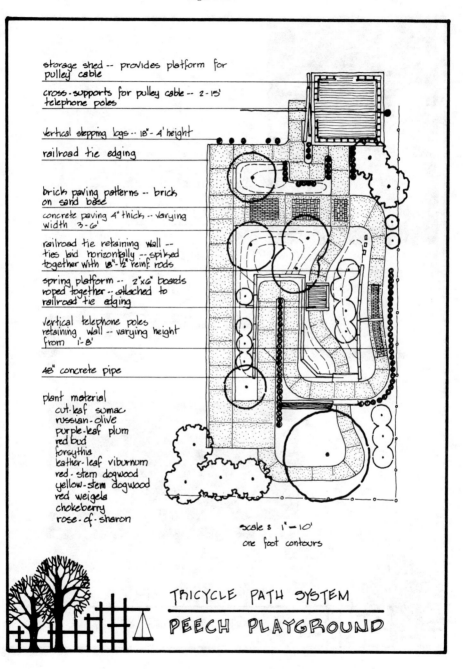

storage shed -- provides platform for pulley cable

cross-supports for pulley cable -- 2-15' telephone poles

vertical stepping logs -- 18"-4' height

railroad tie edging

brick paving patterns -- brick on sand base

concrete paving 4" thick -- varying width 3-6'

railroad tie retaining wall -- ties laid horizontally -- spiked together with 18"-½" reinf. rods

spring platform -- 2"x6" boards roped together -- attached to railroad tie edging

vertical telephone poles retaining wall -- varying height from 1'-8'

48" concrete pipe

plant material
cut-leaf sumac
russian-olive
purple-leaf plum
red bud
forsythia
leather-leaf viburnum
red-stem dogwood
yellow-stem dogwood
red weigela
chokeberry
rose-of-sharon

scale : 1"-10'
one foot contours

TRICYCLE PATH SYSTEM
PEECH PLAYGROUND

Figure 12

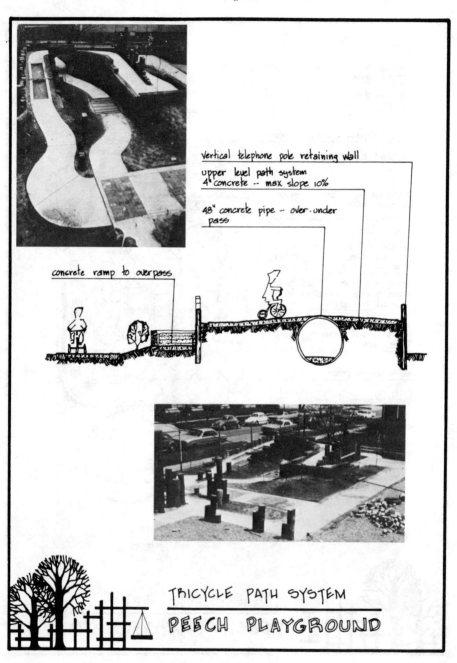

Figure 13

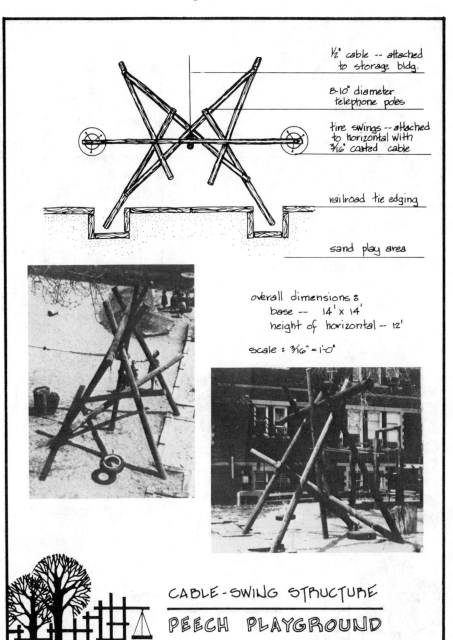

½" cable -- attached to storage bldg.

8-10" diameter telephone poles

tire swings -- attached to horizontal with 3/16" coated cable

railroad tie edging

sand play area

overall dimensions:
    base -- 14' x 14'
    height of horizontal -- 12'

scale : 3/16" = 1-0"

CABLE-SWING STRUCTURE
PEECH PLAYGROUND

Figure 14

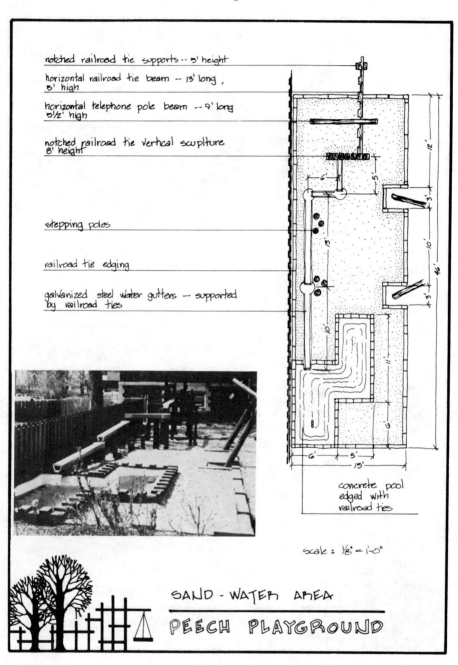

notched railroad tie supports -- 5' height

horizontal railroad tie beam -- 13' long , 5' high

horizontal telephone pole beam -- 9' long 5½' high

notched railroad tie vertical scuplture 8' height

stepping poles

railroad tie edging

galvanized steel water gutters -- supported by railroad ties

concrete pool edged with railroad ties

scale : ⅛" = 1-0"

SAND - WATER AREA

PEECH PLAYGROUND

Figure 15

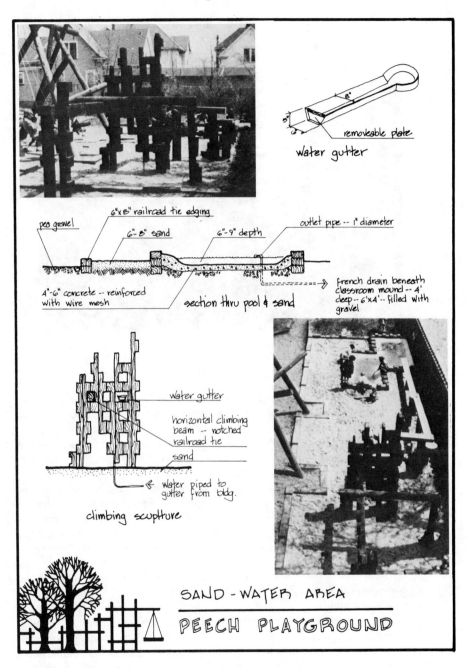

removeable plate

water gutter

peg gravel

6"x8" railroad tie edging

6"-8" sand

6"-9" depth

outlet pipe -- 1" diameter

4"-6" concrete -- reinforced with wire mesh

section thru pool & sand

french drain beneath classroom mound -- 4' deep -- 6'x4' -- filled with gravel

water gutter

horizontal climbing beam -- notched railroad tie

sand

water piped to gutter from bldg.

climbing scupiture

SAND - WATER AREA

PEECH PLAYGROUND

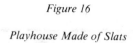

Note. From "Early Education for Multihandicapped Children" by B. Rafael, *Children Today*, January-February 1973, p. 24.

A brochure entitled *A Priceless Playground for Exceptional Children,* published by the Early Childhood Learning Center in El Paso, Texas, describes various pieces of homemade equipment, such as the "walking trough" shown in Figure 17. Traffic cones or 3 gallon ice cream cartons can be used to teach children directionality (see Figure 18). If the cartons are used, they should be filled with sand and painted with poster paint.

Experience with toddlers and infants has indicated that placement in close proximity in a walled off play area (confined space) leads to increased communication (Jones, Barrett, Olonoff, & Andersen, 1969). A small enclosed area can be made by using a large (5 × 6 foot) packing carton or by building a three sided wall that can be placed against a one way viewing mirror (see Figure 19).

In the corner of a room or in a separate structure, a "fun house" (such as Thera-Play shown in Figure 20) may be constructed. If the walls are lined with resilient materials and all inside pieces of equipment are made entirely of foam covered with vinyl or other washable synthetic material, a "responsive environment" is provided, which gives the child feedback as he pushes against it and is completely safe for falling in any area. It is designed to provide for independent exploration, for climbing, and for rolling. The teacher remains outside the enclosure making

Figure 17

Walking Trough

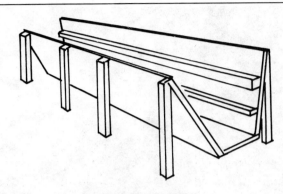

WALKING TROUGH

The walking trough is an excellent means of teaching balance and coordination. The trough is 8 feet long and is a V-shape set in a 2 × 4 framework.
It is 30 inches high. 1 × 6's form the sides. The floor boards are 8 inches above the ground. The children walk on the sides of the V, achieving a difficult task.

Note. From *A Priceless Playground for Exceptional Children* by P. G. Adkins, El Paso TX: Learning Resources Press, 1973. Copyright 1973 by Learning Resources Press. Reprinted by permission.

Figure 18

Traffic Cones

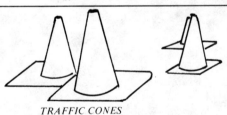

TRAFFIC CONES

A zig-zag course made with poly-plastic traffic cones is an ideal pathway for teaching children directionality.
The cones were donated by a local construction company, but three gallon ice cream cartons can be substituted for the cones.
Fill cartons with sand and paint with poster paint.
The children play follow-the-leader through the maze of cones or cartons.

Note. From *A Priceless Playground for Exceptional Children* by P. G. Adkins, El Paso TX: Learning Resources Press, 1973. Copyright 1973 by Learning Resources Press. Reprinted by permission.

Figure 19

Children in Confined Space, with Teacher

Note. From "Two Experiments in Training Handicapped Children at Nursery School" by M. H. Jones, M. L. Barrett, C. Olonoff, and E. Andersen. In P. Wolff and R. MacKeith (Eds.), *Clinics in Developmental Medicine* (No. 33), London: Spastics International Medical Publications in association with William Heinimann Medical Books Ltd., 1969, p. 109. Copyright 1969 by Spastics International Medical Publications. Reprinted by permission.

Figure 20

Thera-Play

plan

Obstacle area

Note. Thera-Play™ is a product of Industrial Educational Design, 5231 Cushman Place, No. 7, San Diego, California 92110.

records and being available in case of need. The children are invited to enter the area and are entirely free to do whatever they wish with no suggestion or direction.

Water activities are recommended and can be made available through the use of small plastic bathtubs for infants, wading pools, and full sized pools if suitable steps, parallel walking rails, and other safety features are provided. Volunteers can participate in the program very effectively, but their activities should be under the direct supervision of a teacher familiar with the individual children's problems. The objectives of the water activities are to help the children feel safe and happy in this environment, to help them develop balance, and to facilitate gross motor activity. Interventions need to be determined for each child since children's responses vary. The following teacher's report illustrates the gains from a pool program for three very young handicapped children with different types of problems.

A dramatic change was seen in the behavior of one severely involved child with congenital anomalies. She would not move when placed on the floor, had extreme difficulty in separating from the mother in the classroom. In the pool, on a partially submerged table, for the first time she was able to get into and to maintain a crawling position. She separated easily from her mother on the first session, was happy and cooperated with the volunteers readily whereas in the classroom fussing and crying was frequent. A spastic quadriplegic cerebral palsied child not only learned to stand and walk in the parallel bars in the water but he developed enough confidence to reach both hands overhead to throw a ball. He learned to blow bubbles in the water. Of all the children in the pool program a young autistic boy made the most striking gains. Attention span increased. Vocalization increased, including words such as "no," "row, row, row," "bub" for bubbles. He made direct eye contact and followed basic level instructions. All this was accomplished in eleven weekly one hour sessions. One important factor was the continuity of instructor, in this case a male student. (Kehr, 1974, p. 220)

Practical as well as theoretical considerations regarding physical facilities and environments for normal young children and discussions of the functions of play are provided by the following authors: Bengtsson, 1970; Ellis, 1974; Friedberg and Perry, 1970; Hurtwood, 1967; and Lederman and Trachfel, 1959.

CRITERIA FOR EVALUATING PHYSICAL FACILITIES AND ENVIRONMENTS

In evaluating a physical facility or environment, the following questions should be considered:
1. Does the facility provide adequate space for staff, parents, and children to carry out the various aspects of the program plan?
2. Is the space arranged so as to provide optimal use of the area available?
3. Does the decor promote relaxation but at the same time motivate exploration and look inviting and comfortable?
4. Is the equipment appropriate for the specific needs of the population and for the program to be provided?

CONCLUDING COMMENTS

Motivation for both learning and movement is basically related to success in achievement. The physical facility can provide opportunity for decision making and opportunity for the development of independence. Handicapped children have the same needs as all children as well as some needs that are uniquely their own. Not only physical development but also learning and social and psychological growth are aided or limited by the physical facility, the equipment, and the environment to a greater extent in children with physical and/or other handicaps than in normal children.

REFERENCES

Bengtsson, A. *Environmental planning for children's play.* New York: Praeger & Praeger, 1970.

Berkeley, E. P. Pioneering nursery school. *Forum,* March-April 1969, pp. 68–69.

Cratty, J. B. *Motor activity and the education of retardates* (2nd ed.). Philadelphia: Lea & Febiger, 1974.

Ellis, M. *Why men play.* Englewood Cliffs NJ: Prentice-Hall, 1974.

Friedberg, P. M., & Perry, E. *Play and interplay.* London: Collier-MacMillan Ltd., 1970.

Hurtwood, L. O. A. *Planning for play.* London: Thames & Hudson, 1967.

Jones, M. H., Barrett, M. L., Olonoff, C., & Anderson, E. Two experiments in training handicapped children at nursery school. In P. Wolff and R. MacKeith (Eds.), *Clinics in developmental medicine* (No. 33). London: Spastics International Medical Publications in association with William Heinimann Medical Books Ltd., 1969.

Kehr, K. Pool program, UCLA Pre-Nursery. In *The first three years—Programming for atypical children* (A United Cerebral Palsy Nationally Organized Collaborative Project). United Cerebral Palsy Association, Inc., 66 East 34th Street, New York, New York 10016, 1974.

Lederman, A., & Trachfel, A. *Creative playground and recreation centers.* New York: Praeger & Praeger, 1959.

Rafael, B. Early education for multihandicapped children. *Children Today,* January-February 1973, pp. 22–26.

Schiffer, M. *The therapeutic play group.* New York: Grune & Stratton, 1969.

Swan, W. W. *The physical plant.* The Georgia Psychoeducational Center Network, 698 North Pope Street, Athens, Georgia 30601, 1974.

RESOURCES

Fun House (film). A Nationally Organized Collaborative Project to Provide Comprehensive Services for Atypical Infants and Their Families, New York, New York. (Available from UCPA, Inc., 66 E. 34th Street, New York NY 10016. $76.50; rental, $10 for three days.)

PEECH Learning Playground (sample lesson plans). PEECH Project, Urbana-Champaign, Illinois. (Available from the project, Institute for Child Behavior and Development, 403 E. Healey, Champaign IL 61820. Free.)

The Physical Plant. Rutland Center, Athens, Georgia. (Available from the center, Technical Assistance Office, 698 N. Pope Street, Athens GA 30601.)

Play Lot (blueprints and construction plans for indoor-outdoor preschool playground). Comprehensive Children's Services for Rural and Non-Urban Areas, Fargo, North Dakota. (Available from Southeast Mental Health and Retardation Center, 700 First Avenue South, Fargo ND 58102. $45.00.)

A Priceless Playground for Exceptional Children. Early Childhood Learning Center, El Paso, Texas. 1973. (Available from Learning Resources Press, 609 La Cruz, El Paso TX 79902. $1.75.)

9
PARENT INVOLVEMENT

Marsha S. Shearer
David E. Shearer

☐ No longer can the parent involvement component be viewed as simply a nice adjunct to an early childhood program. There was a time when it was the unusual program that made efforts to directly involve and train the parents of the children being served. Parent training programs were once viewed as "the frosting on the cake."

RATIONALE FOR PARENT INVOLVEMENT

Research is now showing that effective parent involvement is, in fact, a main ingredient in long term effective early childhood intervention. In summarizing an extensive survey of the research literature, Brofenbrenner (1974) stated:

> The involvement of the child's family as an *active participant* is critical to the success of any intervention program. Without such family involvement, any effect of intervention . . . appears to erode fairly rapidly once the program ends. In contrast, the involvement of the *parents as partners* in the enterprise provides an ongoing system which can reinforce the effects of the program while it is in operation, and help to sustain them after the program ends. (p. 55; emphasis added)

In too many studies, significant gains in IQ have been made by children in early intervention programs only to be "washed out" after the intensive program ended and the children entered school or remained at home (Brofenbrenner, 1974, p. 14). One of the key variables in changing these sad and costly results appears to be the effective involvement of parents.

There are many reasons to involve parents in their child's education. First, parents are the consumers. They pay, either directly or indirectly, for the program and service their child is receiving. Many parents are saying they want a voice in what and how their child is being taught. Often parent training programs begin as a result of pressure from parents. They want to participate in the teaching of their child; thus parents must be taught *how* to teach their child (Fredericks, Baldwin, & Grove, 1974).

Second, parents, if knowledgeable about the program their child is receiving, can be the best advocate for program continuation and extension (Hayden, 1974; Shearer & Shearer, 1974). School boards, advisory councils, and state legislatures throughout the nation have substantially changed policy and laws as a direct result of parental advocacy.

Third, according to government figures, there is currently a deficit of 58,500 teachers to provide service to the nation's preschool handicapped population (Ackerman & Moore, 1974). Certainly, parent training programs can and should be developed to help meet this huge manpower need.

There are a vast number of additional reasons, perhaps more human and more individual in nature, for developing effective parent involvement programs:

• Parents of a handicapped child will have more responsibility for their child over a significantly longer period of time than parents of a normal child. They need parenting and teaching skills that parents of a normal child need not necessarily possess (Shearer & Shearer, 1972).

- Parents usually know their child better than anyone else. Parents can thus serve as a vital resource to program staff in the development of functional program objectives for the child that will be useful in his or her own unique environment.
- Transferring learning from the classroom to the home has been an acknowledged problem. This occurs because there is insufficient and/or ineffective communication between parents and teaching staff. Thus, it is vitally important that there is planned consistency between the center's educational program and the educational experiences provided by the parents. Without effective parent involvement, the best possible program for the child will have little effect (Lillie, 1974).
- Studies have shown that parent training during the preschool years was beneficial not only for the target child but also for his or her siblings (Gilmer, Miller, & Gray, 1970; Klaus & Gray, 1968; Gray & Klaus, 1970). This indicates that parents are able to generalize these learned skills, making them better teachers of all their children.
- The training of parents, who already are natural reinforcing agents, will provide them with the skills necessary to teach new behaviors effectively and to modify inappropriate behaviors that interfere with learning.
- Parent involvement can greatly accelerate the child's rate of learning. The center, working with the child without benefit of parental involvement, cannot begin to accomplish alone what staff and parents can accomplish together. Fredericks and his colleagues (1974) have demonstrated that a systematic program by the parent in conjunction with a school program will almost double the rate of acquisition of a particular skill.

Thus, it appears that one condition necessary for an effective early intervention program is an effective parent involvement and parent training component.

TYPES OF PARENTAL INVOLVEMENT

Parents can be involved in every phase of an early childhood program. Their roles in the BEH First Chance projects vary both in responsibility and extent of involvement. The following is a list of roles that parents are fulfilling within the network.

1. *Administrator*—Parents in every First Chance project are members of that project's advisory council. Obviously, the extent of their involvement depends on how active the council is. However, it is at this level that parents make program decisions that will directly affect the children's total education program.
2. *Disseminator*—Parents have the responsibility, whether implicit or explicit, for public relations and dissemination within the community and perhaps regionally and nationally as well. At one level, parents can talk to friends, relatives, and others within their community about the program in which they and their child are participating. In the past parents have written letters to congressmen and government officials describing the project and their pleas-

ure or displeasure with it. At another level, parents have gone to school board meetings to help assure program continuation after federal funding has ceased. Parents have presented their project to educators at national conferences with impressive results (PCMR, 1972; Airlie House Conference, 1972). Parents as consumers seem better able to effect major changes in policy than educators. As disseminators and consumers, parents are an invaluable resource for program acceptance, continuation, and expansion.

3. *Staff member*—Parents can serve as volunteers or paid staff members. Numerous projects have trained parents to serve in this capacity with excellent results for parents and children alike.

4. *Primary teacher*—Related to the above section, some First Chance projects have trained parents to teach their own child. Many of these programs are centered in the home. Parents are not staff members, as such, but are viewed as primary teachers of the child. Programing of instructional goals is geared for the child. However, it is the parent, not the teacher, who is trained to implement the instructional plan.

5. *Recruiter*—Many First Chance projects use parents as a source of referrals. Parents who are already receiving service can be extremely useful in contacting other parents about the program or in making direct referrals.

6. *Curriculum developer*—Suggestions from parents regarding curriculum are actively sought by the staff of most of the First Chance projects. This serves as an implicit acknowledgement that parents have goals and objectives they would like to see met and that the program has an obligation to both parent and child to develop teaching plans to meet these objectives. It is a waste of time and energy to teach a child a skill that is not functional in the environment in which he or she operates. Parents, because they know their child better, can often suggest curriculum goals, teaching techniques, and reinforcers that are appropriate for their child, thus significantly increasing staff effectiveness.

7. *Counselor*—Many projects use parents as the basis of their counseling and support system. Parents share ideas that work for them and offer each other support and guidance in dealing with the child at home. A bond develops between parents as they realize they are not alone and that they can rely on each other as well as on the project's professional staff. This can significantly increase the effects of the total program. Some projects encourage group parent meetings where the entire content is decided by the parents themselves. Other projects use group meetings as a method of relaying information. Others have encouraged a parent to parent partnership that is particularly valuable for new parents entering the project.

8. *Assessor of skills*—Several First Chance projects use parents in screening and assessment. All testing is done in front of the parents, with both child and parent participating in the testing process. The staff thus exhibits acceptance of the parent as the major source of information relating to the skills and behaviors the child already possesses. Parent involvement in the testing process also indicates to the parents that all information they have about the child is valuable and important.

9. *Evaluator and record keeper*—Recently more First Chance projects have given parents significant responsibility for evaluating the progress their child is making in the program. Parents are taught to keep records of their child's performance on prescribed tasks both in center and home based programs. Based on data collected by parents, teaching objectives are developed, implemented, and modified. In some projects, parents are asked weekly to evaluate in narrative form the progress their child has made. This information can provide important feedback to the staff, which can further aid in curriculum development, implementation, and modification.

Although it is important that parental involvement is sought in all phases of the project's operation, research findings indicate that the key component is direct and ongoing productive parental involvement with their child. It thus becomes mandatory that projects develop training programs for parents with the objective of teaching parents to be effective in working with and teaching their own child.

The following are examples of First Chance projects that have developed exemplary programs with parents in each of the roles described previously.

Administrator

The Vermont Parent/Child Development Center in Brattleboro, Vermont, organized parents into task forces that took over some roles traditionally assigned to a project director. According to a project paper, these task forces "include the areas of fund raising, legislation, teacher assistants, building improvements and trustees, among others" (Devoid & Mills, 1972). Each task force of parents made work timetables, assigned responsibilities, and determined systems of communication.

Goals and objectives were outlined, discussed, and agreed upon. Examples of some of the goals, as stated in the project paper, were to "find permanent quarters for the program by the end of the first year," "develop and aim for improvement in state legislation for the handicapped by the end of the second year," and "outline a refunding and project continuation plan by the end of the second project year." Procedures for implementing these and other objectives were agreed upon between the parents and the project director.

Parents have made major contributions to the administration of this project. The first and a necessary step toward this success was giving the parents an opportunity to be involved in the administrative process and then planning well to maximize the results.

Disseminator

The Julia Ann Singer Preschool Early Education Program for Handicapped Children in Los Angeles, California, has used the talents of parents in numerous dissemination activities. Parents have aided staff in dissemination of the program to the larger community, both professional and nonprofessional. A parent who was participating in this project was its sole speaker at a BEH conference

(Airlie House Conference, 1972). She described the program as well as her involvement in learning how to teach and live effectively with her emotionally disturbed child. The project director had no need to make any additional comments. The general feedback indicated that the parent had provided a unique educational experience to project directors and BEH officials.

Julia Ann Singer parents have participated in fund raising activities for the school and have been given responsibility for representing the agency to local television, radio, and news media. Additionally, the parents have been a potent force in disseminating the Singer teaching techniques to the public schools so that their children will continue to receive quality educational services after leaving the First Chance program. Another aspect of their dissemination program is encouragement of parental attendance at professional conferences and seminars. Parents then report on the content to the full staff and other parents. Parents themselves are disseminating what they have learned to professionals and other parents.

Staff Member

The Down's syndrome program of the Model Preschool Center for Handicapped Children at the University of Washington in Seattle believes that parent involvement in the classroom is valuable both to the program and to the parents. Thus, parents must assist in the classroom a minimum of once per week. Parents are taught techniques in observation, recording, and behavior modification. At each daily staffing, parents and teachers evaluate the day's events and determine how the child's gains can be continued at home. The staff views the parent as an important team member and an invaluable help and resource in program planning and implementation.

The Early Childhood Learning Center in El Paso, Texas, requires family participation in the classroom setting. Any family member is welcome. The staff has found family assistance to be vital as it provides more individualized planning and instruction and increases the adult-child ratio. A second advantage is that parents learn teaching techniques through modeling and imitation of professional staff. Parents are then better able to carry out learning activities for their child in the home setting.

The PEECH Project (Precise Early Education of Children with Handicaps) in Urbana-Champaign, Illinois, also trains parents to teach in the classroom setting. Parents are prepared through discussions with staff members, observation of the classroom, and role playing activities. When a parent is ready, he or she performs direct teaching under the supervision of professional staff.

The Chapel Hill (North Carolina) Training Outreach Project has trained several parents to become paid aides in the classroom. The training includes teaching parents skills such as behavior modification techniques and task analysis.

There is no doubt that parents can be a valuable asset as aides or volunteers in the classroom. However, several conditions seem necessary before this can occur. Merle Karnes, director of the PEECH Project, has stated (ABT Associates, 1973, p. 6) that parents become directly involved in programs if:

- *"The involvement is meaningful."* Giving parents cleanup jobs and bathroom duty is not particularly meaningful. Teaching a child to name two colors or to unbutton his jacket without help is meaningful.
- *"Parents are included in the decision-making process."* For example, the teacher may say to the parent, "What do you think Johnny is ready to learn next?" or "Is there a certain behavior you and I can work on together here at school that will be especially helpful to Johnny and you at home?"
- *"Parents receive feedback from the program staff."* For example, the teacher may say to the parent, "You were great! I really appreciate the time you're giving, and you reinforce the children so well. I particularly liked the way you smiled and touched Mary when you rewarded her with the goodie" or "I like the way you're giving Tom only the help he really needs."
- *"The program is individualized to meet parental needs."* Project directors have emphasized that programs for parents should be based on their needs and skills just as program goals are individualized for the children.

The major consideration underlying this section involves parent training. In order for anyone—professional, paraprofessional, community volunteer, or parent—to be effective as a staff member, preservice and inservice training is mandatory. Fredericks and his colleagues (1974) have found the following guidelines for parent volunteer training effective in their programs at the Teaching Research Infant and Child Center (Monmouth, Oregon):

- Time must be taken to train volunteers. This training must be concise and simple. A short lecture describing the center, the things a volunteer must do, and some principles of teaching is an excellent way to begin. This lecture would be followed by observation and demonstration. Finally, the volunteer would be placed in a practicum situation, teaching children under supervision of a teacher or an aide.
- Volunteers must be given teaching tasks in the classroom comparable to their level of training. It will take time for parents to learn how to teach all parts of the curriculum. Starting them in one area—e.g. self-help, motor, or arithmetic—will allow them to master that area before they are required to teach in another.
- A continuous system of feedback as to the adequacy of the volunteers' performance must exist. This rule requires that the center have a system of observation of volunteers that allows center supervisory personnel to monitor the quality of the volunteer's teaching and to give feedback to volunteers.
- A simplified system of communication, not requiring verbal instruction, between the teacher and the volunteer must exist. This rule requires that the teacher have specified detailed directions on how instruction is to be delivered to children. It further requires that the volunteer record in some systematic way the performance of the child and that the recorded data be examined on a regular basis by the teacher in order to provide timely updating of children's programs. (Fredericks et al., 1974, p. 46)

Figure 1

Parent Guide Sheet on Behavior Modification
Comprehensive Early Childhood Project
(Cedar Rapids, Iowa)

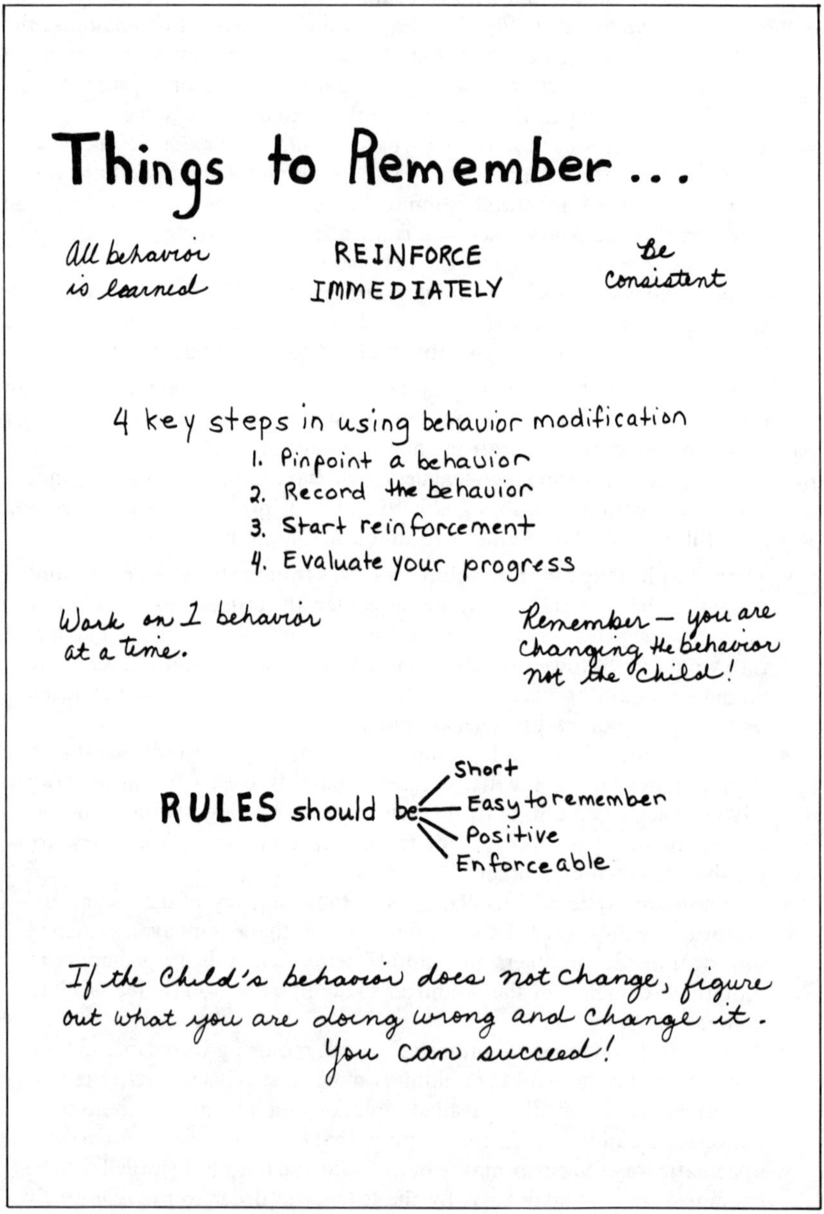

Things to Remember...

All behavior   REINFORCE   Be
is learned   IMMEDIATELY   Consistent

4 key steps in using behavior modification
1. Pinpoint a behavior
2. Record the behavior
3. Start reinforcement
4. Evaluate your progress

Work on 1 behavior   Remember — you are
at a time.   changing the behavior
                            not the child!

RULES should be ⟨ Short
                     Easy to remember
                     Positive
                     Enforceable

If the child's behavior does not change, figure
out what you are doing wrong and change it.
You can succeed!

Figure 2

Parent Guide Sheet on Language Development
Comprehensive Early Childhood Project
(Cedar Rapids, Iowa)

Developing Better Language

Use a sentence rather than just a word.

Example: Child asks, "What's that?" You answer: "THAT IS A RABBIT."
Rather than: "A rabbit."

Give clear directions.

Example: "YOU CARRY THE DOLL AND I'LL CARRY THE TRUCK." Rather than:
"Let's move these."

Find opportunities to help a child understand an idea.

Example: "LET'S LOOK UNDER THE SOFA." "LET'S PUT IT ON TOP OF THE BOOK."

Be precise in how things are similar.

Example: "THESE ARE THE SAME COLOR." or "THESE ARE BOTH RED."
Rather than: "These are the same."

Add words that describe an object.

Example: "THAT IS A GREEN CAR."
Rather than: "That is a car."

Be specific when talking about a place or location.

Example: "THE BALL BELONGS IN THE TOY CHEST BY THE BLUE CHAIR."
Rather than: "It goes over there."

Primary Teacher

A major objective of some First Chance projects is not just to teach the child per se, but also to teach the parent to teach the child. These projects may either be home or center based. Some projects rely primarily on group meetings and written instructions as the major instructional delivery system for parents. Others provide one to one instruction for the parent and child with the teacher modeling

Figure 3

Parent Guide Sheet on Motor Coordination
Comprehensive Early Childhood Project
(Cedar Rapids, Iowa)

Large muscle control is the ability of a child to coordinate his whole body. Coordination takes place as the child grows and learns about his body. Once a child becomes aware of his body, then he can begin to use it. His large muscles and abilities to use these large muscles usually have to develop before he can use his small muscles. A child learns what he does. He needs many experiences and opportunities to use his arms for climbing, hanging, pushing, pulling and to use his legs for kicking, running, jumping and climbing. Such experiences help develop a child's eye-foot and eye-hand coordination.

When you encourage activities that involve the entire body in a physical activity you are also helping develop gross motor coordination. While playing with your child, any time you are having him run, jump, hop, throw a ball or work with his entire body, you are helping him develop his large muscles and his coordination. An infant learning to crawl or scoot can be encouraged or tempted by a toy or object to move forward, sideways or to even turn around.

Taking time to stack blocks and play with a child and his toys helps him learn how to use his body. When a child watches an adult build a tower with blocks, the child will soon start to build a tower. Even knocking down the blocks helps a child use and understand his muscles.

Opportunities for children to use their large muscles are endless. A few to consider are:

Exercise, march, or move freely to music on the radio, television or record players. (They do not have to be designed for children!)

Ascending and descending stairs.

Climbing—even chairs; an indoor slide can be made using the closed ironing board proped at an angle on a chair or low table.

Riding a tyke bike or tricycle or even a board attached to a pair of roller skates.

Encourage those activities that involve the entire body in a physical activity. They are good for children and they are FUN.

Figure 4

Parent Guide Sheet on Dressing Skills
Comprehensive Early Childhood Project
(Cedar Rapids, Iowa)

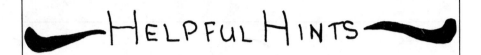

Helpful Hints

Dressing

1. To help your child learn to put on and take off his boots:
   Use plastic bags (bread bags) on shoes to allow them to slip in easier.
   Teach your child to hold his foot in a pointed position.
   When taking off boots, pull off the heel end first; then have your child pull his toes out.
2. Use Velcro tape instead of:
   Pins so diapers can be changed without removing braces.
   Button and zipper for child who could not possibly master them.
3. Avoid:
   Frustration by getting clothing large enough.
   Zippers and snaps by using elastic waistbands. (If zippers are necessary use front zippers, not side ones.)
4. Putting on shoes—use footprints on the floor (draw footprints).
5. Activities to provide large muscle practice at dressing skills:

   Lacing: Beads; Fisher-Price lacing shoe; Dad's large shoes; large eyelet and lacing board.

   Snaps: Snap together toys; pop beads; large snaps found on tents.

   Buttons: Dad's old shirt; use large size buttons and oversized holes on pieces of cloth; pushing poker chips or buttons through a cardboard slit.

   Zippers: Use zippers on garment bags; put a big ring or string on a zipper to make it easier to pull up and down.

or showing the parent how to teach the child a particular skill. The parent then models the same behavior for the teacher, and the teacher provides feedback to the parent to reinforce or improve teaching and recording techniques.

The Cedar Rapids (Iowa) Comprehensive Early Childhood Project uses a combination of center and home based programing along with group meetings to program for parents and their children. They have developed a parent's guide (for examples see Figures 1 through 5) which includes written descriptions of behavior modification, responsive environments, and suggestions for helping to teach motor, language, and self help skills. Programed instruction is provided at group parent meetings and is individualized for the parent during the home visit.

Figure 5

Parent Guide Sheet on Teaching Independence
Comprehensive Early Childhood Project
(Cedar Rapids, Iowa)

PRINCIPLES OF TEACHING INDEPENDENCE

1. Know your child. Know what he can accomplish! Know what frustrates him!
2. See each learning skill as a pleasant one.
3. Teach each skill one step at a time.
4. Allow plenty of time and opportunities to work on each skill.
5. Be consistent.
6. The child needs some reason for doing what you want him to do. If you want your child to learn to put on his coat allow plenty of time each time he is going out to put on his coat. Children do not understand practice without reward.
7. Praise your child at every opportunity for each small accomplishment he makes towards learning the skill.
8. Do not expect perfection. Recognize what the child can and cannot do. Help your child to gain some confidence by letting his attempts stand on their own merit. Do not re-button his shirt for your own personal satisfaction.
9. Be flexible. Try many approaches to a skill until you find one that works.

One phase of the UNISTAPS Project in St. Paul, Minnesota, is the direct teaching of the parent. The teacher (tutor) demonstrates a specific activity with the child while the parent observes. Gradually the parent is encouraged to take the lead role, and feedback is provided to the parent as the tutor observes. These sessions are conducted weekly in a homelike atmosphere. The goal is for the parent to carry out the same activities with the child in the family's own home. The project director, Winifred Northcott, feels it is vital that parents learn teaching skills and apply them to their child since "parents are the child's first and best teachers; the home is the most important learning environment; and daily activities are the most vital sources of language input for young children" (ABT Associates, 1973, p. 9).

The Teaching Research Infant and Child Center in Monmouth, Oregon, uses a unique system of transferring information from classroom to home or from home to classroom. The system has been used with children in a center based program as a vehicle for involving parents in the direct teaching of their child at home. The parent is shown precisely what to do and how to do it, including the delivery of consequences to the child for the emitted behavior. Again, modeling is stressed as a key element. The daily reporting system (see Figure 6) passes information about the child's progress back and forth between the parent and the center and is dubbed the "lunch box data system." Staff and parents have found this to be an effective system, aiding each in the coordination of instructional activities. Face to face contact and phone calls act as a backup for the system.

The Portage Project in Wisconsin is a totally home based program. A home teacher visits each family weekly for 1½ hours. Curriculum goals are individualized for each child and are demonstrated to the parent as baseline data are collected. Again, emphasis is placed on teacher-parent modeling as the key teaching component. The parent then works with the child during the remaining 6 days and records the child's progress daily on activity charts (see Figure 7). The home teacher teaches the parents and the parents teach the child. The precision teaching model that is implemented provides ongoing feedback to both staff and parents, which in turn provides objective data for the continual modification of curriculum objectives.

The Alaska Head Start Special Services Project provides a demonstration home to work with families of hearing impaired or deaf children who come to Anchorage from throughout the state. The intense training covers a 5-day period in which the family is taught specific skills for fostering language development. Followup is provided weekly by a person in the community who has been trained to work with the deaf child and his family. In addition, each family receives idea sheets (see Figure 8), which provide teaching suggestions to the parents.

Project TAPP (Technical Assistance to Preschool Programs) at the University of Wyoming (Laramie) is designed for parents of children with communicative disorders and consists in part of an 8 week summer clinic program. One of the major goals of this intensive training is to provide the opportunity for parents to acquire adequate skills to stimulate their child's speech and language development, both in a clinical situation and a home setting. Parents are then able to implement language therapy and behavior management practices during ses-

Figure 6

Home Recording Sheet
Teaching Research Infant and Child Center
(Monmouth, Oregon)

BEHAVIORAL TREATMENT CLINIC

838–1220, Ext. 401

Data for Dressing Program
being coordinated at home
Removes pants and underpants

Child's Name ____Johnnie____

Steps

5. Child pushes down to ankles, grabs cuffs and removes pants.
4. Child pushes down to ankles, grabs cuffs and removes pants when pulled to thighs.
3. Child pushes down to ankles, grabs cuffs and removes pants when pulled to knees.
2. Child grabs cuffs and removes pants when pulled to ankles.
1. Child grabs cuffs and removes pants when one leg removed.

Date	Reinforcer Used	Phase	Step	1	2	3	4	5	6	7	8	9	10	Comments
home { 2/1/74	Juice - social	II	1	x	o	x	o	x	x	x				
2/1/74	Juice - social		2	o	x	x								

Figure 7

Sample Activity Chart
Cooperative Educational Service Agency 12
(Portage, Wisconsin)

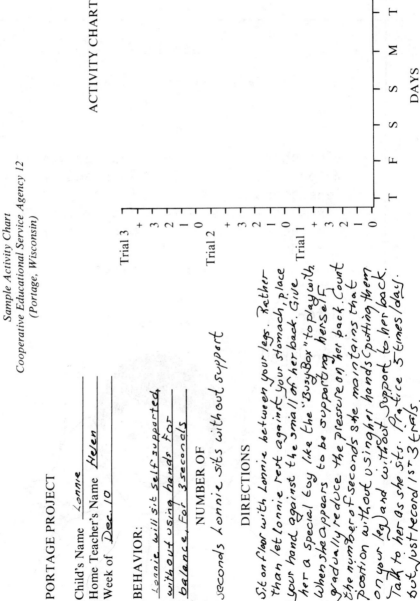

PORTAGE PROJECT

Child's Name _Lonnie_

Home Teacher's Name _Helen_

Week of _Dec. 10_

BEHAVIOR:

Lonnie will sit self supported
without using hands for
balance, for 3 seconds

NUMBER OF

seconds Lonnie sits without support

DIRECTIONS

Sit on floor with Lonnie between your legs. Rather
than let Lonnie rest against your stomach, place
your hand against the small of her back. Give
her a special toy like the "BusyBox" to play with.
When she appears to be supporting herself
gradually reduce the pressure on her back. Count
the number of seconds she maintains that
position without using her hands (putting them
on your leg) and without support to her back.
Talk to her as she sits. Practice 5 times/day.
but just record 1st 3 trials.

ACTIVITY CHART

Trial 3   + 3 2 1 0

Trial 2   + 3 2 1 0

Trial 1   + 3 2 1 0

T F S S M T W T

DAYS

Figure 8

Idea Sheet
Alaska Head Start Special Services Project
(Anchorage, Alaska)

sions with their child while receiving suggestions and reinforcement from the clinician (see Figure 9).

The Preschool and Early Education Project at Mississippi State University (Starkville) has developed the *Parents Can Teach, Too* booklet. It lists content and techniques of teaching so parents can more effectively reinforce and teach their own child.

The services provided by the Rutland Center in Athens, Georgia, focus primarily on assisting parents in implementing a parallel home program and providing parents with information about the child's progress and needs. The individualized parent program typically calls for initial contact and "tuning in" to the child's needs from a developmental reference point, frequent communication with the center's teachers, home programs, and parent observation and actual participation in the classes. Center support and communication are decreased as the parent develops necessary coping skills and a realistic understanding of the child.

The staff of the Julia Ann Singer Preschool Early Education Program in Los Angeles, California, views parents as staff partners. Their goal, too, is to provide parents with specific knowledge and techniques to alter behavioral problems in their children as well as an opportunity to practice these skills in a controlled environment, under the supervision of a staff member. The staff feels this approach is valuable in averting overdependency on the teacher. It also helps to bring out the parents' strengths, reaffirming the agency's message to them that parents are capable people and that the "professionals" *know* that parents can adequately perform their parenting role.

Recruiter

The Model Preschool Center for Handicapped Children at the University of Washington in Seattle has developed a parent to parent program. "Old" parents talk with pediatricians, letting them know they are willing to visit and talk with parents who have recently been told they have a handicapped child. These "new" parents are then informed about resources that are available to help the family and child.

Most projects have not developed such a structured system. However, a great majority welcome and solicit referrals from parents regarding their own child or someone else's child.

Curriculum Developer

The Teaching Research Infant and Child Center (Monmouth, Oregon) encourages parents to select behavior they wish to target for modification. They recommend that the parent's choice be honored if at all possible. Their choices most likely represent skills that, if taught, will be reinforcing to and reinforced by the parent.

The same philosophy underlies the Portage Project (Wisconsin). After assessment, staff offer the parents a choice of at least five behaviors their child is ready

Figure 9

Example of Parent Training Content
Project TAPP
(Laramie, Wyoming)

COMMUNICATIVE DISORDERS AND PARENT TRAINING PROGRAM
UNIVERSITY OF WYOMING

POSITIVE VERBAL GUIDANCE

Using words in guiding children can be helpful or confusing, according to our choice of phrases. Many children develop a protective "deafness" against adult directions because they hear too many of them.

In helping young children learn through verbal directions one must first get the child's attention. Then use clear, short, meaningful phrases that are expectant and encouraging. Directions are positive rather than negative in form, and are always specific. One should give just what verbal help is needed by the child.

She will usually say this:	Instead of saying this:
"You may hold your glass." (Specific, positive, expectant)	"Oh, aren't you going to drink your water?" (Negative, raises doubt)
"You need to turn off the faucet." (Specific, positive)	"Don't turn on so much water." (Negative)
"Yes, you may go walking after you take your nap." (Encouraging)	"No, you can't go walking until after you take your nap." (Discouraging)
"We stay inside the fence." (Positive, specific, tells what to do)	"Don't go out in the street." (Negative, fails to tell what to do)
"Let's stack the long, red blocks on the shelf. There's a green block." (Specific, expectant)	"Get your blocks out of the way now." (Not interesting)
"You are ready to lie still and rest." (Specific, expectant)	"Aren't you ever going to be quiet?" (Does not tell what to do)
(To child painting) "We just paint on the paper. That's a lovely red, isn't it?" (Positive, appreciative)	"Now don't get paint on your clothes. That doesn't look much like a dog." (Negative, discouraging)
"Hold the pitcher steady and walk slowly." (Specific, tells what to do to avoid accident)	"Be careful. You are going to spill that water." (Negative, discouraging, not helpful)

to learn next. Parents are asked to select or target the goal they believe to be most important as they perceive the child and his needs.

The Rutland Center in Athens, Georgia, has parents help the staff by listing objectives they believe to be important to them and their child.

The Gila River Indian Community Handicapped Children's Early Education Program in Sacaton, Arizona, actively solicits parental help in planning curriculum goals by asking, "What are some of the things you think are important for your child to learn?"

Counselor

The UNISTAPS Project in St. Paul, Minnesota, has a program component called "Pop-n-Parents." This is a group of former parents of the early intervention program who visit new parents in their homes. The purpose of the visit is to provide emotional support and encouragement to new families and to help them understand the program's benefits for the child as well as themselves. The parents are trained to fulfill this supportive role and to work closely with the project staff informing them of the family's needs, problems, and progress.

The Julia Ann Singer Preschool Program in Los Angeles, California, has used parents both to teach new parents what the program has to offer and also to teach actual teaching techniques.

Parent meetings have often served as a vehicle for parent to parent support programs. The Cedar Rapids (Iowa) Comprehensive Early Childhood Project has weekly parent meetings as a major component. Parents help each other set up behavior modification programs for their children to be implemented by them in their own home. Group members help each other target behaviors for change and reinforce each other when the behavioral goals are met.

Project TAPP at the University of Wyoming (Laramie) in its summer workshop for parents provides the opportunity to share experiences and ideas with other parents.

United Cerebral Palsy of New York City, Inc., has also sponsored summer workshops for parents with the major objectives of teaching the family to understand the handicapping condition and involving the family in the child's rehabilitation program.

Assessor of Skills

The Schaumburg (Illinois) Early Education Center encourages parents to evaluate their own child through a list of screening questions included in the project's brochure, *Early Childhood Education for Children with Unique Emotional Needs* (see Figure 10). Parents are then asked to contact project staff if they believe their child might benefit from the program.

The Portage Project in Wisconsin uses knowledge the parents have in the screening and assessment process of their child. All testing is done in front of the parents in the familiar environment of the home. One of the instruments selected is a parent questionnaire. Parents are thus encouraged to be immediately and

Figure 10

List of Screening Questions from Parents Brochure
Schaumburg Early Education Center
(Schaumburg, Illinois)

AM I INVOLVED?

Yes, if you are of the opinion that your child has unique **needs**. If you are not sure, compare your child's present development with this list of behaviors that are characteristic of three to four year olds.

All children have strengths and weaknesses. However, if you answer "no" to five or more of these questions, you may wish to seek further help, to see if he qualifies for an early childhood program. If your concerns are not reflected by this list, please feel free to contact the public school nearest your home.

A child of age three to four can do these things: **Can Mine?**

1. Can walk on a line   _____
2. Can walk up and down stairs   _____
3. Can throw a big ball   _____
4. Can walk on tiptoes   _____
5. Can touch thumb to each of the other finger-
    tips on the same hand   _____
6. Can cut paper with scissors   _____
7. Can say at least one nursery rhyme, poem, or
    song from memory
8. Can whisper   _____
9. Can brush teeth   _____
10. Can wash hands unassisted   _____
11. Can care for self at toilet   _____
12. Can undress self   _____
13. Can tell how simple objects are used (i.e.,
    fork, crayon, ball)   _____
14. Can speak in three to four word sentences   _____
15. Can copy drawings of horizontal lines,
    vertical lines, and circles   _____
16. Can initiate own play   _____
17. Can hold up fingers to signify age   _____
18. Can count three objects   _____
19. Can repeat three digits (say 1, 3, 9; 3, 5, 1)   _____
20. Can give an account of a recent event   _____
21. Can tell his or her own sex   _____
22. Can show five body parts: head, mouth, nose, ears,
    eyes, arms, hands, fingers, legs, feet, toes   _____
23. Can be understood by playmates and adults   _____
24. Can imitate movements (i.e., raise your arms;
    shake your head)   _____
25. Can listen attentively to short, simple stories   _____
26. Can match some colors   _____
27. Can play well with other children   _____
28. Can solve simple play problems independently   _____
29. Can show **appropriate** emotional responses
    (smiling, laughing, crying, anger)   _____
30. Can respond and relate to family friends and
    acquaintances without undue fear or shyness   _____

directly involved with the project from the beginning. Staff have found the information parents have about their child and his present and emerging behaviors to be a valuable resource for individualized curriculum planning.

Evaluator and Record Keeper

One goal shared by several of the First Chance projects is to teach parents to take data and maintain records of their child's performance both at home and in the classroom. The Model Preschool Center at the University of Washington (Seattle) teaches parents to chart their child's performance. This reinforces the parents since they can evaluate the progress their child is making as a result of the program.

Evaluation of curriculum for the parents at home and the teacher at school is one of the purposes of the lunch box data system as it functions in Monmouth, Oregon. Both parent and teacher are provided with objective data concerning the child's progress. Based on this data, curriculum goals are modified so that the child continues to progress and the parents continue to experience success in teaching their child at home.

All parents served by the Portage Project are asked to keep daily records of their child's behavior on activity sheets. Over the past 5 years of project operation, daily recording by the parents has averaged about 91%. This seems to indicate that parents *like* to record. It appears that parents are reinforced by recording since they can then see small gains that might otherwise go unnoticed. Since parents themselves are implementing the project by teaching their own children, recording progress is even more rewarding.

The great majority of First Chance projects use parents as a major resource for measuring program effectiveness. Based on this feedback, projects have modified goals, objectives, and procedures as they relate to the services they are providing to parents and children.

The Chapel Hill (North Carolina) Training Outreach Project solicits feedback from parents using a questionnaire. These questions deal with the amount and degree of parental satisfaction with the project's operations including communication with parents, helpfulness of home programing, staff availability, and the like. The quality of the services provided by the project can then be reassessed and modified to keep up with parental needs and expectations.

THE "HOW TO'S" OF PARENT TRAINING

Because the literature places great stress on meaningful involvement of parents as partners in their child's education, this "how to" section will deal with parent training—teaching parents to work effectively with their own child.

First the project staff needs to believe, and to exhibit the belief, that parent involvement is vital and that without parents as allies and partners the program will have little long term effect. However, the development of this belief on the part of staff is not always easy. Earl Jones (1973) from the Julia Ann Singer Preschool (Los Angeles, California) expressed this very well as he described traditional attitudes regarding parents:

There has been an unfortunate tendency on the part of some highly skilled professionals to view parents of disturbed [and handicapped] children as the ones "who made their kids sick" and at the same time, to view the children as "victims" who must be saved from the "bad guys." True, in these agencies parents are usually given social work therapy, but it has been suggested that this just underlines their sense of failure and incompetence particularly as they observe their children interacting more wholesomely with the "professional" parental substitute. Consequently, very little seems to be done in an active demonstrable way to foster the strength of parents. (p. 22)

Many parents do not believe that we are serious about helping them become staff partners. They usually translate this into a belief that we want them to be janitors, file clerks, or second-rate teacher's aides. (p. 24)

Parents probably react this way on the basis of their past experience with school systems and other "helping" agencies. Centers ask for parent volunteers; yet, the responsibilities given to the parents are not meaningful to them or, in fact, to the program. Too frequently they are asked to run ditto machines, toilet the children, and clean up after the teacher. They are asked to repair what someone else has broken or to cut out circles, squares, and triangles by the dozen. This tends to reinforce the parents' belief that they are ineffective since little attempt is made to teach them what they can do to help their own child. Thus parents get the impression that, although their child needs special help, this help can only be provided by someone else.

One project director stated that parents who volunteer in their teaching program generally do not work with their own child. Volunteer parents are viewed as being a significant help in the classroom, and yet it is likely that the parents are more capable of teaching someone else's child than their own.

The authors believe, based on experience in the Portage Project, which teaches parents to teach their own child, that the most effective way of remediating behavioral excesses or deficits is to teach the child's first teacher to become the child's best teacher. And the staff must believe that this can be accomplished. Specific procedures can then be developed to meet this objective.

There are several important techniques or procedures used by the Portage staff that they believe help initiate and maintain parent involvement:

1. Set goals at a level the child and parent will accomplish within a short time, for instance, a week.
2. Model for the parents. Show them, do not just tell them, what to do.
3. After modeling, allow the parents to take over and work on the same activity with the child while the teacher observes.
4. Reinforce the parents. Let them know they are doing it right.
5. Remember that parents are *not* the same. It is as important to individualize for the parents based on their present behavior as it is to individualize for the child based on his.
6. Involve the parents in planning appropriate goals for the child.

Setting Short Term Goals

In planning individualized goals for a child and the parents, who are going to teach him, it is important that the chosen goal be one that can be achieved within a week. There may be times when this goal will not be met; however, it is extremely important that successes come frequently and quickly, especially in the beginning. When the child succeeds, the parents succeed. They are the ones who are doing the teaching.

All parents teach, but the degree of success they achieve (as measured by what the child learns) will be directly related to the goal chosen. If the parent tries to teach a child to walk before he can stand, to say words meaningfully before he understands what the words mean, to comply with all requests when he complies with none, neither the parent nor the child will succeed. Parents will not be systematically reinforced for working with their child on developmental tasks. Behaviors that are not reinforced are eventually extinguished. The Portage staff hypothesizes that this is one reason parents seem eager to turn the responsibility of teaching over to someone else. They have failed so often, they do not want to try again.

The technique of task analysis will help parents and staff to concentrate on one small segment of one behavior. As Fredericks and his colleagues (1974) have pointed out:

> When this task is being taught to the child, the parent is not faced with having to teach the entire task, but only one small step at a time. The chances for the parent to see some progress are greater and thus the parent will be reinforced. (p. 29)

In planning curriculum, the goal of the Portage Project is that the prescribed activity be one that can be achieved by the child in a week, regardless of the severity of the child's handicap. In the beginning, the teacher, using the parent's knowledge of the child, will plan what that activity might be. The premise is that all children are learners and it is just a question of what the child is ready to learn next. "The chosen goal should be based as much on the likelihood of success as on the importance of the skill" (Shearer, 1974, p. 58).

Showing the Parent What To Do

A common complaint of teachers is that when they have made a special effort to involve parents by giving them ideas and suggestions to carry out at home, parents do not follow through. Several programs have found that it is necessary to *show* parents what to do. Teachers certainly would not tell a child, when introducing a new task, "Okay, Susie, stack blocks." The teacher would model the behavior first so the child would have a concrete example to follow. Modeling, then, is an important and necessary step for parents since they too are learning new skills.

The Oregon intervention program in Monmouth and the Portage Project in

Wisconsin stress the importance of modeling and precise instructions to parents. Every aspect of the teaching paradigm is modeled for the parent including the positioning of the child, the physical aid necessary to insure success, the placement of cues or materials, the criteria for success, and the delivery of consequences.

Another major advantage of modeling is that the teacher will get an indication of how likely it is that the child will accomplish the task within the designated time. Perhaps the goal is too advanced. By trying it out, the teacher will be able to adjust the goal, thereby increasing the likelihood of success for parent and child. Targeted behaviors such as temper tantrums may have to be instigated so that the prescribed method of reducing their frequency can be modeled for the parent. Parents are much more likely to follow a "time out" procedure if shown what to do than if told what to do. If the remedial technique does not work, other techniques are tried until one is found that does work. Again, teachers are modeling behavior for parents.

Parents should be asked to practice the same activity with their child that the teacher has just modeled. Visual feedback through the use of videotape and/or verbal feedback from the teacher will increase parental awareness of clues and aid they may be giving inadvertently. Seeing how the child reacts to praise or other rewards can increase their use by parents, which increases frequency of correct response, which in turn increases the likelihood of success by parent and child. The teacher can spot and correct problems and reinforce good parental teaching, and this will increase the likelihood that the parent will continue teaching the child when the teacher is not present. The opportunity to practice in front of a nonthreatening observer who can offer help and reinforcement is an important procedure that helps to teach parents to be a catalyst for change.

Reinforcing the Parents

All people are more likely to perform behaviors that are reinforced. It is important to praise parental involvement and to praise specific behavior. "I like the way you praised Mary when she got it right." "It's great you recorded every day; that helps to see the progress he's making." "He's got it—and you taught him."

It is very important to praise improvement in teaching behavior and not to expect or demand perfection. Applying good teaching techniques may mean breaking long established parental behavior patterns such as frequently doing things for the child that he can do for himself, ignoring "good" behaviors and attending to "bad" ones, and not talking to the child because he never responds anyway. It does take time, practice, and reinforcement to change old patterns, and parents should be praised for small improvements. Eventually the success parents are having with their own child will serve as the major reinforcer—that the child can learn as a result of their own teaching.

Individualizing for Parents

If one of the project's objectives is to teach parents to teach the child, then it should be recognized that the teacher must individualize planning for both the child and the parent. Each parent, like each child, will present different entry skills. Factors such as working parents, number of siblings and their ages, and the parents' educational competency will need to be considered in programing. Portage staff have trained retarded parents to teach their child effectively. Baby-sitters in conjunction with parents have been successfully used as the primary teacher. The special skills of the parents should be taken into account and then used for the good of the project and the child. The teacher should build on the skills the parent already possesses however minimal they may seem, and go on from there.

Involving Parents in Planning

As parents experience success in teaching their child, the teacher should increase their involvement in planning weekly goals and writing objectives. Help can be reduced as the parents gain in skill. In this way, rather than becoming dependent on the teacher, parents will become confident and self reliant in planning the curriculum as well as teaching it. Not everyone learns at the same rate; some parents will reach this stage 6 months after program initiation, some after 6 years. It is possible to fade or reduce aid as the parents demonstrate readiness but the teacher should always be ready to give support and reinforcement, help, and encouragement based on their needs.

A FINAL COMMENT

The authors were impressed with the quality of parental involvement in the First Chance projects. Much of what has been referred to in this chapter is a direct result of BEH's recognition and insistence that parents must be involved in the projects they fund. It is fair to say BEH was the catalyst and the projects took it from there, developing new models for parent involvement.

Through outreach and training efforts of these BEH projects, more educators throughout the country are learning that parents are the child's first teacher and that with appropriate staff training, staff encouragement, and staff respect parents can learn to be the child's best teacher.

REFERENCES

ABT Associates, Inc. *Exemplary programs for the handicapped* (Vol. 3). (ERIC No. ED 079890) 1973.

Ackerman, P., & Moore, M. *The delivery of educational services to pre-school handicapped children in the United States—The state of the art—1974.* Paper presented at Conference on Early Intervention for High Risk Infants and Young Children, Chapel Hill, North Carolina, 1974.

Airlie House Conference on Parent Involvement in BEH Projects, Arlington, Virginia, 1972.

Brofenbrenner, V. *A report on longitudinal evaluations of preschool programs* (Vol. 2) *Is early intervention effective?* Washington, DC: Department of Health, Education, and Welfare, 1974.

Devoid, R., & Mills, P. *A parent task force group.* Brattleboro VT: Winston Prouty Center for Child Development, 1972. (project paper)

Fredericks, H D., Baldwin, V., & Grove, D. *A home-center parent training model.* In J. Grimm (Ed.), *Training parents to teach: Four models.* Chapel Hill NC: Technical Assistance Development Systems, 1974.

Gilmer, B., Miller, J. O., & Gray, S. W. *Intervention with mothers and young children: Study of intra-family effects.* Nashville TN: DARCEE Demonstration and Research Center for Early Education, 1970.

Gray, S. W., & Klaus, R. A. The early training project: The seventh-year report. *Child Development,* 1970, *41,* 909–924.

Hayden, A. H. Educating families of handicapped children in a multidisciplinary center-school environment. In J. Grimm (Ed.), *Training parents to teach: Four models.* Chapel Hill NC: Technical Assistance Development Systems, 1974.

Jones, E. F. *Parents as staff partners.* Los Angeles: Julia Ann Singer Preschool, 1973. (Project paper)

Klaus, R. A., & Gray, S. W. The early training project for disadvantaged children: A report after five years. *Monographs of the Society for Research in Child Development,* 1968, *33* (4, Serial No. 120).

Lillie, D. Dimensions in parent programs: An overview. In J. Grimm (Ed.), *Training parents to teach: Four models.* Chapel Hill NC: Technical Assistance Development Systems, 1974.

President's Committee on Mental Retardation (PCMR) Leadership Training Conference, Ann Arbor, Michigan, 1972.

Shearer, D. E., & Shearer, M. *The Portage Project.* Paper presented at Conference on Early Intervention for High Risk Infants and Young Children, Chapel Hill, North Carolina, 1974.

Shearer, M. The Portage Project—Parent involvement in a home-based model. In J. Grimm (Ed.), *Training parents to teach: Four models.* Chapel Hill NC: Technical Assistance Development Systems, 1974.

Shearer, M., & Shearer, D. E. The Portage Project: A model for early childhood education. *Exceptional Children,* 1972, *39,* 210–217.

RESOURCES

Child Management Materials. Comprehensive Children's Services for Rural and Non-Urban Areas, Fargo, North Dakota. (Available from Southeast Mental Health and Retardation Center, 700 First Avenue South, Fargo ND 58102. $10.00.)

Developmental Levels of Waterbug Swimming Skills. Alaska Head Start Special Services Project, Anchorage, Alaska. (Available from Easter Seal Society, 726 E Street, Anchorage AK 99501. $1.00.)

Early Childhood Education for Children with Unique Educational Needs. Schaumburg Early Education Center, Schaumburg, Illinois. 1973. (Available from SEEC Communications, 804 W. Bode Road, Schaumburg IL 60172.)

Fears in the Preschool Child. Alaska Head Start Special Services Project, Anchorage, Alaska. (Available from Easter Seal Society, 726 E Street, Anchorage AK 99501. Pamphlet, $1.00; slides/audio cassette, $35.00.)

Freddie Fetus. Alaska Head Start Special Services Project, Anchorage, Alaska. (Available from Easter Seal Society, 726 E Street, Anchorage AK 99501. $1.00.)

Giving a Head Start to Parents of the Handicapped: A Resource Book for Preschool Staff Who Counsel Parents. Technical Assistance Resource Center in Early Childhood Education for the Handicapped, Omaha, Nebraska. 1976. (Available from Meyer Children's Rehabilitation Institute, University of Nebraska Medical Center, 444 S. 44th Street, Omaha NB 68131. $3.00.)

Homemade Developmental Toys and Activities. Alaska Head Start Special Services Project, Anchorage, Alaska. 1974. (Available from Easter Seal Society, 726 E Street, Anchorage AK 99501. $3.50.)

Homemade Equipment. Ochlocknee Multi-Handicapped Outreach Project, Ochlocknee, Georgia. (Available from the project, P. O. Box 110-A, Ochlocknee GA 31773. Free.)

Learn and Earn Together Catalog. Comprehensive Children's Services for Rural and Non-Urban Areas, Fargo, North Dakota. (Available from Southeast Mental Health and Retardation Center, 700 First Avenue South, Fargo ND 58102. $3.00.)

Meet Baby. Early Childhood Learning Center, El Paso, Texas. 1974. (Available from the center, P. O. Box 10716, El Paso TX 79997. $4.50.)

PACT Learning PAC. Comprehensive Children's Services for Rural and Non-Urban Areas, Fargo, North Dakota. (Available from Southeast Mental Health and Retardation Center, 700 First Avenue South, Fargo ND 58102. $15.00.)

A Parent Task Force Group (project paper). Vermont Parent/Child Development Center, Brattleboro, Vermont. 1972. (For availability information contact the center, 2 Oak Street, Brattleboro VT 05301.)

Parental and Classroom Speech Helps for Children. Magnolia Preschool Handicapped Project, Magnolia, Arkansas. 1974. (Available from West Side Preschool Program, P. O. Box 428, Magnolia AR 71753. $2.00.)

Parents Are Teachers Too. A Nationally Organized Collaborative Project to Provide Comprehensive Services for Atypical Infants and Their Families, New York, New York. 1975. (Available from UCPA, Inc., 66 E. 34th Street, New York NY 10016. Rental, $7.50 for three days.)

Parents as Staff Partners (project paper). Julia Ann Singer Preschool Psychiatric Center, Los Angeles, California. 1973. (For availability information contact the center, 8730 Alden Drive, Los Angeles CA 90048.)

Parents Can Teach, Too. Preschool and Early Education Project, Starkville, Mississippi. (In *Selected Readings in Early Education of Handicapped Children.* Available from The Council for Exceptional Children, 1920 Association Drive, Reston VA 22091. Order no. 85. $4.25.)

Preschool Personality Traits. Alaska Head Start Special Services Project, Anchorage, Alaska. (Available from Easter Seal Society, 726 E Street, Anchorage AK 99501. Slides/audio cassette, $35.00; rental, $10.00.)

Sharing Ideas of Family Involvement in Programs for Atypical Infants. A Nationally Organized Collaborative Project to Provide Comprehensive Services for Atypical Infants and Their Families, New York, New York. 1976. (Available from UCPA, Inc., 66 E. 34th Street, New York NY 10016. Rental, $7.50 for three days.)

Talking and Listening. Alaska Head Start Special Services Project, Anchorage, Alaska. (Available from Easter Seal Society, 726 E Street, Anchorage AK 99501. Book, $2.00; slides/audio cassette, $45.00.)

Toys and Other Things for Children by Parents. Comprehensive Children's Services for Rural and Non-Urban Areas, Fargo, North Dakota. (Available from Southeast Mental Health and Retardation Center, 700 First Avenue South, Fargo ND 58102. $2.00.)

Who Cares? Alaska Head Start Special Services Project, Anchorage, Alaska. (Available from Easter Seal Society, 726 E Street, Anchorage AK 99501. Slides/audio cassette, $45.00.)

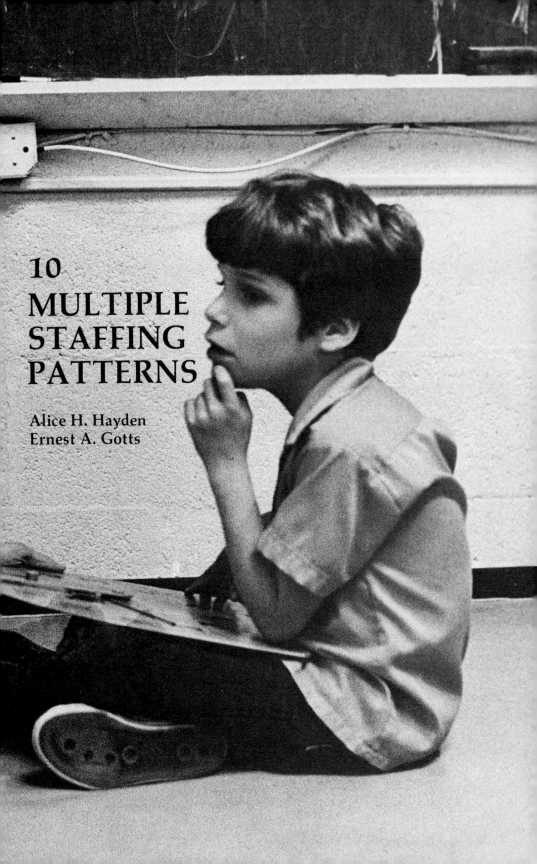

10
MULTIPLE
STAFFING
PATTERNS

Alice H. Hayden
Ernest A. Gotts

□What factors influence or determine staffing patterns and costs for providing education and other services for young handicapped children? This is not an easy question to answer, but it is obvious that those attempting to provide such programs must take into account a number of considerations essential to providing an exemplary program or programs for children with different types of handicapping conditions, for example, the severity of the handicapping conditions and the age level or levels of the children to be served. What is feasible in one geographic area or setting may not be feasible in another setting. Those in programs that seek to serve young handicapped children in rural areas may need to cope with situations that are quite different from those serving children in an urban area. Available resources vary from one setting to another. What mode or modes of service delivery can best meet the needs of young handicapped children and their families in a particular community? How much service is needed, over what period of time? What type of schedule or schedules are most appropriate for the age range of the children served? What staff competencies and levels of training are essential to effective programs?

Some staffing patterns are prescribed to a degree by the nature of the setting or by the funding agency or agencies, but there are usually some opportunities for innovative planning and effective deployment of resources. At least one thing is abundantly clear—no single staffing pattern will suffice for all programs. Adaptations may need to be made as data on pupil progress are gathered and analyzed and as parents request changes or additions in services.

But there are many other factors that influence and determine staffing patterns and costs of programs. There are also other variables that may have influence or impact on programs for early childhood/special education.

INFLUENCES ON EARLY CHILDHOOD/SPECIAL EDUCATION PROGRAMS

Federal Legislation, Mandates, and Certification Requirements

The Handicapped Children's Early Education Assistance Act of 1968 provided opportunities for the development of exemplary programs to provide education and services to young handicapped children. The benefits of these programs and the efforts of the Bureau of Education for the Handicapped (BEH) to provide and to improve programs serving handicapped children from 0 to 8 years of age are well known to those in the field of special education. The First Chance Network and other networks of projects delivering technical assistance and outreach services have grown out of this legislation. Projects have been funded in practically every state; some have served handicapped children from 0 to 3; others have served handicapped children in other early childhood age brackets. Some projects have had multiple programs; others have served only a particular group of children. All of the project staffs have had responsibilities for evaluation and dissemination.

More recent federal legislation, Public Law 94–142, the Education for All Handicapped Children Act of 1975, will gradually extend education and other services to all handicapped children age 3 and over. Every person interested in programs for handicapped children should become well acquainted and be in compliance with the provisions of this new legislation.

Head Start Mandate

The Economic Opportunity Act Amendments of 1972, Public Law 92–424, mandated the inclusion of at least 10% of children with handicapping conditions in Head Start. Such children were to be recruited, enrolled, and integrated or mainstreamed. Head Start had certainly not excluded handicapped children from their programs previously, but there had been no special mandate to enroll a certain percentage of children with handicapping conditions. Initially, the mandate carried no special or additional funding to implement this new requirement, and many staff members felt ill prepared to cope with this new mandate.

Fortunately, the Congress later recognized the need to provide additional funding to implement this mandate. The Bureau of Education for the Handicapped and the Office of Child Development have endeavored to coordinate and further efforts to serve handicapped children in Head Start and other programs. Procedures have been developed for verifying the handicapping conditions of the children included in the 10% figure. Some programs actually enroll a greater percentage of handicapped children. The necessity for technical assistance and additional staff training has been recognized and such services are being provided through a number of channels.

Certification and Standards

Certification requirements for some personnel are determined at the national level by different organizations. For example, there are national requirements for certification in deaf education, in the education of the blind, and in the area of speech pathology and audiology. Staff who meet these national certification requirements do have special training regarded as essential in working with certain types of handicapped children. In some instances, programs must be in compliance with national standards (Head Start); in other instances, programs and facilities for the children served must be in compliance with standards set by state agencies. Teachers may need to meet different types of state certification requirements, particularly if the programs serving young handicapped children are operated within a school district. Support personnel and paraprofessionals may also need to meet certification requirements or to hold certain types of certificates. Such requirements may vary from state to state.

State Legislation Regulations

A number of states have passed legislation requiring services to handicapped children and youth from birth or specific ages to different upper age limits such as 18, 21, or 25. Many other states have recognized the importance of providing services and education for children below 3 years of age and have either required them or made such programs permissive. Some agencies or special projects have recognized the need for identifying and serving infants at risk. There is an increasing awareness of the need to provide treatment and services to children and their families in those early and crucial weeks, months, and years. There is also increased recognition that "formal schooling" usually intervenes only *after* this critical period has passed, but leaving potentially damaging impressions and effects on the child's physical, cognitive, social, communication, and language development.

In many states, rules and regulations have been formulated to help implement various types of legislation and to set standards with regard to facilities, programs, and staff-pupil ratios. The latter may vary considerably depending upon age level and the nature and severity of the handicapping condition(s).

Staff certification requirements may also be stipulated for teachers, paraprofessionals, and various support personnel such as psychologists, physical and occupational therapists, communication disorders specialists, social workers, school nurses, and other specialized personnel. Usually, the more qualified a staff member is, the higher he or she is on the pay schedule.

Affirmative Action Requirements

National and state efforts to provide equal employment opportunities for members of minority groups have had their influence on staffing patterns. There has also been an effort to provide career and training opportunities for staff serving in Head Start, Indian and migrant programs, bilingual programs, and other types of programs. Training programs in special education and in programs for the severely and profoundly handicapped have offered special opportunities to students entering these fields.

Parent Involvement

There has been an increasing awareness that parent involvement is important to all programs for young handicapped children. Parent involvement is integral to every effective program for handicapped children; parents serve in many different capacities: as child advocates, as members of advisory councils, as members of "parent to parent" programs, as classroom aides, as volunteers performing a variety of roles, and as effective agents applying procedures in the home setting. But parents have played many other important roles—they have influenced legislation, funding and staffing patterns, delivery systems, organizations, the professions, and the general public. They have demanded quality services and programs for their children. Without their help and assistance, many of the programs available today would not have been possible. Their efforts have been critical in the development of the concept of the right to education for all children and youth.

PROGRAM STAFFING: THE TEAM APPROACH

Thus it becomes evident that no one staffing pattern will suffice as a model for those attempting either to implement a new program serving young handicapped children or to reorganize a program already in existence. Every situation will differ in at least some parameters of the many factors that influence the staffing pattern: types of handicapping conditions, geographic setting, type of service delivery, goals of the program, requirements of funding agencies, and parent involvement, to name but a few. BEH exemplary early childhood education programs can be used as models of several different staffing patterns, each designed to provide aid for young exceptional children under a particular set of conditions, each with its own specific goals, each with a particular mode of service delivery. Several chapters in this volume deal with the particulars of the work done by various BEH projects. (Readers are referred to Chapter 3 by Merle Karnes in particular.) Program administrators and others involved in setting a staffing pattern for a program can look to these chapters for a model that would suit their needs, or form a composite by picking out those points from several examples that apply to their unique situation.

Yet some considerations apply to the implementation of any staffing pattern. Before staff can be hired, trained, or promoted, the roles to be filled and the qualifications for such staff must be specified.

A systematic and focused approach to defining staff roles, staff qualifications, staff competencies, and staffing requirements is possible. One prerequisite to developing behavioral descriptions of the competencies needed by staff members is a clear understanding of the scope of the work to be accomplished. The basic principle which underlies the definition of the work to be done is that the needs of the children and their families have preeminence in defining rules, staff to child ratios, and program goals. (For the purposes of this discussion the term *staff* refers only to full and part time paid employees. Parents and other volunteers are frequently involved and contribute a significant proportion of the work. But unless they are *paid* the discussion here does not necessarily relate to them.)

DEFINITION OF STAFF ROLES

Ordinarily when one thinks about employing staff or retraining existing personnel, some specific or essential area of work is envisioned. This is at times not entirely true in emerging programs for the early education of exceptional children since all of the work to be done may not be clearly defined or conceptualized by the program leadership. As a result, staff are frequently employed and existing staff are involved in somewhat indistinct and open ended undertakings. This makes for indistinct roles, overlapping or even conflicting responsibilities, gaps in assignment of responsibilities, and other related problems. Much staff time can be lost and much anxiety experienced because of a failure to develop a systematic and focused approach to staff role definition.

The program staff should play an integral part in the development of job descriptions. Together, the different roles and expectations of teachers and assistant teachers are developed. There is real merit in including the staff in role planning, as the whole staff then has an appreciation of the specific duties and relationships of each team member. When roles are reviewed, teachers should participate in revising them, and opportunities to move "within the program" should be available for staff members as they increase their preparation and skills in the performance of roles.

A Process for Role Defining

While it is impossible to formulate or establish specific role descriptions that will work in any setting, it is possible to suggest a *process* for working together as a staff to define and clarify roles. The steps in the process should help to:

1. Define the specifics of the scope of the work to be done. Develop a description of the program model specifying the intake, diagnostic, individualized program planning, direct services, and followup processes. Determine which specific objectives relate to intake (casefinding and the identification of the population to be served), diagnosis, and individualized planning and describe the activities necessary to achieve the objectives; that is, determine what work is implied by the kinds of activities necessary to achieve the program goals. Describe leadership roles in developing, supporting, monitoring, and evaluating the important areas of the work to be done.
2. Analyze areas of work and assign them in meaningful units to staff members. (Staff take responsibility for different areas of the work and begin to develop their areas of responsibility. They call on the leadership for assistance, resources, and feedback.)
3. Develop behavioral descriptions of the work staff who are actually involved and make some estimation of the time spent in various efforts.
4. Evaluate the work that is actually being done in terms of meeting all of the objectives and compare this with the general model of the work that needs to be done to identify gaps.
5. Develop the areas in which gaps were identified and, should the staff already be fully utilized in other areas, employ additional staff.
6. Formulate job or role descriptions from the second round of behavioral descriptions of staff work which follow Step 5 above.

Role of the Teachers

A specifically defined role for a teacher that might result from the process just described would include:

1. Designing the learning environment and scheduling changes in its arrangement to meet educational developmental objectives.
2. Designing the overall instructional pattern for the classroom including subject matter, selection of materials and media, development of learning activities, and cycling and recycling of learning modules.
3. Assessing and recording evaluations of children's development in all relevant developmental domains.

4. Managing child behavior problems.
5. Teaching individual children.
6. Teaching groups of children.
7. Performing routine child care activities.
8. Supervising any assistant teacher (e.g., teacher aide, parent or other volunteer, university student) in his or her various roles.
9. Relating to parents in order (a) to elicit information relevant to a child's welfare and educational programing and (b) to give information regarding the child's needs and progress and family support required.
10. Participating in training parents to extend objectives and activities of the school into the home environment.
11. Relating to other teachers and support staff in operating the service program and in professional efforts to increase early educational opportunities and to improve the quality of existing services.
12. Keeping records related to the operation of the classroom.

Role of the Assistant Teacher

Since many times assistant teachers are involved in early education programs for exceptional children, the following description of duties might result from the role definition process:

1. Setting up the learning environment with specific materials, equipment, and toys under the guidance and supervision of the teacher.
2. Helping the teacher maintain class and child records.
3. Helping the teacher in routine child care (dressing, toileting, washing routine, snack time, etc.)
4. Helping the teacher manage child behavior according to a preconceived plan of verbal and nonverbal controls.
5. Teaching individual children or small groups of children under direct supervision of the teacher.
6. Assisting the teacher at clean up time to prepare the learning environment for the coming day.
7. Relating to teachers, support personnel, and others to plan and operate the service program.
8. Developing new skills and knowledge bases to perform his or her role to a better extent.

Instructional Leader or Coordinator Role

Outside the direct area of the classroom, a program that is large enough to employ several teachers and assistant teachers may have a head teacher or coordinating teacher. A role definition for such a person might include the following:

1. Assisting in integrating the roles of teachers and teacher assistants as well as any specialized personnel such as occupational therapists, physical therapists, and speech therapists.

2. Maintaining overall planning and integrity of the instructional program design.
3. Modeling appropriate child care, child management, and teaching procedures for inservice training purposes.
4. Supervising teachers in the program.
5. Organizing teachers for parent work and education activities.
6. Keeping records of the planning and implementation process in cooperation with teachers.
7. Developing agenda for special meetings of staff or staff and parents.
8. Conducting educational staffings following sessions with children.
9. Working with the preschool coordinator/director to verify that all child and financial records of the classroom are up to date and complete.

Program Director Role

Some programs will be large and complex enough to require a leader who has little to do with direct instruction or direct services. A role definition for such a person that might come from the process defined earlier would include duties something like these:

1. Handling all business affairs (purchasing, maintenance, relationships to funding sources) or delegating as appropriate.
2. Keeping financial records for the program.
3. Seeking new funds for the program's development.
4. Preparing interim and final reports with the cooperation and assistance of the staff.
5. Working with the instructional coordinator to plan and schedule people and space.
6. Handling "external affairs" relations with other agencies.
7. Working with teachers and instructional coordinators in referral, followup, parent involvement, community education, and so forth.

Meeting Specific Program Requirements

Any definition of staff roles must include a caveat against applying general position descriptions to all types of settings; for example, universities and university affiliated facilities may have established channels that govern certain aspects of the project, such as the channel for handling finances or the one for reporting on budget expenditures. There are also different requirements of funding agencies that make it necessary to stay within certain boundaries within different categories of the budget. Role descriptions like those just given need to be adapted to the unique characteristics and requirements of the individual program. Some examples of specific staff role descriptions and competencies follow.

Competencies for an Intern

Under the supervision of a classroom teacher, an intern should:

1. Respond appropriately to (teacher) supervision and direction.
2. Work cooperatively with other program personnel.

3. Identify and define behaviors that promote learning.
4. Identify and define behaviors that interfere with learning.
5. Assess pupil skill levels for selection of or placement in curriculum.
6. Develop long range and short range learning and behavior objectives for pupils.
7. Write comprehensive, individualized instructional plans.
8. Implement individualized instructional plans on a one to one basis.
9. Collect daily performance data on children's instructional and social behavior tasks.
10. Use individual performance data to determine when to alter a child's instructional and management programs.
11. Alter individual instructional plans to facilitate pupil's achievement of objectives.
12. Collect periodic summative data on pupil performance gains.
13. Demonstrate child performance gains through direct daily data as well as with summative data.
14. Prepare quarterly reports of pupil progress.
15. Confer with parents regarding pupil progress.
16. Manage an educational program for 5 to 20 children (depending on degree of handicap) incorporating the preceding competencies.

Competencies for a Classroom Teacher

Under the general supervision of the principal, vice principal, or a coordinator, a classroom teacher should:

1. Demonstrate all competencies required of interns.
2. Respond to organizational priorities, needs, and objectives.
3. Plan and conduct single subject and/or small group research projects.
4. Demonstrate ability to utilize data analysis procedures on individual pupil data.
5. Analyze and interpret data and write reports of research results on these research projects (at least one project per quarter).
6. Demonstrate ability to evaluate, modify, devise, or write instructional programs.
7. Know and use objective procedures for establishing pupil performance criteria.
8. Demonstrate child performance gains for all pupils through summative or formative data.
9. Supervise trainees including graduate level interns, student teachers, project students, visiting teachers, volunteers, etc.
10. Plan, assign, and monitor the work of trainees assigned to the classroom.
11. Provide instruction and assistance to trainees assigned to the classroom regarding methods, procedures, etc.
12. Confer with parents, district personnel, and other professionals regarding pupil placement, progress, changes, or problems.
13. Know and use the sequence of activities by which children are referred to and enrolled at the program and returned to their home school districts.

14. Assist with the actual return of pupils to public school programs.
15. Initiate suggestions for improvements in organizational functioning including training, management, community relations, etc.
16. Demonstrate familiarity with literature and resources relevant to current population.
17. Utilize appropriate instructional methods, materials, and media for current population.
18. Utilize appropriate prosthetic and/or adaptive equipment.
19. Demonstrate and describe project and classroom procedures to visiting personnel.

Competencies for a Coordinator

Under the general supervision of the director, associate director, or principal, a coordinator should:

1. Demonstrate all competencies required of teachers and interns.
2. Anticipate and respond to organizational needs, priorities, and objectives.
3. Supervise subordinates in such a way as to procure high productivity and maintain positive attitudes.
4. Manage the training of graduate and undergraduate trainees using a training sequence, including both didactic and practicum experiences and providing written, audio, video, or other feedback.
5. Consult with other agencies, including local school districts, regarding project procedures whose effectiveness has been demonstrated.
6. Assist in staffing organization and changes and in recruiting and advancement of personnel.
7. Facilitate communication among staff members under coordinator's supervision to achieve effective and efficient program management.
8. Facilitate communication between the coordinator and administrative and teaching personnel to achieve effective and efficient program management.
9. Initiate suggestions for improvement in instructional and management techniques for pupils.
10. Initiate suggestions for program improvement to relevant administrative and/or instructional personnel.
11. Oversee parent conferencing and coordination activities.
12. Provide training of persons under coordinator's supervision, i.e., teachers, staff interns, etc., including didactic and practicum (with appropriate observation and feedback).
13. Supervise planning for total classroom management.
14. Approve classroom and purchase requests and work orders before forwarding them to administration.
15. Plan and implement followup activities to be completed when a pupil is returned to referring district.
16. Coordinate all services for individual children, e.g., communications, nursing, occupational therapy, medical, family concerns, etc.

17. Familiarize instructional team members with training research, development, and service priorities that affect program operations.
18. Assist in establishing, evaluating, and implementing admission and monitoring procedures for referred children.
19. Prepare quarterly reports summarizing the coordinator's and the team's activities and responsibilities.

Competencies for an Administrator

An administrator should:

1. Know university and funding agencies' priorities, goals, and objectives, and develop program priorities, goals, and objectives.
2. Know and be in compliance with legal and fiscal responsibilities.
3. Assess program and personnel needs based on external and internal constraints.
4. Develop training objectives, strategies, and policies.
5. Develop research objectives, strategies, and policies.
6. Develop service/demonstration objectives, strategies, and policies.
7. Formulate general plan/strategy for achievement of objectives.
8. Formulate task and time line sequence for achieving general plan.
9. Formulate evaluation/monitoring procedures to determine progress en route to program objectives.
10. Assign responsibility for achievement of objectives.
11. Monitor personnel progress toward objectives for decision making purposes.
12. Provide ongoing feedback and reinforcement to personnel as they complete activities and objectives.
13. Provide opportunities for staff to participate in programs, conferences, and workshops.
14. Encourage team approach, professional development, and publication.

DEVELOPING TEAM APPROACHES

The foregoing discussions imply throughout that early childhood programs are staffed by teams of individuals whose responsibilities interlock and whose roles are interdependent. Also implied are different levels of training from paraprofessional to very high levels of professional preparation. Various professions, with their different points of view, are involved. The complexity of exceptional children's unique needs determines the complexity of the staffing situation. Nowhere in the present discussion have the vast areas of medical treatment, health, and habilitation efforts been touched upon. Yet these areas are integral parts of most comprehensive service programs for the exceptional child in early childhood. Also not included has been the large area of parent-family counseling.

Rather than attempt to deal with the immense problem of interdisciplinary teaming in comprehensive programs, this discussion focuses primarily on those individuals who are most directly involved in the educational or developmental intervention programs. This delimitation is artificial but necessary. Many of the points made here about the educational or developmental team will apply to all service areas included in a program.

Because levels of training are different, the professional backgrounds varied, and the roles differentiated, a picture may emerge of individuals going about their specialized individual responsibilities and having little to do with the work of others. This is neither an ideal nor practical image of an effective program staffing situation.

The concept of team work has been worked and reworked many times. Little new can be said with respect to early childhood programs for exceptional children. It holds true here as elsewhere that program staff need to work in a coordinated, cooperative, and goal directed fashion.

Essentials for the Team Approach

Leadership style is perhaps the crucial factor in promoting a team effort. A program director who understands team effort to mean, "I make the decisions, call the shots, and you, the staff, carry out my plans," is unlikely to be able to help a group of individuals begin to become a team. The essentials for developing an effective team approach are discussed briefly in the following paragraphs.

All staff are oriented to the "big picture" of the program. Although roles are differentiated, each staff member needs a general understanding of how the program is operated. The teacher aide, for example, needs to understand how the program fits into the local service delivery picture as well as the major components of the program and its operational procedures. Perhaps the teacher aide will be the one to serve a public education function when everyone else is otherwise occupied and that important surprise visitor arrives for a tour. Understanding the big picture tends to increase the meaningfulness of a given person's work and make for greater personal satisfaction.

Staff roles are differentiated and professional development ladders are defined. "Team effort" means cooperative effort toward commonly agreed upon goals. A frequent distortion of the concept is that everyone does the same work (or stated differently, all team members have the same or interchangeable roles). The concept of "team" in no way implies that everyone has the same role or that all must be able to do everyone else's work. The team concept works so well because in fact the individuals who make up a staff have many different interests, talents, skills, and capabilities, and these are drawn upon and utilized. Team work does imply that each individual has a clearly defined role to play and that the roles are related to each other in such a way as to ensure the accomplishment of the common goals. Roles that build on other roles (for example, the teacher role is based upon the skills and knowledges of the assistant teacher role) are identified and individual ambition to develop and advance is encouraged.

Staff participate in development and interpretation of major program goals or major changes in direction. Team work is facilitated when staff develop a consensus over the directions and major developments in a program. This does not mean that individual staff members should always be able to block or veto decisions, but rather that prior to making major decisions, time is devoted to open discussion of the issues. The program leadership then has at its disposal the ideas, comments, and insights of the individuals who will later have to implement whatever decisions are reached and can take action accordingly.

Individual differences and characteristics are valued. A positive contribution to team work is made when the individual qualifications of staff members and their unique potentials for contributing to the program's development are recognized. Efforts should be made early on to identify special talents or skills of staff and to encourage them to use those skills on behalf of the programmatic effort. For example, one of the teachers may have a real talent for drawing. This skill can be given appropriate recognition and directed to program goals if the teacher is requested to illustrate newsletters, brochures, or other program media. Perhaps one of the teacher aides has a penchant for videotape equipment. Such an individual can be encouraged to develop this interest and through technical assistance and perhaps some formal training make a real contribution to the program through videotaping services.

Communication channels are kept open and honest. The key to successful team work is communication. Time must be provided for all individuals involved to talk together and to understand information related to program operations. Written memoranda should be supplemented by face to face contact at least weekly. Every effort should be made to be sure that essential messages concerning program operations flow back and forth in a clear, undistorted fashion. Leadership personnel should take time to *listen* to staff concerns. The informal communication system of the "grapevine" may be inevitable, but the state of the formal channels need not cause staff to come to rely on the informal system to acquire basic information about program operation.

There is a real hazard in larger programs that the operational units become so large that good communication becomes difficult. Program leadership should give careful consideration to forming teams and subteams so that the size of the operational team unit is kept between six to eight people. Once a larger group is involved more formal communication is inevitable.

Overall careful selection of staff in the beginning and the establishment of trust between leadership and line staff lay a foundation for team work. An honestly recognized and openly expressed need to bring to bear the skills of each staff member for the program's success builds on that foundation. The time and effort involved in providing for face to face communication of staff members (including the leadership personnel) will assure the soundness of the team structure being built. Promoting real team effort does take more time in the initial phases of program development, but it pays off in increased individual responsibility taking and heightened commitment to program goals later on.

Personal Characteristics Needed by Staff

In making staffing decisions, a number of personal characteristics have wide applicability for most programs. Staff need to be:

- Oriented to personal growth.
- Flexible.
- Open to change and to new ideas.
- Oriented to team work as well as to individual effort.
- Tolerant of stress and long hours.
- In good health.
- Of high energy level.
- Child and family oriented.
- Endowed with a fine sense of humor.
- Optimistic concerning the change potential of children and families.
- Representative of the community in terms of ethnic composition.
- Of various experiential and education backgrounds.
- Willing to learn.
- Able to admit mistakes and to accept praise for success.
- Committed to a developmental perspective of exceptional children and their families.

Ackerman and Moore (1974) have reported that preservice training efforts cannot begin to fill the need for qualified and competent staff. They say that individuals who seem to "fill the bill" in terms of desirable general characteristics will need to be selected, from wherever they can be found. Whatever the skills of staff may be, program leadership personnel should expect to devote significant resources and considerable efforts toward inservice training and technical assistance. A rich resource of training potential and technical expertise may be tapped by contacting the projects developed under the Handicapped Children's Early Education Program (see Appendix A). These projects have a major training and dissemination emphasis. Experienced staff members from these projects can offer much in the way of assistance and guidance for developing the potential of a program's staff.

CONCLUDING COMMENTS—PROGRAM RESPONSIBILITIES TO STAFF

When John Kennedy took office as President in 1961, he composed an inaugural address in which he admonished his listeners, "Ask not what your country can do for you; ask what you can do for your country." Throughout this chapter on staffing patterns we have taken his advice only too well. We have described staff roles and staff responsibilities that concern what the staff will do for the program. We really have devoted little attention to what the program can do for the staff. As a final note to all that we have had to say on staffing patterns, we would like to add a few words about what the program *must* do for the staff if staffing patterns are to achieve the goals set for the preschool program.

Specifying Objectives

Every preschool teacher realizes that for every child in every program there must be behavioral objectives specified. If the child is ever to reach the goal of nearly normal behavior, the best procedure in working toward the goal is to set out in advance concrete steps that the child can achieve, so that the teacher can recognize when the child reaches them. Similarly, the staff in a program require precise descriptions of exactly what is wanted of them. They have more skills than do preschool children in setting objectives for themselves; but, at least in the beginning, and particularly with paraprofessional staff, it is imperative that practical guidelines be laid down and precise job descriptions be given to those who are assuming new responsibilities for the first time.

The descriptions must not only include an *overall* job description, but in the beginning should include exactly what is wanted on specific *tasks.* Describing what is wanted on a task in behavioral terms may need to be followed by a session in which a project director or coordinator *models* the appropriate behavior for a teacher or other staff person.

Providing Consequences

If it is important to let the staff know what is wanted, it is equally important to let them know when they have produced what is wanted—and to provide appropriate positive consequences for adequate performance. Adequate compensation for good performance is one way to promote improved performing in the future.

Compensation will take the form, first of all, of an adequate living wage. It is often difficult, given the tight budget constraints under which so many preschool programs operate, to provide adequate compensation for staff. Nevertheless, the recent high turnover rate among staff in Head Start centers and other preschool programs that enroll handicapped children is almost certainly owing in part to the undercompensation of work that has characterized these programs from the beginning. Staff members who leave Head Start routinely give as a reason for giving up employment the low pay that they have been receiving. Supporting a family on paraprofessional salaries has proved extremely difficult. The well being of the staff must be considered as relevant to performance.

But compensation is not merely a matter of financial compensation. Often a preschool teacher receives little feedback from supervisors or peers when performing appropriately in the preschool. We would suggest that another kind of staffing—the educational staffing that follows a routine preschool session— could provide a natural opportunity for the project director, the trainer, or other supervisory person to offer positive feedback immediately following a teacher's correct performance in the classroom.

Teachers should also be encouraged to reinforce each other. Often a teacher will notice another teacher doing "exactly what is needed" for a particular child on a given day. All staff members should be encouraged to comment on these appropriate responses of their peers. They should be *discouraged* from commenting at length on inappropriate responses. Instead, they should be directed to present "team problems," which *all* of the team members must "put their heads together" to help solve. In this way a more positive atmosphere will grow and eventually predominate in the preschool center. This kind of atmosphere, this kind of positive encouragement of good performing can come to be an important source of adequate compensation for good performance.

Providing for Staff Development

Probably the topic of providing a means for staff to undertake additional training and perhaps to acquire additional certification in their chosen field is something that might come under the heading of adequate compensation. But we have chosen to discuss it under a separate heading because it is so very important; it is particularly relevant to Head Start staff who often begin at the bottom of the career ladder.

Of course, every program must begin with considerable *inservice training,* since much on the job learning needs to be done by every member of a Head Start center or other preschool for handicapped children. That form of staff development we almost take for granted. But the project director and the training coordinator frequently are aware of local educational programs that provide credit to paraprofessionals enrolled in programs—particularly in community colleges. They often are able to facilitate enrollment, to offer advice, and to provide moral support to staff who might never have considered enrolling in educational programs without some form of encouragement by a person known to them. Ultimately, the whole field stands to benefit from the professional advancement of those who begin at the bottom of the career ladder.

One way of encouraging staff development is to provide opportunities for advancement as programs expand or change. Those who are prepared and who have served the program well should be the first to be considered for the assumption of new responsibilities or for advancement within the program. Such a policy should be made known to the staff and should be followed when opportunities to promote it arise. Every program has, or at least should have, a considerable investment in staff development. It is far better to build on this investment of time and monies expended than to be in the position of having to "start over" in training new staff to replace those who have not found their work appreciated, rewarded, or challenging. Such an investment also provides dividends in improved staff morale and enthusiasm for the program. Of course, professional advancement is a reward in itself for good performance in that most people seem to relish the opportunity to receive recognition and advancement.

Other staff members may *resist* advancement and even recognition quite strenuously. If it is not possible to make their work loads more satisfying and productive to them by increasing responsibility and adding opportunities for widening the scope of their tasks or by advancing them educationally, it should be possible to find means of making their everyday working lives interesting and challenging without these avenues.

We raise these issues concerning staff knowing that most of those who supervise or those who train workers in preschool programs for the handicapped will already be aware of them. But we do feel, from what we have observed ourselves in various settings, that these ideas need particular emphasis and repetition. Too often, there is a feeling that the adults in the program should constantly *give* to the children and to each other—that this is "what they are supposed to do." Their own very human needs are not taken into account. But failing to take these needs into account is failing to do one thing that can contribute much to the overall success of the program. A staff person who feels appreciated and needed in the program is in a position to do a much better job of meeting children's needs and the needs of other staff than one who feels ignored or unappreciated. The ultimate success of any staffing pattern may depend on the ability of all the staff to realize that not only are children people but adults are people too. As educators, we recognize the value of applying the principles of positive reinforcement in our work with children, but these principles can serve us well in our work with staff and with parents. A positive atmosphere is a happier one for all of us. A positive, shared, constructive approach can do much to improve morale and programs and create an environment that is not only stimulating for children but for adults as well.

REFERENCE

Ackerman, P., & Moore, B. *Early childhood education for handicapped children: The state of the art.* Paper presented at the National Conference on Handicapped and High Risk Infants and Young Children. Chapel Hill, North Carolina. University of North Carolina, President's Committee on Mental Retardation, and the Association for Childhood Education International, May 1974.

RESOURCES

Programming for Atypical Infants and Their Families (Monograph 1). A Nationally Organized Collaborative Project to Provide Comprehensive Services for Atypical Infants and Their Families, New York, New York. 1976. (Available from UCPA, Inc., 66 E. 34th Street, New York NY 10016. $1.25.)

Rural Area Head Start Teacher Training Model. Alaska Head Start Special Services Project, Anchorage, Alaska. 1975. (Available from Easter Seal Society, 726 E Street, Anchorage AK 99501. $2.00.)

Staff Development: A Resource for the Transdisciplinary Process. A Nationally Organized Collaborative Project to Provide Comprehensive Services for Atypical Infants and Their Families, New York, New York. 1976. (Available from UCPA, Inc., 66 E. 34th Street, New York NY 10016. $3.50.)

The Staff Training Prototype Series. Program for Staff Training of Exemplary Early Childhood Centers for Handicapped Children, The University of Texas, Austin. (Available from ERIC, LEASCO Information Products, Inc., P. O. Drawer O, Bethesda MD 20114.)

Training Program for Communication Aides. Project TAPP, Laramie, Wyoming. 1976. (Available from the project, University of Wyoming, Box 3224 University Station, Laramie WY 82071. $52.50.)

11
EVALUATION OF PROGRAMS

Carl J Huberty
William W. Swan

☐In the past, an evaluation component has perhaps been one of the most over-looked aspects of many educational programs. This is particularly true in the case of treatment programs for exceptional children. Relatively little effort, com-pared to other aspects of most programs for exceptional children, was devoted to evaluation, possibly because (a) it was not expected or required, (b) it was diffi-cult to carry out due to child assessment problems, (c) a commitment was not made to it, (d) it was not seen as being particularly beneficial, and/or (e) the number of individuals having evaluation expertise and available to work with these programs was somewhat limited.

Various notions have given rise to recent changes in emphasis and contribution of evaluation in educational programs. The role of an evaluation component in programs has recently been recognized as being a significant one. The notions of accountability and "return for the dollar" demands from various concerned groups have influenced the increased emphasis on evaluation. Also, recent considerations of, and technical developments in, theory and applications have brought on a more positive outlook toward evaluation practices in pro-grams for exceptional children.

It is the purpose of this chapter to discuss some theoretical aspects of evalu-ation, including meaning and importance, as well as to suggest how an evalu-ation system might be designed and how it can be implemented. Evaluation ideas, plans, and activities that have been employed in ongoing programs will be cited as exemplary practices.

EVALUATION IN GENERAL

Evaluation Theory

Much has been stated about both evaluation theory and evaluation methodology. It is not the purpose here to review all such statements. It behooves the reader of this handbook, however, to be aware of selected writings dealing with some evaluation theories and methods. Such a knowledge background should provide the reader with a broader perspective on evaluation issues and problems, which in turn may prove helpful in practical ways.

A theory of evaluation supposedly identifies what actions, occurrences, and behaviors are to be observed and appraised. Alkin (1969) stated:

> A theory of evaluation should: (1) offer a conceptual scheme by which eval-uation areas or problems are classified; (2) define the strategies including kinds of data, and means of analysis and reporting appropriate to each of the areas of the conceptual scheme; (3) provide systems of generalizations about the use of various evaluation procedures and techniques and their ap-propriateness to evaluation areas or problems. (p. 2)

What has been typically included in a statement of an evaluation theory is a definition of evaluation, a symbolic "model," and the methodology, or how the observations and appraisals are made. Various evaluation theories, models, and methodologies have been reviewed and illustrated by Worthen and Sanders

(1973); the publications edited by Taylor and Cowley (1972) and by Tyler, Gagné, and Scriven (1967) also contain excellent papers on evaluation theories. Specific approaches to evaluation have been discussed by Cronbach (1963), by Stake (1967), by Stufflebeam, Foley, Gephart, Guba, Hammond, Merriman, and Provus (1971), and by Provus (1969). Alkin (1969) compared and contrasted his evaluation model with the latter two approaches to evaluation.

Areas of evaluation of four models proposed by Alkin (1969), Stufflebeam et al. (1971), Provus (1969), and Huberty, Quirk, and Swan (1973) are summarized in Figure 1. A much more detailed comparison of the first three models in Figure 1 and five other formal evaluation models is reported by Worthen and Sanders (1973, pp. 209–217). This latter comparison spells out a number of definitions of evaluation, purposes of evaluation, and roles of an evaluator. (See the list of additional readings at the end of this chapter for other references on evaluation theory and methodology.)

Evaluation to many practitioners has, in the past at least, implied only one area of evaluation as depicted in Figure 1, namely, program certification, product evaluation, or appraisal. In the sense of basic meaning, three definitions of evaluation have been used. The first involves the equating of evaluation with measurement. The second involves determining the congruence between performance and objectives. The third definition states that evaluation is professional judgment. Elaborations of these definitions, along with advantages and disadvantages of each, are given by Stufflebeam et al. (1971, pp. 9–16).

It is reasonable to expect the "evaluation coordinator" of a program to be cognizant of various theoretical approaches to and definitions of evaluation; complete knowledge of the various approaches and definitions is, of course, not expected. A familiarization with many evaluation ideas should, however, provide the evaluation coordinator with some suggestions regarding the development of an evaluation plan or design for the program or project. It is not at all inconceivable that a coordinator would formulate an eclectic evaluation system of his own, based on various aspects of the general theories, in order to meet his specific program needs. In so doing he could, based on his constraints, make decisions regarding a number of issues in the field of program evaluation, for example, formative versus summative evaluation (Scriven, 1967), program portrayal versus program comparison, short term versus longitudinal evaluation, and internal versus external evaluation.

Reasons for Evaluation

Before proceeding to a detailed discussion of how one might develop an evaluation system for a program, some of the reasons for considering evaluation and some of the benefits to be gained from program evaluation will be briefly reviewed. Five interrelated reasons for including evaluation activities in the overall operation of an educational program are that evaluation (a) is expected and/or mandated, (b) can lead to an examination of program worth, (c) can lead to program improvement, (d) can enhance intraprogram communication, and (e) can add to the knowledge base pertaining to exceptional child education.

Figure 1

Commonalities of Four Evaluation Models

Model Author

Area of Evaluation	Alkin (1969)	Stufflebeam et al. (1971)	Provus (1969)	Huberty et al. (1973)
	Systems assessment	Content		Planning
	Program planning	Input	Definition	
	Program implementation	Process	Installation	Monitoring
	Program improvement		Process	
	Program certification	Product	Product	Appraising
			Cost-benefit analysis	

A leading reason for considering evaluation in the planning and budgeting of an educational program is that such consideration is, or will be, expected. It is expected, first of all, by the agency funding and supporting the program. In fact, the inclusion of an evaluation component in each project of the First Chance Network is not only expected but required. During the current emphasis on accountability, evaluation is also expected more and more by congressmen, state officials, various community groups, school board members, school administrators, teachers, and parents. These people are demanding some measures of accountability from those who administer educational programs—not only in terms of what is being done but also how effectively it is being done.

Evaluation information collected in anticipation of such demands for justifying the existence and continuation of a program may lead to determining the worth of the program. An intent of evaluation is to document the accomplishments of a program; evaluation data can provide a documentation of the extent to which stated goals have been attained and documentation of some unintended attainments. Such evidence is usually presented at or near the end of a year or a funding period or after adequate time has elapsed so that overall program goals may be related to collected evaluative information.

An evaluation plan should yield information on which decisions may be based at interim points of a program as well. Such informational feedback can lead to modifications and, it is hoped, improvements in the program. Periodic data collection can also provide information on various aspects of a program for purposes of examining the direction it is headed in terms of the clientele served, program administration, staff training, and so forth.

Having an evaluation system internal to an educational program can lead to a better understanding of what is going on in the program. One function of a program evaluation component is to provide a comprehensive description of the program, its objectives, and its efforts. The information exchange leading up to, and resulting from, such a description can greatly enhance understanding by those concerned about what is going on. The evaluation process itself, which should be integral to the overall program, can result in increased interstaff dialogue and enhanced interprogram communication. Such communication can create better interstaff working relations.

Finally, written evaluation reports, which include program descriptions as well as outcome data, can contribute to the knowledge base of exceptional child education (Swan & Wood, 1975). (Such reports should be made readily available to various audiences.) This contribution can be made with respect to (a) learning and adjustment of children and (b) implementation of an educational program for children.

DEVELOPING AN EVALUATION SYSTEM

Planning

Suggestions in this section will be presented with the assumption that a commitment in terms of personnel and other resources is made for an evaluation component in the proposal for an educational program.

The position of evaluation coordinator may be full time or part time depending on the scope of the overall program and its various components. It is imperative to have additional staff members who take responsibility for carrying out the various evaluation activities; these members include such persons as typists, data clerks, and data analysts. (See Chapter 10, "Multiple Staffing Patterns," for a more detailed discussion of staffing patterns, including how paraprofessionals may be helpful in evaluation; see also Provus, 1972, pp. 126–127.)

It would be most desirable for evaluation personnel to become familiar with the concept of evaluation in general and with alternative approaches to evaluation. This is particularly true for the evaluation coordinator, as pointed out in a previous section. Inservice training sessions dealing with evaluation in general and involving all evaluation personnel would be one means of exchanging ideas. It may be helpful to enlist the services of a professional consultant in evaluation, and such is recommended if resources allow it.

Becoming Familiar with the Program

One of the first tasks of the evaluation coordinator in formulating an evaluation system for an educational program is to become familiar with the model and/or philosophy of the treatment program itself. This includes the overall administration of the program, the general goals and/or objectives of the program, and at least some of the activities and materials used in the program. This familiarization, which can be accomplished through readings and/or discussions with the program director, should prove helpful in recognizing needs and problems in terms of evaluation. It might be pointed out that knowledge of more than just the purposes of a program enables the evaluator to suggest modifications of stated goals, to be alert for unintended effects and/or changes, and to have some input regarding the worth of the goals. (See Chapters 3, 6, and 9.)

In Depth Discussions with Nonevaluation Staff

Program familiarization would then be followed by more formal evaluation planning activities. These activities might begin with in depth discussions involving the program administrator(s) plus other program component coordinators. One purpose of these discussions would be to assess the needs of the program, including the specification of program goals and/or objectives. An end product here may be statements of objectives in terms of outputs of the program. These outputs must be directly related to the ultimate behavior of the clients being served—children, parents, teachers, and so forth.

Typical questions of concern at this point are: What are the general goals of the program? Based on these goals, what are some typical specific objectives? Can the goals and/or objectives be grouped or categorized in some way? Are the stated objectives meaningful? What types of evaluative information do the administrator(s) and staff members see as being important? (See White, Day, Freeman, Hautman, & Messenger, 1973, for other guidelines on program planning.)

The needs determined must be related to program resources and constraints. Needless to say, if resources—time, money, personnel—are not adequate so that program needs can be expected to be met, a reassessment of needs is necessary. Compatibility of needs and resources is, indeed, an important consideration in the planning of an evaluation system.

A second purpose of the planning discussion is to arrange for the integration of the evaluation component into the overall program, in terms of roles, functions, and efforts (see Gallagher, Surles, & Hayes, 1973). It is desirable that the evaluation procedures and activities blend smoothly into the everyday functioning of the program. An evaluation system that takes an inordinate amount of extra effort and does not facilitate the functions of the program will soon be discarded. Practicing educators need evaluation procedures with which they can be comfortable and which help them to deal more effectively with children's problems. Some questions of concern here may be: How can the evaluation and other components, in particular the administration, work together in organizing the overall program? What are some possible strategies for getting staff members to use the information to be collected?

Planning Discussions with Evaluation Staff

Once the basic planning discussions with nonevaluation staff are completed, the next step for the evaluation coordinator is to initiate and conduct planning sessions with the evaluation staff. The thinking and discussing would focus on the needs and constraints of the evaluation component. Decisions would be made regarding the overall evaluation approach to be used, this being determined by the needs of the program and the constraints under which the evaluation component must operate. An activity that would yield some input to this decision making process is a review of writings dealing with evaluation of programs similar to the one of concern. If feasible, an Educational Resources Information Center (ERIC) search might yield some helpful information.

Some questions of concern at this point are: How can the stated objectives be assessed in terms of relevance, scope, and meaningfulness? Which evaluation focus is to be used—formative, summative, portrayal, comparative? Are the resources for a satisfactory evaluation process adequate? What kinds of data—achievement, attitudes, behaviors, skills, numbers of hours—are needed? What types of data collection instruments need to be considered—standardized (group and individual) tests, questionnaires, observational forms? How much personnel training is necessary in the data collection process? How often need data be collected? Should a child sampling or time sampling data collection plan be devised?

Development of Strategies

As mentioned above, if an (internal) evaluation system is to be effective, it must be an integral part of the overall program. It must be accepted and favorably received by most, if not all, staff members. Staff members must be involved in the system, in its planning as well as in its implementation. A next step, then, in the planning stage is the development of strategies for getting as many staff members as possible involved in the evaluation process. Of course, one way to get them involved is to ask for staff input in the evaluation plans. This can be done through individual or group discussions or through a brief questionnaire. It is also advisable to develop, with the assistance of the staff members, a system of information exchange between the evaluation personnel and others. A few questions of pertinence are: How can positive attitudes of staff members toward the evaluation process be developed? How can nonevaluation staff members become involved in the evaluation process? What information feedback would be helpful to the staff members? How often is feedback desired?

Development of Work Schedule

As a final step in the planning process, the evaluation coordinator should develop a "work schedule," which would cover, say, 12 months. Such a schedule would include the evaluation tasks to be completed—develop instruments and forms, collect data, write reports—at tentatively specified time points.

Of course, concurrent with the work on the various evaluation tasks specified in the work schedule will be ongoing efforts that require continuous attention on the part of the evaluation staff. For example, the problem of maintaining good rapport with nonevaluation personnel needs constant attention. Continuous effort must also be extended in formulating and revising statements of objectives for the program.

A close eye must always be kept on the direction of the program as a whole, as well as on the direction of the evaluation component. Continually asking such questions as the following is imperative in keeping the proper perspective: Is what was proposed being done? Has there been a shift in emphasis in any component in the program? Has the evaluation system been effectively implemented? What has been accomplished in terms of the clients served? In terms of individual components?

Implementation

Two dimensions of the implementation of an evaluation system will be considered. The first dimension relates to the type of evaluative information: input, process, and output information. The second dimension relates to the processing of evaluative information: collecting, summarizing, reporting, and storing information. These two dimensions provide a means of examining the various problems, issues, and concerns in the implementation process. The discussion that follows is based on the assumption that a commitment to evaluation has been made and that planning activities, at least related to evaluation, have been completed. The concerns of each dimension will be reviewed along with relationships within and between dimensions.

Type of Information

A concern common to most evaluation models is the collection of input, process, and output information. Briefly stated, input information is used to determine "where one is" at a particular point in time with respect to client characteristics and to specific treatment objectives; for example, baseline performance data may be collected upon entry into a program (see Chapter 4, "Identification, Screening, and Assessment"). Process information is used to determine "how far one has progressed to date" and to assess the rate and direction of progress of individuals as well as of a group; program monitoring activities yield such information (see Chapter 5, "Record Keeping"). Output information is used to assess end of term progress of individuals and/or of a group; a term may be a quarter of a year, a full year, or longer depending upon program enrollment. Output information may also refer to the impact a program has on a community.

Most of the information of each type should be directly related to one or more treatment objectives, which are to be previously specified. However, it might be well to consider information that is not directly related to prespecified objectives but is related to some unintended worthwhile outcomes (see Scriven, 1972).

Processing of Evaluative Information

There are several important questions pertaining to the collection of evaluative information: Why? What? On whom or on what? By whom? How? When? A response to the first question ("why?") was given in an earlier section of this chapter.

What information is to be collected (second question) is generally covered in the immediately preceding subsection. This question should be answered during the planning phase. Input information would include such items as client and family characteristics, teacher or therapist characteristics, baseline academic achievement data, and mastery level of self help skills. Process information might include continuous and/or periodic performance data (e.g., reading competencies and socialization skills), program direction indicators, and treatment implementation assessments. Output information would include summary data—frequency counts of children or objectives attained, descriptions of clients served, group data on achievement tests, other performance scores, and so forth.

In response to the third question, information is collected on clients being served (children, parents, trainees), on physical facilities, and on various community agencies.

An answer to the fourth question depends on the staffing patterns in a program. Typically, program staff members, including evaluation personnel, collect both input and process information. This may also be the case in collecting output information; however, sometimes it is advisable to have an external evaluator—a nonstaff member who is knowledgeable in evaluation methods and in exceptional children—collect and summarize evaluative information.

The fifth question on how evaluative information is collected pertains to the type of instrument used. Input information is often collected by using simple intake forms (dealing with client and family characteristics), checklists, and medical and psychiatric reporting forms. Observation forms, rating scales, and developmental forms are often used in obtaining process information. Output information may be collected through the use of standardized or locally developed instruments measuring academic achievement, developmental progress (psychomotor, affective, and cognitive), medical changes, and progress in home and school.

Considerations to be made regarding the question of *how* to collect information refer, of course, to *what* information is to be collected. A first consideration is to thoroughly seek out prior developed instruments; these may be commercial standardized instruments, instruments appearing in professional journals, or those developed in other educational programs (see Appendix B; see also Buros, 1972; Technical Assistance Development System, 1974).

Numerous books have recently been published which serve as excellent references for assessment instruments. Many of these are of the handbook variety, containing extensive inventories of tests, scales, and indexes. They are particularly helpful in locating published measures of affective behavior of young children. (See the references on instrumentation in the list of additional readings at the end of this chapter.) Sometimes such instruments are not satisfactory for local use because of incongruence between items or questions and program objectives and emphasis. In this case, developing an instrument may be a viable alternative. This may merely involve modifying and adapting previously developed instruments; for example, using subsets of previously written items or sections of forms already in use. A word of caution is needed: Locally developed instruments should be kept simple. If most of the resources of a program are to be devoted to service, minimum effort should be put into development of instruments, and outside help should be solicited in locating or developing instruments.

An answer to the sixth question, pertaining to when information will be collected, will, of course, vary from program to program. At first glance it appears that input information is collected at the initiation of program operation, process information during the program operation, and output information at the conclusion of program operation. However, the same sequence of information collection may occur within a shorter period of time, say, 3 months. In this situation output data from one period may be used as input data for a subsequent period. It may be noted, parenthetically, that some of the information that has been considered process information here may be considered output information in some settings.

The methods of summarizing and reporting evaluative information are a function of the audience for which these activities are being done. One audience may call for information summarized in the form of frequency counts and percents, while another may call for mean gains, correlation matrices, or even factor analyses. Information may be requested monthly, quarterly, or annually; on individual children or on groups of children; and on all program components or merely on specified components by staff members, project offices, or school superintendents. Reporting may take the form of formally written reports, simple summary tables, or even verbal reports (see Hawkridge, Campeau, & Trickett, 1970; Worthen & Sanders, 1973, pp. 300–316).

It is strongly recommended that simple, yet systematic, procedures be developed for the storage of evaluative information. This may be accomplished using an index card system for each client, with storage by client or by groups of clients. If a program is large in the sense of resources and number of clients served, it may be advisable to use computer storage (cards, magnetic tapes, or discs) or storage in microform. The important considerations in storage are simplicity and accessibility.

Criteria to Consider

There are numerous criteria that could be considered in order to determine whether or not a given evaluation system is acceptable for a particular educational program. Following is a set of criteria that is not to be taken as exhaustive or prescriptive, but merely suggestive (Stufflebeam et al., 1971, pp. 28–30):

1. *Relevance*—Evaluative information should be collected with purposes or objectives in mind, and the information should relate to these purposes.
2. *Importance*—The purposes or objectives for which evaluative information is collected should be significant and worthwhile.
3. *Scope*—The range of information collected should be compatible with staff background and other resources, and it should not dominate the total program.
4. *Credibility*—All aspects of an evaluation system should be open, with the evaluation coordinator being in full trust of all staff members.

5. *Timeliness*—The best of information is of little value if presented too late (or too soon).
6. *Pervasiveness*—Summarized evaluative information should be disseminated to all persons who need it, taking into consideration varying audiences.

These criteria ought to be seriously considered during the planning stages of developing an evaluation system. They should also be reexamined periodically during the implementation process.

EXEMPLARY PRACTICES

Different evaluation systems have been used in the First Chance Network; each system is designed and implemented to provide its users with the information needed. Built into *The Rutland Center Model for Treating Emotionally Disturbed Children* (Athens, Georgia) are the planning, monitoring, and appraising activities of Huberty, Quirk, and Swan (1973), while only the two latter activities are explicitly emphasized in the *Evaluation Plan* and *Program Evaluation* of the Magnolia (Arkansas) Preschool Handicapped Project. "Quality and impact" are stressed in the evaluation of the Seattle (Washington) Model Preschool *(Assistance to Programs for Handicapped Young Children)*.

In the First Chance Network different evaluation systems are used, with different evaluation staffing patterns being used as well. The Seattle Model Preschool receives program evaluation services from a project consultant; the Magnolia Preschool Handicapped Project uses an external evaluation; and the Rutland Center has used a combination of an internal evaluation team and an external evaluation consultant.

Specific planning activities of the evaluation component in each project have been dependent upon local situations—personnel, administrative structure, project proposal, and so forth. To give some idea of the practices in planning in the Network, examples of work schedules are presented: the Activity and Accomplishment Schedule of the Seattle Model Preschool (Figure 2) and the work schedule of the Rutland Center (Figure 3).

Input Information

Most programs in the Network specify input information obtained from the child, parents, sources of previous treatment, and various special assessment consultants. Often this input information is described as screening, intake, diagnostic, or basic assessment information (see Chapter 4, "Identification, Screening, and Assessment"). For example, a center could use a combination of information obtained from diagnostic and evaluative instruments by the medical profession, occupational therapists, psychometrists, and speech pathologists. The Gary (Indiana) Special Preschool Outreach and Training Program *(Summary and Evaluation Report)*, the Magnolia Preschool Handicapped Project, and the Rutland Center use input information from combinations of standardized and locally developed assessment instruments gathered by a variety of professionals, including psychologists, social workers, and psychiatrists.

Figure 2

Activity and Accomplishment Schedule
Seattle Model Preschool Center for Handicapped Children
(Seattle, Washington)

Following is a brief outline of projected third year activities and quarterly accomplishments. Additionally, during the first and last quarters, one of the planned activities is a complete review of project status for purposes of plan revision.

Year 1976–77
First quarter activities

1.0 *Expand project* as necessary, hire additional staff, complete third year plan, make staff assignments, train and prepare staff as necessary. Schedule: To be completed no later than 1 September, 1976.

2.0 *Identify all preschool and day care centers serving Down's children* which might provide children for the third year Seattle Public Schools classes; establish working relationships with those agencies. Schedule: To be completed no later than 1 August, 1976.

3.0 *Expand and revise as necessary all child and program description forms* for collecting and recording data. Schedule: To be completed by 15 August, 1976.

4.0 *Review, expand and revise as necessary developmental assessment battery.* Schedule: Completed 1 July, 1976; tested in 1976–77.

5.0 *Revise assessment procedures if necessary and schedule assessments* for all children registered for entrance into the Seattle Public Schools classes. Schedule: 1 July to 15 September, 1976.

6.0 *Review and revise, as necessary, data evaluation plan and computer development schedule for all evaluations, based on second year computer development.* By the end of the first quarter, 1976–77, it is expected that correlational, discriminate and significant testing routines will be fully functional. Schedule: 15 June to 1 September, 1976 (ongoing thereafter as indicated below).

7.0 *Obtain child and present/planned program description information and developmental level assessment data* on all children to be enrolled in the Seattle Public Schools classes during the third year. Schedule: 1 August, 1976, to 1 October, 1977. (Assessments will be scheduled to correspond as closely as possible to the opening of public school classes.)

8.0 *Summarize activities and accomplishments to date,* including at least a basic summary of program and child data collected. Schedule: 15 August to 1 October, 1976.

First Quarter Products and Accomplishments

1.0 New and replacement staff hired and detailed project plan for third year established.

Figure 2 continued

2.0 All programs in Seattle area from which children for third year of Seattle Public Schools classes might be recruited will have been identified, and working agreements will have been finalized.

3.0 Additional forms will have been completed for child and program characteristics.

4.0 Descriptive data will have been collected on all of the children in the public school classes and on the planned programs for those children.

5.0 The assessment battery for developmental levels will have been reviewed, revised if necessary, and compiled; and a schedule of assessments for all children enrolled in, or expected to be enrolled in, the public school classes will have been determined.

6.0 Assessments of the developmental levels of all children enrolled in the public school classes will have been completed.

7.0 Initial correlational and discriminate routines will have been computerized and tested.

8.0 Results from all of the above will have been summarized.

Second Quarter Activities

1.0 *Continue and complete developmental level assessments and child and present program descriptions* of children enrolled in the public school classes. Schedule: To be completed by 1 November 76.

2.0 *Conduct direct class and program observations,* assist classroom staff as necessary in implementing Model Preschool procedures; implement family programs, data collection, and observations for all children enrolled in public school classes. Collect past program information for all children enrolled in public school classes, such as type of program: institution, day care, Head Start, preschool (private or public) and length of time in program. Schedule: 15 September to 15 November 76.

3.0 *Continue computer development,* complete initial outputs for discriminate and correlational studies. Schedule: 15 September to 1 December 76.

4.0 *Output computer summaries* of: child and program characteristics, and assessed developmental levels, preliminary and discriminate and correlational studies.

5.0 *Conduct first review of project's third year activities* with the assistance of members of the review committee. (The committee includes two representatives from the Seattle Public Schools' Special Education Departments; two representatives from Epton Day Care Centers, including state agency representatives; two parents, one from Green Lake Elementary School and one from the Model Preschool Down's Syndrome Programs; two staff members

(continued on next page)

Figure 2 continued

from the Experimental Education Unit's Model Preschool Center; and one representative from the Child Development and Mental Retardation Center, University of Washington.) Schedule: 15 November to 1 December 76.

6.0 *Summarize project activities and accomplishments* to date, compile outputs and products. Schedule: To be completed by 15 November 76.

7.0 *Review plans* for placement and progression of pupils reaching CA 12 years. Schedule: 15 November to 1 December 76.

Second Quarter Products and Accomplishments

1.0 Child and present program descriptions completed for all new children enrolled in public school classes.

2.0 Past program information for all children newly enrolled in the public school classes.

3.0 Direct classroom observation data on all pupils enrolled in the public school classes.

4.0 Records from at least one parent-teacher conference for each child enrolled in the public school classes.

5.0 Computer produced summaries of all project data collected and analyses conducted to date.

6.0 The comments and suggestions resulting from the review committee's analysis of project progress.

7.0 A brief summary of preliminary plans for placement and progression of pupils reaching CA 12 years.

Third Quarter Activities

1.0 *Continued development of computer capabilities,* revising where necessary, and completing at least the programs to perform significance and stability analyses of the assessed developmental levels of children and their developmental gains between administrations of the assessment battery. Schedule: Program completed no later than 1 March 77.

Third Quarter Products and Accomplishments

1.0 *Additional summaries of developmental levels and gains* made by all children enrolled in public school classes.

Fourth Quarter Activities

1.0 *Begin regular computer runs* on all discriminate, correlational, significance testing, and stability of gain analyses.

2.0 *Conduct second review of project activities,* with assistance of review committee. Schedule: 15 June to 1 July 77.

Fourth Quarter Products and Accomplishments

1.0 A complete summary, by quarters, of each child's gains, program and individual characteristics; and an analysis of the differences in gains achieved by

Figure 2 continued

children with broad differences in personal characteristics and program histories (i.e., by age groups within 6 months, and a comparison of children with one, two, three, etc., years of preschool experience).

2.0 A brief description of the review committee's findings and suggestions regarding the project's relevance to the needs of handicapped children, and its progress in meeting those needs.

Recurring or Continuous Activities and Products

1.0 *Continue direct classroom observations,* assist in the implementation of Model Preschool procedures, and collect data on child, present program, and past program information of children newly admitted to the public school classes (or scheduled for admission); and update, as necessary, the information collected previously on children who have been enrolled in the public school classes for one or more quarters. Schedule: Between the middle of the first month of each quarter, and the middle of the last month of each quarter.

2.0 *Schedule and conduct assessments of developmental levels* for children enrolled in the Seattle Public Schools classes or scheduled for transfer into those classes during the course of the study. Schedule: All children in the public school classes will be assessed at least twice yearly, as close to the beginning of the first and end of the third quarters as is possible; children identified as having potential for transfer will be assessed twice each year, as close to the beginning and ending dates of those years (first and third quarters) as is possible.

3.0 *Develop plans for continuing the program* with children who have received continuous intervention since infancy. Since our Down's Program at the Experimental Education Unit started in January 1971 with children who were 2 ½ years old, we have not yet moved into the public schools a group that has had early and continuous intervention from 0 to 6. The first such group will move into the public schools in 1978–79. Refer to Appendix for accompanying chart on pupil enrollment summary information. Schedule: Complete no later than 1 June 77, with plan produced.

4.0 *Input, summarize, and analyze all data collected each quarter, and make comparisons* with previously collected data. Schedule: within the last two weeks of each quarter.

5.0 *Arrange for the project review committee's meetings.* Schedule: during the last two weeks in November of each year; and during the last two weeks of June each year.

6.0 *Review project activities and products, and modify, revise, and update pro-*

(continued on next page)

Figure 2 continued

ject plan. Schedule: continuously, but with emphasis during April and May of each year (i.e., the last two months of each project year), to be completed by 1 June of each year.

7.0 *Prepare all materials for dissemination.* These materials will fall into three general classes: (1) standard publications or media products describing the project's work and findings, to be disseminated through such avenues as journal articles and presentations at professional meetings and symposia; (2) information papers that can be used to answer the voluminous requests (average: two letters or phone calls daily) for information about project components and activities; and (3) materials concerning replication of the project's basic model for those who request information or assistance in such replication efforts.

These materials will undergo constant review and revision as new developments occur and as our data pool increases. The project staff look forward to collaborating with professionals from other disciplines in preparing materials for dissemination under category (1) above, with the expectation that such products will appear in journals or at meetings of more than one discipline. The interest in our project that has been expressed by specialists from many disciplines (particularly pediatric nursing and medicine) suggests the need for such cross-disciplinary dissemination. Schedule: Ongoing throughout the project year.

8.0 *Write and submit annual reports* including complete summary interpretations of all analyses, recommendations for utilization of study findings, statements regarding the potential impact of study findings on Down's children and handicapped children in general, and complete plans for the next year's operation.

Locating appropriate measurement instruments appears to be a significant problem in program evaluation as evidenced by the large number of locally developed instruments. (The Technical Assistance Development System publications, *Evaluation Bibliography* (1973) and *First Chance Projects: A Catalogue of Instructional and Evaluative Materials* (1974), provide brief descriptions of instruments used by various programs.) Most programs use a combination of standardized and locally developed instruments to meet their needs in obtaining appropriate input information.

Many of the programs summarize and report input information not only to determine whether or not a child is appropriate for its services, but also to use as

Figure 3

Evaluation Work Schedule
The Rutland Center
(Athens, Georgia)

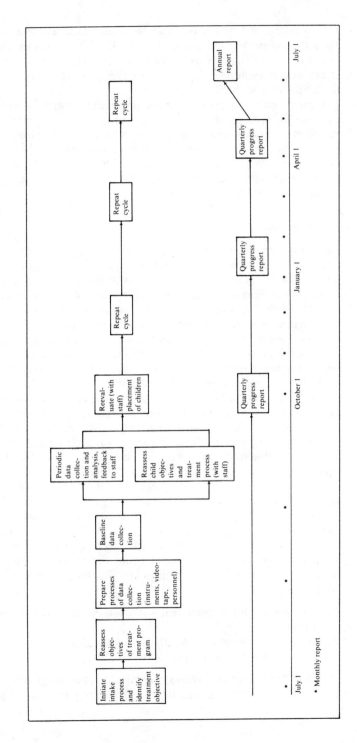

before-treatment data in a pre- and posttreatment assessment design. (See the *Final Report on Products and Results of a Year's Work* and the *Report to Advisory Committee* from Project PUSH, Keyser, West Virginia; and see evaluations already mentioned for the Seattle Preschool, the Gary Project, the Magnolia Project, and the Rutland Center.)

Some programs collect sets of input, process, and output information by using the same instruments (the Gary Project and the Rutland Center). This common thread of instrumentation simplifies the collecting, summarizing, reporting, and storing of information and leads to an effective and efficient program evaluation design. Typically, summarizing the collected input information is done by a narrative report; reporting is accomplished by a verbal discussion; and information is stored in folders in file cabinets.

Process Information

Collecting, summarizing, reporting, and storing of process information depend on the program resources committed to evaluation. While the collection of input information is a generally accepted necessity, the collection of process information in a structured format is often considered an alternative rather than a necessity. However, the significant benefits of process information are program improvement and enhanced intraprogram communication.

All programs are required to collect, summarize, and report process information on proposal goals, objectives, and procedures. Some programs emphasize the collection of process information related to specific individuals or to groups. An effective means of collecting process information is through curriculum referenced measures. For example, the Gary (Indiana) Project uses the rather extensive Learning Accomplishment Profile; the Rutland Center (Athens, Georgia) uses the Developmental Therapy Objectives Rating Form (see Figure 20 of Chapter 5, "Record Keeping") and an observational instrument, Systematic Who-to-Whom Analysis Notation, both of which are based on the Developmental Therapy treatment model; the Magnolia (Arkansas) Project records the program's progress in meeting objectives, problems encountered, and uses of specific techniques. Typically, summarizing process information is accomplished by a chart of number of objectives achieved; reporting is done by verbal explanations of the data; and information is stored in a folder in a file cabinet.

While appropriate instruments for collecting input information are not abundant, appropriate instruments for collecting process information are nearly nonexistent for newly developed curricula. Thus the project director has a choice of three alternatives:

1. Use available instruments that approach the ideal instrument as much as possible.
2. Develop instruments specifically for a curriculum.
3. Use a combination of the first two alternatives.

Standardized instruments generally require long periods of time for administration and other extra resources. Thus most programs that depend on standardized instruments to collect input and output data do not emphasize the collection of process information. Measurement instruments for collecting process information are almost always locally developed due to the varying natures of processes. Again, the reader is referred to the two Technical Assistance Development System publications.

Output Information

The Gary (Indiana) Project reports pre- and posttreatment comparisons for individual children using three standardized instruments (Stanford-Binet Intelligence Scale, Developmental Test of Visual-Motor Integration, and Peabody Picture Vocabulary Test) and one instrument developed by the Chapel Hill (North Carolina) Project (the Learning Accomplishment Profile). Project PUSH (Keyser, West Virginia) uses a matrix sampling technique in collecting pre- and posttreatment data; these data are summarized and reported in percents and mean gain scores. The Seattle (Washington) Model Preschool and the Rutland Center (Athens, Georgia) additionally report selected "cost data." Typically, summarizing output information is done by recording frequency counts or percents along with narrative statements, and information is stored in file cabinets. The format for reporting output information, as well as for reporting some input and some process information, has been specified by the funding agent for all Network projects. These reports have included objectives, procedures, and outputs. See Figure 4 for an example of such a report from the Magnolia (Arkansas) Project.

The linkage of input, process, and output information specifically referenced to a curriculum is demonstrated in such projects as the Rutland Center and the Gary (Indiana) Projects.

References of exemplary evaluation practices in other programs for exceptional children may be obtained through the Educational Resources Information Center (ERIC). An ERIC search refers the user both to reports in professional journals (indexed in the *Current Index to Journals in Education)* and to other reports (indexed and abstracted in *Resources in Education).* Many of the latter reports are those of programs receiving federal support.

A set of papers dealing with "real world" evaluation practices in school programs may also be found in Payne (1974).

EXTERNAL EVALUATION OF EXEMPLARY PRACTICES

An additional phase of evaluation in addition to the monitoring by federal project officers of the First Chance projects has recently been initiated. The Joint Dissemination Review Panel (US Office of Education/National Institute of Education) reviews summaries of data from "output evaluations" and determines whether a project's model should be validated for national dissemination by the US Office of Education. This panel represents an additional audience for summative evaluation information.

Figure 4

Evaluation Design Summary Chart
Magnolia Preschool Handicapped Project
(Magnolia, Arkansas)

PERFORMANCE OBJECTIVES	MEASUREMENT INSTRUMENTS			DATA COLLECTION PROCEDURES			DATA ANALYSIS TECHNIQUES	Evaluator's Report Due
	Name/Type of Instrument	Date Instrument to be Completed	Baseline Data	Target Group	Scheduled Date(s)	Person Responsible		
1. By May 1, 1973, the participating teachers and administrators will increase their skills in identifying specific characteristics of exceptional children as measured by a pretest/posttest score on a staff-made evaluation scale. The minimum level of expectancy will be that 80% of the teachers and administrators will correctly identify all nine of the items presented on the posttest and a minimum of 10% gain by the total group will be made.	Staff-made evaluation scale	Already completed	Items on staff-made evaluation scale answered correctly	30 teachers 10 administrators	Pretest September 1972 Posttest May 1973	Teacher trainer and social worker	The scores on the pretest and posttest staff-made evaluation scale will be compared to determine if level of expectancy is achieved.	June 30, 1973
2. By May 1973 the participating administrators will increase their awareness of special services available to handicapped children as indicated on a pretest/posttest staff-made evaluation scale. The minimum level of expectancy will be 10% mean increase on the posttest score.	Staff-made evaluation scale	September 30, 1972	Items on staff-made evaluation scale answered correctly	30 teachers 10 administrators	Pretest September 1972 Posttest May 1973	Teacher trainer and social worker	The scores on the pretest and posttest staff-made evaluation scale will be compared to determine if level of expectancy is achieved.	June 15, 1973

Figure 4 (continued)

PERFORMANCE OBJECTIVES	MEASUREMENT INSTRUMENTS			DATA COLLECTION PROCEDURES				DATA ANALYSIS TECHNIQUES	Evaluator's Report Due
	Name/Type of Instrument	Date Instrument to be Completed	Baseline Data	Target Group	Scheduled Date(s)	Person Responsible			
3. By May 1973 the participating teachers will demonstrate application of teaching techniques appropriate to handicapped children in their classroom as indicated by a monitoring report completed by the teacher and teacher trainer. The minimum level of expectancy will be as follows: 100% of the participating teachers	Monitoring report	September 30, 1972	Number of appropriate learning activities	30 teachers	Each 6 weeks	Teacher trainer		The completed monitoring reports will be summarized and analyzed to determine if the minimum level of acceptance is achieved.	June 5, 1973
a. Will initiate one or more appropriate learning activities.			Use of specific techniques taught in the training						
b. Will complete and maintain an appropriate daily schedule of learning activities for their class.			Copy of daily schedule of learning activities						
c. Will use at least three of the specific techniques taught in the training session, with at least one technique being judged successful.									

(continued on next page)

Figure 4 (continued)

PERFORMANCE OBJECTIVES	MEASUREMENT INSTRUMENTS			DATA COLLECTION PROCEDURES			DATA ANALYSIS TECHNIQUES	Evaluator's Report Due
	Name/Type of Instrument	Date Instrument to be Completed	Baseline Data	Target Group	Scheduled Date(s)	Person Responsible		
4. After participating in the Outreach activities the participants will respond positively to the project as indicated by the results of a staff-made feedback questionnaire completed in May 1973. The minimum level of expectancy will be that 70% of the responses will be positive to each item on the questionnaire.	Staff-made feedback questionnaire	February 1, 1973	Items on staff-made feedback questionnaire	30 teachers 10 administrators 60 day care workers	May 1973	Social worker	The percentage of positive responses to each item on the staff-made feedback questionnaire will be computed and analyzed to determine if 70% responded positively to each item.	June 15, 1972

SUMMARY AND CONCLUSION

In conclusion, a reiteration of several points on program evaluation, which were mentioned previously, will be made. First, the importance of a serious commitment to evaluation cannot be overemphasized. The integration of evaluation thinking and plans into the program should be made at the outset. All of the benefits yielded by a sound evaluation system cannot be realized if evaluation is merely an adjunct to the rest of the program. Such a commitment of the program administration to evaluation will result in someone assuming the responsibility of carrying out the evaluation activities. It is recommended that this "evaluation coordinator" become familiar with some aspects of evaluation theory—models, systems, issues. This background, plus that on the program itself, should enable the coordinator to arrive at a workable meaning of evaluation in the local context. This thinking coupled with considerable planning should lead to a sound local program evaluation system.

Second, the success of implementing the devised system is, of course, contingent upon the cooperation among evaluation and other program personnel. This cooperation will be enhanced if nonevaluation personnel view the evaluation activities as useful and helpful. A primary means of bringing this view into focus is to implement a program referenced evaluation system, one that is directly related to the program goals and objectives. Furthermore, it should be made clear how evaluation information feedback might lead to program modification and improvement. The administration personnel can be shown how evaluation information can demonstrate the impact of the program on various communities, local and professional.

Third, and related to the first two points, is the fact that planning is a must for the development of an evaluation system. To have a sound, effective system, planning is necessary, but not sufficient. The resource guide edited by Meierhenry (1969) provides some helpful suggestions in planning.

Last, the evaluation system must be helpful; that is, evaluation should serve a purpose, and not be mere "window dressing."

The discussion of evaluation philosophies and activities in this chapter was presented with a *service* program in mind. This is opposed to a research and/or development program, where emphasis might be on experimental investigation of problems identified by the researchers or on developing instruments, curricular materials, etc.

Evaluation information can be of great assistance to those project directors and staff who choose to implement an evaluation system as an integral part of their program. A program evaluation system can both facilitate the improvement of a particular project's treatment model and provide information needed to assist certain audiences in determining support for the project. This is certainly one of those areas in which "an ounce of planning is worth both a pound of correction and a dollar of continuation."

REFERENCES

Alkin, M. C. Evaluation theory development. *Evaluation Comment,* 1969, *2*(1), 2–7.

Buros, O. K. (Ed.) *Seventh mental measurements yearbook.* Highland Park NJ: Gryphon Press, 1972.

Cronbach, L. J. Course improvement through evaluation. *Teachers College Record,* 1963, *64,* 672–683.

Gallagher, J. J., Surles, R. C., & Hayes, A. E. *First Chance for children.* Vol. 2: *Program planning and evaluation.* Chapel Hill NC: Technical Assistance Development System, 1973.

Hawkridge, D. G., Campeau, P. L., & Trickett, P. K. *Preparing evaluation reports: A guide for authors* (Monograph No. 6). Pittsburgh: American Institute for Research, 1970.

Huberty, C. J., Quirk, J. P., & Swan, W. W. An evaluation system for a psychoeducational treatment program for emotionally disturbed children. *Educational Technology,* 1973, *13*(5), 73–80.

Meierhenry, W. C. (Ed.) *Planning for the evaluation of special education programs.* (BEH Resource Guide No. OEG-0-9-372160-3553 (032)). Washington DC: US Office of Education, September 1969.

Payne, D. A. *Curriculum evaluation.* Lexington MA: Heath, 1974.

Provus, M. Evaluation of ongoing programs in the public school system. In R. W. Tyler (Ed.), *Educational evaluation: New roles, new means* (Sixty-eighth yearbook of the National Society for the Study of Education, Part II). Chicago: National Society for the Study of Education, 1969.

Provus, M. The discrepancy evaluation model. In P. A. Taylor & D. M. Cowley (Eds.), *Readings in curriculum evaluation.* Dubuque IO: Brown, 1972.

Scriven, M. The methodology of evaluation. In *Perspectives of curriculum evaluation* (AERA Monograph Series on Curriculum Evaluation, No. 1). Chicago: Rand McNally, 1967.

Scriven, M. Pros and cons about goal-free evaluation. *Evaluation Comment,* 1972, *3*(4), 1–4.

Stake, R. E. The countenance of educational evaluation. *Teachers College Record,* 1967, *68,* 523–540.

Stufflebeam, D. L., Foley, W. J., Gephart, W. J., Guba, E. G., Hammond, R. L., Merriman, H. O., & Provus, M. M. *Educational evaluation and decision making.* Itasca IL: Peacock, 1971.

Swan, W. W., & Wood, M. M. Making decisions about treatment effectiveness. In M. M. Wood (Ed.), *Developmental therapy—A textbook for teachers as therapists for emotionally disturbed young children.* Baltimore MD: University Park Press, 1975.

Taylor, P. A., & Cowley, D. M. (Eds.). *Readings in curriculum evaluation.* Dubuque IO: Brown, 1972.

Technical Assistance Development System. *Evaluation bibliography* (Tadscript #2). Chapel Hill: University of North Carolina, 1973.

Technical Assistance Development System. *A catalogue of instructional and evaluative materials* (Tadscript #3). Chapel Hill: University of North Carolina, 1974.

Tyler, R. W., Gagné, R. M., & Scriven, M. (Eds.). *Perspectives of curriculum evaluation* (AERA Monograph Series on Curriculum Evaluation, No. 1). Chicago: Rand McNally, 1967.

White, S. H., Day, M. C., Freeman, P. K., Hantman, S. A., & Messenger, K. P. *Federal programs for young children: Review and recommendations* (Summary, Vol. 4, Contract No. HEW-OS-71-170, Publication No. (OS) 74-100). Washington, DC: US Department of Health, Education, and Welfare, 1973.

Worthen, B. R., & Sanders, J. R. *Educational evaluation: Theory and practice.* Worthington OH: Jones, 1973.

ADDITIONAL READINGS

Evaluation Theory and Methodology

Books

Anderson, S. B., Ball, S., Murphy, R. T., et al. *Encyclopedia of educational evaluation.* San Francisco: Jossey-Bass, 1975.

Gottman, J. M., & Clasen, R. E. *Evaluation in education: A practitioner's guide.* Itasca, IL: Peacock, 1972.

Provus, M. *Discrepancy evaluation: For educational program improvement and assessment.* Berkeley CA: McCutchan, 1971.

Stufflebeam, D. L., Foley, W. J., Gephart, W. J., Guba, E. G., Hammond, R. L., Merriman, H. O., & Provus, M. M. *Educational evaluation and decision making.* Itasca, IL: Peacock, 1971.

Suchman, E. A. *Evaluative research.* New York: Russell Sage Foundation, 1967.

Weiss, C. H. *Evaluation research.* Englewood Cliffs NJ: Prentice-Hall, 1972.

Wick, J. W., & Beggs, D. L. *Evaluation for decision-making in the schools.* Boston: Houghton Mifflin, 1971.

Worthen, B. R., & Wiley, D. E. (Eds.) *The evaluation of instruction.* New York: Holt, Rinehart and Winston, 1970.

Edited books of papers

Caro, F. G. (Ed.). *Readings in evaluation research.* New York: Sage, 1971.

House, E. R. (Ed.). *School evaluation: The politics and process.* Berkeley CA: McCutchan, 1973.

Payne, D. A. (Ed.). *Curriculum evaluation.* Lexington MA: Heath, 1974.

Rippey, R. M. (Ed.). *Studies in transactional evaluation.* Berkeley CA: McCutchan, 1973.

Struening, E. L., & Guttentag, M. (Eds.). *Handbook of evaluation research* Vols. 1 and 2. London: Sage, 1975.

Taylor, P. E., & Cowley, D. M. (Eds.). *Readings in curriculum evaluation.* Dubuque IA: Brown, 1972.

Tyler, R. W. (Ed.). *Educational evaluation: New roles, new means.* Sixty-eighth yearbook of the National Society for the Study of Education, Part II. Chicago: University of Chicago Press, 1969.

Walberg, H. J. (Ed.). *Evaluating educational programs.* Berkeley CA: McCutchan, 1974.

Wittrock, M. C., & Wiley, D. E. (Eds.). *The evaluation of instruction.* New York: Holt, Rinehart and Winston, 1970.

Monographs

Gallagher, J. J., Surles, R. C., & Hayes, A. E. *Program planning and evaluation* Vol. 2. First Chance for Children (Technical Assistance Development System), 1973.

Grobman, H. Evaluation activities of curriculum projects. *A.E.R.A. Monograph Series on Curriculum Evaluation,* No. 2. Chicago: Rand McNally, 1968.

Hawkridge, D. G., Campeau, P. L., & Trickett, P. K. Preparing evaluation reports: A guide for authors. *American Institutes for Research Monograph,* No. 6, 1970.

Meierhenry, W. C. (Ed.). *Planning for the evaluation of special education programs.* US Office of Education, BEH Resource Guide, Grant No. OEG–0–9–372160–3553(032), September 1969.

Tyler, R. W., Gagné, R. M., & Scriven, M. (Eds.). Perspectives of curriculum evaluation. *A.E.R.A. Monograph Series on Curriculum Evaluation,* No. 1. Chicago: Rand McNally, 1967.

Periodicals

Educational Technology (Educational Technology Publications, Inc.)
Evaluation Comment (CSE at UCLA)

Instrumentation

Beatty, W. H. (Ed.). *Improving educational assessment and an inventory of measures of affective behavior.* Washington: Association for Supervision and Curriculum Development, 1969.

Bonjean, C. M., Hill, R. J., & McLemore, S. D. *Sociological measurement: An inventory of scales and indices.* San Francisco: Chandler, 1967.

Johnson, O. G., & Bommarito, T. W. (Eds.). *Tests and measurements in child development: A handbook.* San Francisco: Jossey-Bass, 1971.

Lake, D. G., Miles, M. B., & Earle, R. B. (Eds.). *Measuring human behavior.* New York: Teachers College Press, 1973.

Pfeiffer, J. W. & Heslin, R. *Instrumentation in human relations training.* Iowa City: University Associates, 1973.

Shaw, M. E., & Wright, J. M. (Eds.). *Scales for the measurement of attitudes.* New York: McGraw-Hill, 1967.

Walker, D. K. *Socioemotional measures for preschool and kindergarten children: A handbook.* San Francisco: Jossey-Bass, 1973.

Wylie, R. C. *The self-concept. Vol. I: A review of methodological considerations and measuring instruments.* Lincoln: University of Nebraska Press, 1974.

RESOURCES

Assistance to Programs for Handicapped Young Children: A Continuation Proposal. Technical Assistance to Programs for Preschool Handicapped Children, Seattle, Washington. 1973. (Available from Model Preschool Center for Handicapped Children, University of Washington, Seattle WA 98195.)

Evaluation Bibliography (Tadscript #2). Technical Assistance Development System, Chapel Hill, North Carolina. 1973. (Available from ERIC Document Reproduction Service, P. O. Box 190, Arlington VA 22210. ED 082 422.)

Final Report on Products and Results of a Year's Work. Project PUSH, Keyser, West Virginia. 1973. (Available from the project, Mineral Street Annex, Keyser WV 26726.)

First Chance Projects: A Catalogue of Instructional and Evaluative Materials (Tadscript #3). Technical Assistance Development System, Chapel Hill, North Carolina. 1974. (Available from ERIC Document Reproduction Service, P. O. Box 190, Arlington VA 22210. ED 093 116.)

Learning Accomplishment Profile (LAP). Chapel Hill Training Outreach Project, Chapel Hill, North Carolina. (Available from the project, Lincoln Center, Merritt Mill Road, Chapel Hill NC 27514. $2.00.)

Report to Advisory Committee. Project PUSH, Keyser, West Virginia. 1973. (Available from the project, Mineral Street Annex, Keyser WV 26726.)

The Rutland Center Model for Treating Emotionally Disturbed Children. Rutland Center, Athens, Georgia. 1972. (Available from ERIC Document Reproduction Service, P. O. Box 190 Arlington VA 22210, ED 087 703; and from Technical Assistance Office, Rutland Center, 698 N. Pope Street, Athens GA 30601, $5.00.)

Summary and Evaluation Report. Special Preschool Outreach and Training Program, Gary, Indiana. 1973. (Available from the project, 620 E. 10th Place, Gary IN 46402.)

Systematic Who-to-Whom Analysis Notation (SWAN). Rutland Center, Athens, Georgia. (In *The Rutland Center Model for Treating Emotionally Disturbed Children.* Available from ERIC Document Reproduction Service, P. O. Box 190, Arlington VA 22210, ED 087 703; and from Technical Assistance Office, Rutland Center, 698 N. Pope Street, Athens GA 30601, $5.00.)

Appendix A

DIRECTORY OF BEH FIRST CHANCE PROJECTS

ALABAMA

Birmingham

Comprehensive Early Education Program (CEEP)
K. F. King
Division of Child Development
University of Alabama, Birmingham
1720 Seventh Avenue, South
Birmingham, Alabama 35233
(205)934-5241

Tuscaloosa

Rural Infant Stimulation Environment (RISE) Project
Loreta Holder
The University of Alabama
College of Speech
Communicative Disorders Area
P. O. Box 2846
Tuscaloosa, Alabama 35486
(205)348-7340

University

Handicapped Children's Early Education Program
Eugenia Ruth Walker
University of Alabama (Tuscaloosa)
P. O. Box 1982
University, Alabama 35486
(205)348-7131

ALASKA

Anchorage

Alaska Head Start Special Services Project
Marion D. Bowles
Easter Seal Society for Alaska Crippled Children and Adults
726 E Street
Anchorage, Alaska 99501
(907)274-1665

ARIZONA

Sacaton

Gila River Indian Community Handicapped Children's Early Education Program
Cecilia T. Braun
Gila River Indian Community
P. O. Box A
Sacaton, Arizona 85247
(602)562-3423 or (602)963-9697

Tucson

Program Development for Preschool Handicapped Indian Children
Elizabeth Y. Sharp
Department for Special Education
College of Education
University of Arizona
Tucson, Arizona 85721
(602)884-3806 or (602)884-3214

ARKANSAS

Magnolia

Magnolia Preschool Handicapped
  Project
Louise Phillips
Magnolia Public Schools
P. O. Box 428
Magnolia, Arkansas 71753
(501)234-3511

Sherwood

Family Life Services
L. J. McCaffery, Jr.
North Hills Exceptional Children's
  School, Inc.
207 Rainbow Lane
Sherwood, Arkansas 72116
(501)758-0432

CALIFORNIA

Carmel

Accountable Re-Entry Model (ARM)
Bruce Ryan
Behavioral Sciences Institute
72 Fern Canyon Road
Carmel, California 93921
(408)625-2222

Kentfield

Agency for Infant Development (AID)
Susan Collins
1030 Sir Francis Drake Boulevard
Kentfield, California 94904
(415)456-2184

Los Angeles

Dual Educational Approach to Learn-
  ing (DEAL)
Bea Gold
Los Angeles Unified School District
Special Education Division, Room H-
  104

450 North Grant Avenue
Los Angeles, California 90012
(213)687-4784

Handicapped Early Childhood Assis-
  tance Program
Robert A. Wright
Child Care and Development Services
Child Care Division
1450 W. Venice Boulevard
Los Angeles, California 90006
(213)747-9618

Infant Intervention in a Chicano Barrio
Alicia Noriega
EL ARCA, Inc.
P. O. Box 2976, Terminal Annex
Los Angeles, California 90051
(213)269-8471

Julia Ann Singer Preschool Psychiatric
  Center
Frank Williams
8730 Alden Drive
Los Angeles, California 90048
(213)855-3618

A Model for the Early Education of
  Handicapped Children and Their
  Families
Patricia Simmons, Annette Tessier
California State University
Los Angeles Foundation
5151 State University Drive
Los Angeles, California 90032
(213)224-3631

UCLA Intervention Program for Developmentally Handicapped Infants
  and Children
Judy Howard
UCLA School of Medicine
1000 Veteran Avenue
Room 23-33 Rehab. Center
Los Angeles, California
(213)825-4821

Napa

Atypical Infant Development and Educational Systems Project (AIDES)
Sarge Kennedy
AIDES Project
Napa County Superintendent of
  Schools
Wintun School
74 Wintun Court
Napa, California 94558
(707)255-0143

North Hollywood

Handicapped Children's Early Education Program at the Dubnoff Center
Ruth Pearce
Dubnoff Center for Child Development and Educational Therapy
10526 Victory Place
North Hollywood, California 91606
(213)877-5678

Piedmont

Preparing Handicapped Children for
  Normal Classrooms
Jack Hailey
Circle Preschool
9 Lake Avenue
Piedmont, California 94611
(415)655-0633

Pomona

Casa Colina Preschool for Multi-Handicapped
Elizabeth M. Neumann
Casa Colina Hospital
Children's Developmental Services
255 East Bonita Avenue
Pomona, California 91767
(714)593-7521 Ext. 275

San Diego

The Early On Program
Donovan McClard
Longfellow School
5055 July Street
San Diego, California 92182
(714)275-1844 or 286-6246

San Francisco

Infant Special Education Project
Judith Lewis
Family Service Agency of San Francisco
Family Development Center
1010 Gough Street
San Francisco, California 94109
(415)626-0171

Langley Porter Neuropsychiatric Institute
Hilde S. Schlesinger
Mental Health Services for the Deaf
University of California
San Francisco, California 94122
(415)731-9150

COLORADO

Alamosa

San Luis Valley Early Education and
  Home Intervention Project for the
  Handicapped
Shelley Griffee
San Luis Valley Board of Cooperative
  Services
22nd & San Juan
Alamosa, Colorado 81101
(303)589-2536

Boulder

Inclass Reactive Language Therapy
  (INREAL)
Rita S. Weiss
University of Colorado
Boulder, Colorado 80302
(303)492-6445

Denver

Comprehensive Support Program for Handicapped Children in Day Care Settings
Arlene Merkey
Mile High Child Care Association
1575 Gilpin Street
Denver, Colorado 80218
(303)355-1618

Early Education Developmental Program (SEED)
Diana N. Pefley
Easter Seal Society of Denver
1360 Vine Street
Denver, Colorado 80206
(303)399-1800

Durango

Telecommunications of Educational Diagnosis and Prescription Regarding Pupils' Learning Disorders
Lawrence J. Putz
Ft. Lewis College
Miller Student Center
Durango, Colorado 81301
(303)247-7010

Ignacio

Sheila M. Rogers
Southern UTE
Children's Center
Box 523
Ignacio, Colorado 81137
(303)563-4566

CONNECTICUT

New Haven

New Haven Preschool Program for Handicapped Children
Murray Rothman
New Haven Board of Education
Celentano School

400 Canner Street
New Haven, Connecticut 06511
(203)787-0107

DISTRICT OF COLUMBIA

Early Childhood Learning Center of Federal City College
Shirley Fields
1420 New York Avenue, N.W.
Washington, D.C. 20005
(202)727-2314

Grouping Handicapped and Nonhandicapped Children
Michael J. Guralnick
National Children's Center, Inc.
6200 Second Street, N.W.
Washington, D.C. 20011
(202)726-1090

Infant and Child Development Program for Visually Impaired and Blind Children
Donna Zadnik
Columbia Lighthouse for the Blind
2021 14th Street, N.W.
Washington, D.C. 20009
(202)265-6290

Project "GOOD START"
Constance Cole Mair
D. C. Public Schools
Division of Special Education
Watkins Elementary School, Room 402
12th and E Streets, S.E.
Washington, D.C. 20016
(202)282-0146 or 282-0150

Special Education in a Day Care System Project
Mattye P. Jackson
National Child Day Care Association
537 Kentucky Avenue, S.E.
Washington, D.C. 20003
(202)547-5119

FLORIDA

Bristol

Selective Early Education for the Handicapped
Shirley Bateman
Liberty County Preschool
P. O. Box 415
Bristol, Florida 32321
(904)643-3361

Tallahassee

Handicapped Children's Early Education Program
Landis Stetler
Florida Department of Education
319 Knott Building
Tallahassee, Florida 32304
(904)488-1570

GEORGIA

Athens

Outreach Assistance for Utilization of the Rutland Center Developmental Therapy Model
William W. Swan
Rutland Center
698 N. Pope Street
Athens, Georgia 30601
(404)549-3030

Atlanta

Milton Avenue Handicapped Youth Services Project
Paula Calhoun
Milton Avenue School
202 Milton Avenue S.E.
Atlanta, Georgia 30315
(404)627-8476

Martin Luther King, Jr., Child Development Center, Diagnostic Resource Unit
Vera C. Hillian

380 Martin Street, S.E.
Atlanta, Georgia 30312
(404)659-8274

Decatur

Project KIDS (Kindergarten and Preschool Identification Diagnostic Teaching System)
Mary Janet Harden
Coralwood Center
2477 Coralwood Drive
Decatur, Georgia 30033
(404)325-9618

Ochlocknee

Ochlocknee Multi-Handicapped Outreach Project
G. Harold Smith (Director), Bob Kibler (Outreach Coordinator)
S.W. Georgia Program for Exceptional Children
P. O. Box 110-A
Ochlocknee, Georgia 31773
(912)574-4801

Sparta

Hancock County Preschool Education Program
Gerry Woods
Hancock County Board of Education
P. O. Box J
Sparta, Georgia 31087
(404)444-6920

HAWAII

Honolulu

Enrichment Project for Handicapped Infants
Setsu Furuno
University of Hawaii
School of Public Health
1960 East-West Road
Diomed C105M

Honolulu, Hawaii 96822
(808)948-7265

Therapeutic School and Training Home
Barbara A. Rutter
The Salvation Army Residential Treatment Facilities for Children and Youth
Our House, 2950 Manoa Road
Honolulu, Hawaii 96817

IDAHO

Coeur d'Alene

Intervention and Prevention—Early Education Program for Rural Areas
Joan Dickerson
Panhandle Child Development Association
421½ Sherman Avenue
Coeur d'Alene, Idaho 83814
(208)667-9478

Gooding

Project Vision-Up
Lee Robinson
Idaho State School for the Blind and Deaf
14th and Main Streets
Gooding, Idaho 83330
(208)934-4457

ILLINOIS

Chicago

Infant-Toddler Trauma Nursery
Ramona D. Fogerty
Potential School for Exceptional Children, Inc.
7222 South Exchange Avenue
Chicago, Illinois 60649
(312)221-9711 or 9712

DeKalb

EACH (Early Action for Children) Project
Sherry Kinsley
DeKalb County Special Education Association
405 Gurler Road
DeKalb, Illinois 60115
(815)758-0651

HELP (Help Ease Learning Problems in Early Childhood)
Marge Stewart
DeKalb County Special Education Association
Early Childhood Division
405 Gurler Road
DeKalb, Illinois 60115
(815)758-0651

Macomb

Rural Early Childhood Handicapped Child/Parent Service
D. L. Edinger, P. L. Hutinger
Western Illinois University
Macomb, Illinois 61455
(309)298-1634

Peoria

An Interdisciplinary Approach to Early Education for Handicapped Children
Arthur J. Moreau
United Cerebral Palsy of Northwestern Illinois and Peoria Association for Retarded Children
320 East Armstrong Avenue
Peoria, Illinois 61603
(309)673-6481

Peoria Achievement Station System (PASS)
Eleanor Norton
Peoria Public Schools
District No. 150

3202 N. Wisconsin Avenue
Peoria, Illinois 61603
(309)672-6594

Rockford

Project RHISE (Rockford Handicapped Infant Services Expansion)
Shirley K. Frank
Children's Development Center
5350 Springbrook Road
Rockford, Illinois 61111
(815)877-1866

Schaumburg

Schaumburg Early Education Center (SEEC)
Jennie E. Swanson
Community Consolidated School District 54
804 W. Bode Road
Schaumburg, Illinois 60172
(312)885-4200 Ext. 22

Urbana-Champaign

PEECH Project (Precise Early Education of Children with Handicaps)
Merle B. Karnes
University of Illinois
403 East Healey
Champaign, Illinois 61801
(217)333-4890

RAPYTH Project (Retrieval and Acceleration of Promising Young Talented and Handicapped)
Merle B. Karnes
The Board of Trustees
The University of Illinois
Urbana, Illinois 61801
(217)333-4890

INDIANA

Bloomington

Facilitative Environments Encouraging Development (FEED)

Nicholas J. Anastasio
Institute for Child Study
10th Street & By-Pass #46
Bloomington, Indiana 47401
(812)337-1733

Community Program for *Pre*school and *Pare*nt Education (PREPARE)
Henry J. Schroeder
Indiana University Foundation
Bloomington, Indiana 47401
(812)337-8311

Gary

Special Preschool Outreach and Training Program (SPOT)
Alpha Rogers, Carrie Dawson
620 East 10th Place
Gary, Indiana 46402
(219)886-3111

Muncie

Home Training Center for Hearing Impaired Children of 0 to 3 Years and Their Parents
Emily Wallace
Ball State University
Department of Special Education
201 North Talley Avenue
Muncie, Indiana 47306
(317)285-4940

IOWA

Ankeny

Access to Success Project
Robert C. Gibson
J. R. Phillips
Heartland Education Agency
1932 Ordnance Road
Ankeny, Iowa 50021
(515)964-2550

Cedar Rapids

Cedar Rapids Comprehensive Early Childhood Project
Myron W. Rodee
Joint County School System
4401 6th Street, SW
Cedar Rapids, Iowa 52401
(319)366-7601

Marshalltown

The Marshalltown Project
Jack Montgomery
Area Education Agency #6
9 Westwood Drive
Marshalltown, Iowa 50158
(515)752-1723

Mason City

Preschool Education Reaches Special Needs (PERSN)
Bonnie Lucido
Mason City Community Schools
120 East State Street
Mason City, Iowa 50401
(515)423-3860 Ext. 37

KANSAS

Topeka

The Observational Recording of Performance in the Early Intervention of Preprimary Physically Handicapped Children
Benith MacPherson
The Capper Foundation for Crippled Children
3500 West 10th Street
Topeka, Kansas 66604
(913)272-4060 Ext. 35

KENTUCKY

Lexington

UCPB Outreach for Preschool Handicapped Children

Rhea A. Taylor
United Cerebral Palsy of the Bluegrass, Inc.
465 Springhill Drive
Lexington, Kentucky 40503
(606)278-0549

LOUISIANA

Ruston

North Central Louisiana Model Preschool Program for Handicapped Children
Gertrude L. Simonton
Lincoln Center, Arlington Street
Ruston, Louisiana 71270
(318)255-6071

MAINE

Cumberland Center

Project Maine Stream
Frances H. Hale
School Administrative District #51
Cumberland Center, Maine 04021
(207)829-5541

Harrington

Project Let's Move Ahead
Jane Weil
School Administrative District #37
Post Office Building
Harrington, Maine 04643
(207)483-2734

Waterville

HELP ME (Handicapped Early Learning Program: Model Education)
Sally Doxtater
Brookside Elementary School
Drummond Avenue
Waterville, Maine 04901
(207)873-5184

MARYLAND

Baltimore

Baltimore Early Childhood Learning Continuum
Larry A. Magliocca
Baltimore City Schools
Area for Exceptional Children
Educational Annex
23rd and Calvert Streets
Baltimore, Maryland 21218
(301)396-7004

Infant-Parent Program for Communicatively Impaired Children
Barbara A. Hanners
Hearing and Speech Agency of Metropolitan Baltimore, Inc.
928 N. Charles
Baltimore, Maryland 21201
(301)243-3800

Rockville

A Remedial Program for Children with Language and Speech Disabilities
Beverely Whitlock
Montgomery County Society for Crippled Children & Adults, Inc.
1000 Twinbrook Parkway
Rockville, Maryland 20851
(301)424-5200

MASSACHUSETTS

Allston

Infant Stimulation Program for Multi-Handicapped and Deaf Children
Eleanor Semel
Boston University/Sargent College
Infant Stimulation Project
Horace Mann School
500 Cambridge Street
Union Square
Allston, Massachusetts 02134
(617)254-5700

Boston

Boston Center for Blind Children
Eunice Kenyon
147 South Huntington Avenue
Boston, Massachusetts 02115
(617)232-1710

Framingham

Development and Coordination of Regional Service Centers for Young Handicapped Children
Frank Skinnell
Integration Model at Framingham State College
Education Department
Framingham, Massachusetts 01701
(617)872-3501 Ext. 283

Medford

Learning in Integrated Classrooms (LINC)
Eliot Pearson
Eliot-Program Children's School
Department of Child Study
Tufts University
Medford, Massachusetts 02155
(617)628-5000

Newton

Demonstration in Four Child Service Sites Providing Statewide Training of Public Schools
Marian Hainsworth
Allen Leitman
Education Development Center, Inc.
55 Chapel Street
Newton, Massachusetts 02160
(617)969-7100

Quincy

OPTIMUS (Optimizing Potentials through Intensive Multiservices)
Joseph Bleiberg
Cerebral Palsy of the South Shore Area

105 Adams Street
Quincy, Massachusetts 02169
(617)479-7443

MICHIGAN

Alpena

Telstar Project
Herbert Baker
Alpena-Montmorency-Alcona
Intermediate School District
Department of Special Education
P. O. Box 497
Alpena, Michigan 49707
(517)354-3101

Ann Arbor

Early Intervention Project
Martha S. Moersch
Institute for Study of Mental Retardation and Related Disabilities
130 South First Street
Ann Arbor, Michigan 48108
(313)764-4115

Mason

Infant Program for the Visually
Impaired Child
Sherry Raynor
Ingham Intermediate School District
2630 West Howell Road
Mason, Michigan 48854
(517)676-1051

Saginaw

Preparing Mentally Handicapped Chil-
dren for Public School Placement
(Project PAR)
Nels M. Andersen
Saginaw County Child Development
Centers, Inc.
Box 3224
Saginaw, Michigan 48605
(517)752-2193

Saginaw D.O.E.S. Care Program
Kayte M. Fearn
Saginaw Board of Education
550 Millard Street
Saginaw, Michigan 48601
(517)755-6501

Ypsilanti

High/Scope Demonstration Preschool
Project
Bernard Banet
High/Scope Educational Research
Foundation
600 North River
Ypsilanti, Michigan 48197
(313)485-2000

MINNESOTA

St. Paul

Handicapped Children's Early Educa-
tion Program
Mary V. Hubbard
Early Education Program, Mattocks
School
447 Macalester
St. Paul, Minnesota 55105
(612)298-5862

UNISTAPS Project
Winifred H. Northcott
Minnesota Department of Education
550 Cedar Street
St. Paul, Minnesota 55101
(612)296-6013 (project director)
(612)336-8908 (lab program)

MISSISSIPPI

Jackson

Early Education Center Infant Pro-
gram: Developmental Training for
Handicapped Infants Aged 0-3 and
Parent Education and Training
Lois E. White

Christian Education Services, Inc.
Early Education Center
4601 Kirkley Drive
Jackson, Mississippi 39206
(601)366-8025

Natchez

Preschool Resource Program for the Handicapped
Mary Cecelia Lee
Adams-Jefferson Improvement Corporation
P. O. Box "L"
Natchez, Mississippi 39120
(601)445-9442

Starkville

Preschool and Early Education Project (PEEP)
Ernestine W. Rainey
Preschool and Early Education Resource Center
Drawer EP
Starkville, Mississippi 39206
(601)325-2185

MISSOURI

Sedalia

Delivery of Services to Rural Preschool Children
Ralph Kenneth Wilcox
Children's Therapy Center
P. O. Box 1565
Sedalia, Missouri 65301
(816)826-4400

St. Louis

Parent-Infant Program
Audrey Simmons Martin
Central Institute for the Deaf
818 South Euclid
St. Louis, Missouri 63110
(314)652-3200

NEBRASKA

Omaha

Coordinated Early Education Program (CEEP)
Charles N. Galloway
Eastern Nebraska Community Office of Retardation
885 South 72nd Street
Omaha, Nebraska 68131
(402)444-6500 or 444-6557

Technical Assistance Resource Center in Early Childhood Education for the Handicapped
Meyer Children's Rehabilitation Institute
444 S. 44th Street
Omaha, Nebraska 68131

NEW HAMPSHIRE

Hanover

Project Prevent
J. Bertrand E. Nadeau
Department of Psychiatry
Dartmouth Medical School
Hanover, New Hampshire 03755
(603)643-4000 Ext 3637

NEW MEXICO

Albuquerque

Vista Larga Therapeutic School Project
Lawrence Harris
2600 Marble Avenue, N.E.
Albuquerque, New Mexico 87106
(505)265-1251

Clovis

Responsive Environment Early Education Program (REEEP)
Gay Herman
Clovis Municipal Schools

420 West Grand Avenue
Clovis, New Mexico 88101
(505)762-5250

Las Cruces

Las Palomitas Early Childhood Education for the Handicapped Project
Joy A. Brown
New Mexico State University
Box 3AC, O'Donnell Hall
Las Cruces, New Mexico 88003

NEW YORK

Bronx

Integrated Model for Handicapped Early Childhood Development
Miriam S. Sour
Community School District 9
1787 Weeks Avenue
Bronx, New York 10457
(212)878-6666

Commack

Total Milieu Approach to Handicapped Infant Education
Claire Salant
Suffolk Rehabilitation Center
159 Indian Head Road
Commack, New York 11725
(516)543-2200 Ext. 60 or 61

Guilderland

Bobbi L. Kamil
Guilderland Elementary School
Western Avenue
Guilderland, New York 12084
(518)474-6892 (office)
(518)456-3356 (preschool)

Manhasset (Long Island)

A Language Development Program for Preschool Children
Barbara Wilson

North Shore Hospital
400 Community Drive
Manhasset, New York 11030
(516)627-5000 Ext. 271

New York City

First Chance Child Development Center
Beverly R. Fischer
Hospital for Joint Diseases and Medical Center
Neuromuscular Service, Department of Orthopaedics
1919 Madison Avenue
New York, New York 10035
(212)876-7000 Ext. 295

Mini Community for Disturbed Children
Joy D. Glickman
The Educational Alliance, Inc.
197 East Broadway
New York, New York 10002
(212)GR5-6200

A National Organized Collaborative Project to Provide Comprehensive Services for Atypical Infants and Their Families
Una Haynes
United Cerebral Palsy of New York City
66 East 34th Street
New York, New York 10016
(212)889-6655

NORTH CAROLINA

Chapel Hill

Chapel Hill Training Gifted Project
Anne R. Sanford
Chapel Hill–Carrboro Schools
Lincoln Center
Merritt Mill Road
Chapel Hill, North Carolina 27514
(919)967-8295

Chapel Hill Training Outreach Project
Anne R. Sanford
Chapel Hill-Carrboro City School System
Lincoln Center
Merritt Mill Road
Chapel Hill, North Carolina 27514
(919)967-8211

Technical Assistance Development System (TADS)
David Lillie
University of North Carolina
500 NCNB Plaza
Chapel Hill, North Carolina 27514
(919)967-9221

Conover

Catawba County Children's Center
Albert Yoder
207 6th Street, S.W.
Conover, North Carolina 28613
(704)464-3191

Morganton

Parent Training Project
Clarita King
Western Carolina Center
Morganton, North Carolina 28655
(704)433-2660

Powellsville

Access to Mainstream Project
Susan Thomas
Alliance for Progress, Inc.
P. O. Box 160
Powellsville, North Carolina 27967
(919)332-3819

NORTH DAKOTA

Bismarck

Bismarck Early Childhood Education Program (BECEP)
Roger Schultz

400 Avenue E. East
Bismarck, North Dakota 58501
(701)255-4067

Fargo

Comprehensive Children's Services for Rural and Non-Urban Areas
William Gingold
Southeast Mental Health and Retardation Center
700 First Avenue South
P. O. Box 2083
Fargo, North Dakota 58102
(701)237-4513

OHIO

Athens

Normalization Programming for Young Children Project
Lloyd H. Inglis
Ohio University
Center for Human Development
College of Education
Athens, Ohio 45701
(614)594-2561

Columbus

Developmentally Delayed Infant Education Project
Ann Bardwell
The Nisonger Center
The Ohio State University
1580 Cannon Drive
Columbus, Ohio 43210
(614)422-8365 or 9844

Mantua

Early Education for Institutionalized Multi-Handicapped Young Children Project
Jeanette Reuter
First Chance Project
Kent State University

Hattie Larlham Foundation
9772 Diagonal Road
Mantua, Ohio 44255
(216)274-2272

OKLAHOMA

Oklahoma City

Putnam City Early Childhood Prevention Program (PEPP)
Marion L. Thornhill
Director of Special Services
Putnam City Public Schools
5417 N.W. 40
Oklahoma City, Oklahoma 73122
(405)789-5151

OREGON

Medford

The Medford Preschool (no longer in operation)
Information may be obtained from Bruce Metzger
Lone Pine School
3158 Lone Pine Road
Medford, Oregon 97501
(503)776-8847

Monmouth

Teaching Research Infant and Child Center
H. D. Fredericks, William G. Moore
Teaching Research Preschool
Division of the Oregon State System of Higher Education
345 N. Monmouth
Monmouth, Oregon 97361
(503)838-1220 Ext. 401

PENNSYLVANIA

Hazleton

A Program and Services Grant for Developmentally Delayed and Language Impaired Preschool Age Children
John S. Seaman
Easter Seal Society
Hazleton, Pennsylvania 18101
(717)455-9514

Philadelphia

Center for Preschool Services in Special Education
Louise Sandler
The Franklin Institute
20th and Parkway
Philadelphia, Pennsylvania 19103
(215)448-1508

Infant Stimulation and Parent Training Program
Byron Wight
Special People in the N.E.
8040 Roosevelt Blvd., Room 219
Philadelphia, Pennsylvania 19152
(215)333-6262

Pittsburgh

Early Identification and Comprehensive Rehabilitation Outreach Project
Gladys Russell
Home for Crippled Children
1426 Denniston Avenue
Pittsburgh, Pennsylvania 15217
(412)521-9000 Ext. 315

University Park

Comprehensive Outreach Model Program (COMP)
John T. Neisworth
College of Human Development
S-24 Human Development Building
Pennsylvania State University
University Park, Pennsylvania 16802
(814)863-0267

Laboratory of Early Education Program
Karen Laub
S-24 Human Development Building
Pennsylvania State University
University Park, Pennsylvania 16802
(814)863-0267

York

Systems Network for Preschool Emotionally Disturbed Children
Donald Klein
Jefferson Child Development Center
501 Pershing Avenue
York, Pennsylvania 17404
(717)848-5820

PUERTO RICO

Hato Rey

Early Childhood Education for the Handicapped Project
Ramon A. Cruz
Commonwealth of Puerto Rico
Department of Education
Hato Rey, Puerto Rico 00919
(809)765-3493

SOUTH CAROLINA

Clinton

Early Education for Multi-Handicapped Children
Evelyn White
Whitten Village, Drawer 239
Clinton, South Carolina 29325
(803)833-2733 Ext. 191 or 195

Ladson

Parent Tape Training Program
Mary Deecie Laney
South Carolina Department of Mental Retardation
Coastal Center, Jamison Road
Ladson, South Carolina 29456
(803)873-5750

Lancaster

Early Education for Speech and Hearing Handicapped Project
Louis J. Rosso
Region V Educational Services Center
P.O. Box 1069
102 East Arch Street
Lancaster, South Carolina 29720
(803)285-2001

SOUTH DAKOTA

Pierre

South Dakota Preschool Program for Handicapped Children
Norena A. Harrold
State Capitol Building
Pierre, South Dakota 57501
(605)224-3678

TENNESSEE

Harrogate

Preschool Handicapped Program
Emma Jo Hurst
Clinch-Powell Educational Cooperative Special Education
P. O. Box 97
Harrogate, Tennessee 37752
(615)869-3605

Memphis

PEACH Project (Program for Early Attention to Children with Handicaps)
Rutha D. Pegues
Board of Education, Memphis City Schools
Division of Special Education
584 Lester Street, Lester Center
Memphis, Tennessee 38112
(901)454-5527

Project MEMPHIS (Memphis Educational Model Providing Handicapped Infants Services)
Alton D. Quick
Memphis State University
Memphis, Tennessee 38152
(901)454-2731

Nashville

Parent Teaching Program for Language Handicapped Children
Kathryn B. Horton
The Bill Wilkerson Hearing and Speech Center
1114 19th Avenue South
Nashville, Tennessee 37212
(615)327-2565

TEXAS

Amarillo

Rural Demonstration Project for Preschool Handicapped
Wendell Jones
Peso Education Service Center
Region 16
1601 S. Cleveland
Amarillo, Texas 79102
(806)372-8721

Austin

A Comprehensive Service Delivery System for Preschool Multi-Handicapped Children
Mildred O. Stokes
Austin Independent School District
Casis Elementary School
2710 Exposition
Austin, Texas 78703
(512)474-6461

Infant-Parent Training Program
Madeline Sutherland
Austin-Travis Co. MHMR Center

Infant Parent Project
1226 E. 9th
Austin, Texas 78702
(512)472-3142

Dallas

Project KIDS (Kindling Intellectual Development Stages)
Joe W. Ward
Dallas Independent School District
Division of Development
3700 Ross Avenue
Dallas, Texas 75204
(214)824-1620

Del Rio

San Felipe Del Rio Project
D. Leverman
San Felipe Del Rio Consolidated Independent School District
P. O. Box 1229
Del Rio, Texas 78840
(512)775-9561 Ext. 301 or 302

El Paso

Early Childhood Learning Center
Patricia G. Adkins
1308 Zuni
P. O. Box 10716
El Paso, Texas 79905
(915)778-7044

Houston

Children's Mental Health Services of Houston
Cay Cannady
3214 Austin Street
Houston, Texas 77004
(713)524-9111

Demonstration Diagnostic Intervention Model for Early Childhood
Ronald L. Klinger

Center for Human Resources Development
Houston Independent School District
3830 Richmond Avenue
Houston, Texas 77027
(713)623-5131

Demonstration Training Center for Mentally Retarded Infants of Teenage Mothers
Dixie Kendrix
2501 Dunstan
Houston, Texas 77006
(713)526-2871

Lubbock

Developmental Education, Birth through Two (DEBT) Project
Gloria Galey
Lubbock Independent School District
Special Education
1628 19th Street
Lubbock, Texas 79410
(806)747-3838

San Antonio

Edgewood School's Early Childhood Education for the Handicapped Program
Barbara Schmidt
José Cardenaz Early Childhood Center
3300 Ruiz
San Antonio, Texas 78228
(512)433-2361

Wichita Falls

Region IX Education Service Center
Lois A. Cadman
3014 Old Seymour Road
Wichita Falls, Texas 76309
(817)322-3108 or 322-3100

UTAH

Logan

MAPPS (Multi Agency Preschool Program for the Handicapped)
Glendon Casto
Utah State University
Affiliated Exceptional Child Center
Logan, Utah 84322
(801)752-4100, ext. 7753

Project SKI*HI
Thomas C. Clark
Department of Communication Disorders
Utah State University
Logan, Utah 84322
(801)752-4100, ext. 7582

Salt Lake City

A Model Demonstration Project for Home Based Early Education of Handicapped Children
Lester Coon
Granite School District
340 East 3545 South
Salt Lake City, Utah 84115
(801)268-8142

VERMONT

Montpelier

Vermont Parent/Child Development Center
Jean Garvin
State of Vermont
Department of Special Education
120 State Street
Montpelier, Vermont 05602
(802)257-7852

Demonstration site:
2 Oak Street
Brattleboro, Vermont 05301

VIRGINIA

Alexandria

Parent Cooperative Sheltered Classroom
Janet Chitwood
Resurrection Preschool
2280 N. Beauregard Street
Alexandria, Virginia 22311
(703)578-1314

School for Contemporary Education
David L. Williams
2912 King Street
Alexandria, Virginia 22302
(703)548-2770

Arlington

Northern Virginia Parent-Infant Education Program
Carl J. Dunst
Arlington County Department of Human Resource
1800 North Edison Street
Arlington, Virginia 22207
(703)558-2812

Charlottesville

Infant Education for Multihandicapped Children Project
Sharon L. Hostler
University of Virginia
Medical Center
Box 232
Charlottesville, Virginia 22901
(804)924-5281 or 924-5282

Norfolk

Model Program for Early Education for Handicapped Children
Ken Reavis
Old Dominion University
Box 6173

Norfolk, Virginia 23508
(804)424-9606

Norfolk State College
Ruth Diggs
2401 Couprew Avenue
Norfolk, Virginia 23504
(804)623-8714

Norton

Dilenowisco Educational Cooperative
Jonathan Van Tassel
1032 Virginia Avenue
Norton, Virginia 24273
(703)679-2180

Williamsburg

Williamsburg Preschool for Special Children
Corrine W. Garland
P. O. Box 774
Williamsburg, Virginia 23185
(804)229-8626

WASHINGTON

Seattle

Communication for Multiply Handicapped Blind Children
Kathleen Pendergast
Seattle Public Schools
815 4th Avenue North
Seattle, Washington 98109
(206)587-3431

Technical Assistance to Programs for Preschool Handicapped Children
Alice H. Hayden
Model Preschool Center for Handicapped Children
Experimental Education Unit
Child Development and Mental Retardation Center

University of Washington
Seattle, Washington 98195
(206)543-7583

Toppenish

Project Palatisha
Jacqueline Walker
Yakima Indian Nation
P. O. Box 509
Toppenish, Washington 98948
(509)865-5700

WEST VIRGINIA

Keyser

Project PUSH (Parents Understanding
   Student Handicaps)
April Beavers
Mineral Street Annex
Keyser, West Virginia 26726
(304)788-5160

WISCONSIN

Madison

A Community Based Model for Inter-
   vention with Infants, Toddlers, and
   Preschoolers
Lisbeth J. Vincent
Madison Public Schools, Emerson
   School
2421 E. Johnson
Madison, Wisconsin 53703
(608)244-7766

Milwaukee

Comprehensive Training Program for
   Infant and Young Cerebral Palsied
   Children

Michael Murnane
Curative Workshop of Milwaukee
10437 West Watertown Plank Road
P. O. Box 7372
Milwaukee, Wisconsin 53901
(414)257-5100

Portage

Portage Project
David Shearer
Cooperative Educational Service
   Agency #12
412 E. Slifer, Box 564
Portage, Wisconsin 53901
(608)742-5342

WYOMING

Laramie

Project TAPP (Technical Assistance to
   Preschool Programs)
Janis A. Jelinek
University of Wyoming
Box 3224, University Station
Laramie, Wyoming 82071
(307)766-6426

TRUST TERRITORIES

Saipan, Marians

Deaf-Blind Programs in Truk
William Sewell
Director of Education
Office of the High Commission
Trust Territory of the Pacific Islands
Headquarters Department
Attn: David Piercy, Coordinator of
   Special Education

STANDARDIZED TESTS

USED BY BEH FIRST CHANCE PROJECTS

The ABC Inventory to Determine Kindergarten and School Readiness. N. Adair and G. Blesch. Muskegon MI: Research Concepts.

Adaptive Behavior Scales. K. Nihira, R. Foster, M. Shellhaas, and H. Leland. Washington DC: American Association on Mental Deficiency.

The APELL Test: Assessment Program of Early Learning Levels. E. V. Cochran and J. L. Shannon. Orange CA: Edcodyne Corporation.

Auditory Discrimination Test. J. Wepman. Chicago: Language Research Associates.

The Basic Concept Inventory. S. E. Engelmann. Chicago: Follett Publishing Co.

Bayley Scales of Infant Development. N. Bayley. New York: The Psychological Corporation.

Bender Visual Motor Gestalt Test. L. Bender. New York: American Orthopsychiatric Association, Inc.

Boehm Test of Basic Concepts. A. E. Boehm. New York: The Psychological Corporation.

Burks' Behavior Rating Scales. H. F. Burks. Huntington Beach CA: Arden Press.

The Bzoch-League Receptive-Expressive Emergent Language Scale. K. R. Bzoch and R. League. Gainesville FL: The Tree of Life Press.

Cain-Levine Social Competency Scale. L. F. Cain, S. Levine, and F. F. Elzey. Palo Alto CA: Consulting Psychologists Press, Inc.

California Preschool Social Competency Scale. S. Levine, F. F. Elzey, and M. Lewis. Palo Alto CA: Consulting Psychologists Press, Inc.

Carolina Developmental Profile. D. Lillie. Available from Technical Assistance Development Systems, 500 NCNB Plaza, Chapel Hill NC 27514.

The Cassel Developmental Record. R. N. Cassel. Jacksonville IL: Psychologists and Educators, Inc.

Cattell Infant Intelligence Scale. P. Cattell. New York: The Psychological Corporation.

Children's Self-Social Constructs Test. R. Ziller, B. Long, and E. Henderson. Available from author: R. Ziller, Department of Psychology, University of Oregon, Eugene.

Cincinnati Autonomy Test Battery. T. J. Banta and T. S. Banta. Available from author: T. J. Banta, Department of Psychology, University of Cincinnati, Cincinnati OH.

Communicative Evaluation Chart From Infancy to Five Years. R. Anderson, M. Miles, and P. Matheny. Cambridge MA: Educators Publishing Service, Inc.

Comprehensive Identification Process (CIP). R. R. Zehrbach. Bensenville IL: Scholastic Testing Service, Inc.

Cooperative Preschool Inventory. B. M. Caldwell. Princeton NJ: Cooperative Tests and Services, Educational Testing Service.

Denver Developmental Screening Test. W. Frankenburg and J. B. Dodds. Denver CO: Ladoca Project and Publishing Foundation, Inc.

Detroit Tests of Learning Aptitude. H. J. Baker and B. Leland. Indianapolis: Bobbs-Merrill Co., Inc.

Developmental Guidelines. M. Karnes. Unpublished. Available from Technical Assistance Development Systems, 500 NCNB Plaza, Chapel Hill NC 27514.

Developmental Profile. C. D. Alpern and T. J. Boll. Indianapolis: Psychological Development Publications.

A Developmental Screening Inventory. H. Knobloch, B. Pasamanick, and E. S. Sherard, Jr. Albany NY: Hilda Knobloch, Albany Medical College.

Developmental Test of Visual-Motor Integration. K. Beery and N. Buktenica. Chicago: Follett Publishing Co.

DIAL (Developmental Indicators for the Assessment of Learning). Highland Park IL: DIAL, Inc.

Early Detection Inventory. F. E. McGahan and C. McGahan. Chicago: Follett Publishing Co.

Educational Evaluation of Preschool Children. E. Haeussermann. New York: Grune & Stratton, Inc.

Evanston Early Identification Scale. M. Landsman and H. Dillard. Chicago: Follett Publishing Co.

Gesell Action Agent Test. A. Gesell. Unpublished. Available from Technical Assistance Development Systems, 500 NCNB Plaza, Chapel Hill NC 27514.

Gesell Developmental Schedules, 1940 Series. A. Gesell and Associates. New York: The Psychological Corporation.

Goldman-Fristoe Test of Articulation. R. Goldman and M. Fristoe. Circle Pines MN: American Guidance Service, Inc.

Goldman-Fristoe-Woodcock Test of Auditory Discrimination. R. Goldman, M. Fristoe, and R. Woodcock. Circle Pines MN: American Guidance Service, Inc.

Goodenough-Harris Drawing Test. F. Goodenough and D. Harris. New York: Harcourt Brace Jovanovich, Inc.

The Houston Test for Language Development. M. Crabtree. Houston TX: The Houston Test Co.

Illinois Test of Psycholinguistic Abilities. S. Kirk, J. McCarthy, and W. Kirk. Urbana: University of Illinois Press.

Infant Behavior Inventory. E. Schaefer, M. Aaronson. Available from Technical Assistance Development Systems, 500 NCNB Plaza, Chapel Hill NC 27514.

Kindergarten Evaluation of Learning Potential. J. A. R. Wilson and M. C. Robeck. New York: Webster Division, McGraw-Hill Book Co., Inc.

The K-Q: Kindergarten Questionnaire. S. Berger and E. Periman. Available from Susan Berger and Evelyn Periman, 10 Tyler Road, Lexington MA 02173.

Learning Accomplishment Profile. A. Sanford. Available from Kaplan School Supply Corp., Winston-Salem NC.

Marianne Frostig Developmental Test of Visual Perception. M. Frostig. Palo Alto CA: Consulting Psychologists Press, Inc.

The Meeting Street School Screening Test. P. Hainsworth and M. Siqueland. Providence RI: Crippled Children and Adults of Rhode Island, Inc.

Metropolitan Readiness Tests. G. Hildreth, N. Griffiths, and M. McGauvran. New York: Harcourt Brace Jovanovich, Inc.

Minnesota Child Development Inventory. H. R. Ireton and E. J. Thwing. Minneapolis: NCS Interpretive Scoring Systems.

Minnesota Preschool Scale. F. L. Goodenough, K. M. Maurer, and M. J. Van Wagenen. Circle Pines MN: American Guidance Service, Inc.

The Missouri Children's Picture Series. J. Sines, J. Pauker, and L. Sines. Available from Jacob O. Sines, P. O. Box 1031, Iowa City IA 52240.

Move-Grow-Learn Survey. R. E. Orpet and T. L. Heustis. Chicago: Follett Publishing Co.

Oseretsky Tests of Motor Proficiency. E. A. Doll, Editor. Circle Pines MN: American Guidance Service, Inc.

Parent Readiness Evaluation of Preschoolers. A. E. Ahr. Skokie IL: Priority Innovations, Inc.

Peabody Individual Achievement Test. L. M. Dunn and F. Markwardt. Circle Pines MN: American Guidance Service, Inc.

Peabody Picture Vocabulary Test. L. M. Dunn. Circle Pines MN: American Guidance Service, Inc.

Piagetian Tasks. N. Kohn, L. Kohlberg, and R. DeVries. In *The Cognitive Environment of Urban Preschool Children* (2 volumes). Graduate School of Education, University of Chicago.

Preprimary Profile. H. J. Schiff and M. I. Friedman. Chicago: Science Research Associates, Inc.

Preschool Attainment Record. E. A. Doll. Circle Pines MN: American Guidance Service, Inc.

Preschool Language Scale. I. L. Zimmerman, U. G. Steiner, and R. L. Evatt. Columbus OH: Charles E. Merrill Publishing Co.

School Readiness Survey. F. L. Jordan and J. Massey. Palo Alto CA: Consulting Psychologists Press, Inc.

SRA Primary Mental Abilities. T. G. Thurstone. Chicago: Science Research Associates, Inc.

Stanford-Binet Intelligence Scale. L. M. Terman and M. A. Merrill. Boston: Houghton Mifflin Co.

Stanford Early School Achievement Test: Level I. R. Madden and E. F. Gardner. New York: Harcourt Brace Jovanovich, Inc.

Tests of Basic Experiences. M. H. Moss. Monterey CA: CTB/McGraw-Hill.

Valett Developmental Survey of Basic Learning Abilities. R. E. Valett. Palo Alto CA: Consulting Psychologists Press, Inc.

Verbal Language Development Scale. M. J. Mecham. Circle Pines MN: American Guidance Service, Inc.

Vineland Social Maturity Scale. E. A. Doll. Circle Pines MN: American Guidance Service, Inc.

Walker Problem Behavior Identification Checklist. H. M. Walker. Los Angeles: Western Psychological Services.

Watson and Pickles Scale for Receptive Language. A. G. Ewing. Xeroxed, available from TADS, or in *Educational Guidance and the Deaf Child* by A. G. Ewing, Manchester University Press, 316 Oxford Road, Manchester, England.

Wide Range Achievement Tests. J. F. Jastak, S. R. Jastak, and S. W. Bijou. Wilmington DE: Guidance Associates of Delaware, Inc.

Yellow Brick Road. Austin TX: Learning Concepts.

INDEX